Visual QuickPro Guide

Mac OS X

Maria Langer

Peachpit Press

Visual QuickPro Guide

Mac OS X

Maria Langer

Peachpit Press
1249 Eighth Street
Berkeley, CA 94710
510-524-2178 · 800-283-9444
510-524-2221 (fax)

Find us on the World Wide Web at: http://www.peachpit.com/
To report errors, please send a note to errata@peachpit.com
Peachpit Press is a division of Pearson Education

Editor: Clifford Colby
Technical Editor: Victor Gavenda
Indexer: Emily Glossbrenner
Cover Design: The Visual Group
Production: Maria Langer, Connie Jeung-Mills

Colophon

This book was produced with Adobe PageMaker 6.5 and Adobe Photoshop 5.5 on a Power Macintosh G3/300. The fonts used were Kepler Multiple Master, Meta Plus, and PIXymbols Command. Screenshots were created using Snapz Pro X on a Strawberry iMac and G4/867.

ISBN 0-201-74577-1

9 8 7 6 5 4 3 2 1

Printed and bound in the United States of America.

Dedication

To Victor Gavenda,
Tech Editor Extraordinaire

Thanks!

To Cliff Colby, for his incredible patience while I worked on this book. I've never had a book slip so far off the original deadline and I appreciate Cliff's calmness—even when I started getting uncharacteristically whiny! Next time will be better—I promise!

To Victor Gavenda, for his technical editing skill. Victor cleared up a few misunderstandings I had about Mac OS X and provided a more up-to-date diagram of the Mac OS X architecture. He confirmed what I've suspected for some time: that Mac OS X is more complex than it appears on the surface.

To the two other Peachpit authors who helped me with this book: Ron Hipschman and Ethan Wilde. Ron was the Unix guru on this project, churning out brand new material about Unix for Mac OS users. He wrote so much, we had to turn it into two chapters. Ethan, the Peachpit AppleScript expert, provided a customized excerpt from his book, *AppleScript for Applications: Visual QuickStart Guide*.

To Nancy Ruenzel, Marjorie Baer, and the other powers-that-be at Peachpit Press, for continuing to put up with me, despite ever-more-frequent whining. I *will* stop.

To Connie Jeung-Mills, for her sharp eyes and gentle layout editing. We make a great team!

To the rest of the folks at Peachpit Press—especially Gary-Paul, Mimi, Trish, Hannah, Paula, Zigi, and Keasley—for doing what they do so well.

To Grace Kvamme at Apple Computer, Inc., for helping me get the software I needed to complete this book on a timely (well, sort of) basis. And to the rest of Apple Computer, Inc., for reinventing and continuing to improve the world's best operating system.

Finally, to Mike, for the usual reasons.

www.marialanger.com

Table of Contents

TABLE OF CONTENTS

Foreword

Before We Begin...

Let me start by saying that I've written over forty computer books since 1992 and this is the first one I felt needed a Foreword. Why? Well, I felt a need to share a few thoughts with readers.

Hooray for Mac OS X 10.1

First of all, I want to let everyone know how excited I am about Mac OS X 10.1.

I was one of the people in the audience (via Webcast) when Steve Jobs showed off Mac OS X at Macworld Expo in January 2001. *Oohs* and *ahs* came from my office as I remained glued to my screen, wishing my Internet connection was faster than 128kbps ISDN. I was just as excited about Mac OS X as I was with the release of System 7, Mac OS 8, and Mac OS 9. (Yes, I do go back a few years as a Mac user.)

But when I finally got the software into my hot little hands to write the prequel to this book, *Mac OS X: Visual QuickStart Guide*, I was somewhat disappointed. Although Mac OS X did everything Apple claimed it would, and it was just as beautiful in real life as it was at the Apple booth at Macworld Expo, it just didn't *feel* right to me. As I worked with and wrote about its features, I decided that I *wouldn't* upgrade. It would change the way I worked, making it impossible to take advantage of some of the productivity features in Mac OS 9 that I've come to depend on. And with very little "Built for Mac OS" software out there, I knew I'd be spending more time in the Classic Environment than in Aqua.

I'm sure I wasn't the only person who was disappointed. And I'm sure many of the others were a lot more vocal about it than I was. But Apple listened to its critics. And months later, it delivered the software that this book was based on: Mac OS X version 10.1.

What a difference a decimal makes! At first glance, it may not seem very different, but there are definite improvements in performance and the feature set. It's more customizable, making it easier to set up your computer with the kinds of features that increase your productivity.

And a few months made a difference in third-party software, too. Developers are flocking to Mac OS X, rewriting most of my favorite software so it's built for Mac OS X. Intuit's Quicken 2002 was among the first; Microsoft Office v. X for the Mac will be available when this book goes to print. (I start work on *Microsoft Word X: Visual QuickStart Guide* tomorrow.)

With the release of Mac OS X 10.1, the idea of upgrading suddenly feels *right*. Am I ready to upgrade? You bet I am!

Start or Pro?

Although I've written literally dozens of Visual Quick*Start* Guides since 1995, this is the first Visual Quick*Pro* Guide I've written. It certainly was a challenge.

It all started when Cliff (my editor at Peachipit Press) and I realized that the Mac OS Visual QuickStart Guides I'd been writing (since the release of Mac OS 8) had been getting fatter and fatter. As Mac OS became more complex, many of the topics the books covered also became complex. We decided that some of the topics—such as networking and AppleScript—were beyond the needs of the average Visual QuickStart Guide reader. At the same time, we realized that with the release of Mac OS X, even more complex topics—such as Unix and the intricacies of a true multiple-user system — would need to be discussed. It seemed that the time was right to split the book into two: a slightly pared down Visual QuickStart Guide and a brand new Visual QuickPro Guide.

The first challenge was deciding what material should appear in each book. We decided that *Mac OS X: Visual QuickStart Guide* should cover the basics: what every new Mac OS user needs to know. *Mac OS X: Visual QuickPro Guide* would cover any material cut from previous Visual QuickStart Guides, as well as the new, more advanced concepts and features introduced in Mac OS X.

Mac OS X: Visual QuickStart Guide was released just after Mac OS X—in fact, it was the first Mac OS X book out there. The book has gotten great reviews and has won numerous awards, which make me extremely happy and proud.

But within a month, I started getting e-mail from readers looking for the more advanced material promised in *Mac OS X: Visual Quick-Pro Guide*. I started work just as Apple was fine-tuning Mac OS X 10.1.

No computer book author is an island

I'll be the first to admit that I know very little about Unix. In fact, nearly everything I learned about Unix I learned while editing the chapters written by Ron Hipschman. Ron's Unix chapters are an important part of this book because—let's face the awful truth—Mac OS X can't exist without Unix.

Although the average Mac OS X user doesn't need to know a thing about Unix (which is why it wasn't covered in *Mac OS X: Visual Quick-Start Guide*), anyone who wants to poke around in the inner workings of Mac OS X does. And since this book is for that type of user, we called in Ron to fill in the holes of my "Swiss cheese" knowledge.

We also called in Ethan Wilde, author of *AppleScript for Applications: Visual QuickStart Guide*, to write a chapter about using Apple-Script with Mac OS X 10.1. Although I'd touched upon AppleScript in previous Mac OS Visual QuickStart Guides, I couldn't begin to provide the depth of coverage that Ethan can. His chapter helps round out this book.

I'm feeling better

For a while, I was losing my Mac enthusiasm. It may have started when Apple Computer was struggling for its survival (I was loyal enough to buy stock back then) or when the Newton was put to rest (want to buy one cheap?) or when I realized that my QuickTake camera took pretty bad pictures (at least I unloaded *that* on eBay). For whatever reason, I was not nearly as happy with Apple or Mac OS as someone who earns a living writing about it should be.

But the magic is coming back. I just bought a G4 with a SuperDrive and am excited about creating my first DVD movie. Although I'm finally getting used to the keyboard on my iBook, I'm starting to think about a real Power-Book again. And I'm getting ready to upgrade all of my computers to Mac OS X 10.1.

I've come a long way with Apple since System 6.0.3 running on a Mac IIcx with 1 MB of RAM and a 20 MB hard drive. And I'm just as excited about the future of the Macintosh operating system now as I was in 1989.

I hope you are, too.

— *Maria Langer, Wickenburg, AZ*
November 2001

Introduction to Mac OS X

Figure 1 The About This Mac window for Mac OS X.

Introduction

Mac OS X ("X" is pronounced "ten"; **Figure 1**) is the latest version of the computer operating system that put the phrase *graphic user interface* in everyone's vocabulary. With the slick new look and feel of the Aqua interface and Unix under the hood, Mac OS X is sure to please Mac OS users at any experience level.

This Visual QuickPro Guide picks up where the *Mac OS X: Visual QuickStart Guide* leaves off. Written for intermediate to advanced Mac OS users, it goes beyond the basics to cover more advanced topics, such as Unix, networking, multiple users, security, AppleScript, system preferences, fonts, utilities, speech features, and iDisk. The first two chapters should be especially helpful for experienced Mac OS users just getting started with Mac OS X; they explain many of the differences between Mac OS X and Mac OS 9.x and tell you how you can take advantage of the Classic environment to work with application software that wasn't built for Mac OS X.

Like the Visual QuickStart Guide, this book provides step-by-step instructions, plenty of illustrations, and a generous helping of tips. It was designed for page flipping—use the thumb tabs, index, or table of contents to find the topics you want to learn more about.

If you're interested in information about new Mac OS X and Mac OS X 10.1 features, be sure to browse through this **Introduction**. It'll give you a good idea of what you can expect to see on your computer.

✔ Tips

- If you're brand new to Mac OS and need more basic information about using Mac OS X, check out *Mac OS X: Visual QuickStart Guide*, the prequel to this book.
- This book covers Mac OS X 10.1, a revision to the original release of Mac OS X.

New Features in Mac OS X

Mac OS X was a major revision to the Macintosh operating system. Not only did it add and update features, but in many cases, it completely changed the way tasks are done. With a slick new look called "Aqua" (**Figure 2**) and with preemptive multitasking and protected memory that make the computer work more quickly and reliably, Mac OS X is like a breath of fresh air for Macintosh users.

Here's a look at some of the new and revised features you can expect to find in Mac OS X.

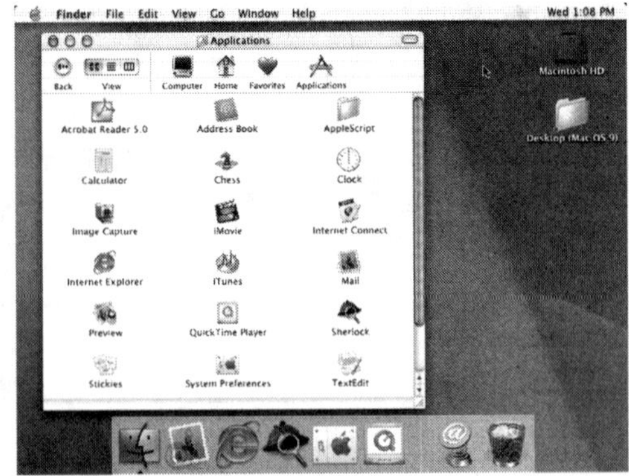

Figure 2 A look at the new Aqua interface.

✔ Tips

- Most of these features are covered in this book and its prequel, *Mac OS X: Visual QuickStart Guide.*
- This section discusses the new features in the original release of Mac OS X. New features in Mac OS X 10.1 are covered later in this **Introduction**.

Installer changes

- The Mac OS X installer automatically launches when you start from the Mac OS X install CD.
- The installer offers fewer customization features for installation.
- The Mac OS X Setup Assistant, which runs automatically after the installer restarts the computer, has a new look and offers several new options.

System changes

- System extensions and control panels no longer exist.
- By default, Mac OS X is set up for multiple users, making it possible for several people to set up personalized work environments on the same computer without the danger of accessing another user's files.

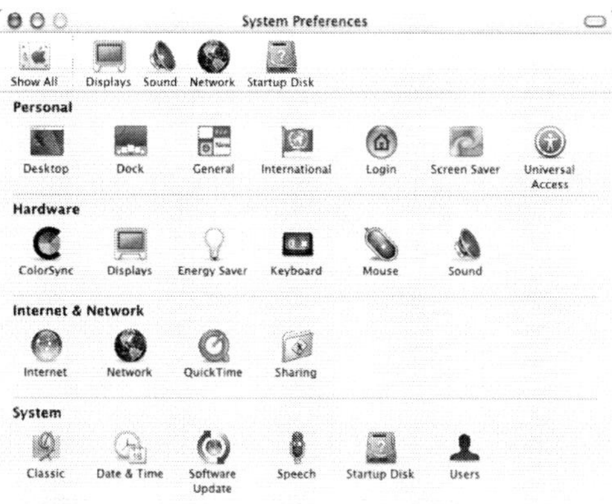

Figure 3 The System Preferences application. In Mac OS X 10.1, preferences were organized logically by function, as shown here.

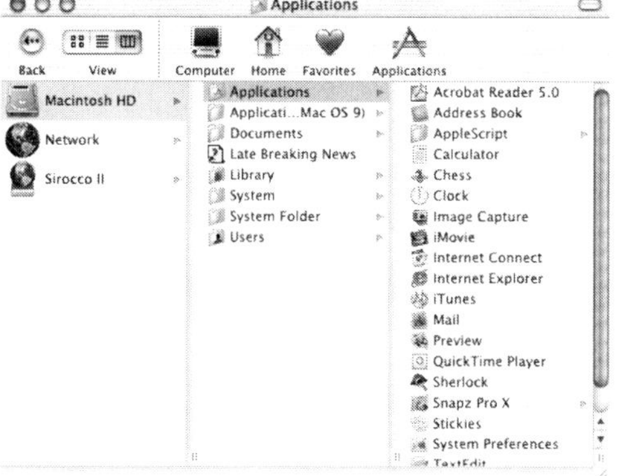

Figure 4 A window in column view. In Mac OS X 10.1, arrows appear to the right of folder names, as shown here.

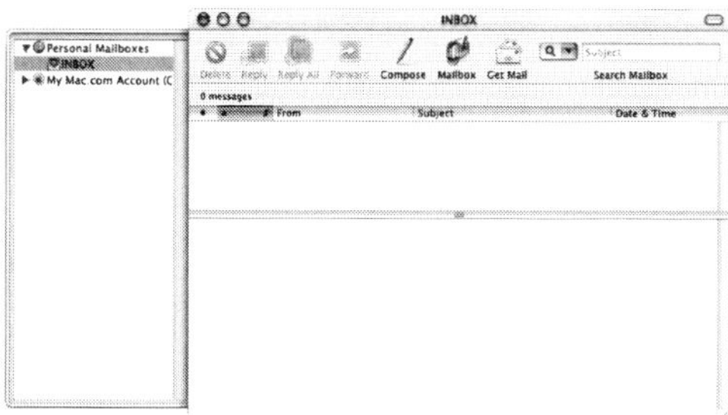

Figure 5 The new Mail application utilizes the drawer interface.

- A new Log Out command enables you to end your work session without shutting down the computer.
- A new System Preferences application (**Figure 3**) enables you to set options for the way the computer works.
- The default system font has been changed to Lucida Grande.
- Finder icons have a new "photo-illustrative" look (**Figure 2**).
- A new, customizable Dock (**Figure 2**) enables you to launch and switch to applications.

Window Changes

- Finder windows offer a new column view (**Figure 4**). Button view is no longer available.
- Pop-up windows and spring-loaded folders are no longer supported.
- Window controls have been changed. The left end of a window's title bar now includes Close, Minimize, and Zoom buttons (**Figure 2**).
- *Drawers* (**Figure 5**) are subwindows that slide out the side of a window to offer more options.
- Document windows for different applications each reside on their own layer, making it possible for them to be intermingled. (This differs from previous versions of Mac OS which required all document windows for an application to be grouped together.)
- You can often activate items on an inactive window or dialog with a single click rather than clicking first to activate the window, then clicking again to activate the item.

Menu changes

- Menus are now translucent so you can see underlying windows right through them.
- Sticky menus no longer disappear after a certain amount of time. When you click a menu's title, the menu appears and stays visible until you either click a command or click elsewhere onscreen.
- The Apple menu, which is no longer customizable, includes commands that work in all applications (**Figure 6**).
- A number of commands have been moved to the revised Apple menu (**Figure 6**) and new Finder menu (**Figure 7**). There are also new commands and new keyboard equivalents throughout the Finder.
- A new Go menu (**Figure 8**) makes it quick and easy to open windows for specific locations, including favorite and recent folders.

Dialog changes

- Dialogs can now appear as *sheets* that slide down from a window's title bar and remain part of the window (**Figure 9**). You can switch to another document or application when a dialog sheet is displayed.
- The Open and Save Location dialogs have been revised.
- The Save Location dialog can appear either collapsed (**Figure 10**) or expanded (**Figure 11**).

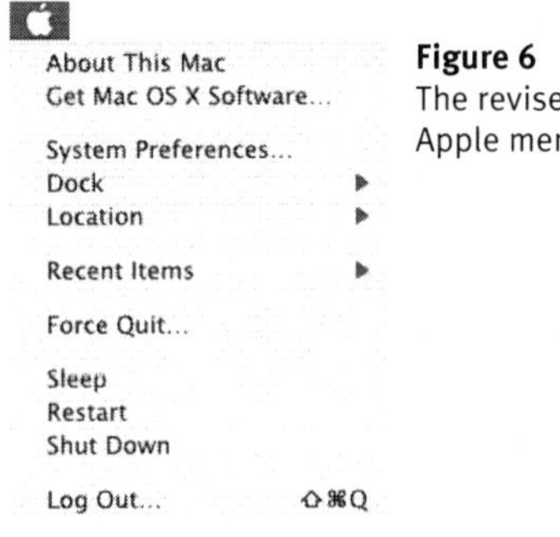

Figure 6 The revised Apple menu.

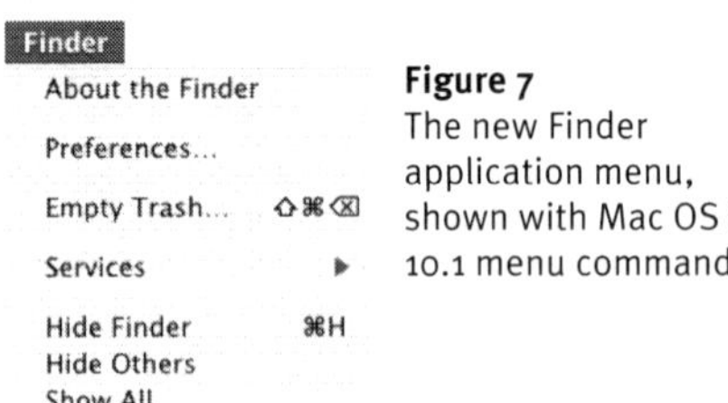

Figure 7 The new Finder application menu, shown with Mac OS X 10.1 menu commands.

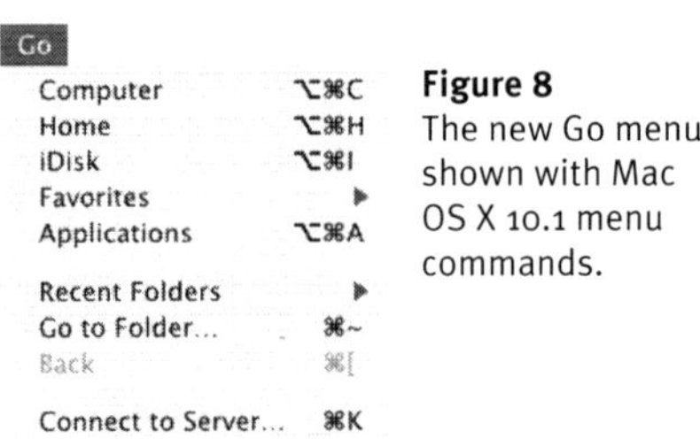

Figure 8 The new Go menu, shown with Mac OS X 10.1 menu commands.

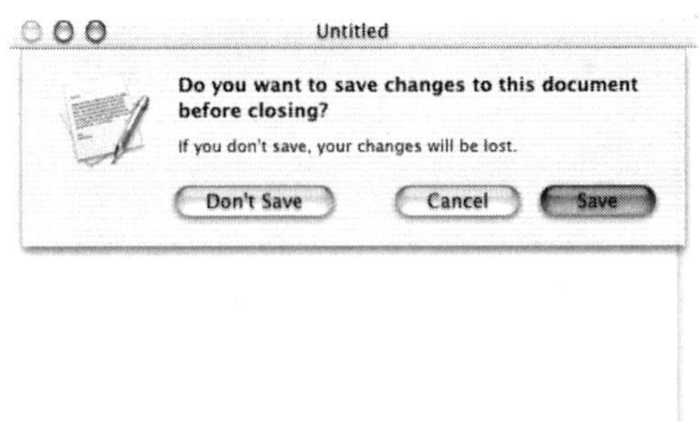

Figure 9 A dialog sheet is attached to a window.

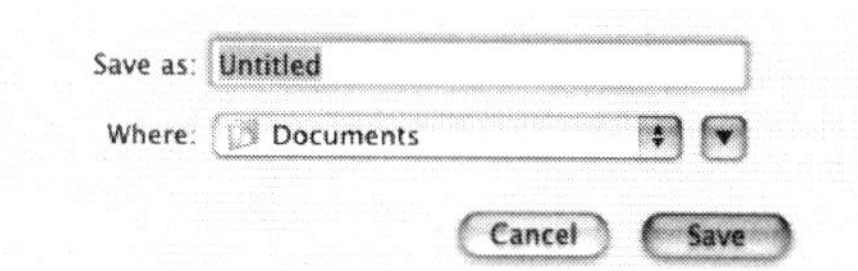

Figure 10 The Save Location dialog box collapsed to show only the bare essentials...

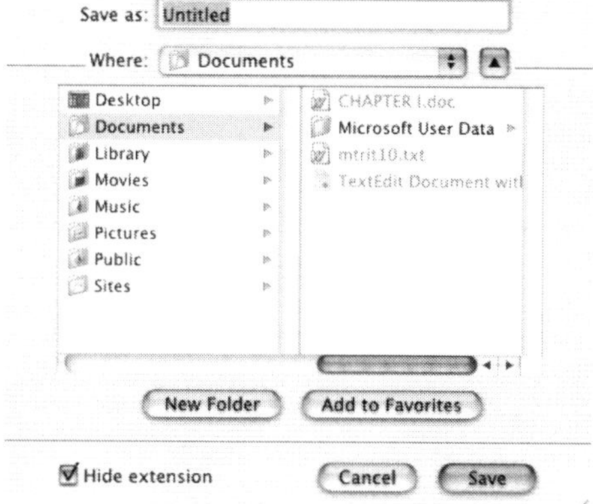

Figure 11 ...and expanded to show everything you need to save a file.

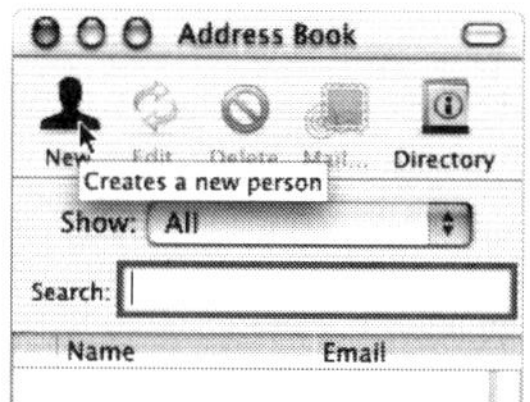

Figure 12 Help Tags replace Balloon Help.

Application changes

- Applications that are not Mac OS X compatible run in the *Classic environment*, which utilizes Mac OS 9.1 and later.
- The list of applications and utilities that come with Mac OS has undergone extensive changes to add and remove many programs.

Help changes

- Balloon Help has been replaced with Help Tags (**Figure 12**).
- The Help Viewer offers more options for searching and following links.
- Guide Help is no longer available.

New Features in Mac OS X 10.1

Mac OS X 10.1, the Mac OS X revision released in Autumn of 2001, improves performance and features. Here's a quick summary of some of the changes.

Performance improvements

- Apple programmers tweaked Mac OS X to make it faster and more responsive. Improved performance is most noticeable when launching applications, resizing or moving windows, displaying menus, and choosing menu commands.
- OpenGL, which is responsible for 3D graphics, is 20 percent faster. It also has full support for the nVidia GeForce 3 graphics card.

Finder & Aqua enhancements

- The columns in the Finder's list views can be resized by dragging the column border (**Figure 13**).
- Long file names in the Finder's icon view wrap to a second line (**Figure 14**).
- Arrows now appears to the right of folder names in the Finder's column view (**Figure 4**). This makes it easy to distinguish between folders and files in column view.
- File name extensions are turned off by default. You can display the extension for a file by setting an option in its Info window (**Figure 15**) or in the Finder Preferences window (**Figure 16**).
- You can now customize the Dock to display it on the left, right, or bottom of the screen.
- The new Burn Disc command makes it quick and easy to create data CDs from within the Finder (**Figure 17**).

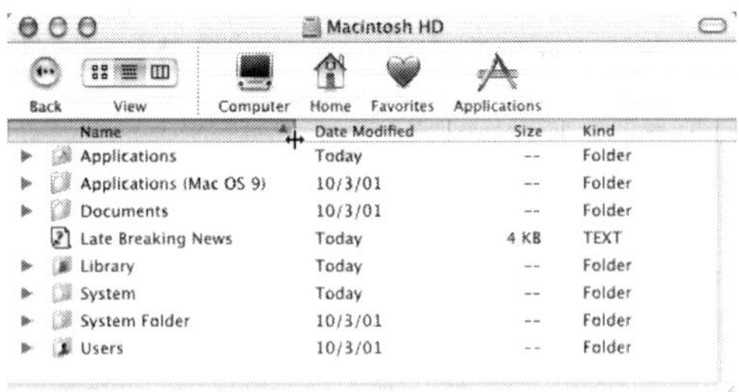

Figure 13 You can now change a column's width by dragging its border.

Figure 14 In icon view, long document names wrap to a second line.

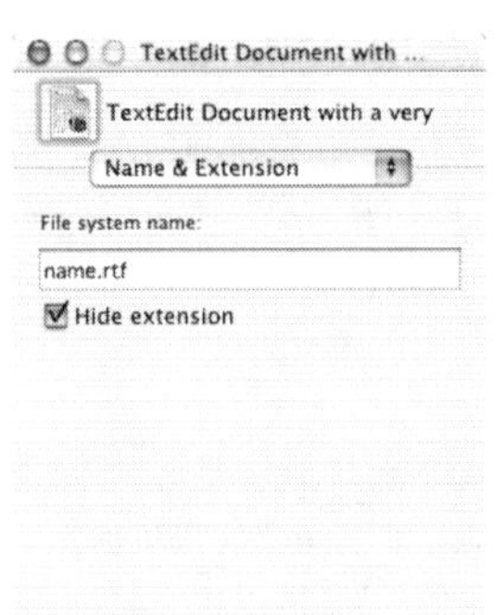

Figure 15 The Name & Extension options in a document's Info window.

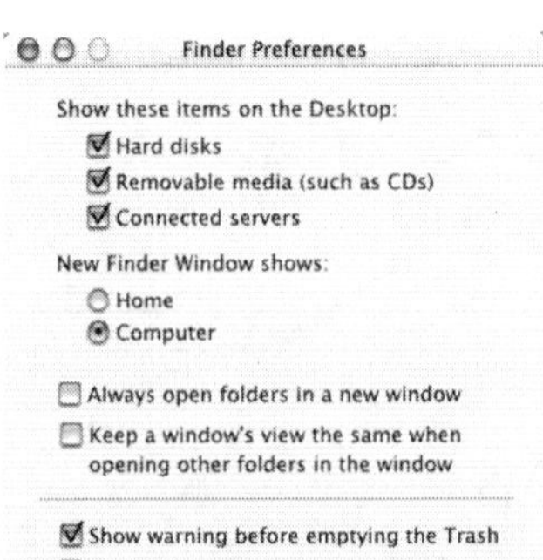

Figure 16 You can use Finder Preferences to specify whether file extensions should show.

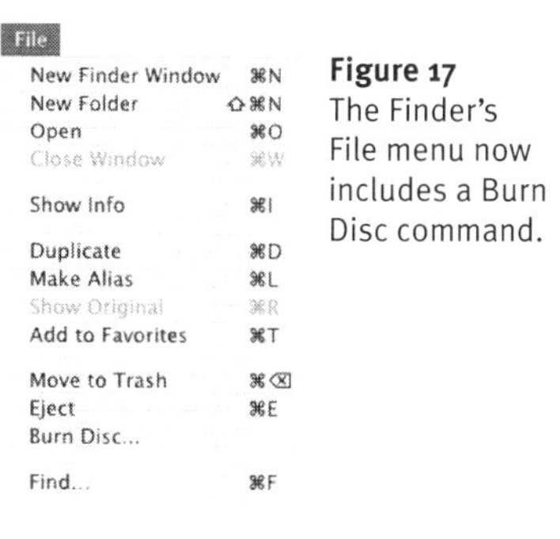

Figure 17 The Finder's File menu now includes a Burn Disc command.

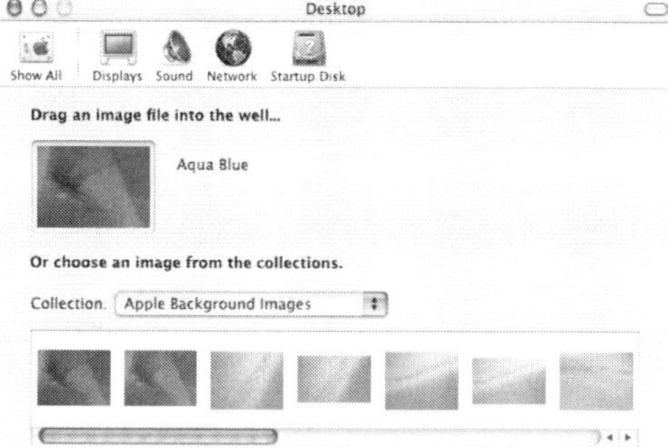

Figure 18 You can use the new Desktop preferences pane to choose a background image.

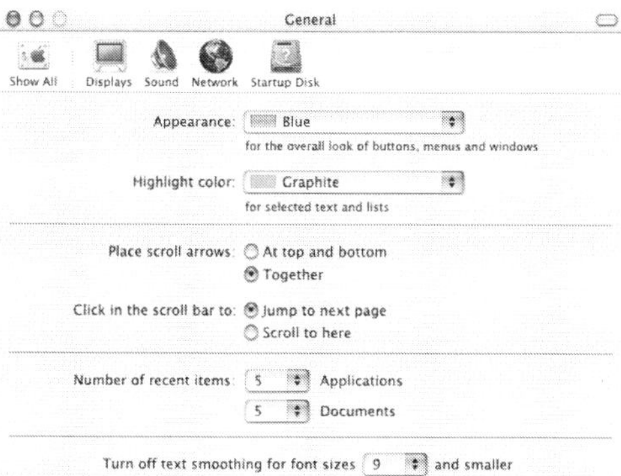

Figure 19 The General preferences pane now enables you to specify how many Recent Items should appear on the Apple menu.

Figure 20 You can add menus for controlling various preferences. This example shows Modem, Displays, Sound, and Date & Time (the menu bar clock) options.

System Preferences improvements

- The System Preferences pane's icons are now organized logically by use (**Figure 3**).
- The Desktop preferences pane, which is brand new in Mac OS X 10.1, enables you to set a desktop picture (**Figure 18**). (This functionality was moved from Finder Preferences.)
- The General preferences pane now enables you to set how many Recent Items should appear on the Apple menu. It also enables you to set a font size threshold for the font smoothing feature (**Figure 19**).
- The Sound preferences pane enables you to select different settings for each output device.
- The Date & Time preferences pane enables you to display the menu bar clock as an analog clock.
- You can now display controls for a variety of System Preferences right in the menu bar (**Figure 20**). You specify whether you want to show or hide the controls in the applicable preferences pane.

Printing improvements

- Mac OS X 10.1 ships with over 200 PostScript printer description files, including files from Hewlett-Packard, Lexmark, and Xerox.
- In most cases, the driver for a USB printer will automatically be selected when the printer is added to the Print Center.

Networking improvements

- Mac OS X is now more compatible with network systems, including AppleShare, Windows NT, Windows 2000, and SAMBA.
- Mac OS X 10.1 now fully supports AirPort, with the AirPort Admin Utility and the AirPort Setup Assistant.

Application improvements

- Mac OS X 10.1 includes Java 2 for up-to-date Java compatibility.
- Internet Explorer 5.1 fully supports Java within the Web browser.
- iTunes now includes CD burning capabilities so you can create music CDs from your iTunes libraries.
- The new DVD Player application enables you to watch DVD movies on computers with DVD-ROM drives or SuperDrives.
- iDVD 2 includes many enhancements for creating your own DVD discs on SuperDrive-equipped Macs, including background encoding.
- AppleScript is now fully supported by Mac OS X. In fact, the Mac OS X 10.1 Finder is more scriptable than ever.

Moving Up to Mac OS X

Moving Up to Mac OS X

Mac OS X is the latest generation of Macintosh operating system software. Rebuilt from the ground up, Mac OS X has a robust Unix core that offers, among other things, a command-line interface—something brand new for Macintosh users. Fortunately (for those of us who don't want to learn Unix), Mac OS X provides a fully functional graphic user interface that does not require knowledge or understanding of Unix.

Mac OS X also offers innovations in multitasking and memory management. Although its Aqua interface has familiar elements from Mac OS 9.x and earlier, it has a more modern look that includes pulsating buttons and translucent windows and menus. Mac OS X's architecture takes full advantage of the processors on today's Macintosh models to do things never before possible on a Mac OS computer.

If you're upgrading to Mac OS X from a previous version of Mac OS, this chapter is for you. It tells you about the components of Mac OS X and defines many terms related to the new operating system. It explains how Mac OS X differs from previous versions of Mac OS. It also points out how tasks performed in Mac OS 9.x are done in Mac OS X—and what tasks are no longer possible.

✔ Tips

- A fuller discussion of Unix can be found in **Chapters 3** and **4**.
- This book does not cover basic Finder operations. If you need instructions for using the Finder and Mac OS X software and utilities, check out the prequel to this book, *Mac OS X: Visual QuickStart Guide*.

Mac OS X Components

Mac OS X is said to be built in layers. Over the past few years, Apple has illustrated these layers in several different ways; **Figures 1** and **2** show two of them. This layered approach limits software access to programming code; each layer can only access the code of the layer immediately beneath it. (The only exception is Classic, which can access all layers.) This enables Apple and third-party developers to create complex yet stable software that does not require intimate knowledge of all workings of the underlying operating system.

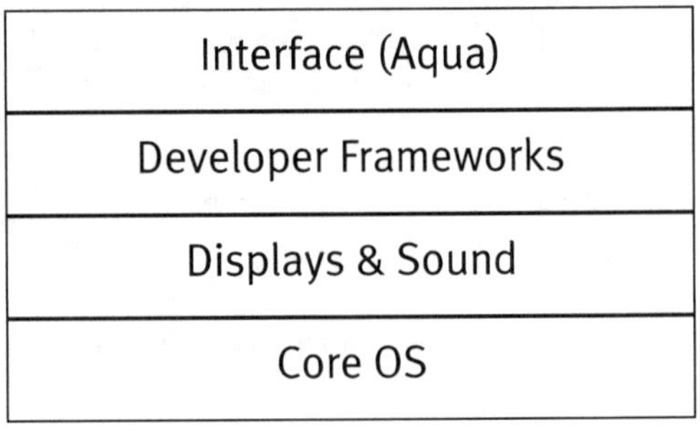

Do you need to know how all these layers work? No! But since you may hear these terms over and over as you work with Mac OS X, here's an explanation so you're not in the dark.

Interface (Aqua)
Developer Frameworks
Displays & Sound
Core OS

Figure 1 A basic representation of the layers of Mac OS X.

Aqua			AppleScript
Cocoa	Java 2	Carbon	Classic
Quartz	OpenGL	QuickTime	Audio
Darwin - Open Desktop			

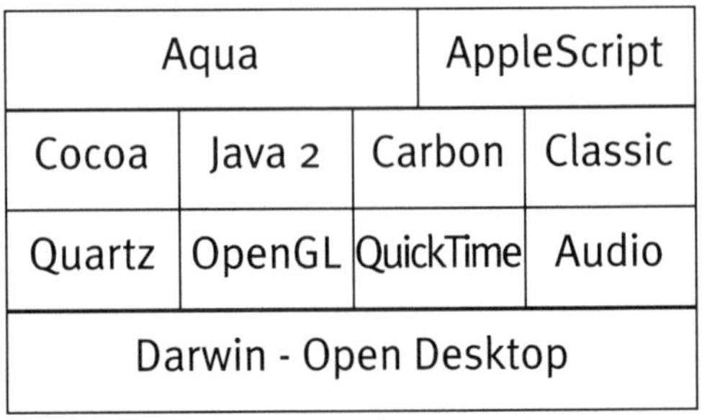

Figure 2 A more detailed representation of the layers of Mac OS X.

✔ Tip

- *Open source*, a phrase used throughout Mac OS X, means that developers outside of Apple are allowed to modify software components at the source code level. You can learn more at www.apple.com/opensource/.

Core OS

The Core OS layer of Mac OS X includes the Unix base and a number of higher-level operating system utilities.

- **Darwin** is part of the bottom or foundation layer of Mac OS X. It is made up of two technologies:
  - **Mach** is a Unix kernel technology that was developed at Carnegie Mellon University in the 1980s and 1990s. It is an open source operating system that provides memory management, memory protection, process scheduling, and interprocess communication services to Mac OS X.
  - **BSD** stands for Berkeley Standard Distribution. It is a version of Unix adapted by Berkeley University from AT&T's System III. BSD provides file system support, network services, symmetric multiprocessing support, and multi-threading facilities to Mac OS X.
- **Core utilities** handle interapplication communication and related tasks, including networking, Internet communication, and security.

Displays & Sound

The Core Services layer of Mac OS X includes a number of higher-level operating system utilities and graphics services:

- **Quartz**, which replaces QuickDraw and related managers, handles two-dimensional graphics that support the user interface. Quartz is based on Adobe Portable Document Format (PDF).
- **OpenGL**, which replaces QuickDraw 3D, is an Open Source rendering system that handles advanced three-dimensional graphics, especially those used by games, multimedia, and scientific visualization.
- **QuickTime** handles video and sound.
- **Audio** handles sound.

Developer Frameworks

Developer frameworks (which are sometimes referred to as *application frameworks* or *application environments*) enable user and system applications to run.

- **Classic** enables you to launch and run Mac OS 9.1 or later. Once Mac OS 9.x is running, you can launch Mac OS 9.x applications within it. The Classic environment was created to meet one of the main challenges of Mac OS X: to create a new operating system that would still allow older applications to run.
- **Carbon** is a set of application programmer interfaces (APIs) that account for about 70% of the APIs in Mac OS 9.1. When a program uses Carbon APIs, it can run in Mac OS 9.x or Mac OS X and is indistinguishable from any other Mac OS X application.
- **Cocoa** is an object-oriented development platform that allows applications to interact with each other and share libraries of programming code. Users cannot see any difference between Carbon and Cocoa applications, both of which run under Mac OS X.
- **Java** supports Java 2 applications and applets by running a Java Virtual Machine. Java can be used by developers for the Cocoa environment.

✔ Tips

- A Mac OS 9.x application that has been rewritten to use the Carbon environment's APIs is said to be *Carbonized*.
- The Classic environment is discussed in detail in **Chapter 2**. If you regularly work in the Classic environment, you may want to check out *Mac OS 9.1: Visual QuickStart Guide* to learn more about its features and use.

Aqua

Aqua is the overall look and feel, as well as interface elements, available to all Mac OS X applications, including the Finder. Aqua includes extensive use of animation and three-dimensional rendering to enhance the user experience. Aqua features include animated shrinking/expanding windows, bouncing icons in the Dock, shadows around windows and menus, translucent menus, the Dock itself, and extensive support for multiple users.

✔ Tip

- Many of Aqua's basic interface features, including the Dock, are covered in detail in *Mac OS X: Visual QuickStart Guide.*

Other Mac OS X Terms

Mac OS X has brought new terms to the vocabularies of intermediate and advanced Mac OS users. Here are some of the terms you might want to know.

Bundle or Package

A *bundle* or *package* is a collection of application components, such as executable code and resource information, each of which is in a separate file. Mac OS X gathers an application's components together in a directory and then presents them to the user as a single, double-clickable file.

✔ Tip

- To view an application's package contents, hold down Control while clicking the application's icon to display a contextual menu (**Figure 3**), and choose Show Package Contents. A window opens with a Contents folder within it. Open that folder to see the contents (**Figure 4**).

Framework

A *framework* is shared collection of programming code (a library) with related resource information. Framework libraries are said to be *dynamic* because they are only loaded when used. Frameworks are packaged as bundles.

Shell

A shell is an interactive, command-line interface for sending instructions to the operating system. A shell is primarily of interest to programmers, system administrators, and advanced users. Mac OS X includes Terminal, an application that offers a shell (**Figure 5**).

✔ Tip

- Consult **Chapters 3** and **4**, which cover Unix, for more information about the shell.

Figure 3 To view the contents of an application's bundle or package, choose Show Package Contents from its contextual menu.

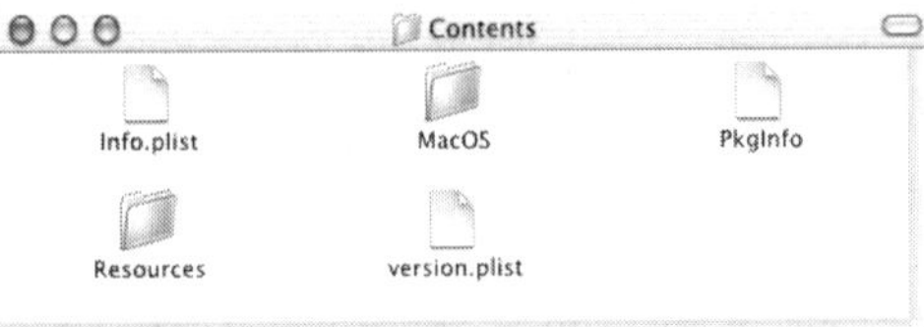

Figure 4 The components of Preview's bundle.

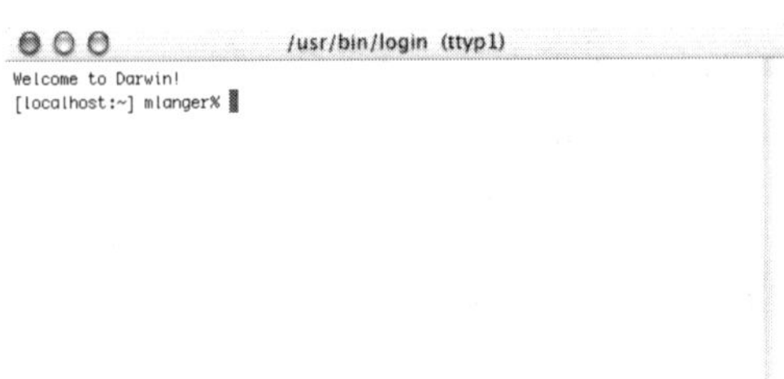

Figure 5 You can use Terminal to access the Unix shell.

Multitasking

Two of the new features of Mac OS X is preemptive multitasking and protected memory. Although some form of multitasking has been in the Macintosh operating system since the late 1980s, the multitasking features of Mac OS X are far more advanced and superior.

In this section, I explain the evolution of Mac OS multitasking and define the different forms of multitasking that Mac OS users have taken advantage of over the years.

Switcher & Context switching

In the late 1980s, Apple introduced a program called *Switcher* that enabled you to load more than one application into memory at a time. Switcher worked by saving the state of one application and restoring the state of another. Although this was not considered true multitasking—only one application was running at a time—it simulated a multitasking environment by enabling you to work with two applications without quitting and launching them repeatedly.

MultiFinder & Cooperative Multitasking

In the early 1990s, Apple developed *MultiFinder*, which did pretty much what Switcher had done, enabling you to load as many applications into memory as your installed RAM would support. Features were added until MultiFinder supported a type of cooperative multitasking.

In *cooperative multitasking*, each time a program pauses to allow the operating system to check the status of the keyboard, mouse, and other operations, it also enables other applications that are loaded into memory, to update their operations. Programs had to be written in

Continued on next page...

Continued from previous page.

such a way that they allowed the operating system and other applications to have some processor time. As the Mac and its software evolved, applications included code that prioritized their importance when they were not running in the foreground. The higher an application's priority, the more processor time it would get. A game, for example, would have a higher priority than a spreadsheet. This is how multitasking works in Mac OS 9.x.

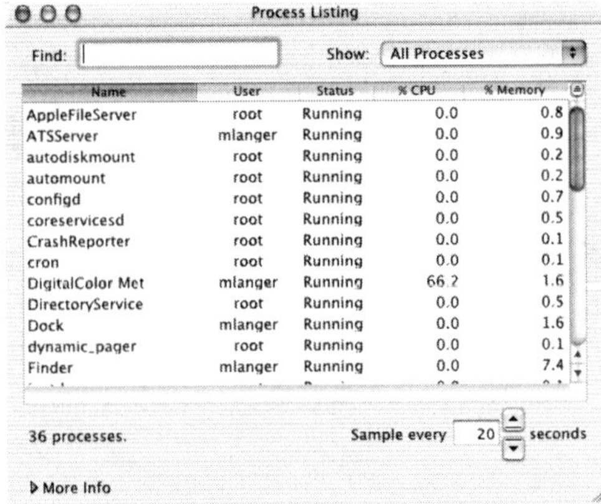

Figure 6 Process Viewer shows all processes running on your computer and the percentage of CPU time and memory each is using.

Preemptive Multitasking & Protected Memory

In Mac OS X, communication between an application and the CPU is handled by a *scheduler*, which is part of Darwin's kernel environment. When a program is launched, the scheduler takes control and allocates a certain percentage of CPU time to the application's processes. When that time is up, the scheduler gives the CPU time to another application's processes, thus *preempting* any running process. This is called *preemptive multitasking*.

For the scheduler to work, your computer's memory must be tightly controlled. As a result, Mac OS X's memory management does not allow an application to write information in another application's space or interfere with certain critical system resources. This concept is called *protected memory* and it prevents your entire computer from crashing or locking up when one application fails.

Symmetric Multiprocessing

Mac OS X's kernel includes built-in support for computers with multiple CPUs, such as the dual processor G4 models Apple introduced in 2000 and 2001. In *symmetric multiprocessing* (SMP), the operating system keeps both CPUs busy, thus increasing system and application performance.

✔ Tip

- You can use Process Viewer to see how much CPU time is allocated to an application's processes (**Figure 6**). I tell you more about Process Viewer in **Chapter 10**.

Installing Mac OS X

A Mac OS X installation should not require detailed instructions for anyone who has installed Apple system software before. There are, however, several things to keep in mind regarding the installation process. Here's a quick look at installation concerns.

✔ Tip

- Although step-by-step instructions for installing and configuring Mac OS X are not included in this book, you can find them in *Mac OS X: Visual QuickStart Guide.*

Initialization Options

Although you don't have to initialize a disk to install Mac OS X—you can do your installation on a disk that already contains a version of Mac OS, as well as existing data—the Mac OS X installer does offer two initialization options:

- **Unix File System** (UFS) is for Unix and Mac OS X operation.
- **Mac OS Extended** (HFS+) is for Mac OS X and Mac OS 9.x operation.

✔ Tips

- Mac OS 9.x cannot read UFS-formatted disks. For this reason, its best to avoid UFS initialization if you expect to run the Classic environment or share files on a network.
- If your disk is formatted as Mac OS Standard (HFS), you must use one of the initialization options to erase the disk and reformat it before installing Mac OS X.

Installation Components & Language Options

If you click the Customize button in the Easy Install screen of the Mac OS X installer, you can pick and choose among the installation components:

- **Base System** and Essential System Software make up the base system software. They must be installed.
- **BSD Subsystem** is the BSD portion of Darwin. If you do not install this part of the system software, certain network and Internet features won't work. Because of this, it's not a good idea to omit this component.
- **Additional Print Drivers** is a set of printer drivers and related files. If you need to save disk space for the installation, you may want to omit this component.
- **Localized Files** are various sets of files necessary to display Mac OS X in languages other than English. They may include Japanese, German, French, Spanish, Italian, and Dutch. Omitting some or all of these components is a good way to reduce the amount of disk space Mac OS X requires.

Mac OS X Setup Assistant

When your computer restarts after a Mac OS X installation, the Mac OS X Setup Assistant appears. Use this assistant to properly configure Mac OS X for your location and your network and Internet connections.

Installing Mac OS 9.x

If you plan to run applications in the Classic environment, you'll need to have Mac OS 9.1 or later installed on your computer. If Mac OS 9.1 or later was already installed on your computer, you're all set; a Mac OS X installation will not remove it (unless, of course, you initialized the disk).

If Mac OS 9.1 or later is not on your disk, start from a Mac OS 9.x installation disc. To do so, use the Startup Disk preferences pane to select the install disk (**Figure 7**) and click Restart. Then use the installer to Install Mac OS 9.x.

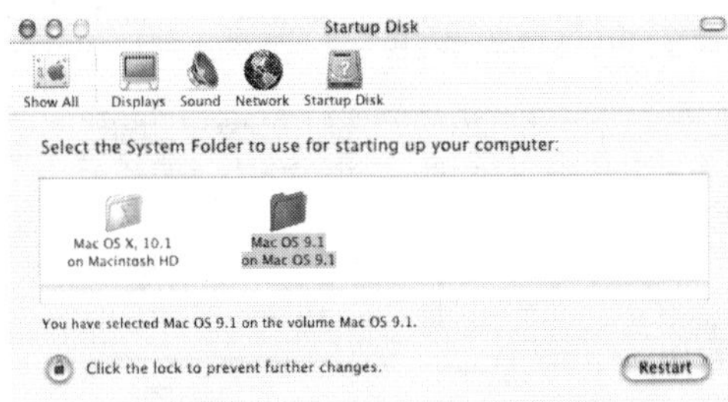

Figure 7 Use the Startup Disk preferences pane to select the Mac OS 9.x installation disk and restart.

✔ Tips

- I explain how to use the Startup Disk preferences pane in **Chapter 2**.
- For complete instructions on installing and configuring Mac OS 9.x, check *Mac OS 9.1: Visual QuickStart Guide.*
- Mac OS X 10.1 prefers Mac OS 9.2 or later. If you try to use the Classic environment with Mac OS 9.1 installed, a dialog like the one in **Figure 8** will appear. You can continue by clicking OK. You can obtain a Mac OS 9.2 updater from Apple's Web site, www.apple.com.
- If you bought the Mac OS X 10.1 Update package, you already have the Mac OS 9.2. updater CD; it's part of the package.

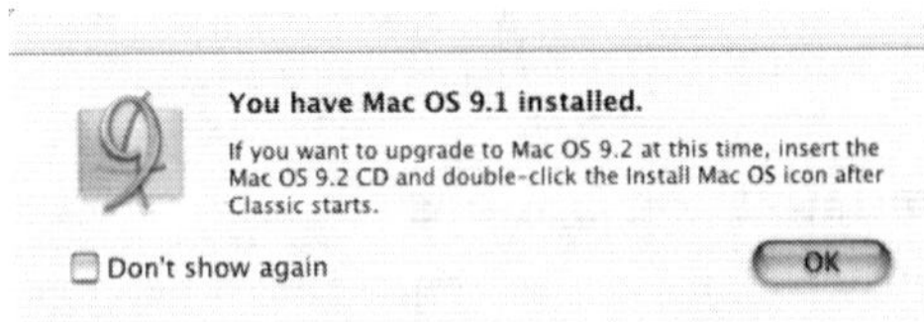

Figure 8 This dialog appears when you launch the Classic environment from Mac OS X 10.1 with Mac OS 9.1 installed.

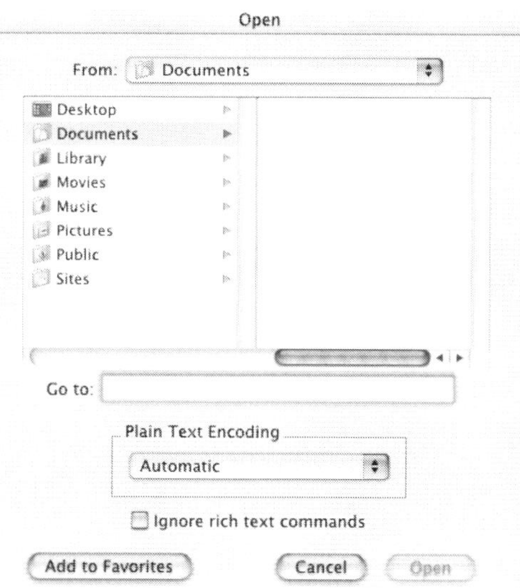

Figure 9 TextEdit's Open dialog includes a Go to edit box, where you can enter the path for the folder you want to open.

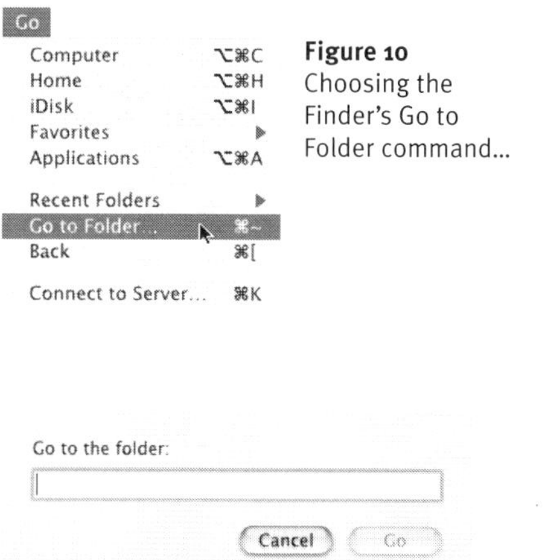

Figure 10 Choosing the Finder's Go to Folder command...

Figure 11 ...displays a dialog you can use to enter the path to the folder you want to open.

Directories

To use familiar Mac OS language, a *directory* is a folder. As you may have gathered, the term *directory* is more commonly used in Mac OS X than in previous versions of Mac OS.

In this section, I discuss the concept of directories and paths, tell you about the standard directories used throughout Mac OS X, and explain how the Mac OS X directory structure compares to that in Mac OS 9.x.

Directories & Paths

In Mac OS, users have always been shielded from the concept of directories by the graphic user interface. In the Mac GUI (and later, in Windows), directories are represented by folder icons. Folders can be nestled inside other folders, thus resulting in multilevel directory structure.

A *path* is textual description of location in the directory structure. So, for example, in Mac OS 9.x, if I wanted to enter the path for the Preferences folder inside the System Folder on a hard disk named Macintosh HD, I'd enter Macintosh HD:System Folder:Preferences. Note the use of a colon (:) in the path to separate each level—that's why colons cannot be used in file names.

In Mac OS 9.x and earlier, the standard Open and Save As dialogs offered just one way to choose a source or destination directory—by manipulating the top half of the dialog. But although the directory portion of dialogs is still available in Mac OS X, you can now specify a directory by typing in a path (**Figure 9**). In the Finder, you can even open a specific folder by choosing Go > Go to Folder (**Figure 10**) and entering the path to the folder in the dialog that appears (**Figure 11**).

Continued on next page...

Continued from previous page.

In Mac OS X, the top-level directory is called *root*. (This comes from the analogy of a directory structure being like a tree.) The root directory is identified with /. Forward slash characters (/) replace the colons throughout the path. So if I wanted to specify the Library folder inside the System folder on my hard disk, I'd enter /System/Library. And if I wanted to specify my Documents folder, I'd enter /Users/mlanger/Documents.

✔ Tips

- A path can also be used to indicate the exact location of a file within a folder. Just include the file name at the end of the path. For example, TextEdit can be found on a Mac OS X computer at /Applications/TextEdit and Process Viewer can be found at /Applications/Utilities/Process Viewer.
- Ever notice how as Windows gets more Mac-like, Mac OS gets more Windows-like? Don't be alarmed by this. Paths and slashes have been used in Unix since it was started, and it's older than both Mac OS and Windows.

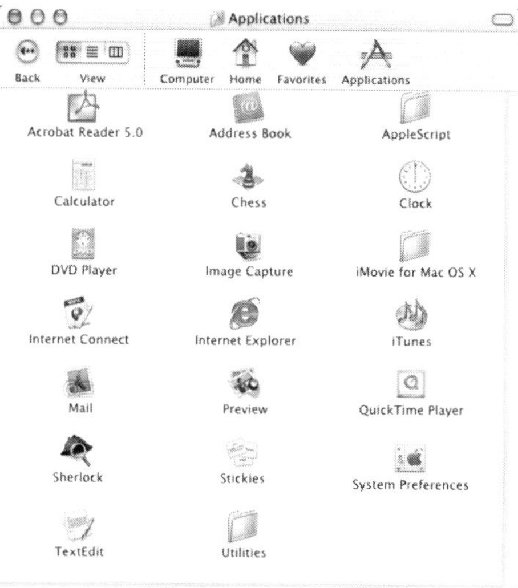

Figure 12 The contents of the Applications folder on a freshly installed Mac OS X 10.1 system.

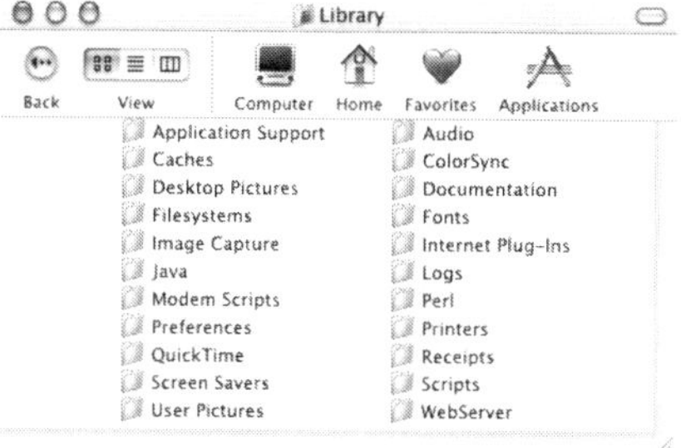

Figure 13 The contents of the Library folder on a freshly installed Mac OS X 10.1 system.

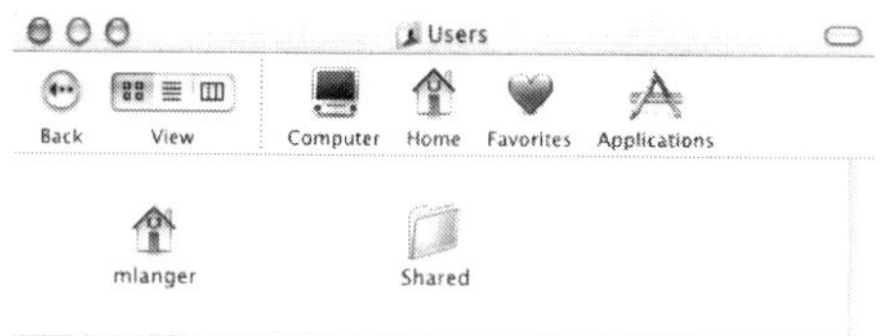

Figure 14 A Users folder with only one user defined.

Standard Directories

Mac OS X includes several directories that did not appear in previous versions of Mac OS:

- **Applications** (**Figure 12**) contains Mac OS X applications. It is distinguished from Applications (Mac OS 9), which contains applications that run in the Classic environment.
- **System** contains Mac OS X system software. It is distinguished from System Folder, which contains Mac OS 9.x system software.
- **Library** (**Figure 13**) contains preference information. Unlike Mac OS 9.x's Preferences folder (inside the System Folder), Library contains fonts, desktop pictures, modem scripts, printer drivers, plug-ins, and other information used by applications and utilities.
- **Users** (**Figure 14**) holds information for a computer's users, whether the computer is used by one person or one hundred.
- **Documents** contains user documents.

In Mac OS X, the Application, Library, and Documents folders are repeated in the directory structure. For example, each user's "Home" folder includes both a Documents and Library folder. If the user installs software, an Applications folder containing that software also appears. These folders are private to the user and cannot be accessed by any other user.

✔ Tips

- System and Users are "owned" by the system and require administrator (or "root") access to manage them.
- You should not change the contents of System (or System Folder, for that matter), unless you know what you're doing.
- I explain how Mac OS X's multiple users features work in **Chapter 6**.

Invisible Directories

If the directory structure that you can see and explore in Mac OS X isn't enough, there's a collection of invisible directories (and files) that exist to support the Unix kernel. These directories are invisible in the Finder because the average user simply doesn't need to see them. In fact, if you saw these directories and files and started messing with them, chances are you'd mess up the operating system and have to reinstall Mac OS. (Not something *I'd* want to do.)

Of course, you can see them if you really want to. Launch the Terminal application, which you can find at /Applications/Utilities/Terminal, enter ls /, and press Return. A list of all folders (and files) within the root directory—including invisible folders and files—appears (**Figure 15**). Compare the list in **Figure 15** with what you see in **Figure 16** to get an idea of what's hiding from you on the root level of your hard disk.

✔ Tip

- If typing Unix commands in a shell is something that gets you excited, be sure to check **Chapters 3** and **4**, which go far beyond the rather pedestrian example here.

Mac OS X File Locations

If you've been using Mac OS for a while but are new to Mac OS X, you're probably wondering how the new directory structure compares to the old structure for storing various types of files. **Table 1** should answer any questions you have.

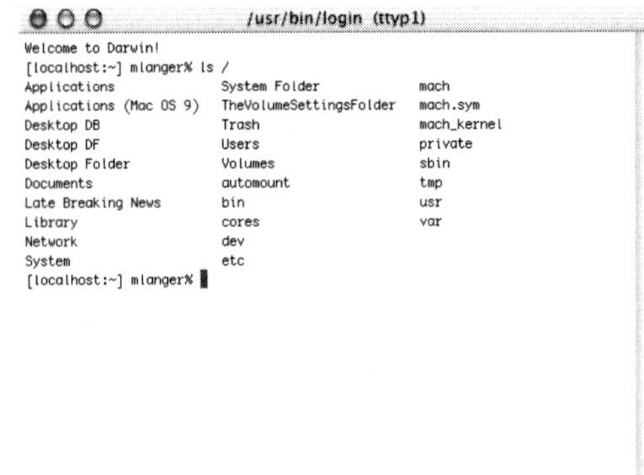

Figure 15 Use the ls command within Terminal to see a list of all directories and files, including invisible ones.

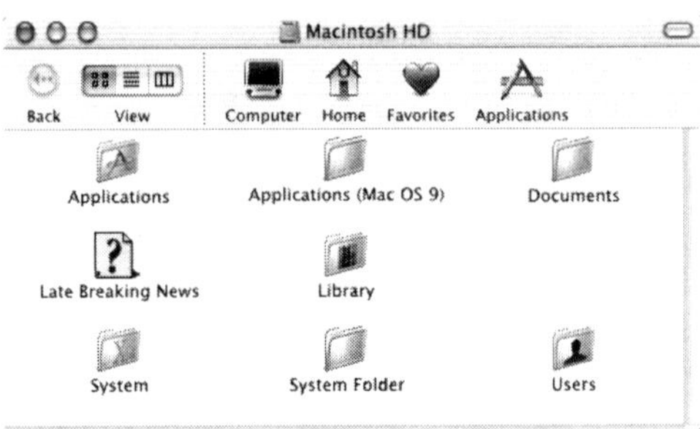

Figure 16 Not all of the folders and files that are listed in Terminal (**Figure 15**) appear in the Finder.

Table 1

Mac OS 9.x vs Mac OS X File Locations

TYPE OF FILE	MAC OS 9.X LOCATION	MAC OS X LOCATION (SHARED) MAC OS X LOCATION (PRIVATE)
Application	Applications (Mac OS 9)	/Applications /Users/*username*/Applications
Document	Documents	/Library/Documents /Users/*username*/Documents
Fonts	System Folder:Fonts	/Library/Fonts /Users/*username*/Library/Fonts
Sounds	System Folder:Sounds	/Library/Audio/Sounds /Users/*username*/Audio/Sounds
Desktop Pictures	anywhere	/Library/Desktop Pictures anywhere
Control Panels	System Folder:Control Panels	n/a n/a
Extensions	System Folder:Extensions	n/a n/a
General Preferences	System Folder:Preferences	/Library/Preferences /Users/*username*/Library/Preferences
Printer Drivers	System Folder:Extensions	/Library/Printers /Users/*username*/Library/Printers
ColorSync Profiles	System Folder:ColorSync Profiles	/Library/ColorSync/Profiles /Users/*username*/Library/ColorSync/Profiles
Modem Scripts	System Folder:Extensions:Modem Scripts	/Library/Modem Scripts n/a
Keychains	System Folder:Preferences:Keychains	n/a /Users/*username*/Library/Keychains
Startup Items	System Folder:Startup Items	n/a Use Login Preferences pane

Other Differences

There are a few other differences between the way Mac OS 9.x and Mac OS X work. Here's a quick rundown of the ones I think are most important.

Figure 17 You can use the About This Mac window to see how much RAM is installed in your computer.

Memory Management

Mac OS 9.x offered a number of features and tools you could use to manage system and application memory. For example, you could use the Memory control panel to set up virtual memory and resize the RAM cache. You could use the Info window to set an application's RAM allocation. You could use the About this Computer window to see how much RAM each application was using.

All this is gone in Mac OS X. Mac OS X has a powerful, sophisticated memory management system that makes it unnecessary for the user to modify memory functions. You can use Process Viewer, which is discussed in **Chapter 10** and earlier in this chapter, to see how much RAM various processes are using (**Figure 6**). You can choose Apple > About this Mac to see how much RAM is installed in your computer (**Figure 17**). But that's it.

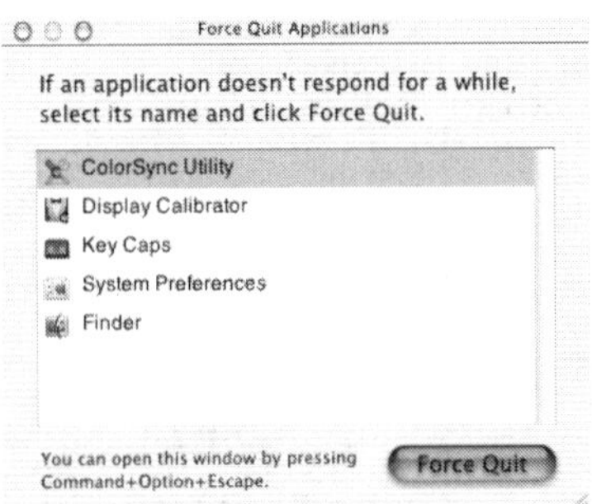

Figure 18 Use the Force Quit Applications dialog to quit unresponsive applications.

Multiuser System

Mac OS 9.x included the Multiple Users control panel, which enabled you to set up a computer so it could be used by more than one person. The multiuser environment was optional and turned off by default.

Mac OS X, on the other hand, is a multiple-user system. It assumes that your computer will be used by more than one person and automatically configures the hard disk to allow for privacy between users files.

✔ Tip

- I tell you more about Mac OS X's multiple-user features in **Chapter 6**.

Fonts

In Mac OS 9.x all fonts were installed in the Fonts folder inside the System Folder. You could double-click a font suitcase to open it, then double-click a font file inside it to see what the font looked like.

In Mac OS X, fonts are scattered all over your hard disk, as discussed in **Chapter 9**. Where they are installed determines who can use them. And you can't see what a font looks like from the Finder; you need to use Key Caps.

Printing

In Mac OS 9.x, you selected a printer with the Chooser and used a Desktop Printer to monitor and cancel print jobs.

In Mac OS X, you use the Print Center utility to manage printers and print jobs.

✔ Tip

- Print Center is discussed briefly in **Chapter 10** and in more detail in *Mac OS X: Visual QuickStart Guide.*

Networking

In Mac OS 9.x, you used a variety of control panels and the Chooser to set up networking and file sharing and connect to a file server.

In Mac OS X, you set up networking and file sharing with the Network and Sharing preference panes, and use the Finder's Connect to Server command to connect to a file server, as discussed in **Chapter 5**.

Disk First Aid & Drive Setup

Mac OS 9.x included two separate utilities for verifying/repairing and formatting a hard disk: Disk First Aid and Drive Setup.

Mac OS X combines these two application into one—Disk Utility—which is discussed in **Chapter 10**.

Force Quit

In Mac OS 9.x, you could force quit an application by pressing [Option][⌘][Esc]. This usually worked, although sometimes it would bring the entire system to a grinding halt that required the [Control][⌘][◁] keystroke to revive by forcing a restart.

In Mac OS X, however, you can force quit an application without knowing any secret keystrokes or hurting other applications. Choose Apple > Force Quit, select the name of the application in the dialog that appears (**Figure 18**), and click the Force Quit button. Because memory is protected, neither the system nor other applications is affected.

Startup Items

In Mac OS 9.x, you could place any item in the Startup Items folder within the System Folder and those items would open when you started your computer.

Mac OS X does not have a Startup Items folder. Instead, you use the Login preferences pane to specify which items you want to open when you log in to the computer. This makes it possible for each user to have his own collection of startup items, as discussed in **Chapter 6**.

Control Panels & Extensions

In Mac OS 9.x, you could modify the way the operating system worked by adding control panels and extensions, many of which came with Mac OS. These items were installed in the Control Panels and Extensions folders within the System Folder.

Guess what? In Mac OS X, there are no control panels and no Control Panels folder. Although there is an extensions folder, it's used strictly by the System for device drivers and kernel extensions and should not be modified.

Doing It in Mac OS X

Table 2 summarizes how specific tasks are completed in Mac OS 9.x and Mac OS X. This should help most experienced Mac OS 9.x users transition to Mac OS X.

Table 2

Completing Tasks in Mac OS 9.x and Mac OS X

Task	Mac OS 9.x Tool	Mac OS X Tool
Set a theme	Appearance control panel	n/a
Set Finder appearance and color	Appearance control panel	General preferences pane
Set font preferences	Appearance control panel	General preferences pane
Set desktop picture	Appearance control panel	Desktop preferences pane
Set sound effects	Appearance control panel	n/a
Set scroll arrow placement	Appearance control panel	General preferences pane
Set collapsible windows	Appearance control panel	n/a
Configure Apple menu	Apple Menu Options control panel	n/a
Set number of recent items	Apple Menu Options control panel	General preferences pane
Configure/enable AppleTalk	AppleTalk control panel	Network preferences pane
Configure ColorSync	ColorSync control panel	ColorSync preferences pane
Configure/use control strip	Control Strip control panel, Control strip	Dock preferences pane, Dock
Set date & time options	Date & Time control panel	Date & Time preferences pane
Set energy saving options	Energy Saver control panel	Energy Saver preferences pane
Select extensions & control panels	Extensions manager control panel	n/a
Configure File Exchange	File Exchange control panel	n/a
Configure/enable file sharing	File Sharing control panel	Sharing preferences pane
Synchronize files	File Synchronization control panel	n/a
Set general system preferences	General Controls control panel	n/a
Configure infrared	Infrared control panel	n/a
Set Internet options	Internet control panel	Internet preferences pane
Set Keyboard options	Keyboard control panel	Keyboard preferences pane
Set up keychain access	Keychain Access control panel	Keychain Access utility
Configure/use Launcher	Launcher control panel	Dock preferences pane, Dock
Set up/manage locations	Location Manager control panel	Network preferences pane
Configure RAM	Memory control panel	n/a
Configure modem	Modem control panel	Network preferences pane
Configure monitor	Monitor control panel	Displays preferences pane

Table 2

Completing Tasks in Mac OS 9.x and Mac OS X (continued)		
Task	**Mac OS 9.x Tool**	**Mac OS X Tool**
Set mouse options	Mouse control panel	Mouse preferences pane
Set up multiple users	Multiple Users control panel	Users preferences pane
Set number options	Numbers control panel	International preferences pane
Configure QuickTime	QuickTime Settings control panel	QuickTime System preferences
Set up Remote Access connection	Remote Access control panel	Network preferences pane
Dial in to Internet	Remote Access control panel or Remote Access status application	Internet Connect application
Get system software updates	Software Update control panel	Software Update preferences pane
Set system sound options	Sound control panel	Sound preferences pane
Set speech options	Speech control panel	Speech preferences pane
Specify the startup disk	Startup Disk control panel	Startup Disk preferences pane
Configure TCP/IP	TCP/IP control panel	Network preferences pane
Configure text behavior	Text control panel	International preferences pane
Configure trackpad	Trackpad control panel	Mouse preferences pane
Configure/enable Web sharing	Web Sharing control panel	Sharing preferences pane
Select a printer	Chooser	Print Center utility
Connect to an IP server	Chooser	Finder, Go > Connect to Server
Connect to an AppleShare server	Chooser	Finder, Go > Connect to Server
Erase a disk	Finder, Special > Erase Disk	Disk Utility
Eject a disk	Finder, Special > Eject	Finder, Finder > Eject
Set application preferences	Edit > Preferences	*Application Name* > Preferences
Switch from one open application to another	Application menu	Dock
Quit an Application	File > Quit	*Application Name* > Quit *ApplicationName*
Force quit an application	Option ⌘ Esc	Apple > Force Quit or Option ⌘ Esc
Create screen shot	Shift ⌘ 3	Shift ⌘ 3 or Grab utility

The Classic Environment

The Classic Environment

One of the goals of the Mac OS X development team was to build an operating system that would allow for compatibility with most existing application software. After all, who would buy Mac OS X if they couldn't use their favorite applications with it?

The developer's strategy was to make it possible for Mac OS 9.1 or later to run as a process within Mac OS X. Users could then run applications that had not yet been updated for Mac OS X within the Mac OS 9.x process, which is called the *Classic environment.*

The Classic environment utilizes a complete Mac OS 9.x System Folder that contains just about all the components you'd find on a computer that doesn't have Mac OS X installed. This System Folder is so complete, you can even start your computer from it—that means you can choose whether to boot from Mac OS 9.x or Mac OS X.

This chapter provides an overview of the Mac OS 9.x installation and configuration process, then explains how you can use the Classic environment and Mac OS 9.x to work with applications that aren't ready for Mac OS X.

✔ Tip

- You can learn more about the differences between Mac OS 9.x and Mac OS X in **Chapter 1**.

Installing Mac OS 9.x

In order to use Mac OS 9.x and the Classic environment, you must install it. How you do this depends on how Mac OS X was installed on your computer:

- If you updated your computer from Mac OS 9.1 or later to Mac OS X and did not initialize your hard disk as part of the installation process, Mac OS 9.x is still installed on your computer, so you probably won't need to do a thing.
- If you updated your computer from Mac OS 9.0 or earlier to Mac OS X, you'll need to update the existing version of Mac OS to 9.1 or later.
- If you initialized your hard disk when you installed or upgraded to Mac OS X, then only Mac OS X is installed. You'll need to install Mac OS 9.1 or later.
- If you purchased a new computer with both Mac OS X and Mac OS 9.1 or later preinstalled, you're all set and probably don' need to do a thing.

This section explains how to install or update to Mac OS 9.1 or later.

✔ Tips

- Although you can use Mac OS 9.1 with Mac OS X 10.1, the first time you start the Classic environment, Mac OS X displays a dialog like the one in **Figure 1**. If you have a Mac OS 9.2 updater disc, follow the instructions in the dialog to update to Mac OS 9.2. If you don't plan to update to Mac OS 9.2, you can turn on the Don't show again check box so the dialog doesn't bother you every time you launch the Classic environment.
- I find it a lot easier to install or update to Mac OS 9.1 or later before installing Mac OS X. So if you haven't installed either on your computer, install Mac OS 9.x first.

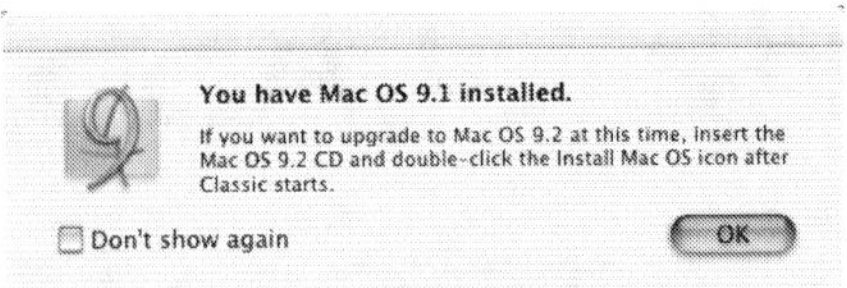

Figure 1 This dialog may appear the first time you run the Mac OS 9.1 Classic environment under Mac OS X 10.1.

Figure 2 The Mac OS Install icon.

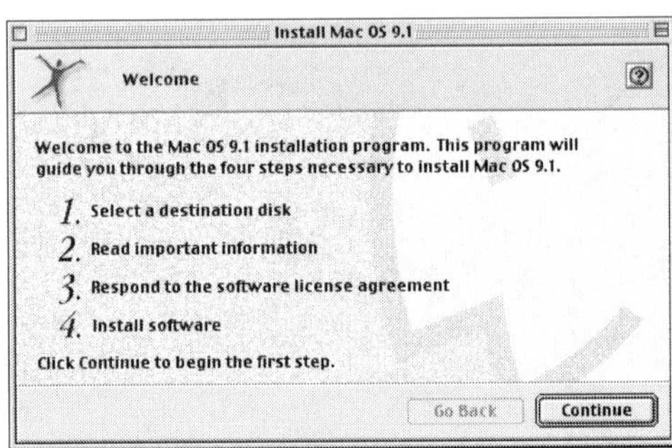

Figure 3 The Welcome window appears when you launch the Mac OS 9.1 installer.

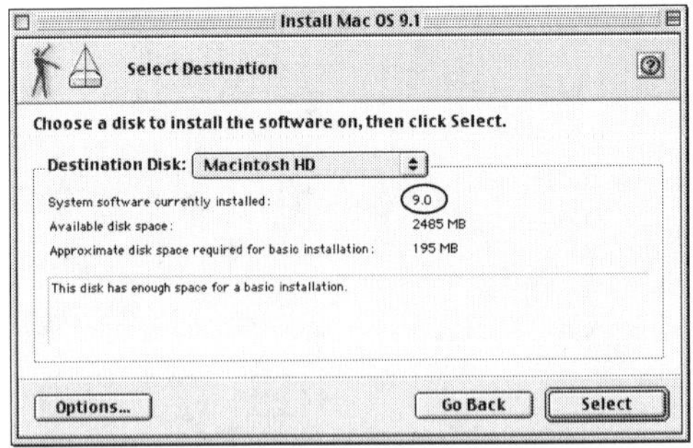

Figure 4 Use this window to select a destination location. The currently installed version of the System software is identified here.

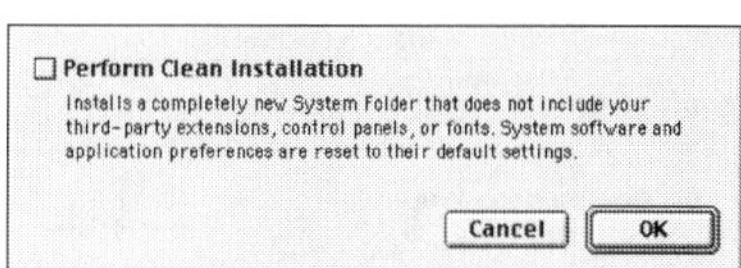

Figure 5 Be sure to perform a clean installation if you're installing Mac OS 9.x on a system that only has Mac OS X installed.

Figure 6 Read this information before you continue the installation.

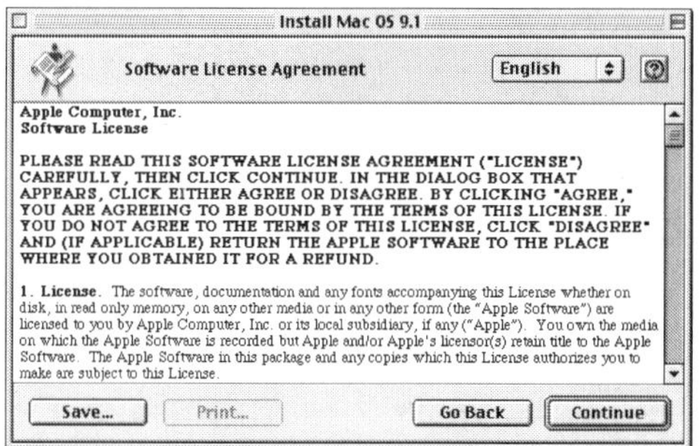

Figure 7 The Software License Agreement window.

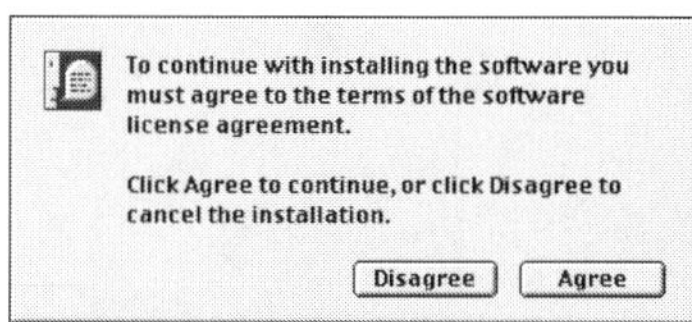

Figure 8 You must click Agree in this dialog to complete the installation.

To install Mac OS 9.1 or later

1. Start your computer from the Mac OS 9.x installation disc. The easiest way to do this is to insert the installation disc, then hold down [C] while restarting your computer.
2. If necessary, open the icon for the Installer disc to display disc contents.
3. Double-click the Mac OS Install icon (**Figure 2**) to launch the installer.
4. In the Welcome window (**Figure 3**), click Continue.
5. In the Select Destination window (**Figure 4**), use the Destination Disk pop-up menu to select the disk on which you want to install Mac OS 9.x. Then:
   - ▲ If Mac OS 9.0 or earlier is already installed on the disk (**Figure 4**), click Select. This tells the installer to update that version of Mac OS.
   - ▲ If Mac OS X is the only system software installed on the disk, click the Options button, turn on the check box beside Perform Clean Installation (**Figure 5**), and click OK. Then click Select. This tells the installer to add a new System Folder for Mac OS 9.x.
6. Read the contents of the Important Information window (**Figure 6**) and click Continue.
7. Read the contents of the Software License Agreement window (**Figure 7**) and click Continue.
8. Click Agree in the dialog that appears (**Figure 8**).
9. Click Start in the Install Software window (**Figure 9**) to start the installation.
10. When the installation is complete, click Quit in the dialog that appears.

Continued on next page...

Continued from previous page.

11. Choose Special > Restart to restart your computer with Mac OS 9.x.

12. The Mac OS Setup Assistant Introduction window appears (**Figure 12**). Follow the instructions on the next page to configure Mac OS 9.x.

✔ Tips

- If the computer was started with Mac OS X and holding down C won't start from the installer disc, follow these steps:
  1. Choose Apple > System Preferences.
  2. In the System Preferences window that appears, click the Startup Disk icon in the Toolbar or in the System row.
  3. In the Startup Disk preferences pane, select the folder icon for the Mac OS 9.x Installer disc (**Figure 10**).
  4. Click Restart.
  5. If a dialog sheet like the one in **Figure 11** appears, click Save and Restart.
- Although these instructions illustrate a Mac OS 9.1 installation, the same steps apply for installing Mac OS 9.2 from an installer disc.
- These instructions assume that you don't want to customize the installation.
- I provide detailed instructions on how to install Mac OS 9.1 in *Mac OS 9.1: Visual QuickStart Guide*. The information provided here, however, should be enough to install Mac OS 9.x for use with Mac OS X.
- Doing a clean installation of Mac OS 9.x on a system that has Mac OS X installed may move the contents of the Applications folder into the Applications (Mac OS 9) folder. If this happens, drag the Mac OS 9 application icons back into the Applications folder; you should be able to identify them by their generic (plain) icons.

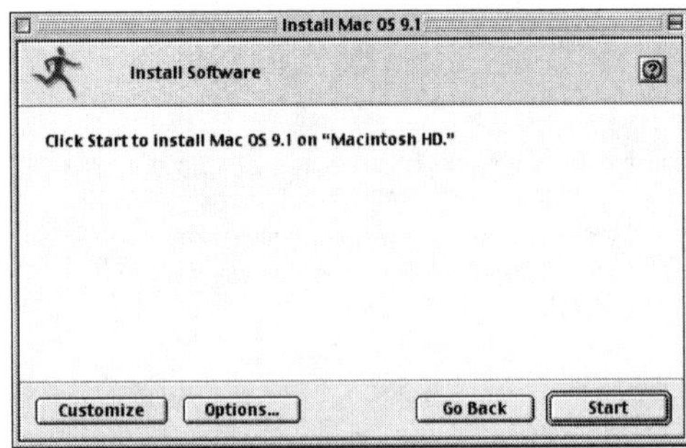

Figure 9 Click Start to begin the installation.

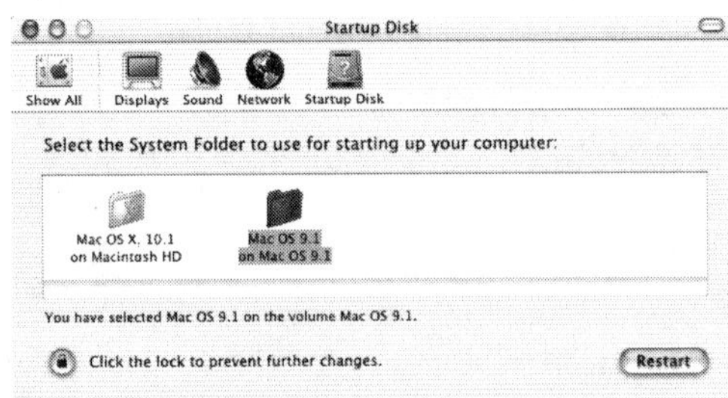

Figure 10 Use the Startup Disk preferences pane to select the Mac OS 9.x installer disk's System Folder.

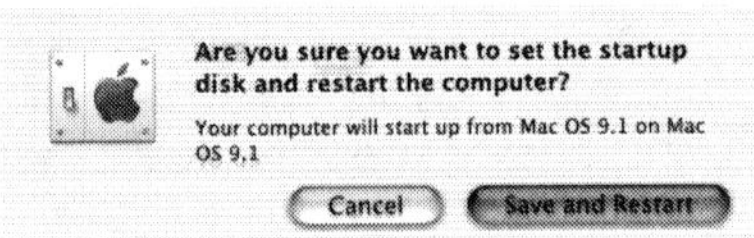

Figure 11 If this dialog appears, click Save and Restart.

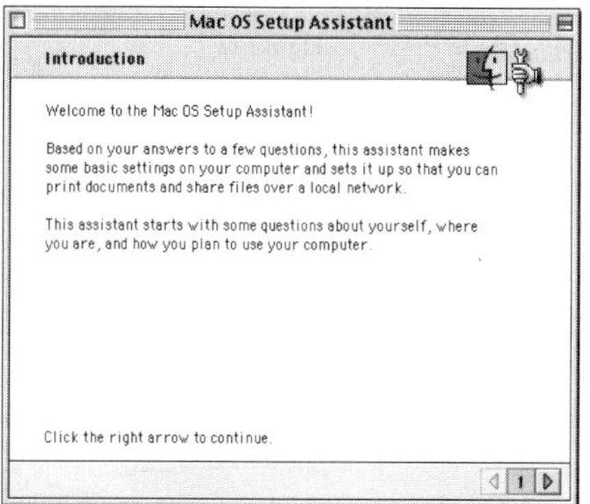

Figure 12 The Introduction window for the Mac OS Setup Assistant.

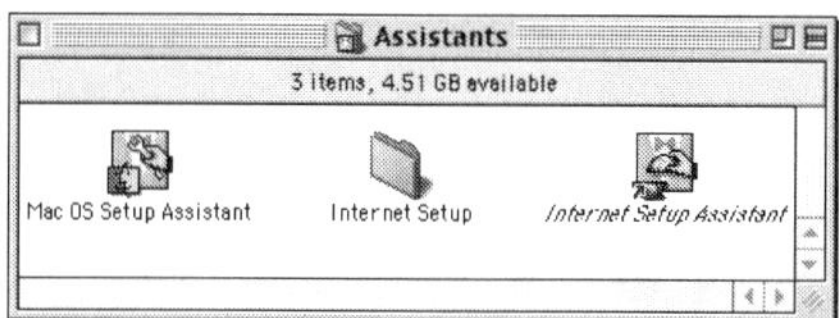

Figure 13 If, for some reason, the Mac OS Setup Assistant doesn't launch automatically, you can open its icon to launch it.

Configuring Mac OS 9.x

When you start your computer for the first time with Mac OS 9.1 or later, the Mac OS Setup Assistant automatically launches. This program steps you through the process of configuring Mac OS 9.x.

✔ Tip

- Use the Mac OS Setup Assistant to configure Mac OS 9.x, even if you are an experienced Mac OS user. The Setup Assistant can properly set all configuration options in Mac OS 9.x control panels; setting control panels manually may interfere with the operation of Mac OS X.

To use the Mac OS Setup Assistant

1. If the Mac OS Setup Assistant does not automatically appear when you first restart your computer with Mac OS 9.x, open its icon. You can find it in *Hard Disk Name*: Applications (Mac OS 9):Utilities:Assistants (**Figure 13**).
2. Read the instructions that appear in each screen of the Mac OS Setup Assistant and enter information when prompted. Click the right-pointing triangle button to move from one screen to the next.

✔ Tip

- If you need step-by-step instructions for configuring Mac OS 9.x with the Mac OS Setup Assistant, you can find it in *Mac OS 9.1: Visual QuickStart Guide* or online, on the companion Web site for *Mac OS X: Visual QuickStart Guide*, www.flyingmproductions/macosxvqs/.

Using the Classic Preferences Pane

In Mac OS X, you set options for the Classic environment with the Classic preferences pane. This pane offers options in two tabs:

- **Start/Stop** (**Figure 16**) enables you to launch the Classic environment within Mac OS X, or to restart or force quit the Classic environment once it is running.
- **Advanced** (**Figure 23**) enables you to set Startup and sleep options for the Classic environment and to rebuild the desktop files used by the Classic environment.

This section explains how to use the Classic preferences pane.

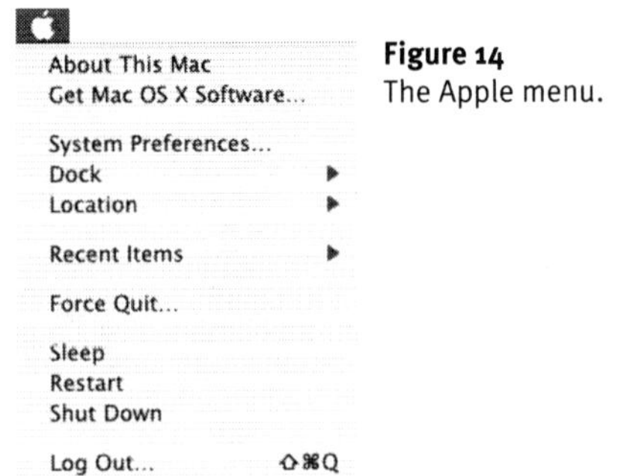

Figure 14 The Apple menu.

Figure 15 You can also open System Preferences by clicking its icon on the Dock.

To open the Classic preferences pane

1. Choose Apple > System Preferences (**Figure 14**), or click the System Preferences icon in the Dock (**Figure 15**).
2. In the System Preferences window that appears, click the Classic icon in the System row. The Classic preferences pane appears (**Figure 16** or **23**).

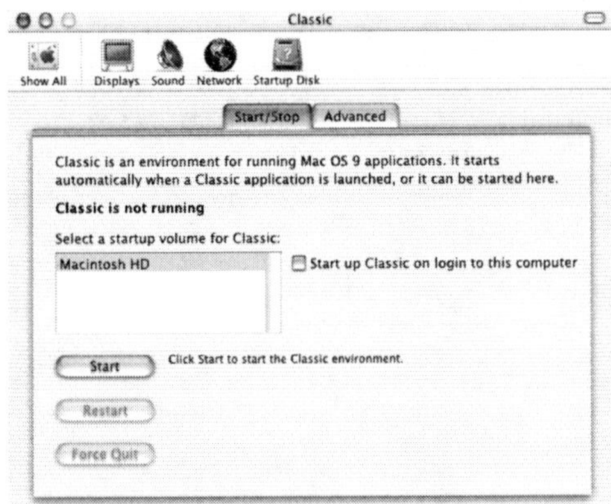

Figure 16 The Start/Stop tab of the Classic preferences pane.

To select a startup volume for Classic

1. Open the Classic preferences pane.
2. Click the Start/Stop tab to display its options (**Figure 16**).
3. Select the name of the disk or volume containing the Mac OS 9.x System Folder you want to use for the Classic environment.

✔ Tip

- In most cases, only one option will appear in the list of startup volumes. In that case, the volume that appears will automatically be selected and you can skip this procedure.

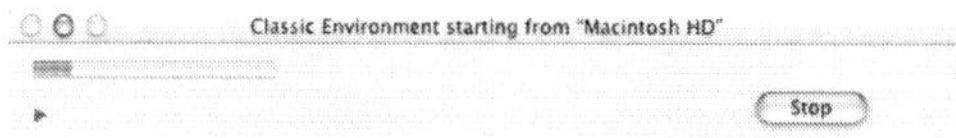

Figure 17 This progress bar...

Figure 18 ...and a Classic icon appear while the Classic environment starts up.

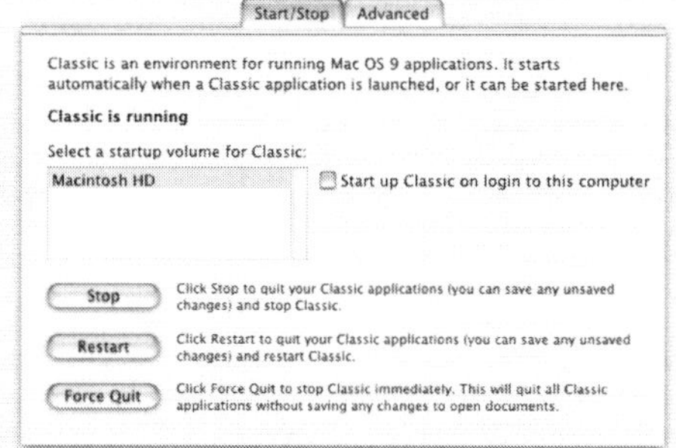

Figure 19 The Start/Stop tab indicates that Classic is running and offers options to stop it.

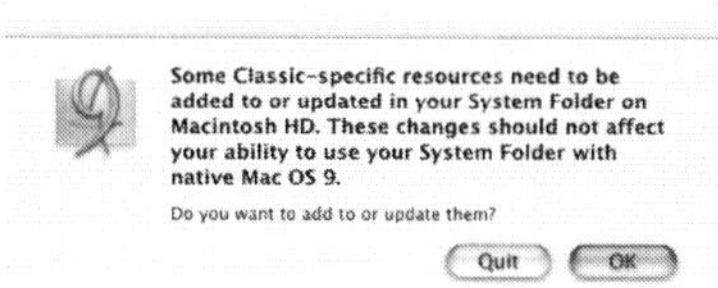

Figure 20 If this dialog appears, click OK.

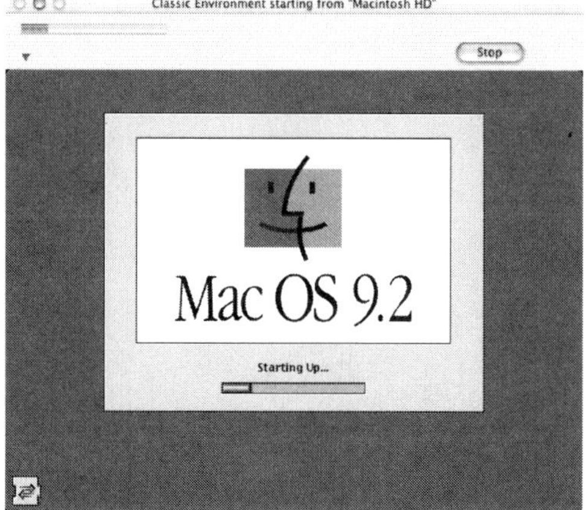

Figure 21 You can expand the progress window to show the Mac OS 9.x startup screen.

To manually start the Classic environment

1. Open the Classic preferences pane.
2. Click the Start/Stop tab to display its options (**Figure 16**).
3. Click the Start button.
4. A short, wide dialog with a progress bar appears (**Figure 17**). The Classic icon appears in the Dock (**Figure 18**).

   When Classic is finished starting, the progress bar and Dock icon disappear. In the Start/Stop tab of the Classic preferences pane (**Figure 19**), the words "Classic is running" appear and the Stop, Restart, and Force Quit buttons become active.

✔ Tips

- If a dialog appears, telling you that you need to update resources (**Figure 20**), click OK. This dialog should only appear the first time you launch the Classic environment after installing or updating Mac OX 9.x.
- If you click the triangle below the progress bar (**Figure 17**), the window expands to show the Mac OS 9.x startup screen (**Figure 21**).
- If you change your mind while Classic is starting, you can click the Stop button beside the progress bar (**Figure 17**) to stop it. As the dialog that appears warns (**Figure 22**), it's better to let Classic finish starting up before you stop it.
- Remember, the Classic environment starts automatically when you launch a Classic application.

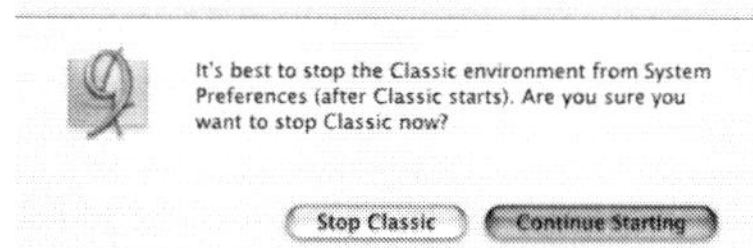

Figure 22 Although you can stop Classic while it's starting, it's best to wait until it's finished.

To automatically start the Classic environment when you log into Mac OS X

1. Open the Classic preferences pane.
2. Click the Start/Stop tab to display its options (**Figure 16**).
3. Turn on the Start up Classic on login to this computer check box.

✔ Tip

- You may want to use this feature if you use Classic applications often. This makes Classic ready anytime you want to use it, so you don't have to wait for Classic to start up when you open a Classic application.

To stop the Classic environment

1. Open the Classic preferences pane.
2. Click the Start/Stop tab to display its options (**Figure 19**).
3. Click the Stop button.
4. If Classic applications with unsaved documents are open, your computer switches to the open applications, one at a time, and offers you an opportunity to save the unsaved documents. Save changes as desired.

   Your computer quits all open Classic applications and stops the Classic environment.

✔ Tip

- If you're having trouble with the Classic environment and the Stop command won't work, you can click the Force Quit button to stop Classic. Doing so, however, automatically quits all Classic applications without giving you an opportunity to save changes to documents. For this reason, you should only click Force Quit if you cannot stop Classic any other way.

To restart the Classic environment

1. Open the Classic preferences pane.
2. Click the Start/Stop tab to display its options (**Figure 19**).
3. Click the Restart button.
4. If Classic applications with unsaved documents are open, your computer switches to the open applications, one at a time, and offers you an opportunity to save the unsaved documents. Save changes as desired.

   Your computer quits all open Classic applications and restarts the Classic environment.

✔ Tip

- Use the Restart button if a Classic application unexpectedly quits. This flushes out memory and can prevent other Classic applications from having related problems.

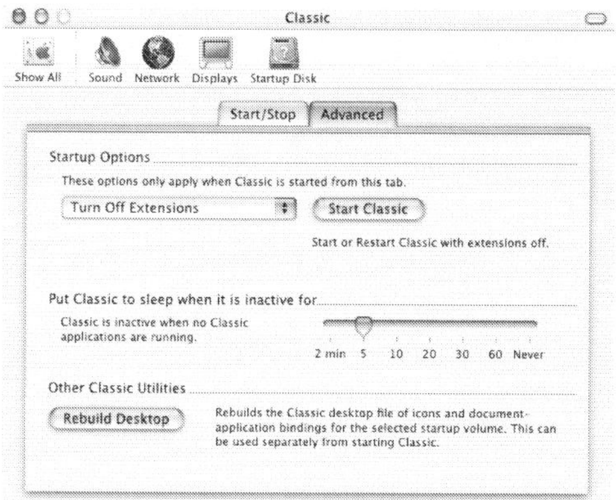

Figure 23 The Advanced tab of the Classic preferences pane.

✓ Turn Off Extensions
Open Extensions Manager
Use Key Combination:

Figure 24 Use this pop-up menu to set startup options.

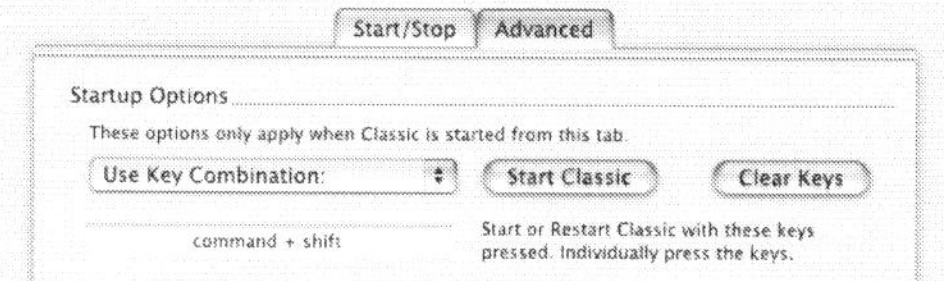

Figure 25 When you choose Use Key Combination, the dialog changes to display a box for entering your keystrokes.

To set Classic Startup options

1. Open the Classic preferences pane.
2. Click the Advanced tab to display its options (**Figure 23**).
3. Choose an option from the pop-up menu in the Startup Options area (**Figure 24**):
   - ▲ **Turn Off Extensions** turns off all Mac OS 9.x extensions when Classic starts or restarts. (This is the same as holding down Shift when starting from Mac OS 9.x.)
   - ▲ **Open Extensions Manager** automatically opens Extensions Manager when Classic starts or restarts. (This is the same as holding down Spacebar when starting from Mac OS 9.x.)
   - ▲ **Use Key Combination** enables you to enter up to five keys to start or restart Classic. If you choose this option, the window changes to display a edit box for your keystrokes and instructions (**Figure 25**). Press the keys, one at a time, to enter them in the box.
4. Click Start Classic (**Figure 23**) or Restart Classic to start or restart Classic with your startup option set.

✓ Tip

- These options only apply when Classic is started or restarted from the Advanced tab of the Classic preferences pane (**Figure 23**).

To set Classic sleep options

1. Open the Classic preferences pane.
2. Click the Advanced tab to display its options (**Figure 23**).
3. Use the slider to specify how long Classic should be inactive before it sleeps.

✔ Tips

- The Classic environment is said to be *inactive* when no Classic applications are running.
- When the Classic environment is sleeping, it uses less system resources. This can increase performance on an older computer, especially one with a slow CPU or the minimum required amount of RAM.
- If you launch a Classic application while the Classic environment is sleeping, it may take a moment or two for Classic to wake and the application to appear. This is still quicker than starting Classic.

To rebuild the Classic desktop

1. Open the Classic preferences pane.
2. Click the Advanced tab to display its options (**Figure 23**).
3. Click Rebuild Desktop. A status bar appears in the bottom half of the Advanced tab (**Figure 26**). When it disappears, the process is complete.

✔ Tips

- You may want to rebuild the Mac OS 9.x desktop if icons are not properly displayed in the Classic environment or when starting your computer from Mac OS 9.x.
- You can use the Rebuild Desktop feature to rebuild the Mac OS 9.x desktop even if the Classic environment is not running.

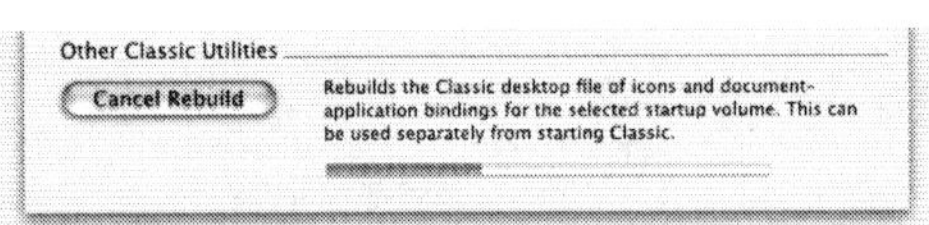
Other Classic Utilities
Cancel Rebuild
Rebuilds the Classic desktop file of icons and document-application bindings for the selected startup volume. This can be used separately from starting Classic.

Figure 26 A progress bar appears in the Advanced tab of the Classic preferences pane when you rebuild the Mac OS 9.x desktop.

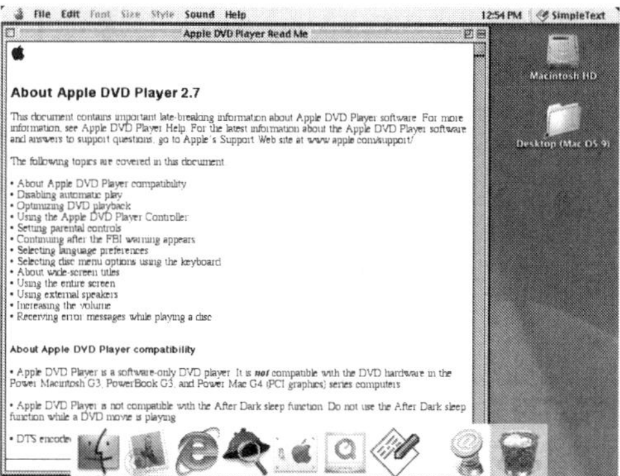

Figure 27 This example shows a SimpleText document open in the Classic environment on a Mac OS X system.

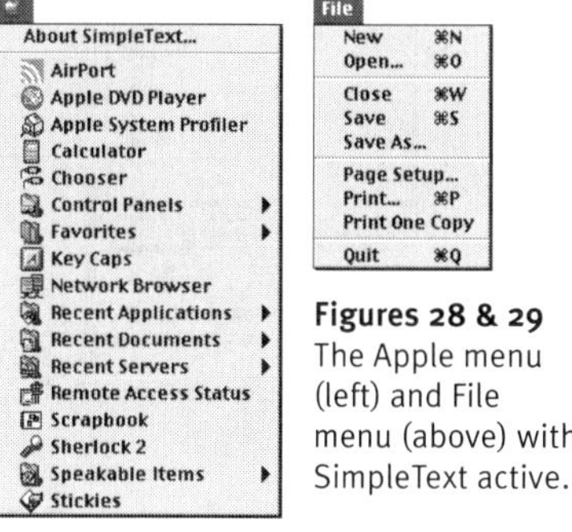

Figures 28 & 29 The Apple menu (left) and File menu (above) with SimpleText active.

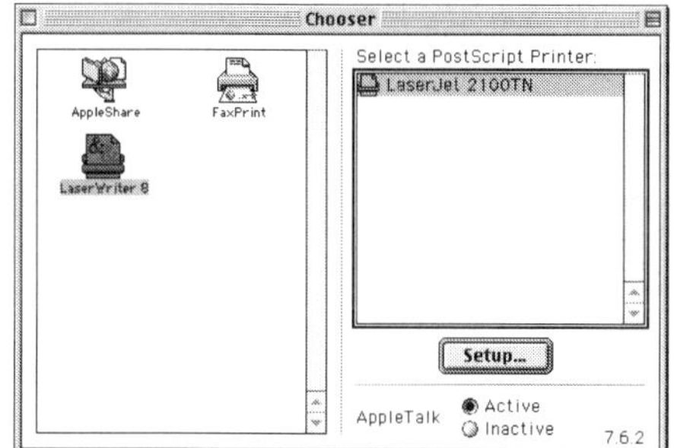

Figure 30 Use the Chooser to set up and select a printer for printing documents from Classic applications.

Running Classic Applications

When you open an icon for a Classic application or a document created with a Classic application, Mac OS X automatically starts the Classic environment and opens the application within it (**Figure 27**). The Mac OS X Aqua appearance disappears, replaced with the more sedate appearance of Mac OS 9.x.

While the Classic environment is in use, certain operations work differently than they do in Mac OS X:

- The Classic Apple (**Figure 28**) and File (**Figure 29**) menus contain different commands than they do in Mac OS X. In addition, Classic applications do not include a menu named after the application; the commands normally under that menu can be found on the File and Window (if available) menus.
- To print from the Classic environment, you must select and set up a printer with the Chooser (**Figure 30**). To open the Chooser, choose Apple > Chooser (**Figure 28**). The Print dialog (**Figure 31**) offers different options than those in Mac OS X.
- To connect to a networked computer from the Classic environment, you must open the network volume with the Chooser (**Figure 32**). To open the Chooser, choose Apple > Chooser (**Figure 28**).
- System preferences can be set with control panels (**Figure 33**).

These are just a few differences between Mac OS X and the Classic environment. As you work with Classic applications, you'll undoubtably find more.

Continued on next page...

Continued from previous page.

✔ Tips

- Not all applications are supported by the Classic environment. If you try to open an application that was not written for Mac OS X and a dialog like the one in **Figure 34** appears, you'll have to restart your computer with Mac OS 9.x to use it.
- You cannot access the Classic Finder from within Mac OS X. To use the Classic Finder, you must restart your computer from Mac OS 9.x, as instructed later in this chapter.
- You can learn more about the differences between Mac OS 9.x and Mac OS X in **Chapter 1**.
- Unfortunately, it is impossible to explore all differences without going into a complete discussion of Mac OS 9.x. If you feel that you need more Mac OS 9.x information, consider picking up a copy of *Mac OS 9.1: Visual QuickStart Guide*, which covers Mac OS 9.1 in detail.

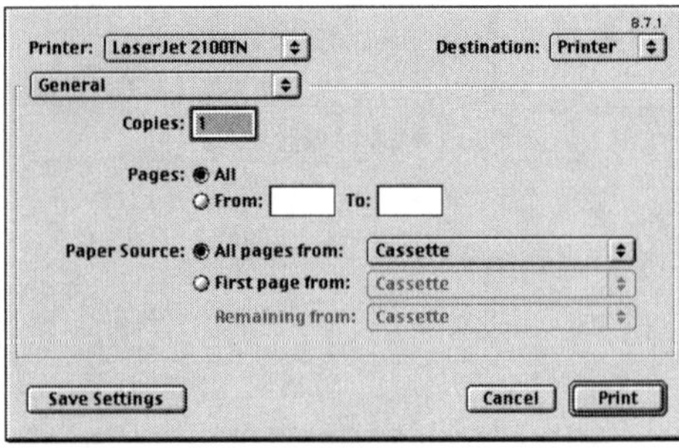

Figure 31 The Classic Print dialog offers different options than the one for Mac OS X.

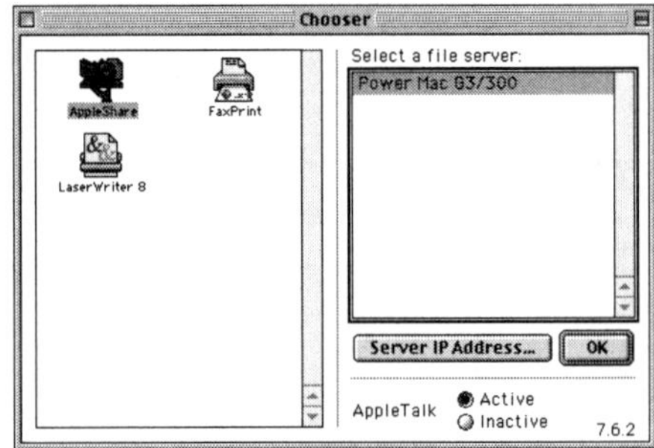

Figure 32 You also use the Chooser to open other disks available via network.

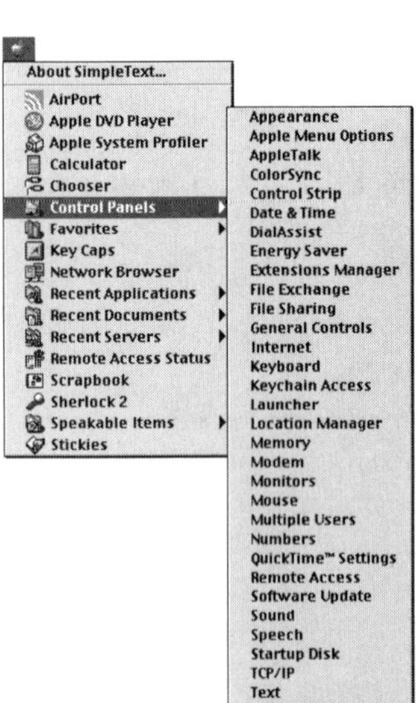

Figure 33 Use control panels to set options that work in the Classic environment.

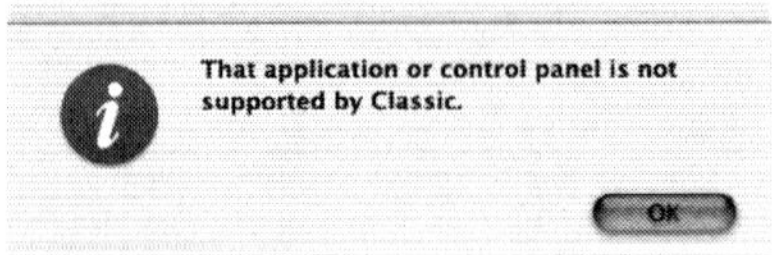

Figure 34 If an application cannot be opened in the Classic environment, Mac OS X tells you.

Starting Your Computer with Mac OS 9.x

If you plan to do a lot of work with Classic applications, you may want to start your computer with Mac OS 9.x and work without using Mac OS X at all. You can do this by selecting your Mac OS 9.x System Folder as the startup "disk" and restarting your computer.

✔ Tips

- You may find that Classic applications—especially large and complex ones—work a bit better when you start with Mac OS 9.x.
- If you start your computer from Mac OS 9.x, you cannot use Mac OS X features and applications. You must restart with Mac OS X to use Mac OS X.
- All the differences discussed on the previous two pages apply when you start your computer from Mac OS 9.x except compatibility issues—all Mac OS 9.x applications will work on your computer when you start with Mac OS 9.x, even those that are not compatible with the Classic environment.
- If you think you'll be using Mac OS 9.x often and want more information, consider picking up a copy of *Mac OS 9.1: Visual QuickStart Guide*, which covers Mac OS 9.1 in detail.

To start from Mac OS 9.x

1. Choose Apple > System Preferences (**Figure 14**), or click the System Preferences icon in the Dock (**Figure 15**).
2. In the System Preferences window that appears, click the Startup Disk icon in the Toolbar or in the System row.
3. In the Startup Disk preferences pane, select the folder icon for the Mac OS 9.x System Folder (**Figure 35**).
4. Click Restart.
5. If a dialog sheet like the one in **Figure 36** appears, click Save and Restart.

   Your computer restarts from the Mac OS 9.x System Folder (**Figure 37**).

To start from Mac OS X

1. Choose Apple > Control Panels > Startup disk (**Figure 33**).
2. In the Startup Disk control panel, select the folder icon for the Mac OS X System folder (**Figure 38**).
3. Click Restart.

   Your computer restarts from the Mac OS X System folder.

✔ Tip

- In step 2, you may have to click the triangle beside the name of your hard disk to display the System folders inside it (**Figure 38**).

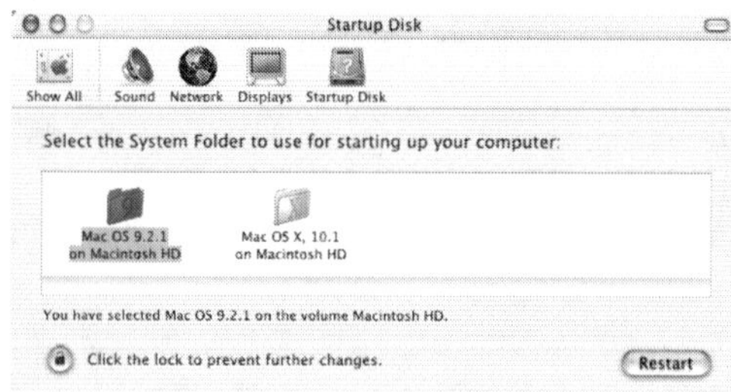

Figure 35 Mac OS X's Startup Disk preferences pane.

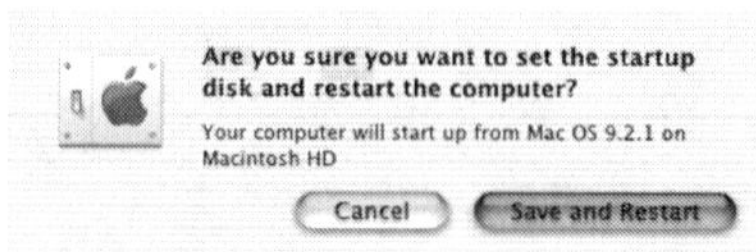

Figure 36 If this dialog appears, click Save and Restart.

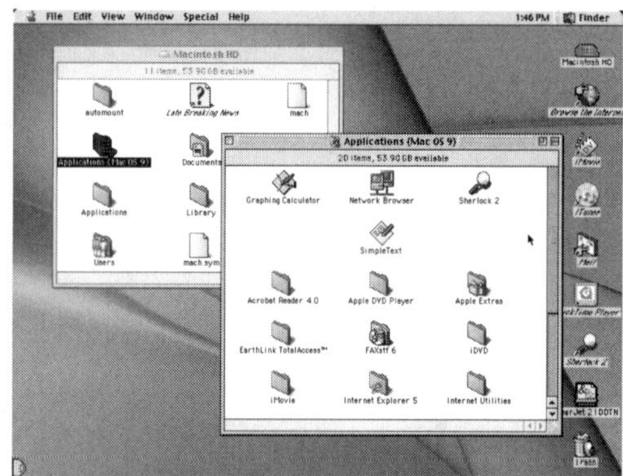

Figure 37 The Mac OS 9.2.1 Finder.

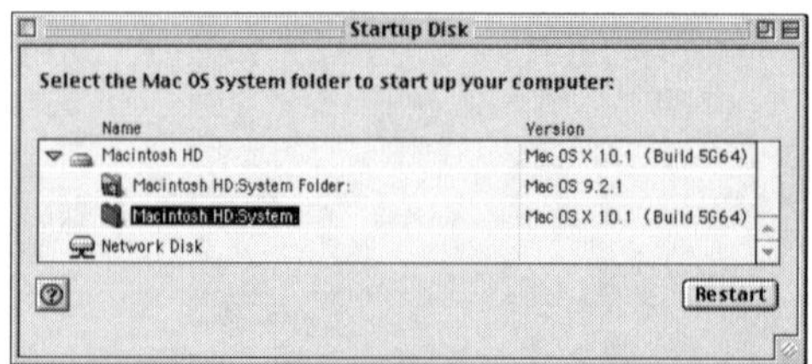

Figure 38 Mac OS 9.2.1's Startup Disk control panel.

UNIX BASICS FOR MAC OS X

BY RON HIPSCHMAN

Ron Hipschman has been playing with computers at the Exploratorium in San Francisco for more years than he wants to admit. At the Exploratorium he has also built exhibits, taught classes, written books, and created the Exploratorium's Web site (www.exploratorium.edu) way back in 1993 when it was among the first 600 sites on the Internet. This is where he learned his Unix (on a Sun Microsystems machine).

Ron's first "real" computer was an IMSAI 8080 that he soldered together from a kit and loaded software (initially) with the toggle switches on the front panel. That computer ran an operating system called CP/M. He became a Mac fanatic in 1985 (he waited for the Mac Plus...). He's on his fifth Mac (A Power Mac G4). He sponsors a local Mac user group that meets at the Exploratorium (www.bmugwest.com). He is now very happy that he has his two favorite operating systems (Mac OS and Unix) all in one system.

Unix & Mac OS X

You probably bought your Macintosh because it was powerful, easy to learn, and easy to use. Sure, more powerful machines were out there, but they all ran this crazy, cryptic Unix or Linux operating system. You thought that Unix was more a lifestyle choice than an operating system, and you swore that you'd never saddle yourself with the task of learning all those arcane commands.

Oops. Now you have Mac OS X.

Guess what? Even though you still have the ease of use for which we all love Apple, you now have the power of Unix under the hood, too. Although it's beyond the scope of this book to teach you everything there is to know about Unix (it really is a lifestyle!), the brief introduction in this chapter and in **Chapter 4** will get you going with some basics and point you to other resources you can explore on your own.

Unix Directories & Files

Before I start my discussion of Unix commands, let's take a look at the structure of the Unix file system.

The directory system

Like the Macintosh file system, the Unix file system starts at the top level with a *root* directory, which can contain files and *subdirectories*. The root directory in Mac OS 9 and earlier is named after your hard disk. The root directory in Unix is named / (a slash without any other characters following it). Subdirectories below the root directory are indicated by listing them after the root slash. Each subdirectory is separated from the subdirectory it resides within by a slash.

For example, my home directory is **/Users/ronh**. That means that in the root directory, /, is a subdirectory called *Users*, inside of which is a subdirectory called *ronh*.

✔ Tips

- On Mac OS, subdirectories are also known as *folders*.
- Unix uses a forward slash (/) to separate subdirectories, not a backslash (\) like in Windows or MS-DOS.
- I discuss the home directory later in this chapter. It is also covered in more detail in **Chapter 1**.

File names

There are two things about Unix file names that you should be aware of.

First, although Unix file names are normally case-sensitive, in the Mac OS Extended file system (HFS+), file names are not case-sensitive. What does this mean to you? Just that you need to be aware of the case of file names, especially if you move files to another Unix machine—for example, to a Unix Web server. Remember, on every other Unix machine in the known universe, upper- and lowercase are different. It's a good idea to pretend that this is the case on your Mac OS X machine, too.

Second, Unix file names do not normally include space characters. Although the Mac OS X Finder has no problem with spaces in file names, the underlying Unix uses spaces to separate commands, options, and operands. Spaces in Unix file names will cause you no end of grief because Unix will misinterpret them as operand separators in the commands you enter and your commands will perform unpredictably. If you need to enter a command that includes a file name with space characters, enclose the file name in single quotation marks so the system recognizes it as a single entity in the command.

Invisible files

File names that begin with a dot (.) are *hidden*. Programs such as the shell, mail, and editors use these files to store preferences s and other data.

Note that Unix has two unusually named subdirectories, one with a single dot (.) and another with double dots (..). These are shorthand ways for Unix to refer to "the current directory" and "the directory above this one" (also called the *parent directory*). The Unix operating system gives these plain files special treatment, as you'll learn later in this chapter in the discussion of the **cd** command.

✔ Tip

- I explain how to include invisible files in a file list later in this chapter.

Terminal, the Shell, & Console

Mac OS X includes a utility called *Terminal* (**Figure 2**). This application is your window into the Unix world lurking deep inside Mac OS X. If you're old enough, you may remember using big, clunky video terminals to communicate with large mainframes. Terminal mimics the operation of those CRT terminals, but it uses your computer's screen, keyboard, and CPU instead of dumb-terminal hardware.

When you run Terminal, it connects to a communication process inside your Mac called a *shell*. The shell is a program that interprets human actions such as the typing of commands and the starting and stopping of jobs. It passes these requests to the computer and is responsible for sending the results of your actions in the Terminal window.

Each shell has its own set of features. The default shell that Mac OS X assigns to new accounts is called the *tcsh* (pronounced "t-shell"). The tcsh is a powerful shell that includes many enhancements, such as a command line editor, file-name completion, spelling correction, and a command history. The tcsh also contains a script command processor that allows you to build interactive programs and preprogrammed command series, similar to what you can do with AppleScript.

The Terminal application and the shell work together, allowing you to communicate with and control your computer. But they are separate entities. Terminal is responsible for accepting commands and displaying results, and the shell is responsible for interpreting and executing commands. You can use Terminal to talk to a variety of shells. You can open as many Terminal windows as you need—they each work independently.

Continued on next page...

Continued from previous page.

Mac OS X also includes a utility called *Console* (**Figure 3**), which is an application that displays system messages. Keeping the console.log window open and watching it can tell you a lot about what's happening on your system.

✔ Tips

- The tcsh is an extended version of the standard *csh*, or "c-shell," that's part of Unix.
- If you are debugging programs, use Console to view error messages.

To launch Terminal

Double-click the Terminal icon in the Utilities folder (**Figure 1**) inside the Applications folder. A Terminal window with a shell prompt appears (**Figure 2**).

✔ Tip

- The shell prompt shown in **Figure 2** (**[localhost:~] ronh%**) includes the following components:
  - ▲ *Computer name* is the name of the computer you're logged into. **localhost** is the local computer.
  - ▲ *Directory* is the current directory. ~ (the tilde character) is Unix shorthand for your home directory.
  - ▲ *User name* is your user name, which, in this example, is **ronh**.

To launch Console

Double-click the Console icon in the Utilities folder (**Figure 1**) inside the Applications folder. The console.log window appears (**Figure 3**).

✔ Tip

- Console is discussed in more detail in **Chapter 10**.

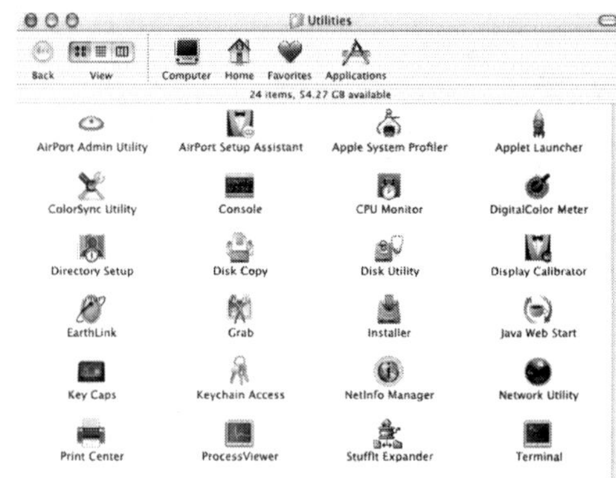

Figure 1 The contents of the Utilities folder includes applications for working with Unix.

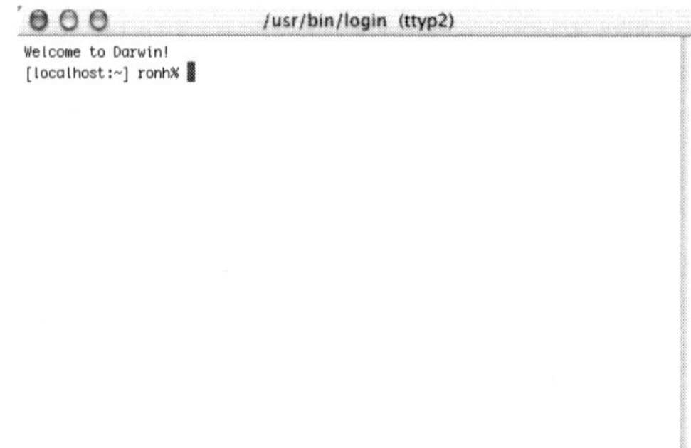

Figure 2 A Terminal window with a shell prompt.

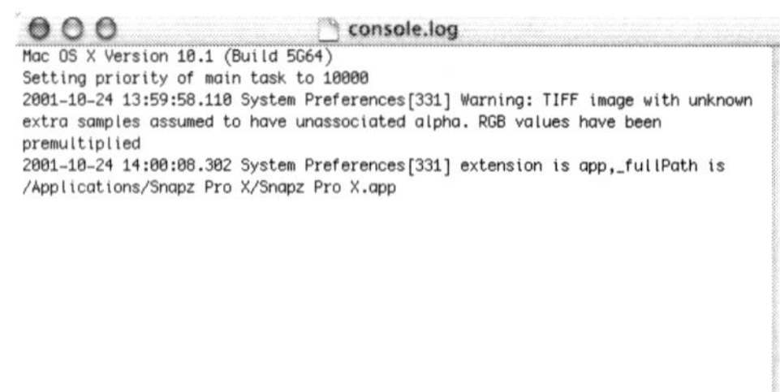

Figure 3 The console.log window displays system messages.

Unix Command Basics

You work with Unix by typing commands into a Terminal window at the shell prompt. You press Return after each command to enter it. The results of the command entry appear in the Terminal window, followed by a new shell prompt.

Most Unix commands can be used with options that make them do slightly different things. For instance, the **ls** command has 25 options in Mac OS X. To include an option with a command, enter the command followed by a space, a hyphen, and the option. For example, to use the **l** option with the **ls** command, you'd enter **ls -l**.

You can use more than one option at a time by stringing them together. Some commands, such as **ls**, let you put all the options together after a single hyphen. Other commands require that you use a separate hyphen for each option.

✔ Tips

- Typing commands into a command-line interface (CLI) offers advantages beyond what is possible with a graphical user interface (GUI) like the Finder.
- If, while working with Unix commands in the Terminal window, you are either flooded with output that you'd like to abort or faced with a command that seems stuck, try pressing Control C to break the current command. If that doesn't work, close the Terminal window and open a new one.
- Throughout this chapter, an ellipsis (...) in command syntax means that you can repeat the previous operand as many times as you wish. For instance, rather than saying **cp *source-file1 source-file2 source-fileN target-directory***, I'll say **cp *source-file ... target-directory***, meaning that you can include as many source files as you like in the command.

Listing Directory Contents with the ls Command

ls is one of the most basic Unix commands. It enables you to list the contents of a directory.

✔ Tip

- The commands in this section assume that the shell prompt is displaying your home directory (~).

To list the contents of your home directory

Type **ls** and press Return.

A list of the contents of your home directory appears (**Figure 4**).

To list the contents of a subdirectory

Type **ls** followed by the subdirectory name (for example, **ls Library**) and press Return.

A list of the contents of the subdirectory you typed appears (**Figure 5**).

To view a long directory listing

Type **ls -l** and press Return.

A list of the contents of your home directory, including permissions, owner, size, and modification date information, appears (**Figure 6**).

✔ Tip

- I tell you more about permissions in **Chapter 4**.

To include invisible items in a directory listing

Type **ls -a** and press Return.

A list of the contents of your home directory, including invisible items, appears (**Figure 7**).

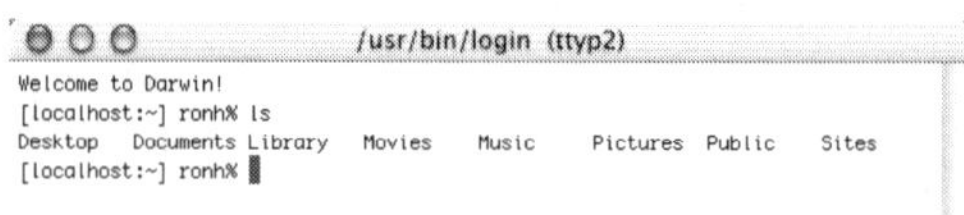

Figure 4 A simple directory listing using the ls command.

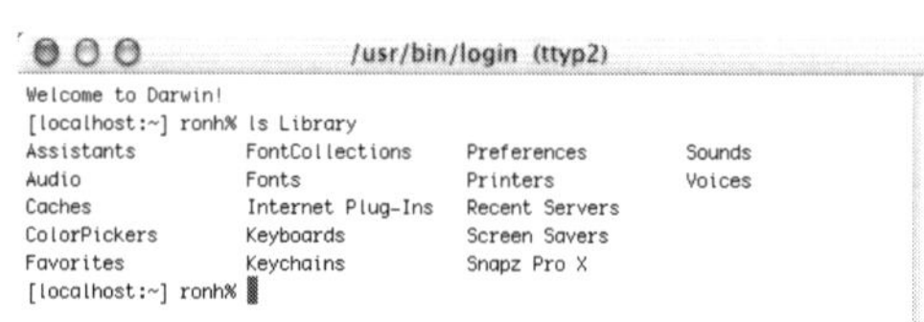

Figure 5 A listing for the library subdirectory.

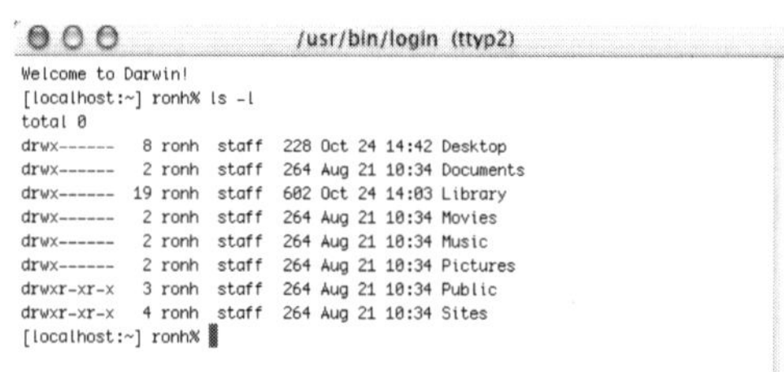

Figure 6 The long version of a directory listing includes permission, owner, file size, and modification date information.

Figure 7 A directory listing that includes invisible subdirectories.

Table 1

man pages Sections

SECTION	TYPE OF COMMAND OR FILE
1	User commands
2	System calls
3	Library routines
4	I/O and special files
5	Administrative files
6	Games
7	Miscellaneous
8	Administrative and maintenance commands

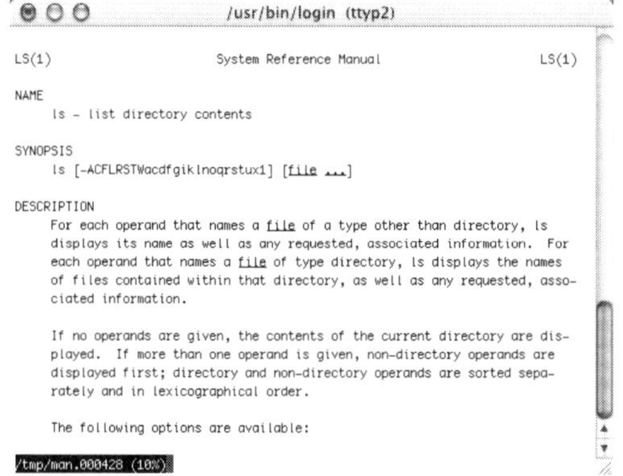

Figure 8 The first man page for the ls command.

Viewing man pages

One important Unix command tells you everything you ever wanted to know about Unix commands and files: the **man** command. It displays information about commands and files documented in the on-line manual pages. These *man pages* are included with every version of Unix.

The man pages present information about a command one page at a time. You can use keystrokes to advance to the next line or page of the man pages. You must quit the man pages feature to enter other Unix commands.

Like a book, man pages are broken into chapters called sections (**Table 1**). Each section is designed for a specific type of user. For example, a programmer will be interested in different man pages than a user or a system administrator. There are some man pages that document identical sounding items, yet are intended for different users.

✔ Tip

- The man pages for commands and files can be lengthy and complex. Don't worry if you don't understand everything on a man page. Just take what you need. As you understand more about Unix, more will make sense.

To view man pages for a command

Type **man** followed by the name of the command (for example, **man ls**), and press Return.

The first page of the reference manual for the command appears (**Figure 8**).

✔ Tip

- The last line of a man page (**Figures 8** and **9**) indicates the percentage of the man pages for the command or file you have viewed.

To view the next line of a man page

Press Return.

The manual advances one line.

To view the next page

Press Spacebar.

The manual advances one page (**Figure 9**).

To quit man pages

Press Q.

Terminal returns you to the shell prompt.

To get man pages for man

Type **man man** and press Return.

The first page of the reference manual for the online manual appears (**Figure 10**).

To list documented commands

Type **man -k directory** and press Return.

A list of documented commands appears (**Figure 11**).

✔ Tips

- When you enter **man -k directory**, you are really running a command called apropos, which does the actual search. I find it easier to remember **-k** for *keyword* instead.
- The numbers that appear in parentheses beside a command name (**Figure 11**) correspond to the man section in which the command appears (**Table 1**).

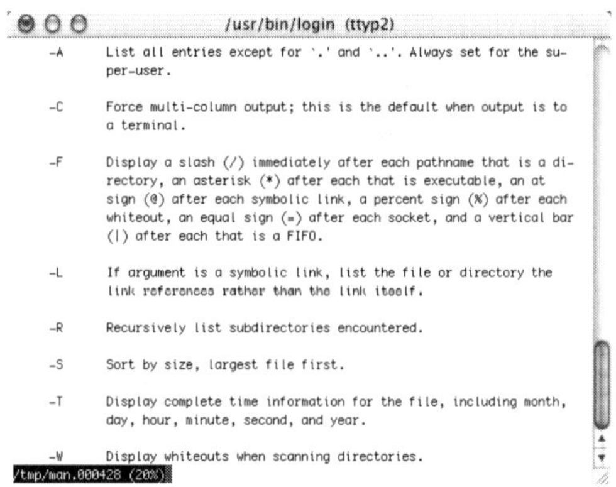

Figure 9 The second page for the ls command.

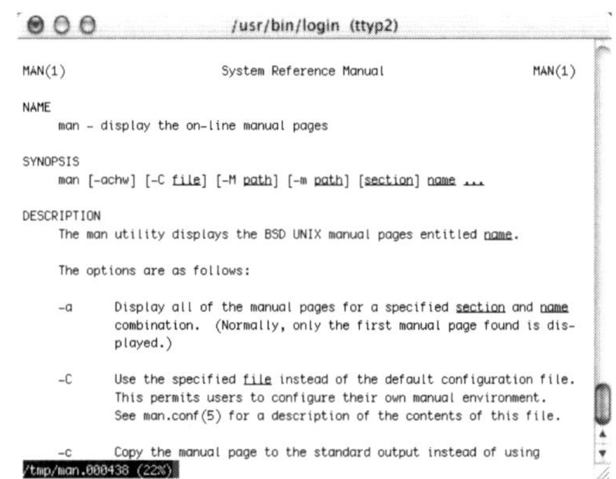

Figure 10 The first man page for man.

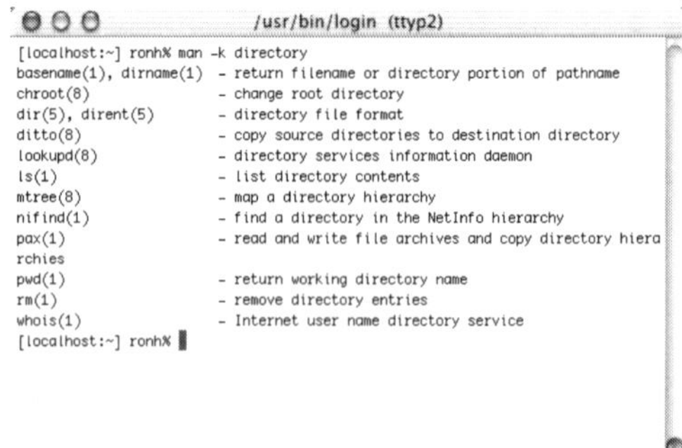

Figure 11 A list of the commands and files for which man pages exist.

Moving Around with the cd Command

Up to now, you haven't moved around in the directory tree. You've been fixed in place in your home directory. Changing directories is easy—just use the **cd** (change directory) command, followed by the destination you want to move to.

You have two ways to indicate a destination: with an *absolute path* or with a relative path.

- An absolute path specifies the location of a file or subdirectory, starting at the root directory and working downward.
- A relative path specifies the location of a file or subdirectory starting at your present location.

Let's look at an example. Suppose I'm currently in my home directory (/Users/ronh) and I want to move to the /usr/bin directory. I could specify the destination with its absolute path: **/usr/bin**. Or I could use the relative path to go up two directories to the root and then down two directories to the one I want. This is where the special "double-dot" (..) directory name that I discussed earlier comes into play; it indicates the directory above the current one. So the relative path from my home directory to /usr/bin would be **../../usr/bin**.

✔ Tips

- The **cd** command does not have any options and has no man page of its own because it's built in to the shell. You can find out more about the shell by using the man pages; enter **man tcsh** and press [Return].
- Absolute paths, which always start with a forward slash (/), work no matter where you are located in the Unix file system because they start from the root directory.
- Relative paths are especially useful if you are deep inside the directory structure and want to access a file or subdirectory just one level up. For example, it's a lot easier to type **../images/flower.jpg** than **/Users/ronh/Documents/ClipArt/Plants/Color/images/flower.jpg**—and it's a lot easier to remember, too!

To change directories using an absolute path

Type **cd** followed by the absolute path to the directory you want (for example, **cd /usr/bin**) and press Return.

The current directory changes and the path to the directory appears in the shell prompt (**Figure 12**).

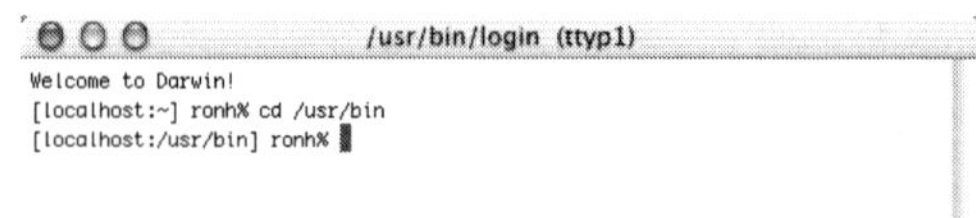

Figure 12 Here's how you can change the current directory to /usr/bin using an absolute path...

To change directories using a relative path

Type **cd** followed by the relative path to the directory you want (for example, from your home directory, type **cd ../../usr/bin**) and press Return.

The current directory changes and the path to the directory appears in the shell prompt (**Figure 13**).

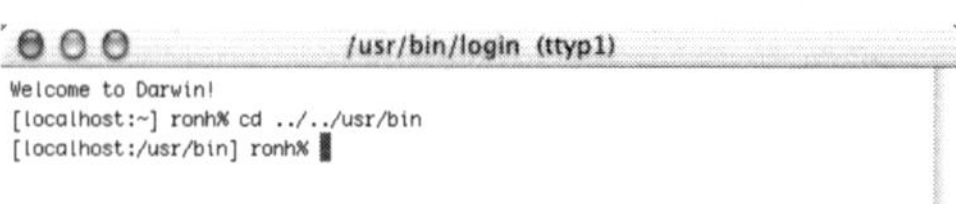

Figure 13 ...and a relative path from your home directory.

To move to a subdirectory using an absolute path

Type **cd** followed by the absolute path to the subdirectory (for example, **cd /Users/ronh/Sites**) and press Return.

The current directory changes and the path to the directory appears in the shell prompt (**Figure 14**).

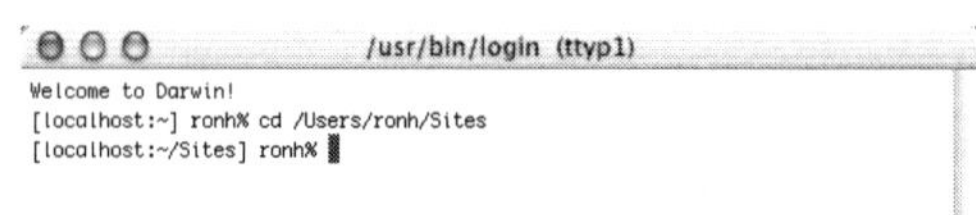

Figure 14 Here's how you can move to a subdirectory using an absolute path...

To move to a subdirectory using a relative path

Type **cd** followed by the relative path to the subdirectory (for example from your home directory, type **cd Sites**) and press Return.

The current directory changes and the path to the directory appears in the shell prompt (**Figure 15**).

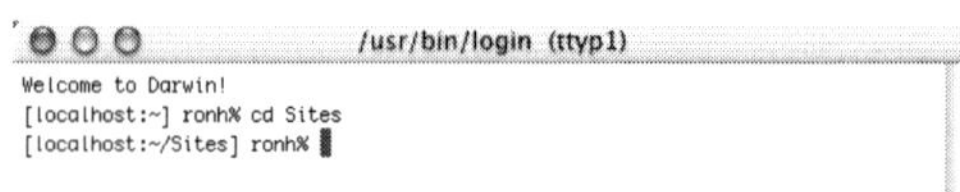

Figure 15 ...and with a relative reference.

✔ Tip

- Do not include a forward slash (/) before a subdirectory name. Doing so tells Unix to start at the root directory (as if you were entering an absolute path) and could result in an error message (**Figure 16**).

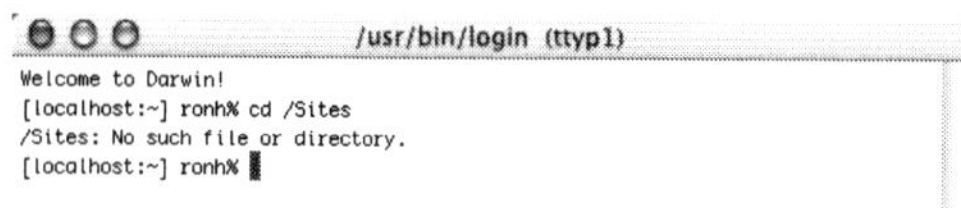

Figure 16 If you enter an incorrect path, an error message appears.

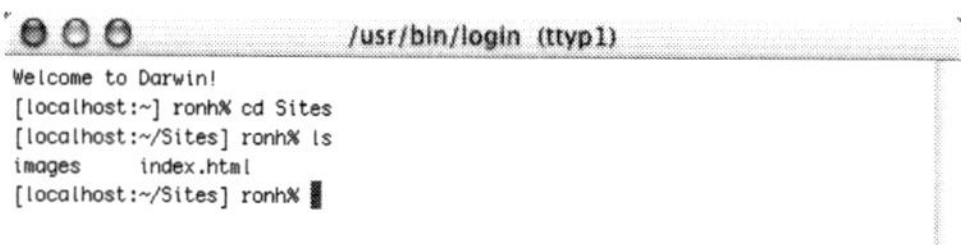

Figure 17 Once you're in a directory, using the ls command by itself displays the contents of that directory.

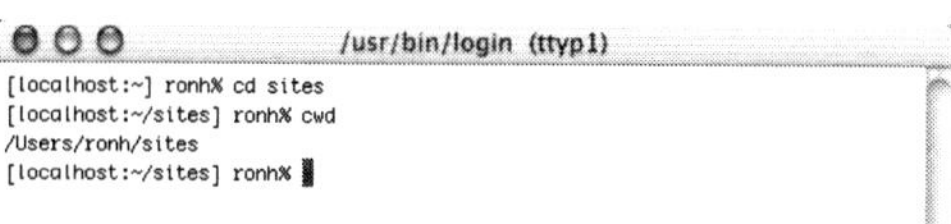

Figure 18 The pwd command displays the complete path to the current directory.

To list the contents of the current directory

Type **ls** and press Return.

The contents of the directory appear in the Terminal window (**Figure 17**).

To return to your home directory

Type **cd** and press Return.

The current directory changes to your home directory and the tilde (~) character appears in the shell prompt.

Getting the Directory Location with the pwd Command

You might be wondering how to find out exactly where you are after doing many **cd** commands. Unix has a spiffy little command just for this: **pwd** (present working directory).

To learn the current directory

Type **pwd** and press Return.

The complete path to the current directory appears, followed by the shell prompt (**Figure 18**).

Wildcards in File Names & Directories

One frustrating activity in Mac OS 9.x and earlier was working with a group of files. Other than shift-clicking or dragging to select the group, you had no good way to select group items by name—for example, to select all files that started with the characters *file* and ended with the characters *.doc*.

Unix, however, makes this easy by enabling you to use three special characters as wildcards:

- **Asterisk** (*), which is referred to as star, is a wildcard for zero or more characters.
- **Question mark** (?) is a wildcard for any single character.
- **Brackets** ([and]) around one or more characters act as a wildcard for any of the enclosed characters.

You can place the wildcard wherever you want in the name you are searching for. As you can imagine, wildcards are a powerful tool for selecting or listing files or subdirectories.

✔ Tip

- The brackets wildcard can include individual characters, such as **[ABCD]** or character ranges, such as **[A-G]** or **[1-6]**.

Using wildcards

The best way to explain how you can use wildcards is to show you some examples.

Suppose your Documents subdirectory contained the following subdirectories and files:

dir1	file03.doc	file12.txt
dir2	file04.doc	file20.txt
dir30	file05.doc	file21.txt
file01.doc	file10.txt	file38.txt
file02.doc	file11.txt	file39.txt

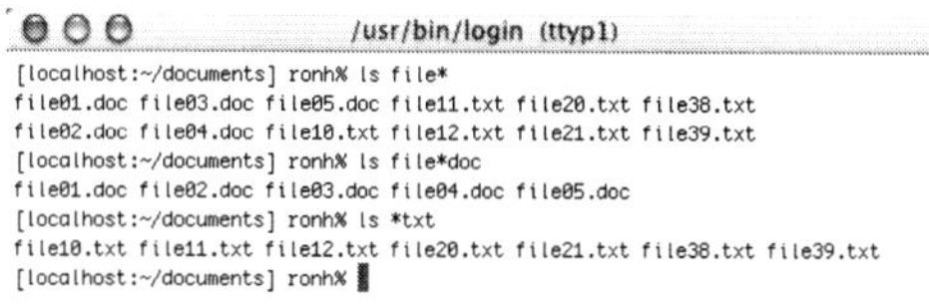

/usr/bin/login (ttyp1)
[localhost:~/documents] ronh% ls file*
file01.doc file03.doc file05.doc file11.txt file20.txt file38.txt
file02.doc file04.doc file10.txt file12.txt file21.txt file39.txt
[localhost:~/documents] ronh% ls file*doc
file01.doc file02.doc file03.doc file04.doc file05.doc
[localhost:~/documents] ronh% ls *txt
file10.txt file11.txt file12.txt file20.txt file21.txt file38.txt file39.txt
[localhost:~/documents] ronh%

Figure 19 These examples show how you can use the asterisk wildcard to list specific files in a directory.

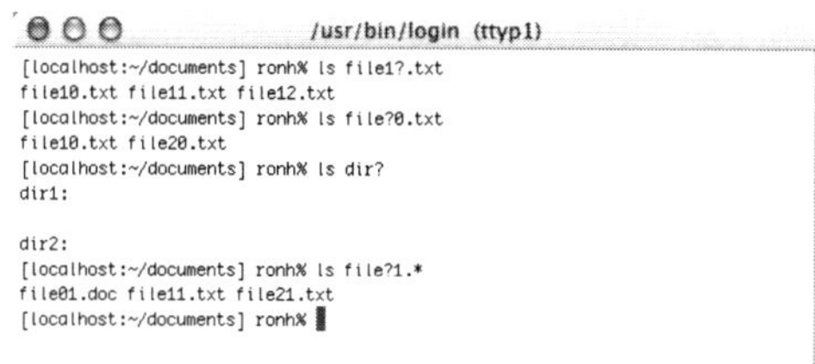

/usr/bin/login (ttyp1)
[localhost:~/documents] ronh% ls file1?.txt
file10.txt file11.txt file12.txt
[localhost:~/documents] ronh% ls file?0.txt
file10.txt file20.txt
[localhost:~/documents] ronh% ls dir?
dir1:
dir2:
[localhost:~/documents] ronh% ls file?1.*
file01.doc file11.txt file21.txt
[localhost:~/documents] ronh%

Figure 20 These examples show the question mark wildcard in action. (Both dir1 and dir2 are empty directories; that's why no files are listed for them.)

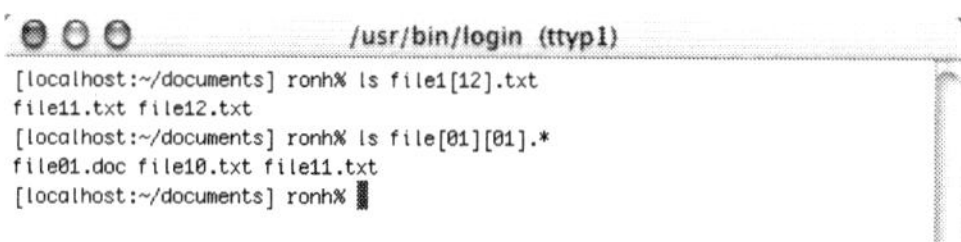

Figure 21 Here are two examples for the bracket wildcard.

Here are some examples to illustrate the asterisk wildcard (**Figure 19**):

- To work with all the files that start with the characters *file*, you'd enter **file***.
- To work with all the files that begin with the characters *file* and end with the characters *doc*, you'd enter **file*doc**.
- To work with all the files that end with the characters *txt*, you'd enter ***txt**.

These examples illustrate the question mark wildcard (**Figure 20**):

- To work with files named *file10.txt*, *file11.txt*, and *file12.txt*, you'd enter **file1?.txt**.
- To work with files named *file10.txt* and *file20.txt*, you'd enter **file?0.txt**.
- To work with subdirectories named *dir1* and *dir2*, you'd enter **dir?**.
- To work with files named *file01.doc*, *file11.txt*, and *file21.txt*, you'd enter **file?1.***. (Okay, so that one uses two wildcards.)

And these examples illustrate the brackets wildcard in action (**Figure 21**):

- To work with files named *file11.txt* and *file12.txt* (but not *file10.txt*), you'd enter **file1[12].txt**.
- To work with files named *file01.doc*, *file10.txt*, and *file11.txt*, you'd enter **file[01][01].***. (Yes, that's another one with multiple wildcard characters.)

To view a directory list using a wildcard

Type the command **ls** followed by the search string for the files or directories you want to display (see previous examples) and press Return.

A list containing only the files and directories that match the search string appear (**Figures 19**, **20**, and **21**).

Copying & Moving Files

Unix also includes commands for copying and moving files: **cp** and **mv**. These commands enable you to copy or move one or more source files to a target file or directory.

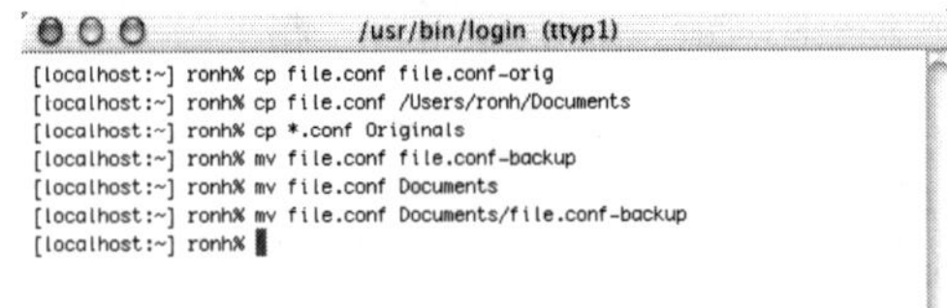

Figure 22 Here's what the cp and mv commands might look like when used. Note that there's no indication if a copy or move was successfully completed.

✔ Tips

- Why copy a file? Usually, to make a backup. For instance, before you edit a configuration file, you should create a backup copy of the original. This way you can revert back to the original if your edits "break" something in the file.
- The ***source-file*** operand can be a file or a directory.
- The **mv** command can also be used to rename a file.
- The **cp** and **mv** commands support several options. You can learn more about them in the man pages for these commands. Type **man cp** or **man mv** and press [Return] to view each command's man pages.
- Unix does not confirm that a file has been copied or moved when you correctly enter a command (**Figure 22**). To check to see if a file has been copied or moved to the correct destination, you can use the **ls** command to get a listing for the target directory. The **ls** command is covered earlier in this chapter.

To copy a file to the same directory

Type **cp *source-file target-file*** and press [Return] (**Figure 22**).

For example, **cp file.conf file.conf-orig** would duplicate the file named *file.conf* and assign the name *file.conf-orig* to the duplicate copy.

✔ Tip

- The ***source-file*** and ***target-file*** names must be different.

To copy files to another directory

Type **cp *source-file ... target-directory*** and press Return (**Figure 22**).

For example **cp file.conf /Users/ronh/Documents** would copy the file named *file.conf* in the current directory to the directory named *Documents* in my home folder.

To copy files using a wildcard

Type **cp** followed by the wildcard search string for the source file and the name of the target directory and press Return (**Figure 22**).

For example, **cp *.conf Originals** would copy all files ending with *.conf* in the current directory to the subdirectory named *Originals*.

To rename a file

Type **mv *source target*** and press Return (**Figure 22**).

For example, **mv file.conf file.conf-backup** would rename *file.conf* as *file.conf-backup*.

To move files to another directory

Type **mv *source ... directory*** and press Return (**Figure 22**).

For example, **mv file.conf Documents** would move the file named *file.conf* in the current directory to the subdirectory named *Documents*.

To move a file to another directory & rename it

Type **mv *source directory/filename*** and press Return (**Figure 22**).

For example, **mv file.conf Documents/file.conf-backup** would move the file named *file.conf* in the current directory to the subdirectory named *Documents* and name it *file.conf-backup* in its new location.

Making Symbolic Links with ln

Mac OS enables you to make aliases to files. It should come as no surprise that Unix does, too. But in Unix, aliases are called *symbolic links*. And rather than use a menu command or shortcut key to create them, you use the **ln** (make links) command with its **-s** option.

✔ Tips

- Mac OS aliases and Unix symbolic links make it convenient to access deeply buried files or to organize files differently than the way the operating system organizes them.
- If you omit the **-s** option, the **ln** command creates a hard link. Hard links can't cross file systems (or partitions) and can't normally refer to directories.
- Unix does not tell you if the source file to which you want to create a symbolic link does not exist. As a result, it's possible to create an alias that doesn't point to anything.
- You can learn more about other options for the **ln** command in its man pages. Type **man ln** and press Return to display them.

To make a link to a file

Type **ln -s *source-file target-file*** and press Return (**Figure 23**).

For example, **ln -s file1 alias1** creates an alias called *alias1* that points to the file called *file1*. In this example, both files (the source and the target) are in the current directory.

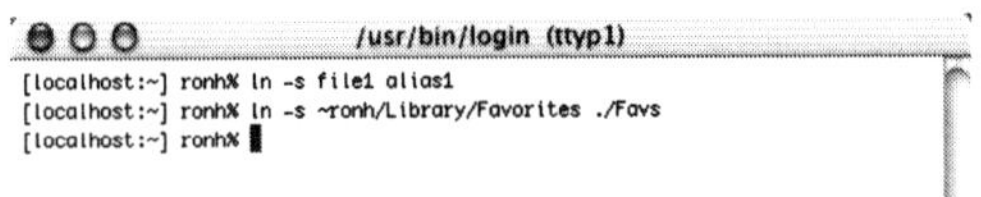

Figure 23 These examples show the commands for creating symbolic links to a file and a directory.

To make a link to a directory

Type **ln -s *source-directory target-file*** and press Return (**Figure 23**).

For example, **ln -s ~ronh/Library/Documentation ./Docs** creates a alias called *Docs* in the current directory (./) that points to the directory called *Documentation*, which is in the directory called *Library*, inside the home directory (~) of the user ronh.

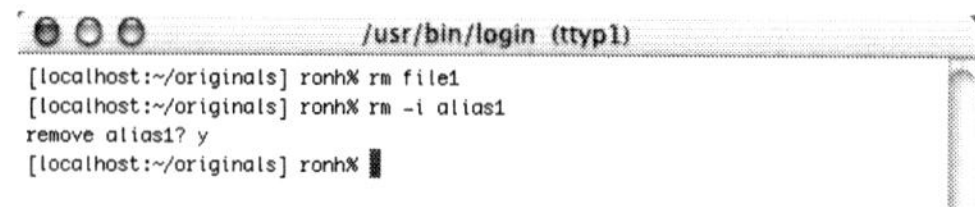
/usr/bin/login (ttyp1)
[localhost:~/originals] ronh% rm file1
[localhost:~/originals] ronh% rm -i alias1
remove alias1? y
[localhost:~/originals] ronh%

Figure 24 The rm command in action, with and without the -i option.

Removing Files & Directories with rm & rmdir

Unix includes two commands that you can use to delete files and directories: **rm** (remove) and **rmdir** (remove directory).

✖ Caution

- **rm** may be the most dangerous command in Unix. Because Unix doesn't have a Trash that lets you recover mistakenly deleted files, when you delete a file, it's gone forever.

✔ Tips

- There are two options that you may want to use with the **rm** command:
  - **-i** tells the **rm** command to ask permission before deleting each file (**Figure 24**). You must press Y and then Return at each prompt to delete the file. This is especially useful when using the **rm** command with wildcard characters, since it can help prevent files from being accidentally deleted.
  - **-R** tells the **rm** command to recursively delete everything within a directory, including its subdirectories and their contents. The **-R** option can be very dangerous; you may want to use it in conjunction with the **-i** option to confirm each deletion.
- The **rm** command's ***file*** operand can be a file or a directory name.
- You can learn more about the **rm** and **rmdir** commands and their options on their man pages. Type **man rm** or **man rmdir** and press Return to view each command's man pages.

To remove a file

Type **rm *file* ...** and press Return. For example, **rm file1** removes the file named *file1* from the current directory (**Figure 24**).

USING RM & RMDIR

To remove files using a wildcard character

Type **rm** followed by the wildcard search string and press [Return]. For example, **rm *.bak** removes all files ending with *.bak* from the current directory.

To remove all files in a directory

Type **rm *** and press [Return] (**Figure 25**).

✔ Tips

- You may want to include the **-i** option (for example, **rm -i ***) to confirm each deletion so you do not delete files by mistake.
- Since the **rm** command cannot remove directories without the **-R** option, an error message may appear when you use the **rm *** command string in a directory that contains subdirectories (**Figure 25**).

To remove all files & subdirectories in a directory

Type **rm -R *** and press [Return] (**Figure 25**).

✔ Tip

- You may want to include the **-i** option (for example, **rm -Ri ***; **Figure 25**) to confirm each deletion so you do not delete files or subdirectories by mistake.

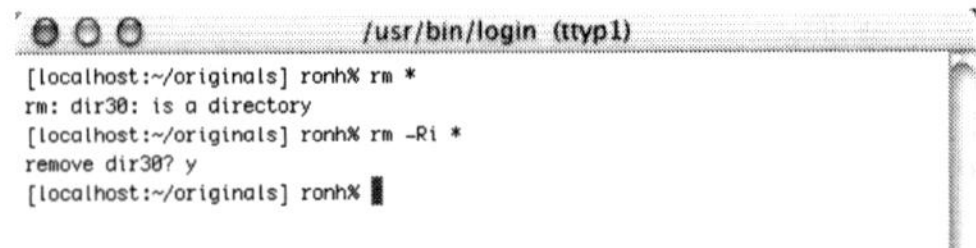

Figure 25 Two more examples of the rm command. In the first, the rm * command string deletes all files in the directory, but not the subdirectory named dir30. In the second, the -Ri options delete all contents with confirmation; the only item still in the directory is the subdirectory named dir30.

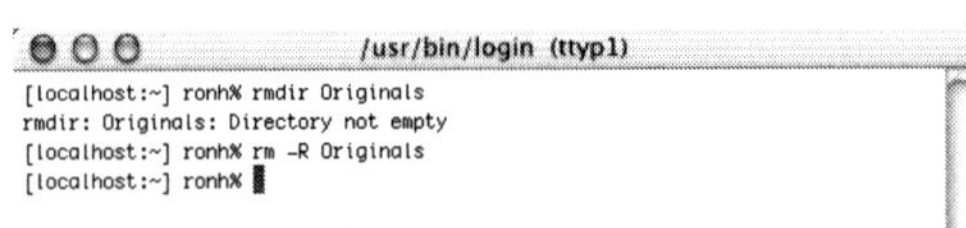

Figure 26 This example shows two attempts to delete a subdirectory. The first, using the rmdir command, is not successful because the directory is not empty. The second, using the rm -R command string, does the job.

To remove an empty directory

Type **rmdir *directory*...** and press [Return]. For example, **rmdir Originals** removes the subdirectory named *Originals* in the current directory (**Figure 26**).

✔ Tip

- The **rmdir** command will result in an error message if the directory you are trying to remove is not empty (**Figure 26**).

To remove a directory & its contents

Type **rm -R *directory*** and press [Return]. For example, **rm -R Originals** removes the directory named *Originals* even if it is not empty (**Figure 26**).

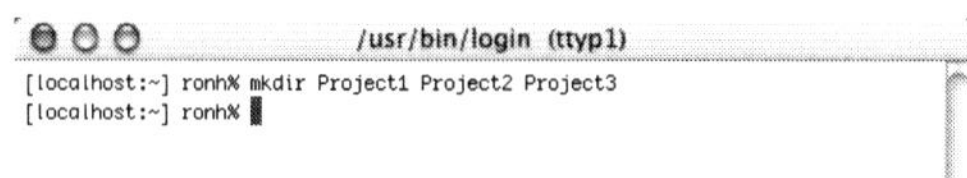

Figure 27 In this example, the mkdir command is used to create three new subdirectories.

Creating a New Directory with mkdir

You can also create new directories. Use the **mkdir** command.

✔ Tip

- You can learn more about the **mkdir** command and its options on its man pages. Type **man mkdir** and press Return to view the command's man pages.

To create a new directory

Type **mkdir *directory-name* ...** and press Return. For example, **mkdir Project1 Project2 Project3** makes three new subdirectories in the current directory: *Project1*, *Project2*, and *Project3* (**Figure 27**).

Viewing File Contents

Unix offers a few tools for examining the contents of files:

- **cat** (concatenate) lists one or more files to the Terminal window.
- **more** outputs files in page-size chunks, enabling you to view the contents of large files one screen at a time.
- **head** displays the first lines of a file.
- **tail** displays the last lines of a file.
- **wc** displays a count of the number of lines, words, and characters in a file.

✔ Tip

- To learn more about these commands, check out their man pages. Type **man cat**, **man more**, **man head**, **man tail**, or **man wc** and press Return to display the command's man page.

Figure 28 In this example, the cat command is used to view the contents of an RTF file. The first few lines of the file—which you wouldn't see when viewing the file with a RTF-compatible word processor (such as TextEdit)—are formatting codes.

To list a file's contents

Type **cat** ***file*** **...** (for example, **cat example.rtf**) and press Return. **cat** lists the entire file in the Terminal window without stopping (**Figure 28**).

✔ Tips

- Do not use **cat** to list binary executable files. Because they contain many nonprintable characters, they could cause Terminal to act strangely. If this happens, close the Terminal window and open a new one.
- If you specify more than one file, **cat** lists them one after another without any indication that it has finished one file and started another one.
- I explain how to use the **cat** command and output redirection to combine multiple files and output them to a new file later in this chapter.
- If you use **cat** to list a long file, Terminal may not be able to store all of the lines. You may prefer to use the **more** command to output the file in page-sized chunks.

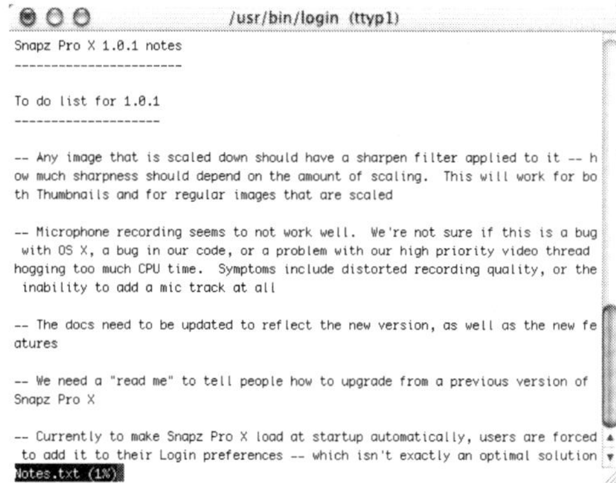

Figure 29 The more command in action.

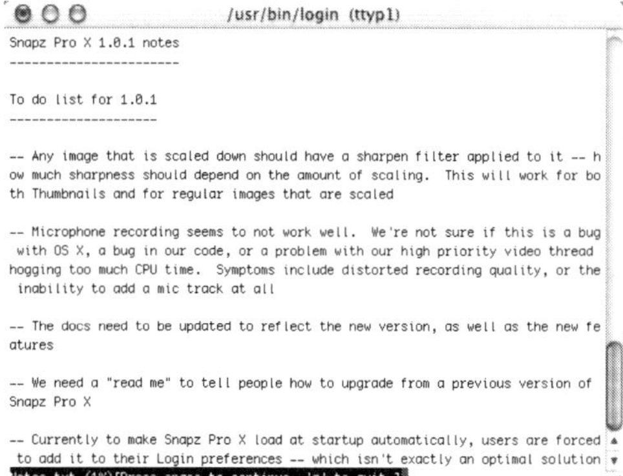

Figure 30 In this example, the -d option was used with the more command. See how the prompt at the bottom of the page changes?

To page through the contents of a file

1. Type **more *file*** (for example, **more Notes.txt**) and press Return. The first page of the file appears in the Terminal window (**Figure 29**). The last line tells you the name of the file and what percentage of the file has been displayed.
2. Press Spacebar to advance to the next screen.

   or

   Press Return to advance to the next line.

   or

   Press D to advance to the next half screen.
3. Repeat step 2 to view the entire file.

   or

   Press Q to return to the shell prompt.

✔ Tips

- You can use the **-d** option to display a more instructive prompt at the bottom of the screen (**Figure 30**).
- You can also use wildcard characters to specify multiple files. If you do, **more** will display the filenames at the start of each file.
- Like the man command discussed earlier in this chapter, the **more** command is a *pager*. A pager displays information one screen at a time, enabling you to page through it.
- Along with the usual pagers, Mac OS X includes a more versatile pager command, which is whimsically called **less**. This newer version has many cool features—including the ability to page backward through a file—so you may want to check out its man page; type **man less** and press Return.
  I emphasize **more** in this section because it appears in all Unix systems.

To show the first lines of a file

Type **head [-n *count*] *file* ...** and press Return, where *count* is the number of lines at the beginning of the file that you want to display. For example, **head -n 15 Sample.txt** displays the first 15 lines of the file named *Sample.txt* (**Figure 31**).

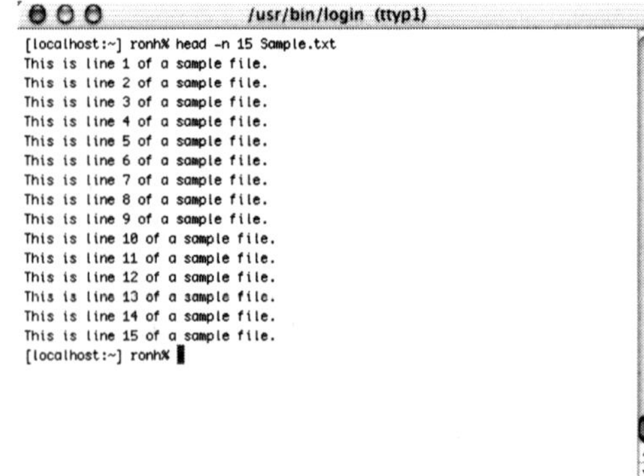

Figure 31 The head command displays the first bunch of lines in a file...

✔ Tips

- If you omit the -n *count* operand, **head** displays the first ten lines of the file.
- You can specify multiple files. If you do, **head** displays the file names at the start of each file.

To show last lines of a file

Type **tail [-n *count*] *file* ...** and press Return where *count* is the number of lines at the end of the file that you want to display. For example, **tail -n 15 Sample.txt** displays the last 15 lines of the file named *Sample.txt* (**Figure 32**).

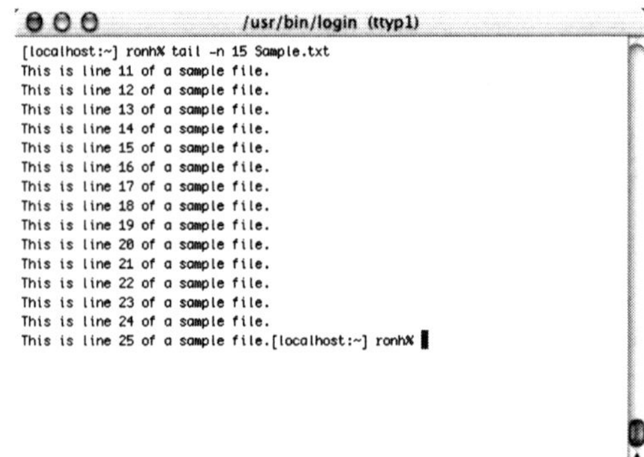

Figure 32 ...and the tail command displays the last bunch.

✔ Tips

- If you omit the -n *count* operand, **tail** displays the last ten lines of the file.
- You can specify multiple files. If you do, **tail** displays the file names at the start of each file.
- The **-f** option (for example **tail -f log.txt**) displays the last lines of the file, but prevents the **tail** command from terminating. Instead, **tail** waits for the file to grow. As new lines are added to the file, **tail** immediately displays them. You may find this useful if you want to watch a log file grow and see the latest entries as they are added. You may also use it to watch an error log file when you are debugging a program. You cannot use the **-f** option if you specify multiple files; to monitor multiple files with the **tail** command, open multiple Terminal windows.

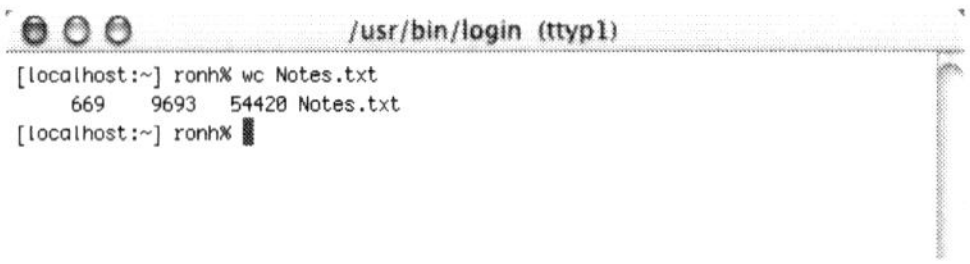

```
/usr/bin/login (ttyp1)
[localhost:~] ronh% wc Notes.txt
     669    9693   54420 Notes.txt
[localhost:~] ronh%
```

Figure 33 The wc command shows the number of lines, words, and characters in a file.

To count the lines, words, & characters in a file

Type **wc *file* ...** (for example, **wc Notes.txt**) and press Return. The number of lines, words, and characters (or bytes) in the file you specified is displayed in the Terminal window (**Figure 33**).

✔ Tip

- You can use any combination of options for the **wc** command:

  -c displays the number of characters

  -w displays the number of words

  -l displays the number of lines

  With no options, **wc** displays all three pieces of information in this order: lines, words, characters, file name (**Figure 33**).

Creating & Editing Files with pico

Although using a GUI text editor in Mac OS X is lots easier than using a Unix text editor, it's a good idea to know a little about them and how they work. This way, if you ever find yourself sitting in front of a Unix system, you'll have a chance at making it usable.

Unix offers a number of text editors: the easy-to-use **pico**, the ever-present **vi**, and the geek-favorite **emacs**. Which one you use is a personal decision: Each has strengths and weaknesses. It is far beyond the scope of this chapter (or book) to help you master any one of these, let alone all three. Because **pico** is the easiest Unix text editor to use, I'll introduce it here.

✔ Tips

- The **emacs** and **vi** text editors are so powerful and complex that entire books have been written about them. You can learn a little more about them in their somewhat inadequate man pages; type **man emacs** or **man vi** and press Return to view them.
- **pico** is normally a piece of the pine email package, but Apple did not make pine part of the standard Mac OS X Unix installation. Apple also did not include the man pages for **pico**. You can download the entire pine-pico package for Mac OS X from **www.osxgnu.org/software/pine/**.

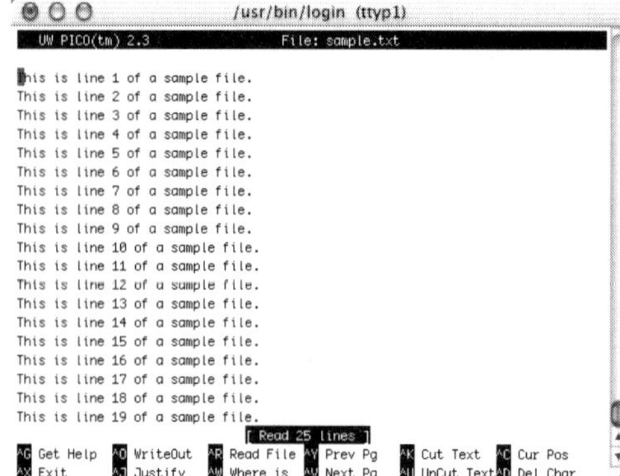

Figure 34 pico can open an existing file...

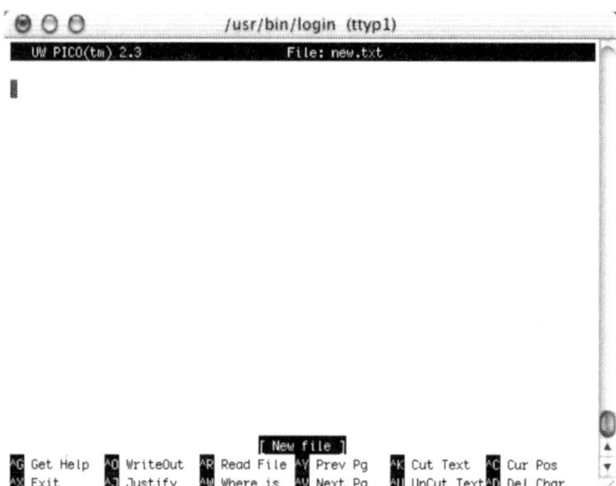

Figure 35 ...or create a new one with the name you specify.

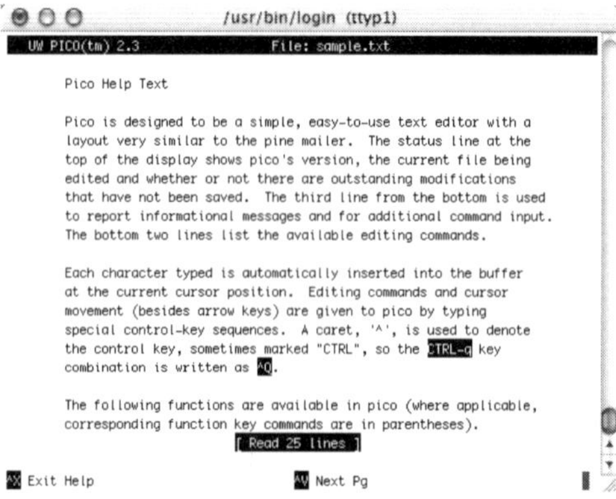

Figure 36 The beginning of pico's onscreen help.

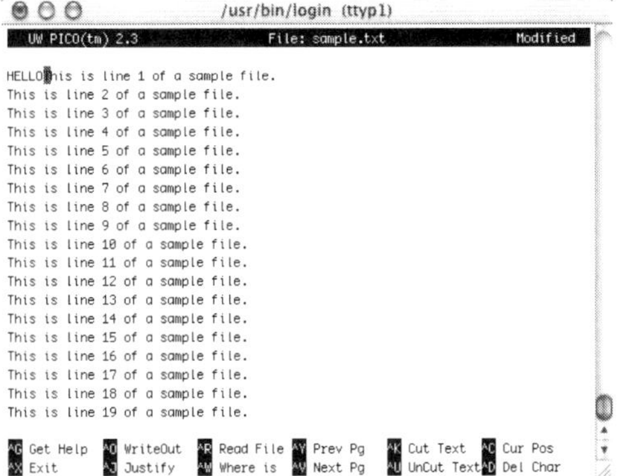

Figure 37 Text is inserted at the cursor.

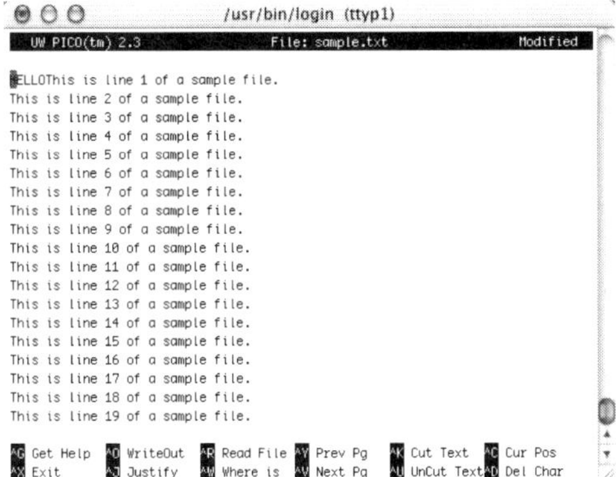

Figure 38 Position the cursor on the character you want to delete.

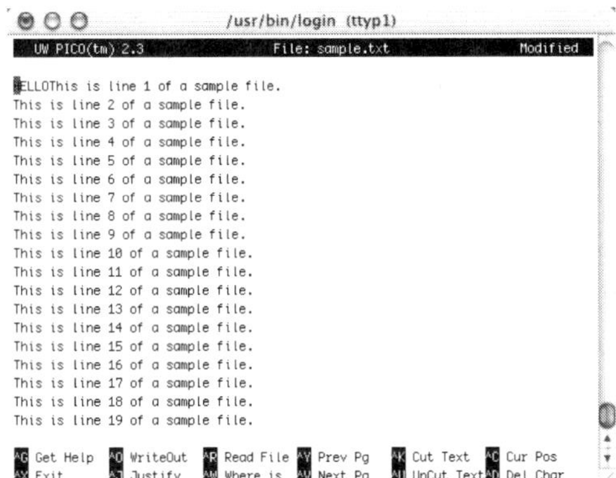

Figure 39 Text at the cursor is deleted.

To open a file with pico

Type **pico *file*** (for example, **pico sample.txt**) and press Return.

pico starts up in the Terminal window. If you entered the name of an existing file, the first 25 lines of the file appear (**Figure 34**). If you entered the name of a file that does not already exist, **pico** creates a new file for you (**Figure 35**). Either way, the **pico** menu appears at the bottom of the window. The cursor appears as a gray box at the beginning of the file.

To use pico menu commands

Press the keystroke for the command you want. Each command includes Control (indicated by ^). For example, you can view onscreen help by pressing Control G (**Figure 36**).

To navigate through text

To move one character in any direction, press the corresponding arrow key.

or

To move to the previous or next page, press Control Y or Control V.

To insert text

1. Position the cursor where you want to insert character(s) (**Figure 34**).
2. Type the character(s) you want to insert. The new text is inserted (**Figure 37**).

To delete text

1. Position the cursor on the character you want to delete (**Figure 38**).
2. Press Control D. The character disappears (**Figure 39**).

To cut & paste text

1. Use the arrow keys to position the cursor at the beginning of the text you want to cut (**Figure 34**).
2. Press Control Shift ^. *[Mark Set]* appears near the bottom of the window (**Figure 40**).
3. Use the arrow keys to position the cursor at the end of the block you want to cut. Text between the starting point and cursor turns black (**Figure 41**).
4. Press Control K (Cut Text). The selected text disappears (**Figure 42**).
5. Position the cursor where you want to paste the text (**Figure 43**).
6. Press Control U (Uncut Text). The cut text appears at the cursor (**Figure 44**).

To insert an existing file

1. Position the cursor where you want to insert the file (**Figure 34**).
2. Press Control R (Read File).
3. The Insert File prompt appears at the bottom of the window. Enter the path name for the file you want to insert (**Figure 45**) and press Return. The contents of the file appear at the cursor (**Figure 46**).

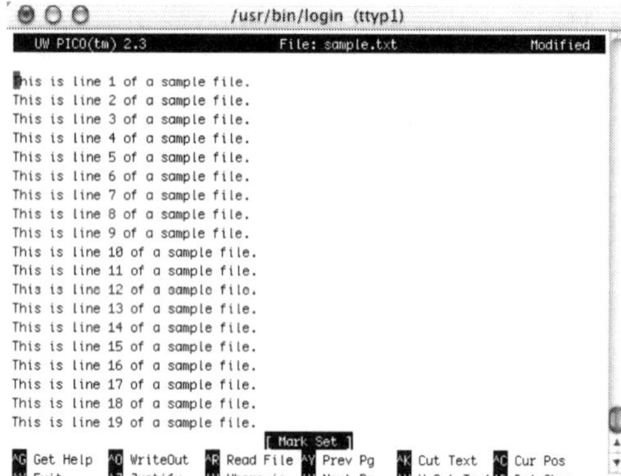

Figure 40 *Mark Set* appears in the window.

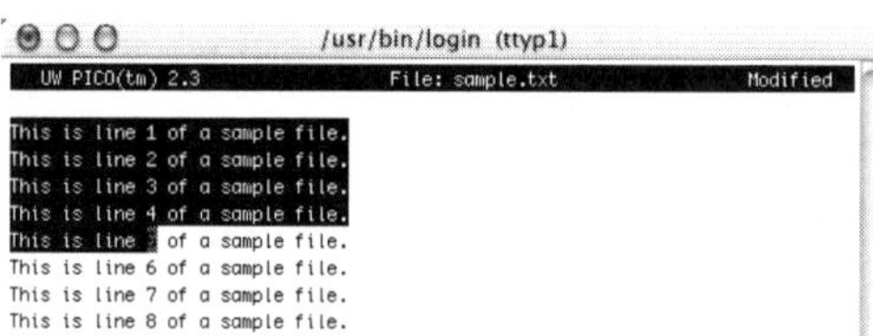

Figure 41 Use the arrow keys to select text.

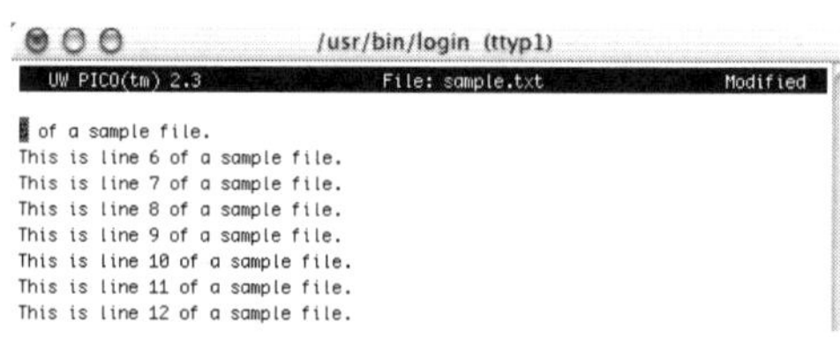

Figure 42 Using the Cut Text command removes the selected text.

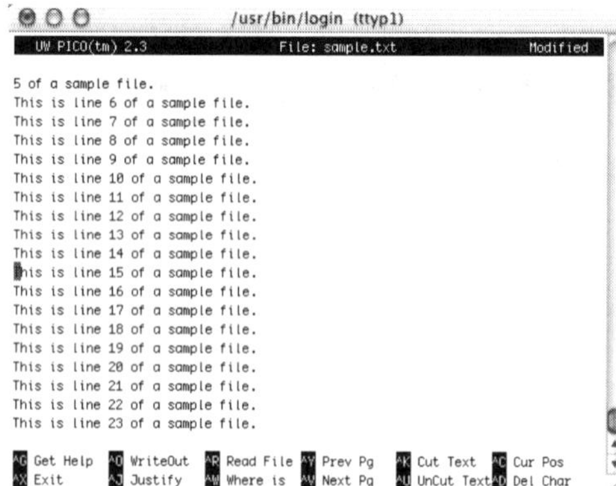

Figure 43 Position the cursor where you want to paste the text.

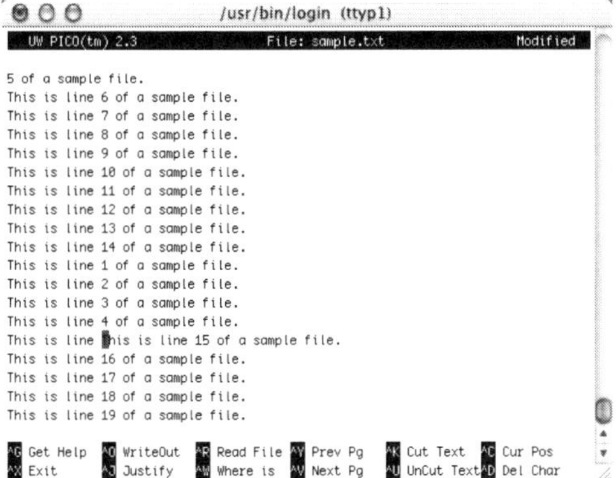

Figure 44 Using the Uncut Text command pastes the text back into the document.

Figure 45 Enter the name of the file you want to insert at the Insert file prompt.

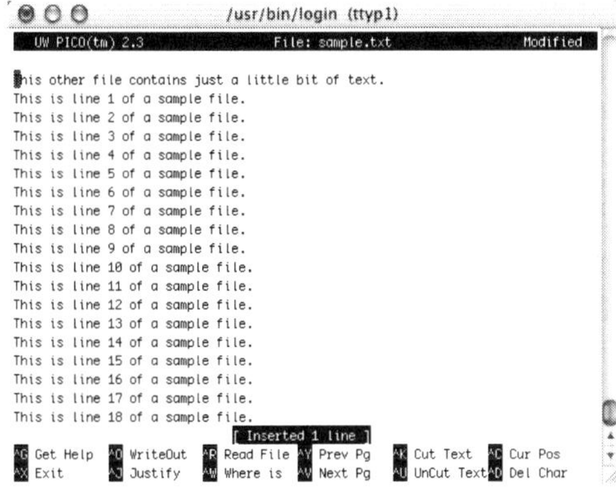

Figure 46 The file is inserted at the cursor.

Figure 47 Use the File Name to write prompt to enter a name for the file.

To save changes to a file

1. Press Control O (WriteOut). The File Name to write prompt appears at the bottom of the window, along with the name of the file you originally opened (**Figure 47**).
2. To save the file with the same name, press Return.

   or

   To save the file with a different name, use Delete to remove the existing file name, enter a new file name, and press Return. The file is saved.

To exit pico

1. Press Control X (Exit).
2. If you have made changes to the file since opening it, the Save modified buffer prompt appears at the bottom of the window (**Figure 48**).
   - ▲ Press Y and then Return to savechanges to the file (**Figure 47**) and exit pico.
   - ▲ Press N and then Return to exit pico without saving changes to the file.

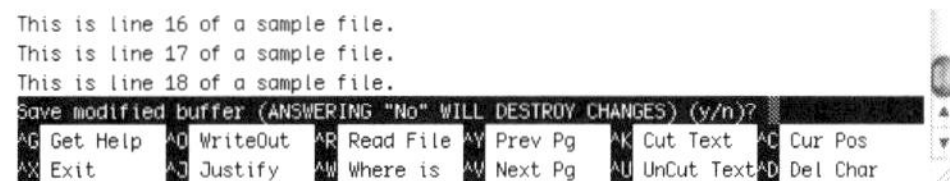

Figure 48 The Save modified buffer prompt enables you to save changes to the file before you exit pico.

The cut Command

The **cut** command enables you to select a list or range of characters or fields in each line of a table or similarly organized file. The option you use with the command determines how file contents are extracted; for example:

- **-c** ***list*** enables you to specify a list or range of character positions.
- **-f** ***list*** enables you to specify a list or range of fields, delimited by a single tab character.

The ***list*** operand can be a list or range. As these examples show, a list consists of numbers separated by commas and a range consists of two numbers separated by a hyphen.

The following examples show how the **cut** command can be used with a tab-delimited text file such as the file named *sales.txt* shown in **Figure 49**.

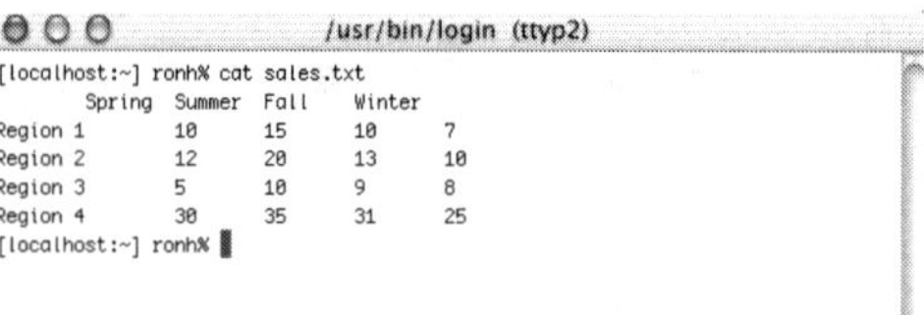

Figure 49 This sample file, sales.txt, has tab-delimited fields of information.

✔ Tip

- To learn more about the **cut** command and its other options, check out its man pages. Type **man cut** and press Return.

To select characters in a file

Type **cut -c** ***list file*** **...** and press Return.

For example, **cut -c 5-10 sales.txt** returns the fifth through tenth character in each line of *sales.txt* and **cut -c 2, 4, 6, 8 sales.txt** returns the second, fourth, sixth, and eighth characters in each line of *sales.txt*. These results are shown in **Figure 50**.

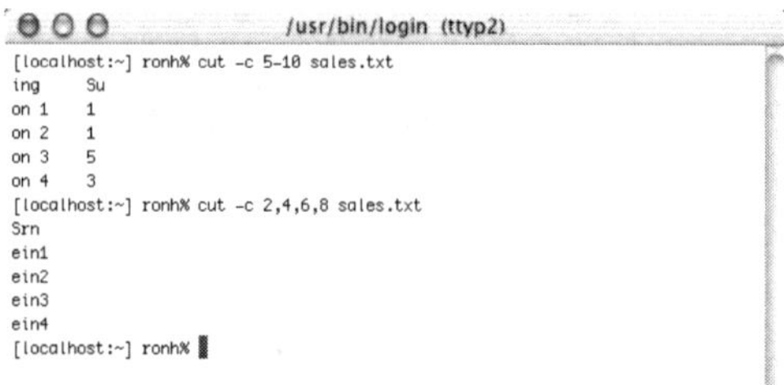

Figure 50 Here's how the cut command can extract characters.

To select fields in a tab-delimited text file

Type **cut -f** ***list file*** **...** and press Return.

For example, **cut -f 1-2 sales txt** returns the first and second field in each line of *sales.txt* and **cut -f 1,4 sales.txt** returns the first and fourth fields in each row of *sales.txt*. These results are shown in **Figure 51**.

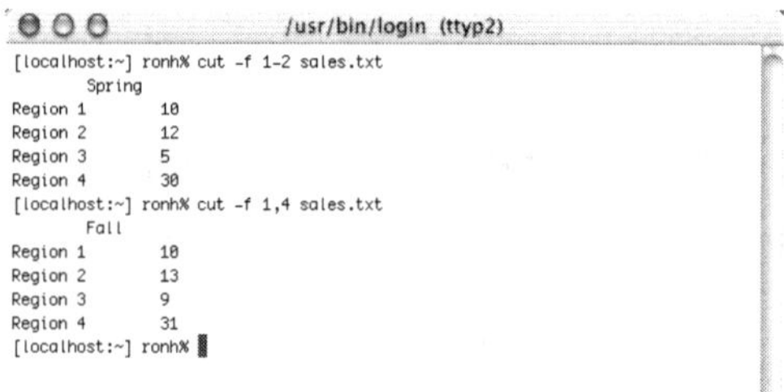

Figure 51 And here's how the cut command can extract fields.

Figure 52 Here are a few names to be sorted. (Recognize them? They're from Italo Calvino's wonderful book, *Cosmic Comics*.)

Figure 53 Here are the names from **Figure 52**, sorted two ways.

Sorting Lines with sort

The **sort** command enables you to sort the lines in a file. Three of its most commonly used options are:

- **-d** sorts in dictionary order, ignoring all characters except letters, numbers, and blanks.
- **-n** sorts in numeric order, ignoring all other characters.
- **-r** sorts in reverse order.

The following examples show how the contents of the file named *names.txt* (**Figure 52**) can be sorted using the **sort** command.

✔ Tip

- To learn more about the **sort** command and its other options, check out its man pages. Type **man sort** and press Return.

To sort alphabetically

Type **sort -d *file*** and press Return.

For example, **sort -d names.txt** sorts the lines in *names.txt* in alphabetical order (**Figure 53**).

To sort in reverse order

Type **sort -r *file*** and press Return.

For example, **sort -r names.txt** sorts the lines in *names.txt* in reverse alphabetical order (**Figure 53**).

Output Redirection

In all of the Unix commands up to this point that produced output—such as **man** and **ls**—the command output appears in the Terminal window. This is called the *standard output device* of Unix.

But the shell can also redirect the output of a command to a file instead of to the screen. This *output redirection* enables you to create files by writing command output to a file.

Output redirection uses the greater than character (>) to tell the shell to place the output of a command into a file rather than listing it to the screen. If the output file already exists, it is overwritten with the new information.

Similarly, a pair of greater than signs (>>) tells the shell to append the contents of one file to an existing file. If the output file does not already exist, the shell creates a new file with the name you specified.

This section offers some examples of output redirection, using commands I have already covered.

To sort a file & output it to another file

Type **sort *file* > *output-file*** and press Return.

For example, **sort sample.txt > alpha.txt** would sort the lines in the file named *sample.txt* and write them to a file named *alpha.txt*.

To save a directory listing as a file

Type **ls > *output-file*** and press Return.

For example, **ls -la > list.txt** creates a file named *list.txt* that contains a complete directory listing in the long format (**Figure 54**).

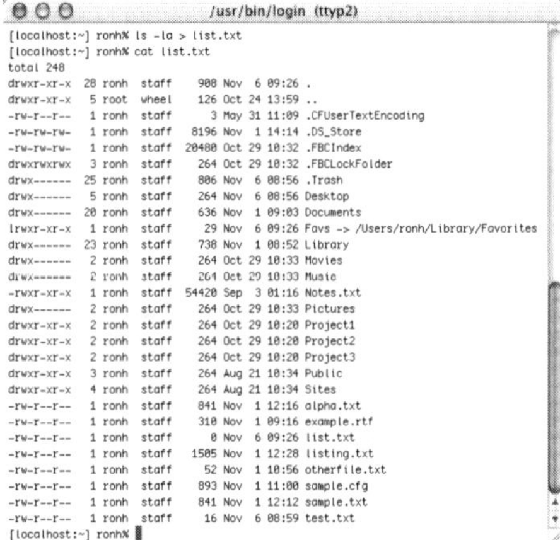

Figure 54 This example shows how the ls command can be used to save a directory listing as a text file. The cat command was used in the illustration to display the contents of the new file.

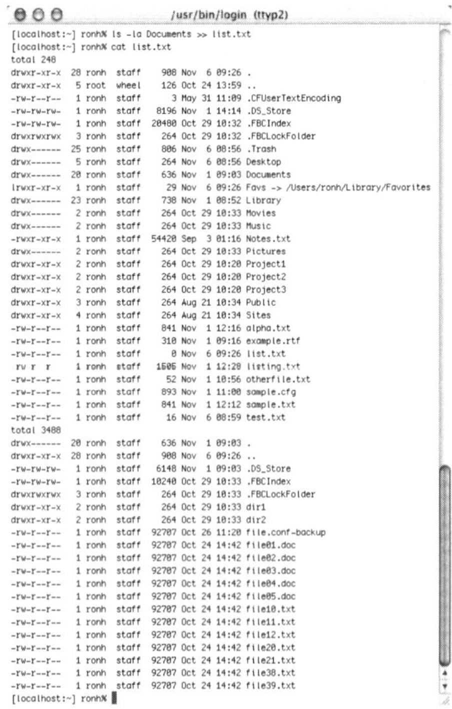

Figure 55 This example uses >> to append another directory to the one in **Figure 49** and display the combined files with the cat command.

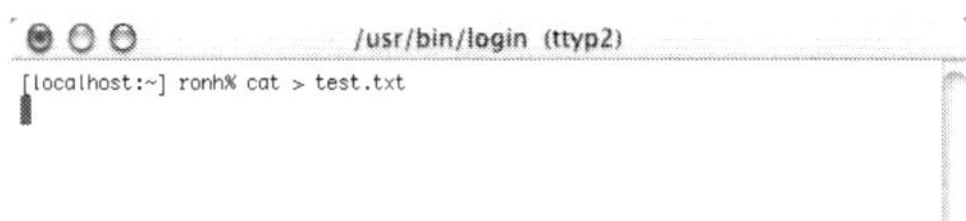

Figure 56 Using the cat command with an output file name starts cat and waits for text entry.

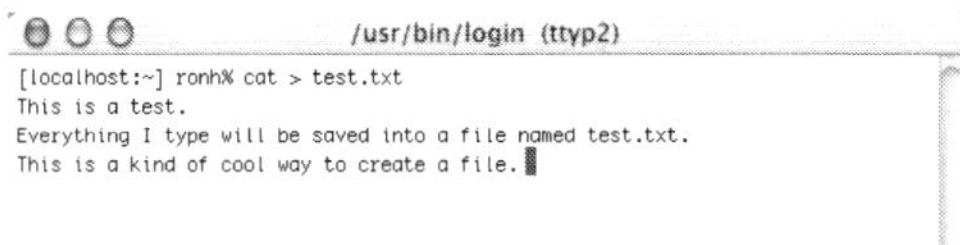

Figure 57 Enter the text you want to include in the file.

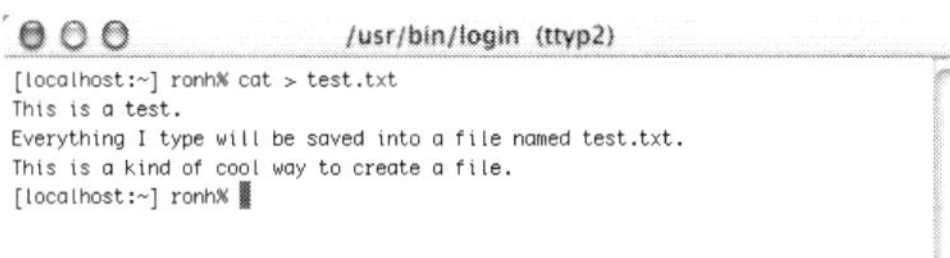

Figure 58 Press Control D to save the file.

To append output to an existing file

Type **ls >>** ***output-file*** and press Return.

For example, **ls -la Documents >> list.txt** would append a directory listing for the Documents subdirectory to the list.txt file (**Figure 55**).

To create a text file with cat

1. Type **cat >** ***output-file*** (for example, **cat > test.txt**) and press Return. The **cat** command starts and waits for you to type text (**Figure 56**).
2. Enter the text you want to include in the file. You can press Return to start a new line if desired (**Figure 57**).
3. When you're finished entering text, press Control D (**Figure 58**). (Control D is the ASCII "End Of Transmission" character.)

   The new file is saved with the name you specified.

✔ Tip

- Normally, the **cat** command uses a source-file argument; that is, you normally tell **cat** to list a specific file to the screen. If you do not specify a source-file for **cat**, it takes source data from the *standard input device*, which is usually the keyboard, and redirects it to the output-file.

To combine files with cat

Type **cat** ***file1*** **... >** ***output-file*** and press Return.

For example, **cat firstfile.txt secondfile.txt thirdfile.txt > combinedfile.txt** combines the files named *firstfile.txt*, *secondfile.txt*, and *thirdfile.txt*, in that order, and saves them as a file named *combinedfile.txt*.

Using Pipes

While reading through this chapter, you may have thought to yourself, "Wouldn't it be nice if I could take the output of one command and feed it into another?" Good thinking! If this were possible, you could take a series of short, specialized commands and string them together into a vast collection of useful tools.

Fortunately, Unix offers this capability with *pipes*. Pipes use the vertical bar character (|), which is called a pipe, to separate commands in a string. The output from the first command is fed to the input of the second command and so forth. You can think of pipes as plumbing you can use to connect commands.

Here's a real-life example I use all the time. On our system, I like to keep tabs on how much mail each user is storing on our machine. Mail files are stored (on our Sun server) in the directory /var/spool/mail. I could enter a simple **ls -la** and look down the list for big files, but we have more than 400 users! Here's the command I use instead:

```
ls -la /var/spool/mail | cut -c15-22,23-31 |
sort -nr +1 | more
```

This command does a directory listing of the /var/spool/mail subdirectory, cuts out the size of the file and the user name (which is the same as name of the file), sorts the result numerically and in reverse order (to put the biggest at the top), and serves it all up in page-size chunks with the **more** command.

Here's what the output looks like with the names changed to protect the innocent:

```
user1   14781064
user2   11389917
user3   10899520
user4   10427310
user5   10231172
user6   9996725
user7   9910928
user8   9235183
user9   9172493
```

Pretty cool, eh?

✔ Tip

- Although you don't need spaces before or after the pipe character, it's a lot easier to read. Unix simply ignores the spaces.

Unix Security & Utilities

by Ron Hipschman

Unix Security

Unix has many built-in security features to help protect your files and your computer. In the first half of this chapter, I cover the following security features:

- **Passwords** enable you to protect your computer from unauthorized access.
- **File and directory permissions** enable you to specify which users or groups can access individual files and directories.
- **Users and groups** enables you to specify access privileges for individual users and groups of users.
- **Information commands** enable you to see who has accessed your computer and what they did.

✔ Tip

- This chapter builds on the information in **Chapter 3**. To get the most out of this chapter, please make sure you read and understand the information in **Chapter 3** before moving on to this one.

Passwords & Security

You may think, "I don't care if someone reads my mail" or "I don't store important files in my directory, so who needs a good password?"

This is exactly what *crackers* count on. Many times, these crackers don't want to read your mail or erase your files; they want to install their own programs that take up your computer time and Internet bandwidth. They steal resources from you and slow down your computer and Internet response time. They also install *Trojan horse* programs that allow them to break into your computer at a future date. These Trojan horses are designed to look and act exactly like other normal programs you expect to see on the machine.

When a cracker breaks into your computer system, your only course of action is to take the machine off the network and rebuild the operating system from scratch. It's virtually impossible to detect Trojan horses, which is why you must rebuild your system. The rebuild process can take days, and you lose communication during that time. Scared? Good. Your first line of defense is to use good passwords.

The object when choosing a password is to pick a password that is easy for you to remember but difficult for someone else to guess. This leaves the cracker no alternative but a brute-force search, trying every possible combination of letters, numbers, and punctuation. A search of this sort, even conducted on a machine that could try one million passwords per second (most machines can try less than one hundred per second), would require, on average, over one hundred years to complete. With this as your goal, here are some guidelines you should follow for password selection.

Dos

- Do use a password with nonalphabetic characters: digits or punctuation mixed into the middle of the password. For example, *ronh3;cat.*
- Do use a password that contains mixed-case letters, such as *ROnIICAt.*
- Do pick a password that is easy to remember, so you don't have to write it down. (And *never* write it on a sticky note and stick it on your monitor.)
- Do use a password that you can quickly type, without having to look at the keyboard. This makes it harder for someone watching over your shoulder to steal your password. If someone is watching, ask them to turn their head.

Don'ts

- Don't use your login name in any form—for example, as it is, reversed, capitalized, or doubled.
- Don't use your first name, last name, or initials in any form.
- Don't use your spouse's, child's, or pet's name.
- Don't use other information that is easily obtained about you. This includes license plate numbers, addresses, telephone numbers, social security numbers, the brand of your automobile, and the name of the street you live on.
- Don't use a password that consists of all digits or all the same letter. This significantly decreases the search time for a cracker.
- Don't use a word contained in dictionaries (either English or foreign language), spelling lists, or other lists of words (for example, the Star Trek series, movie titles, Shakespeare plays, cartoon characters, Monty Python episodes, the Hitchhiker's Guide series, myths or legends, place names, sports words, and colleges). These are all part of the standard dictionaries that come with cracking software, and the crackers can always add their own dictionaries.
- Don't use a word simply prefixed of suffixed with a number or a punctuation mark.
- Don't substitute a zero for the letter O or substitute a numeral one for the letter L or I.
- Don't use a password shorter than six characters.

Password ideas

Although these password rules may seem extreme, you have several methods for choosing secure, easy-to-remember passwords that also obey the rules. For example:

- Choose a line or two from a song or poem and then use the first letter of each word. For example, if you pick, "In Xanadu did Kubla Kahn a stately pleasure dome decree," you would have *IXdKKaspdd*. "Ding dong the Witch is dead" becomes *DdtWid*.
- Create a password by alternating between one consonant and one or two vowels, as long as eight characters. This provides nonsense words that are usually pronounceable and thus easily remembered. For example, *moatdup* and *jountee*.
- Choose two short words and concatenate them with a punctuation character. For example: *dog:rain* or *ray/gun* or *kid?goat*.

To change your password

1. In the Terminal window, type **passwd** and press Return.
2. The shell prompts you to enter your old password (**Figure 1**). Enter it and press Return.
3. The shell prompts you to enter your new password (**Figure 2**). Enter it, and press Return.
4. The shell prompts you to enter your new password again (**Figure 3**). Enter it and press Return.

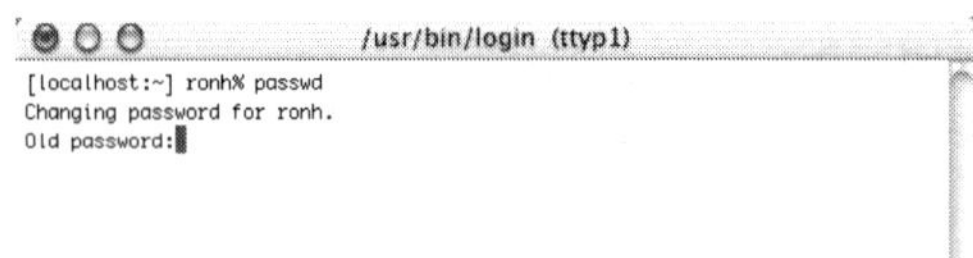

Figure 1 First, the shell prompts you for your current password.

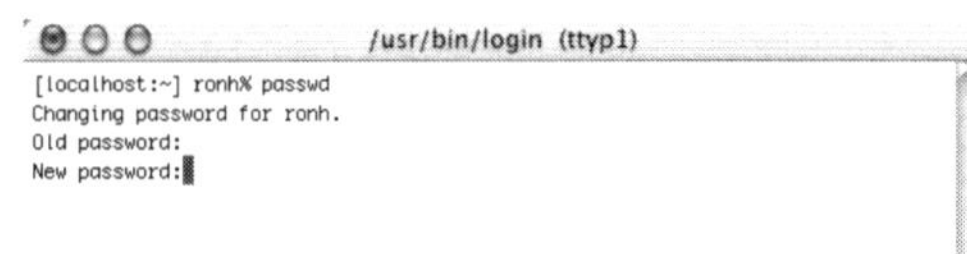

Figure 2 Next, it prompts you to enter your new password.

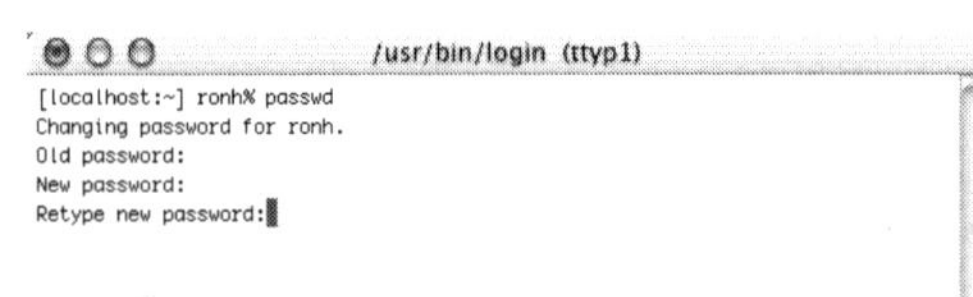

Figure 3 Finally, it prompts you to re-enter your new password.

✔ Tips

- When you enter your old and new password, the cursor in the Terminal window does not move. This is an added security feature; someone looking over your shoulder as you type can't even see how many characters you typed.
- The new password you select must be at least five characters in length.

```
/usr/bin/login (ttyp1)
[localhost:~] ronh% ls -la
total 272
drwxr-xr-x  30 ronh  staff    976 Nov  6 11:09 .
drwxr-xr-x   5 root  wheel    126 Oct 24 13:59 ..
-rw-r--r--   1 ronh  staff      3 May 31 11:09 .CFUserTextEncoding
-rw-rw-rw-   1 ronh  staff   8196 Nov  6 11:09 .DS_Store
-rw-rw-rw-   1 ronh  staff  20480 Oct 29 10:32 .FBCIndex
drwxrwxrwx   3 ronh  staff    264 Oct 29 10:32 .FBCLockFolder
drwx------  37 ronh  staff   1214 Nov  6 12:36 .Trash
drwx------   8 ronh  staff    228 Nov  9 09:32 Desktop
drwx------  20 ronh  staff    636 Nov  6 10:42 Documents
lrwxr-xr-x   1 ronh  staff     29 Nov  6 11:09 Favs -> /Users/ronh/Library/Favorites
drwx------  23 ronh  staff    738 Nov  1 08:52 Library
drwx------   2 ronh  staff    264 Oct 29 10:33 Movies
drwx------   2 ronh  staff    264 Oct 29 10:33 Music
-rwxr-xr-x   1 ronh  staff  54420 Sep  3 01:16 Notes.txt
drwx------   2 ronh  staff    264 Oct 29 10:33 Pictures
drwxr-xr-x   2 ronh  staff    264 Oct 29 10:20 Project1
drwxr-xr-x   2 ronh  staff    264 Oct 29 10:20 Project2
drwxr-xr-x   2 ronh  staff    264 Oct 29 10:20 Project3
drwxr-xr-x   3 ronh  staff    264 Aug 21 10:34 Public
drwxr-xr-x   4 ronh  staff    264 Aug 21 10:34 Sites
-rw-r--r--   1 ronh  staff    841 Nov  1 12:16 alpha.txt
-rw-r--r--   1 ronh  staff    310 Nov  1 09:16 example.rtf
-rw-r--r--   1 ronh  staff   2767 Nov  6 09:36 list.txt
-rw-r--r--   1 ronh  staff   1505 Nov  1 12:28 listing.txt
-rw-r--r--   1 ronh  staff     52 Nov  6 10:58 names.txt
-rw-r--r--   1 ronh  staff     52 Nov  1 10:56 otherfile.txt
-rw-r--r--   1 ronh  staff    107 Nov  6 10:20 sales.txt
-rw-r--r--   1 ronh  staff    893 Nov  1 11:00 sample.cfg
-rw-r--r--   1 ronh  staff    841 Nov  1 12:12 sample.txt
-rw-r--r--   1 ronh  staff    121 Nov  6 09:45 test.txt
[localhost:~] ronh%
```

Figure 4 A directory listing including permissions and other information for files.

File & Directory Permissions & Ownership

If you've ever used file sharing on your Mac, you probably noticed that you can set permissions for folders and files, giving certain users, groups of users, or everyone read-only, read-write, or no access. (This is covered in **Chapter 5**.) Unix has almost the same system with users, groups, and public permissions.

Through the **ls** command, which I cover in **Chapter 3**) you can learn quite a bit more about the ownership and permissions of files on your system. For example, take a look at the **ls -la** listing for a home directory, in **Figure 4**. There's lots of useful information on each line.

The first line (starting with the word *total*) is the number of 512-byte blocks used by the files in the directories that follow. Below that, each line contains information about each subdirectory and file.

Permissions

The group of characters at the beginning of the line (for example, drwxr-xr-x in the first entry) indicates the entry's type and permissions.

The first character indicates the type of entry:

- **d** indicates a directory.
- **-** indicates a file.
- **l** indicates a link to another file.

The next nine characters of the permissions can be broken into three sets of three characters each. The first set of three is permissions for the owner of the file, the second set is permissions for the group owner, and the third set is permissions for everyone else who has access to the entry.

- **r** indicates read permissions. This permission enables the user to open and read the file or directory contents.

Continued on next page...

Continued from previous page.

- **w** indicates write permissions. This permission enables the user to make changes to the file or directory contents, including delete it.
- **x** indicates execute permissions. For an executable program file, this permission enables the user to run the program. For a directory, this permission enables the user to open the directory.
- - indicates no permission.

For example, the file named *listing.txt* can be written to and read by the owner (ronh) and can only be read by the group (staff) and everyone else.

Links

The next number is the number of links. This is a count of the files and directories contained within a directory entry. It's set to 1 for normal files.

Owner

Next is the owner of the file or directory. Normally this will be the name of your account. Sometimes, the system creates files for you, and you may see another owner. For example, the .. directory in **Figure 4** was created by the system, which gave ownership to root, the superuser.

Group

The group is listed next. Just as in file sharing in Mac OS 9.x and earlier, you can create groups of users that have separate permissions. You are, by default, assigned to the staff group, so many of your files are also owned by that group.

File size

The next number gives the size of the entry in bytes.

Modification date

Next is the date and time that the file or directory was last modified. A directory is modified whenever any of its contents are modified.

Filename

Last, you see the name of the file or directory.

More about File & Directory Ownership

Normally when you create a new file, you are given ownership of that file and it is assigned to your default group. Your default group is assigned to you when you are given your user account by the system administrator (sysadmin). You can belong to multiple groups at the same time. Unless the system administrator specifically assigns you to a different group, in Mac OS X, the default group is staff. This applies to single user systems too.

✔ Tips

- A file's ownership can only be changed by the root user (or superuser).
- The root user can use the **chown** and **chgrp** commands to change the ownership of a file or directory. You can learn more about these commands by viewing their man pages. In the Terminal window, type **man chown** or **man chgrp** and press Return to view the command's man pages.

Changing Permissions for a File or Directory

Unix includes a command for setting file or directory permissions: **chmod**. Although this command can be a bit complicated, it is important. The security of your files and subdirectories depend on its proper usage.

The **chmod** command uses the following syntax:

chmod ***mode file ...***

The complex part of the **chmod** command is understanding what can go in the **mode** operand. This is where you specify the owner (also called user), group, and other (everyone else) permissions. You have two ways to do this: numerically and symbolically.

✔ Tip

- You can learn more about the **chmod** command by viewing its man pages. In the Terminal window, type **man chmod** and press Return.

Numeric permission modes

Numeric permission modes uses numbers to represent permissions options.

The best way to explain this is to provide an example. Remember, the nine characters of the permissions coding in a directory listing can be broken down into three sets of three:

```
rwx    rwx    rwx
user   group  other
```

Each character can be represented with an octal digit (a number between 0 and 7) by assigning values to the **r**, **w**, and **x** characters, like this:

```
421    421    421
rwx    rwx    rwx
user   group  other
```

So, if you want to give read and write permission for a file called *file1* to the owner, that would be a 4 (read) plus a 2 (write), which adds up to a 6. You could then give read only permission to the group and others by assigning the value 4 (read). The command to do all this is **chmod 644 file1**. (The 644 permission is one you'll see often on text files that are readable by everyone. A permission of 600 would make a file private.)

USING CHMOD

Symbolic permission modes

Symbolic permission modes enables you to add or remove privileges using symbols. For example, to remove write permission from the group and others, type **chmod go-w file1**. This translates to "take away write permissions from the group and others."

The ownership symbols you use for this are:

u user (owner) of the file or directory

g group owner of the file or directory

o others (everyone)

a all three (user, group, and others)

The symbols for the permissions you can add or take away are:

r read

w write

x execute

Finally, the operations you can perform are:

+ add the permission

- remove the permission

= set (add) the following permissions

You can combine more than one symbol in a mode and more than one "equation" if you separate them with commas. For example, **chmod a+rwx,o-w file1** gives universal read, write, and execute access to all and then takes away write permission from others to file1. (The equivalent numerical permission would be 775.)

To change the permissions for a file or directory

In the Terminal window, **type chmod mode file ...** (for example, **chmod 644 file1**) and press Return.

✔ Tip

- If you include the **-R** option in the command (for example, **chmod -R 644 folder1**), the change is made recursively down through the directory tree. In other words, the change is made to the folder and every file and folder within it.

Learning What's Happening on Your System

A few Unix commands can provide you with answers to questions about your system: "Who is logged in?" "What are they doing?" "What jobs are taking up all my CPU cycles?" "How long has my system been up?"

- **uptime** tells you how long it has been since you last restarted and what your workload is.
- **who** tells you who is logged into your system, where they're logged in from, and when they logged in.
- **w** tells you who is online and what they are doing.
- **last** tells you who has logged onto your computer.
- **ps** and **top** tell you what jobs are running on your computer.

This section explains how to use each of these commands and shows simulated output so you know what you might expect to learn.

✔ Tip

- You can learn more about these commands by viewing their man pages. In the Terminal window, type **man chown**, **man who**, **man w**, **man last**, **man ps**, or **man top** and press Return to view the command's man pages.

Code 1 The results of the uptime command.

```
/usr/bin/login (ttyp1)

7:21PM up 7 days, 17:48, 5 users, load averages:
1.87, 1.80, 1.67
```

Code 2 The results of the who command.

```
/usr/bin/login (ttyp1)

ronh    console  Sep  2 01:35
ronh    ttyp1    Sep  9 19:13  (192.168.1.2)
root    ttyp3    Sep  9 19:13  (192.168.1.2)
ronh    ttyp4    Sep  9 19:16  (isaac.explorator)
```

Code 3 The results of the w command.

```
/usr/bin/login (ttyp1)

7:28PM up 7 days, 17:55, 5 users, load averages: 1.90,
1.80, 1.67
USER  TTY FROM              LOGIN@   IDLE   WHAT
ronh  co  -                 02Sep01  7days  -
ronh  p1  192.168.1.2       7:13PM   0      -
ronh  p2  -                 Thu01AM  13     -
root  p3  192.168.1.2       7:13PM   0      -
ronh  p4  isaac.explorator  7:16PM   0      -
```

To learn how long since you last restarted & your workload

In the Terminal window, type **uptime** and press Return.

The results might look something like what you see in **Code 1**. You see the current time, the time since my last restart, or boot (7 days, 17 hours, and 48 minutes), and load averages of how many active jobs were in the queue during the last 1, 5, and 15 minutes. The load shown here is high because my system is running the SETI@home screensaver. Normally these numbers will be less than 1.

To learn who is on your system

In the Terminal window, type **who** and press Return.

The results might look something like what you see in **Code 2**. In this example, I'm logged in remotely twice from the machine with the IP address 192.168.2.1, once as root and once as myself. I'm also logged in from a remote location (isaac.exploratorium.edu) and at the system console.

To learn who is online & what are they doing

In the Terminal window, type **w** and press Return.

The command's output looks something like **Code 3**. The w command first does an uptime command. Then it gives you information about each user, when they logged in, and how long it's been since they've done anything. (In Unix, you normally would also see what program the users are running, except this feature doesn't seem to work right now in Mac OS X.)

To learn who has logged in to your machine recently

- In the Terminal window, type **last** and press Return.

  The output should look similar to **Code 4**. The last command spews out a list of everyone who has logged in to your machine, when and from where they logged in, how long they stayed, and when you last shut down or restarted your machine.

or

- In the Terminal window, type **last *user*** (where *user* is the user name of a specific user) and press Return.

  If you specify a user, last will show only the logins for that user.

Code 4 The results of the last command.

```
/usr/bin/login (ttyp1)

ronh      ttyp4    isaac.explorator  Sun Sep 9   19:16          still logged in
root      ttyp3    192.168.1.2       Sun Sep 9   19:13          still logged in
ronh      ttyp1    192.168.1.2       Sun Sep 9   19:13          still logged in
ronh      ttyp1    192.168.1.2       Sat Sep 8   23:20 - 00:07  (00:46)
ronh      ttyp1    sodium.explorato  Sat Sep 8   16:05 - 16:13  (00:08)
ronh      ttyp1    192.168.1.2       Sat Sep 8   00:03 - 00:40  (00:36)
ronh      ttyp3    192.168.1.2       Thu Sep 6   22:19 - 00:01  (01:41)
ronh      ttyp1    192.168.1.2       Thu Sep 6   22:01 - 00:01  (02:00)
ronh      ttyp1    192.168.1.2       Thu Sep 6   10:13 - 10:37  (00:23)
ronh      ttyp2                      Thu Sep 6   01:17          still logged in
ronh      ttyp1    192.168.1.2       Thu Sep 6   00:56 - 02:06  (01:09)
ronh      ttyp1    192.168.1.2       Mon Sep 3   23:47 - 01:51  (02:04)
ronh      ttyp1    192.168.1.2       Mon Sep 3   14:12 - 23:19  (09:06)
ronh      console  localhost         Sun Sep 2   01:35          still logged in
reboot    ~                          Sun Sep 2   01:35
shutdown  ~                          Sun Sep 2   01:33
ronh      ttyp2    192.168.1.2       Sun Sep 2   00:53 - 01:23  (00:30)
```

To learn what jobs are running

- In the Terminal window, type **ps** and press Return.

  The **ps** command tells you what you are running at the instant you run the command.

or

- In the Terminal window, type **top** and press Return.

  The **top** command gives you a running commentary of the top ten jobs. If you expand the size of the Terminal window, top shows more than the top ten jobs. Press Q to quit **top**.

✔ Tip

- You may find Process Viewer (in the Utilities folder) a more useful utility to see the processes that are running. Process Viewer is covered in **Chapter 10**.

Archive & Compression Utilities

Long before utilities such as StuffIt existed—long before the Mac existed, in fact!—Unix users could group files together into *archives* and compress the archives to take up less disk space, which was vastly more expensive then. Unix offers several archiving and compression tools:

- **tar** (short for **t**ape **ar**chive) was originally used to combine a collection of files into a single file, which was written to tape. But you don't have to write the file to tape; you can write it to any device your Unix system knows about: disks, tapes, CD-RWs, even the Terminal.
- **compress** and **uncompress** do what you probably expect them to: compress and expand files. Text files are very compressible, sometimes 10 to 1. Files that have already been compressed such as JPEG and MPEG files and QuickTime movies, however, can actually become larger.
- **gzip** is a newer set of utilities that are like **compress** and **uncompress** on steroids. **gzip** includes more options and offers better compression ratios.

✔ Tips

- You can learn more about these commands by viewing their man pages. In the Terminal window, type **man tar**, **man compress**, **man uncompress**, or **man gzip** and press Return to view the command's man pages.
- Experienced Unix users often use **tar** and **gzip** together to produce a compressed archive with a name like *file.tar.gz* or *file.tgz*. A useful way to **uncompress** and **untar** a file uses pipes. For example, **gzcat file.tar.gz | tar xf -** uncompresses the gzipped file and pipes the output to the **tar** command for extraction. The **-** in the **tar** command is necessary to tell **tar** to expect its input from the pipe (its standard input device).
- These tools are useful to know something about because you will encounter them if you download software from Internet archives. If you don't need the GUI interface of StuffIt, the tar/gzip utilities will do the same job for free!

Table 1

tar Options

Option	Description
-c	Creates a new archive
-x	Extracts files from the named archive
-t	Displays a list of files and directories in the named archive
-v	Verbose mode: Tells me everything you are doing
-p	Preserves permissions, owners, and modification dates if possible
-f	Archives files to the following filename or extracts files from the following archive name
-C	Puts extracted files in the specified location

To create an archive from an entire directory tree

Type **tar [-cxtvpf] [-C *directory*] *archive file* ...** and press Return. (Consult **Table 1** for **tar** options.)

Here are some examples using the **tar** command:

- **tar -cf archive.tar file1 directory1 file2** creates and then writes to the archive named *archive.tar*: *file1*, *directory1* and all its contents, and *file2* in that order.
- **tar -tvf old-archive.tar** displays everything in the archive called *old-archive.tar*, but does not extract anything. The **t** option just prints the contents of a tar archive.
- **tar -xpvf old-archive.tar** extracts the files and directories in the archive file called *old-archive.tar* and puts the resulting files in the current directory. The **v** option reports progress and the **p** option preserves the ownerships and modification dates of the original files. (The tar file is unaffected and remains on the disk.)
- **tar -xpvf old-archive.tar -C /usr/local/src** extracts the files and directories in the archive file called *old-archive.tar* and puts the resulting files in the directory */usr/local/src*.

✔ Tip

- It's a standard procedure to end archive names with a .tar suffix, and you should honor this standard to keep evil spirits out of your computer.

To compress & decompress with compress & uncompress

Type **compress *file* ...** (for example, **compress file.txt**), and press Return.

or

Type **uncompress *file* ...** (for example, **uncompress file.z**), and press Return.

✔ Tips

- Your original file is removed if either of the commands successfully complete the compression or decompression.
- By convention, compressed files should have a .Z extension. The compress command will automatically append this extension to the filename.

To compress or decompress with gzip & ungzip

Type **gzip *file* ...** and press Return. This compresses the files, adds the .gz suffix to their names, and removes the original files.

or

Type **ungzip *file* ...** and press Return. This uncompresses the files and removes the original archive.

✔ Tips

- The **gzip** command has several options. The **r** option, for recursive, goes into specified subdirectories and compresses or uncompresses the files. The **v** option, for verbose, tells the command to report its progress.
- **zcat file** lists the contents of a compressed file to the Terminal (or pipes the content to another command) without altering the original archive.

Networking

5

Networking

Networking uses direct connections and network protocols to connect your computer to others on a network. Once connected, you can share files, access e-mail, and run special network applications on server computers.

This chapter looks at *peer-to-peer networking*, which uses the built-in features of Mac OS X to connect to other computers for file and application sharing. It also covers some of the advanced network configuration tools available as Mac OS X utilities.

✔ Tips

- If you use your computer at work, you may be connected to a companywide network; if so, you'll find the networking part of this chapter very helpful. But if you use your computer at home and have only one computer, you won't have much need for the networking information here.
- A discussion of Mac OS X Server, which is designed to meet the demands of large workgroups and corporate intranets, is beyond the scope of this book.
- This chapter does not discuss using networks to connect to the Internet. Connecting to the Internet is discussed in detail in *Mac OS X: Visual QuickStart Guide*.

AppleTalk & Ethernet

AppleTalk is the networking protocol used by Macintosh computers to communicate over a network. It's the software that makes networking work. Fortunately, it's not something extra you have to buy—it's part of Mac OS X (and most previous versions of Mac OS).

Ethernet is a network connection method that is built into all Mac OS X-compatible computers. It uses Ethernet cables that connect to the Ethernet ports or network interface cards of computers and network printers. Additional hardware such as *transceivers* and *hubs* may be needed, depending on the network setup and device.

Ethernet comes in three speeds: 10, 100, and 1000 megabits per second. The maximum speed of the computer's communication with the rest of the network is limited by the maximum speed of the cable, hub, and other network devices.

✔ Tips

- Network hardware configuration details are far beyond the scope of this book. The information here is provided primarily to introduce some of the network terms you might encounter when working with your computer and other documentation.
- If your computer is on a large network, consult the system administrator before changing any network configuration options.
- *TCP/IP* is a networking protocol that is used for connecting to the Internet. Mac OS X computers can use both AppleTalk to communicate with local networks and TCP/IP to communicate with the Internet.
- *LocalTalk* is an older Mac OS-compatible network method. Slow and supported only by older Macintosh models with serial ports, it is rarely used in today's networks and is not covered in this book.

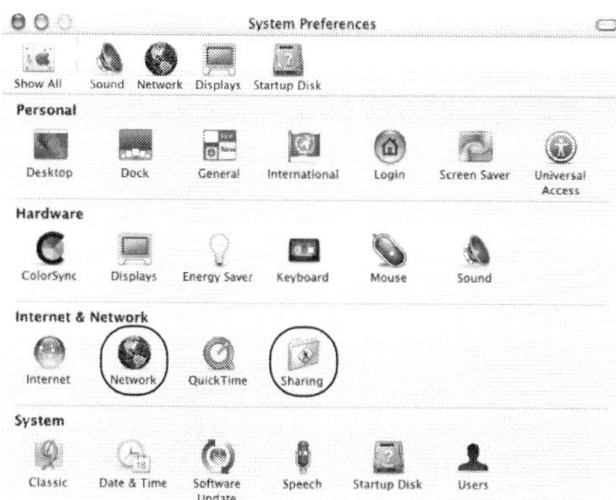

Figure 1 You set configure sharing with two System Preferences panes: Network and Sharing.

Sharing Files & Applications

To use AppleTalk to share files and applications with other network users, you must set options in two System Preferences panes (**Figure 1**):

- **Network** allows you to enable AppleTalk and choose your AppleTalk zone and configuration.
- **Sharing** allows you to name your computer, enable types of sharing and access, and control how other users can run applications on your computer.

This part of the chapter explains how to set up sharing via an AppleTalk Ethernet connection. It also explains how to share files and applications once the configuration is complete.

✔ Tip

- Although file and application sharing is possible with other protocols and types of connections, it is impossible for me to cover all configuration options here. If you're using a different type of network and don't have instructions for using it with Mac OS X, read through the instructions here. Much of what you read may apply to your setup.

To set AppleTalk Network preferences

1. Choose Apple > System Preferences (**Figure 2**), or click the System Preferences icon in the Dock (**Figure 3**).
2. In the System Preferences window that appears (**Figure 1**), click the Network icon in the toolbar or in the Internet & Network row.
3. In the Network preferences pane that appears, choose an Ethernet option (such as Built-in Ethernet) from the Show menu (**Figure 4**).
4. If necessary, click the AppleTalk tab to display its options (**Figure 5**).
5. Turn on the Make AppleTalk Active check box.
6. If necessary, choose a zone from the AppleTalk Zone pop-up menu.
7. Choose an option from the Configuration pop-up menu:
   - ▲ **Automatically** automatically configures your computer with the correct network identification information.
   - ▲ **Manually** displays Node ID and Network ID edit boxes for you to enter network identification information (**Figure 6**).
8. Click Apply Now.

✔ Tips

- AppleTalk zones are normally only present in large networks.
- In step 7, if you choose Manually, you must enter the correct information for AppleTalk to work.

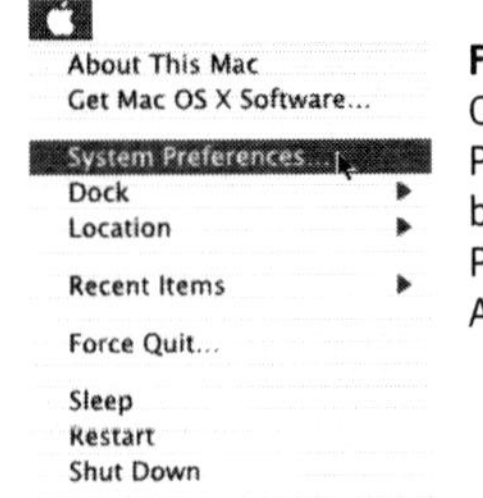

Figure 2 Open the System Preferences window by choosing System Preferences from the Apple menu...

Figure 3 ...or by clicking the System Preferences icon in the Dock.

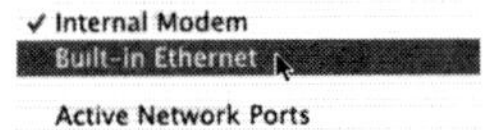

Figure 4 Choose an Ethernet option from the Show pop-up menu.

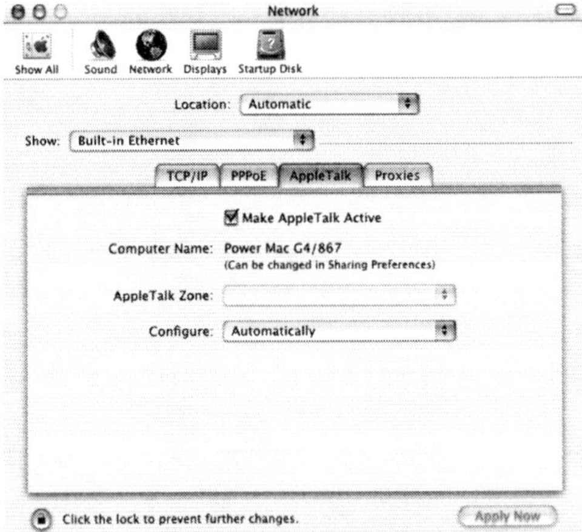

Figure 5 The AppleTalk tab of the Network preferences pane.

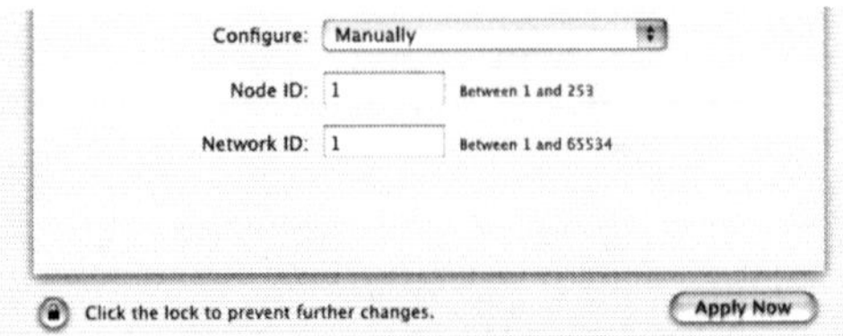

Figure 6 If you choose Manually, you have to enter correct network identification information.

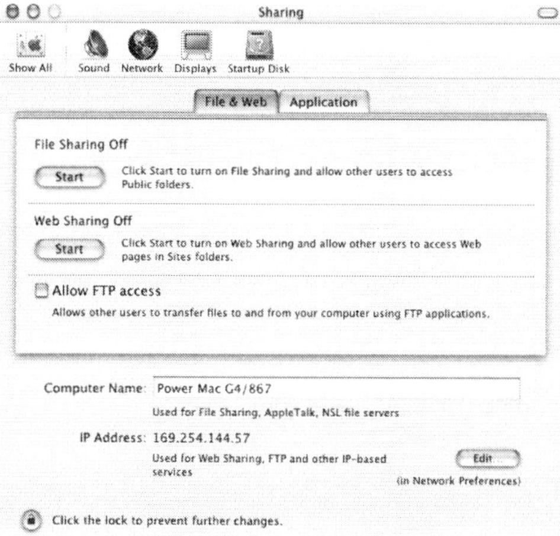

Figure 7 The Files & Web tab of the Sharing preferences pane.

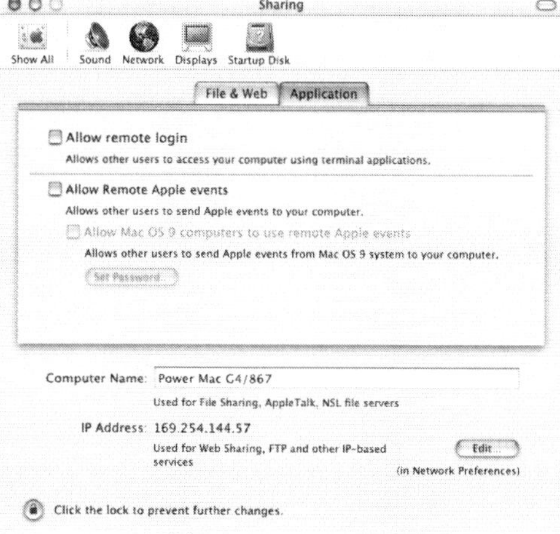

Figure 8 The Application tab of the Sharing preferences pane.

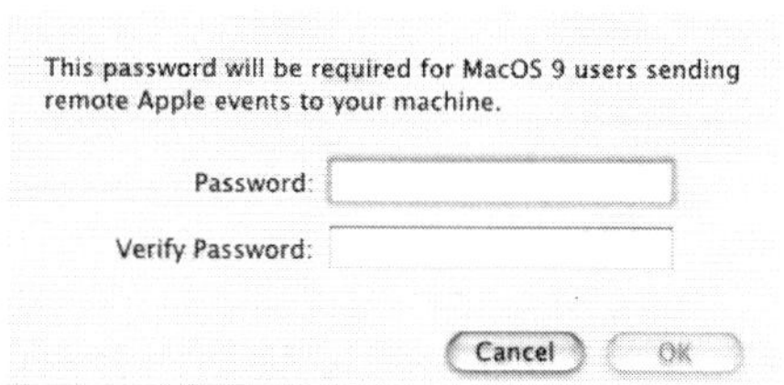

Figure 9 Use this dialog sheet to set up a password that Mac OS 9 users must enter to send Apple events to your computer.

To set Sharing preferences

1. Choose Apple > System Preferences (**Figure 2**), or click the System Preferences icon in the Dock (**Figure 3**).
2. In the System Preferences window that appears (**Figure 1**), click the Sharing icon in the Internet & Network row to display the Sharing preferences pane.
3. If necessary, click the File & Web tab to display its options (**Figure 7**).
4. To allow other users to access Public folders on your computer, click the Start button in the File Sharing area.
5. To allow other users to access Web pages in Sites folders on your computer, click the Start button in the Web Sharing area.
6. To allow other users to transfer files to and from your computer using file transfer protocol (FTP), turn on the Allow FTP Access check box.
7. Click the Application tab to display its options (**Figure 8**).
8. To allow other users to access your computer with terminal applications, turn on the Allow remote login check box.
9. To allow other users to send Apple events to your computer, turn on the Allow Remote Apple events check box. With this option enabled, you can also turn on the Allow Mac OS 9 computers to use remote Apple events check box. Doing so displays a password dialog sheet like the one in **Figure 9**; enter the same password twice and click OK to enable this option.
10. To set the name that identifies your computer on a network, enter a name in the Computer Name edit box.

Continued on next page...

Continued from previous page.

✔ Tips

- When you click the Start button in the File Sharing and Web Sharing areas, a message appears in that area, first telling you that sharing is starting up (**Figure 10**) and then telling you that sharing is on (**Figure 11**).
- To disable file or Web sharing, click the Stop button in the File Sharing (**Figure 11**) or Web Sharing area.
- Web Sharing and FTP utilizes TCP/IP. You can set a computer's TCP/IP address in the TCP/IP tab of the Network preferences pane. TCP/IP settings are covered in *Mac OS X: Visual QuickStart Guide.*
- With Web Sharing enabled, the contents of all Sites folders within user home folders are published as Personal Web Sharing Web sites. To access a user's Web site, use the following URL: http://*IPaddress*/~*username*/ where *IPaddress* is the IP address or domain name of the computer and *username* is the name of the user on that computer.
- When a user accesses your computer with a terminal application, he accesses the UNIX shell underlying Mac OS X.
- Set the options in the Application tab of the Sharing preferences pane with care! Allowing other users to access to your computer with terminal applications or Apple events could pose security risks.

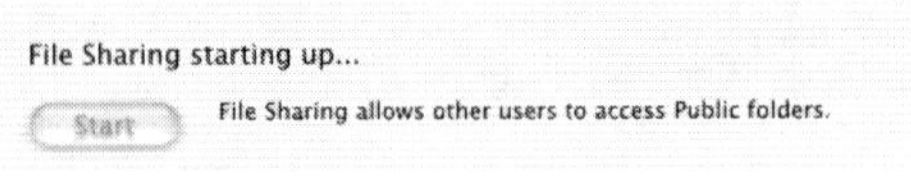

Figure 10 The sharing status appears in the File & Web tab as it starts up...

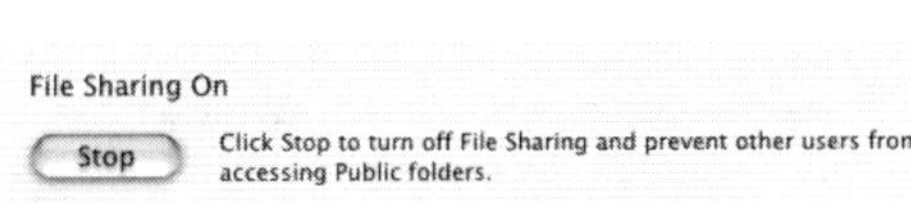

Figure 11 ...and is fully enabled.

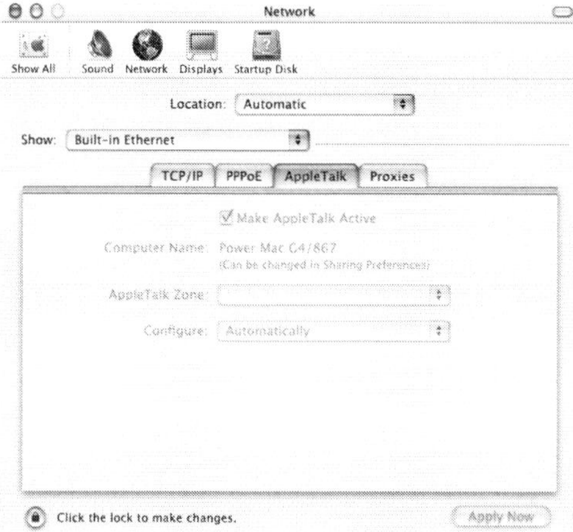

Figure 12 When a preference pane is locked, its contents turn gray.

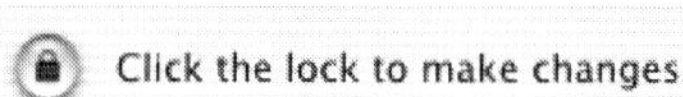

Figure 13 The lock looks closed when you can't make changes.

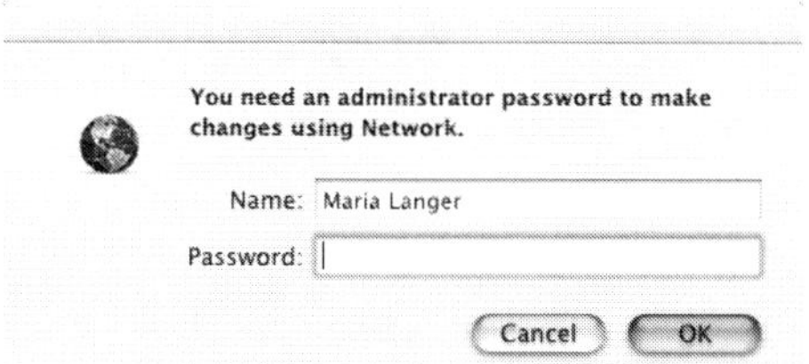

Figure 14 You must enter an administrator name and password to unlock the preferences pane.

To lock Network or Sharing preferences

At the bottom of the Network (**Figure 5**) or Sharing (**Figures 7** and **8**) preferences pane, click the lock button. The window's contents turn gray (**Figure 12**), indicating that they cannot be changed, and the lock button's icon looks closed or locked (**Figure 13**).

To unlock Network or Sharing preferences

1. Click the locked lock button at the bottom of the Network or Sharing preferences pane (**Figure 13**).
2. A dialog like the one in **Figure 14** appears. Enter the name and password for an administrative user and click OK.

   The locked icon changes so it looks open (unlocked) and the options in the preferences pane can be changed.

✔ Tip

- If you're in charge of administering a computer used by other people, it's a good idea to lock the network settings after you set them. This can prevent unauthorized or accidental changes by other users.

To connect to another computer for file sharing

1. In the Finder, choose Go > Connect to Server (**Figure 15**), or press [⌘][K].
2. In the Connect to Server dialog that appears, select the network on which the other computer resides. A list of available computers appears on the right side of the dialog (**Figure 16**).
3. Select the server you want to connect to. Its Address appears in the Address edit box (**Figure 17**).
4. Click Connect.
5. A login dialog like the one in **Figure 18** appears.
   - ▲ If you are registered as a user on the other computer, select the Registered User radio button (**Figure 18**) and enter your user name and password.
   - ▲ If you are not registered as a user on the other computer and it allows Guest access, select the Guest radio button.
6. Click Connect.
7. If necessary, wait while the computer authenticates your user name and password.
8. A dialog like the one in **Figure 19** appears next. Select the volumes you want to mount.
9. Click OK.
10. An icon for the mounted volume appears on your desktop (**Figure 20**). Open the icon to access its contents.

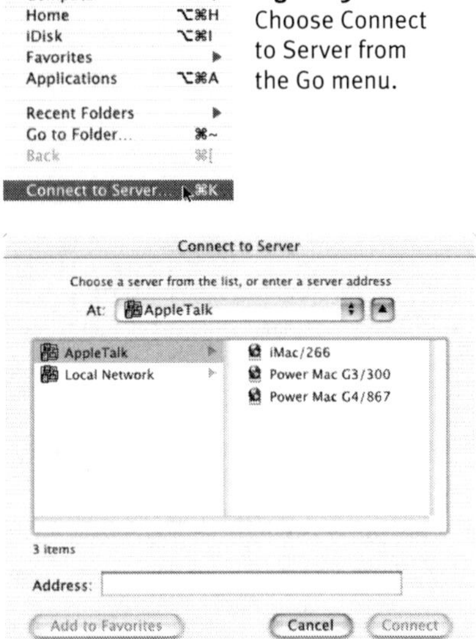

Figure 15 Choose Connect to Server from the Go menu.

Figure 16 Select the network to display a list of computers.

Figure 17 When you select the name of a computer, its address appears in the Address edit box.

Figure 18 Use this dialog to enter login information.

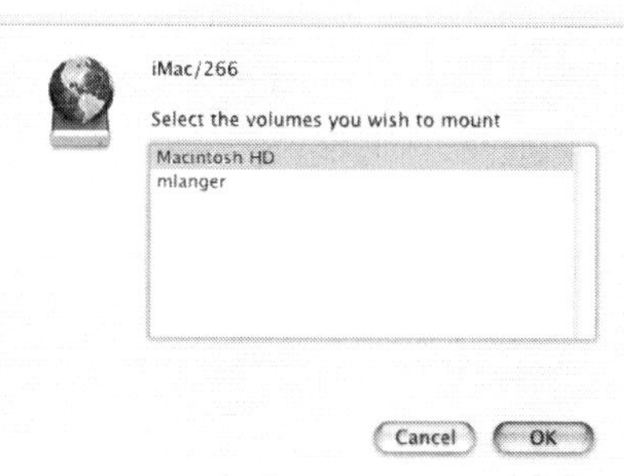

Figure 19 Use this dialog to select the volume or folder you want to access.

Figure 20 An icon for the mounted volume appears on your desktop.

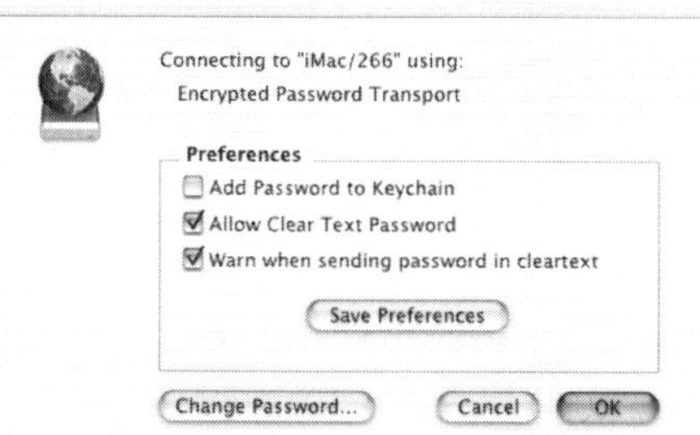

Figure 21 Clicking the Options button in the login window (**Figure 18**) displays login options.

Figure 22 Use this dialog to change your password on the networked computer.

✔ Tips

- If you know the address of the computer you want to connect to, you can enter it in the Address edit box of the Connect to Server dialog (**Figure 16** or **17**) and skip steps 2 and 3.
- After step 3, you can click the Add to Favorites button to add the selected computer to your Favorites folder.
- In step 5, if you are a registered user, you can click the Options button (**Figure 18**) to display login options (**Figure 21**):
  - ▲ **Add Password to Keychain** adds your login information to your keychain. I tell you about the keychain feature in **Chapter 6**.
  - ▲ **Allow Clear Text Password** allows your password to be displayed as you enter it, rather than shown as bullets, if it is configured to show that way.
  - ▲ **Warn when sending password in clear text** warns you before displaying your password as you enter it.
  - ▲ Change Password displays a dialog like the one in **Figure 22**, which you can use to change your password on the other computer.
- In step 8, you can hold down [⌘] and click volume names to select more than one volume.
- The list of volumes that appears in step 8 depends on the disks mounted on the computer you are accessing and your access privileges. In **Figure 19**, the dialog lists the computer's hard disk and the user's Home folder.
- The access privileges you have for network volumes varies depending on the privileges set for that volume or folder. I tell you more about privileges starting on the next page.

Users, Groups, & Privileges

Network file and application sharing access is based on how you fit into the users and groups setup for that computer, as well as the privileges set for the file or its enclosing folder. Let's take a closer look at how all this works.

Users & Groups

Each person who connects to a computer (other than with Guest access) is considered a *user*. Each user has his own user name or ID and a password. User names are set up by the computer's system administrator, using the Users preferences pane. The password is also assigned by the system administrator, but in most cases, it can be changed by the user himself to enhance security.

Each user can belong to one or more group. A *group* is one or more users who have the same privileges. Some groups are set up automatically by Mac OS X when you install it and add users with the Users preferences pane. Other groups can be set up by the system administrator using a program such as NetInfo Manager.

✔ Tips

- Setting up users is discussed in detail in **Chapter 6**. Setting up groups is an advanced network administration task that is beyond the scope of this book.
- I discuss NetInfo Manager briefly near the end of this chapter.

Privileges

Each file or folder can be assigned a set of privileges. Privileges determine who has access to a file and how it can be accessed.

There are four possible privileges settings:

- **Read & Write** privileges allow the user to open and save files.
- **Read only** privileges allow the user to open files, but not save files.
- **Write only (Drop Box)** privileges allow the user to save files but not open them.
- **None** means the user can neither open nor save files.

Privileges can be set for three categories of users:

- **Owner** is the user or group who can access and set access privileges for the item. In Mac OS X, the owner can be you (if it's your computer and you set it up), system, or admin.
- **Group** is the group that has access to the item.
- **Everyone** is everyone else on the network, including users logged in as Guest.

✔ Tips

- In previous versions of Mac OS, which were not designed as multiuser systems, you were the owner of most (if not all) items on your computer.
- You can check or set an item's privileges in the Privileges Info window for the item (**Figures 24**, **25**, and **26**).

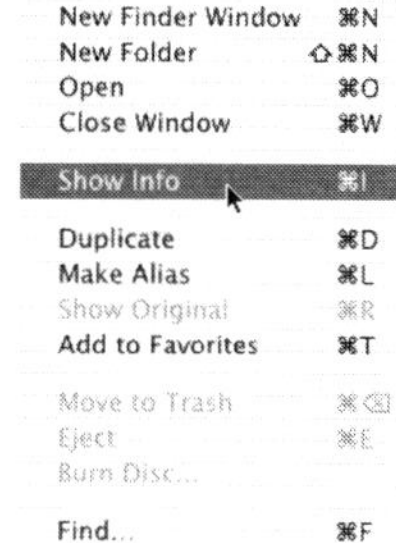

Figure 23 Choose Show Info from the File menu.

Figure 24 Privileges settings for the Applications folder, ...

Figure 25 ...my Public folder, ...

Figure 26 ...and the Drop Box folder inside my Public folder.

To set an item's privileges

1. Select the icon for the item for which you want to change privileges.
2. Choose File > Show Info (**Figure 23**), or press [⌘][I].
3. In the Info window that appears, choose Privileges from the pop-up menu to display privileges information (**Figures 24**, **25**, and **26**).
4. Use the pop-up menus (**Figure 27**) to change the privileges for each category of user.
5. If the item is a folder, to apply the settings to all folders within it, click the Apply button.
6. Close the Info window to save your changes.

✔ Tips

- You cannot change privileges for an item if you are not the owner (**Figure 24**).
- The Write only (Drop Box) privilege is not available for files—just for folders and disks.
- The privileges you assign to one category of users will affect what privileges can be assigned to another category of user. For example, if you make a folder Read only for Everyone, you can only make the same folder Read & Write or Read only for the Group and Owner.

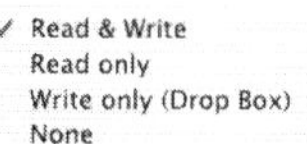

Figure 27 Use this pop-up menu to set privileges for each category of user.

AirPort

AirPort is Apple's wireless local area network technology. It enables your computer to connect to a network or the Internet via radio waves instead of wires.

Most AirPort configurations consist of two components:

- **AirPort Base Station** is an external device that can connect to a network via Ethernet cable or can act as a modem for connecting to the Internet via phone lines.
- **AirPort card** is a networking card inside your computer that enables your computer to communicate with a base station or another AirPort-equipped computer.

There are two ways to use AirPort for wireless networking:

- Use an AirPort-equipped computer to connect to other AirPort-equipped computers.
- Use a base station to link an AirPort-equipped computer to the Internet or to other computers on a network. This makes it possible for a computer with an AirPort card to communicate with computers without AirPort cards.

Mac OS X includes two programs for setting up an AirPort network (**Figure 28**):

- **AirPort Setup Assistant** offers an easy, step-by-step approach for configuring a base station. In most cases, this is the only tool you'll need to set up a base station.
- **AirPort Admin Utility** enables you to set advanced options that cannot be set with the AirPort Setup Assistant.

This part of the chapter explains how to configure an AirPort base station and connect to an AirPort network with an AirPort-equipped computer.

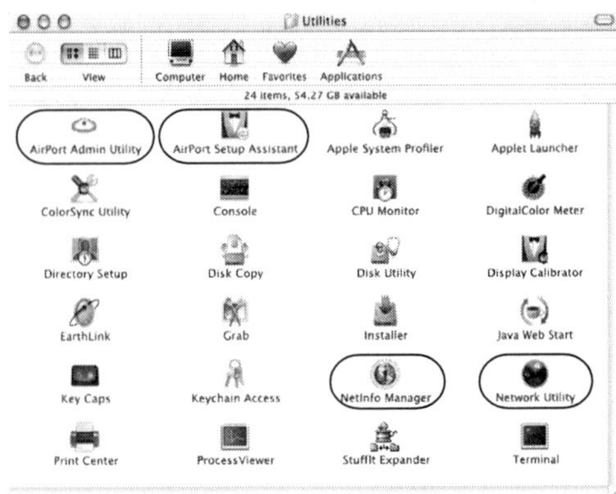

Figure 28 The Utilities folder includes a number of utility applications for working with networks.

✔ Tips

- AirPort is especially useful for PowerBook and iBook users who may work at various locations within range of a base station.
- An AirPort network can include multiple base stations and AirPort-equipped computers.
- You can learn more about AirPort networking at Apple's AirPort home page, www.apple.com/airport/.

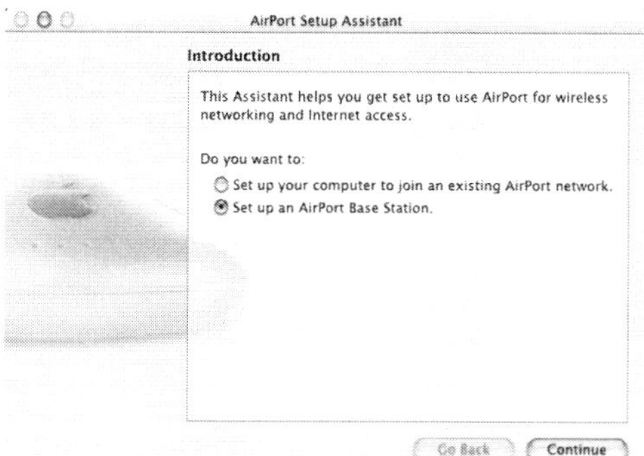

Figure 29 In the Introduction window, tell the Assistant what you want to do.

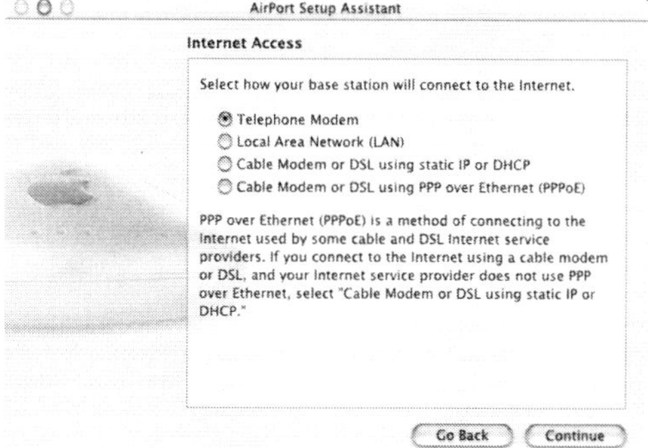

Figure 30 Indicate how you connect to the Internet.

To set up an AirPort base station

1. Open the AirPort Setup Assistant icon in the Utilities folder (**Figure 28**) inside the Applications folder.
2. The AirPort Setup Assistant uses the computer's AirPort card to scan for base stations. It then displays the Introduction window (**Figure 29**). Select the Set up an AirPort Base Station radio button and click Continue.
3. The Internet Access window appears next (**Figure 30**). Select the radio button for the type of Internet access you will have and click Continue.
4. The window that appears next depends on what you selected in Step 3:
   - ▲ If you selected Telephone Modem, the Modem Access window appears (**Figure 31**). Enter information needed to access the Internet via modem.
   - ▲ If you selected Local Area Network (LAN) or Cable Modem or DSL using static IP or DHCP, the Ethernet Access window appears (**Figure 32**). Enter information needed to access the Internet via LAN or cable modem.

Continued on next page...

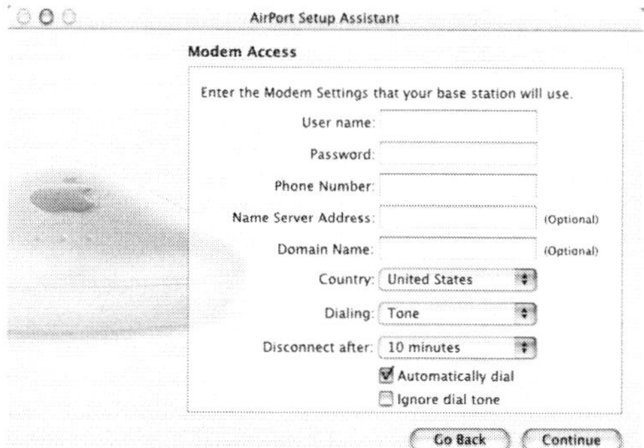

Figure 31 If the AirPort base station's modem will provide Internet access, enter the information it will need to dial in to and connect to the Internet.

Figure 32 If you'll be connecting to the Internet via LAN and Ethernet, enter network information.

Continued from previous page.

- ▲ If you selected Cable Modem or DSL using PPP over Ethernet (PPPoE), the PPPoE Access window appears (**Figure 33**). Enter the information needed to access the Internet via PPPoE.

  When you are finished setting options, click Continue.

5. The Network Name and Password window appears next (**Figure 34**). Enter a name for the network in the Network Name box and then enter the same password in each of the Password boxes.
6. The Base Station Password window appears next (**Figure 35**). Select one of the options and click Continue:
   - ▲ **Use the same password** uses the same password for the base station as you entered for the AirPort network.
   - ▲ **Assign a separate password** enables you to enter a different password for the Base Station than the AirPort network. When you click Continue, a different Base Station Password window appears (**Figure 36**). Enter the same password in each edit box and click Continue.
7. The Conclusion window appears next. Click Continue.
8. Wait while the settings are copied to the base station and the station is reset.
9. The Conclusion window summarizes what was done (**Figure 37**). Click Done.

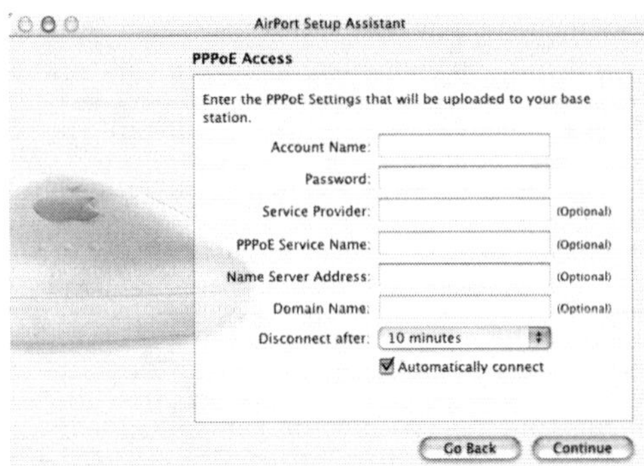

Figure 33 If you'll be connecting to the Internet via PPPoE, enter login information.

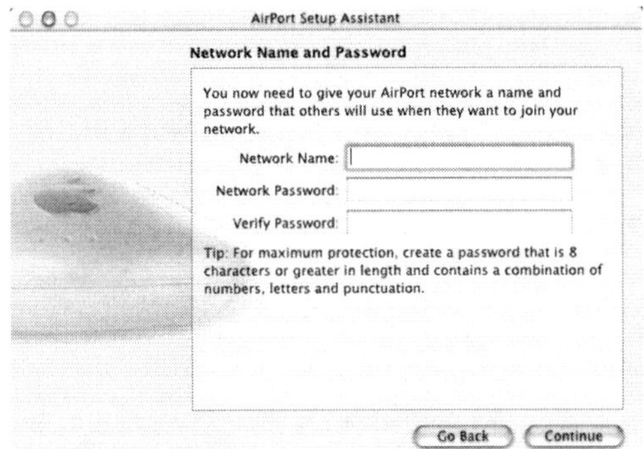

Figure 34 Enter a name and password for the AirPort network.

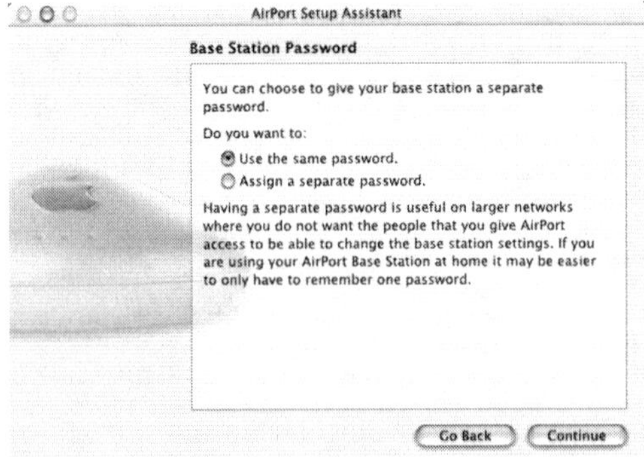

Figure 35 Indicate whether the base station should have a different password than the AirPort network.

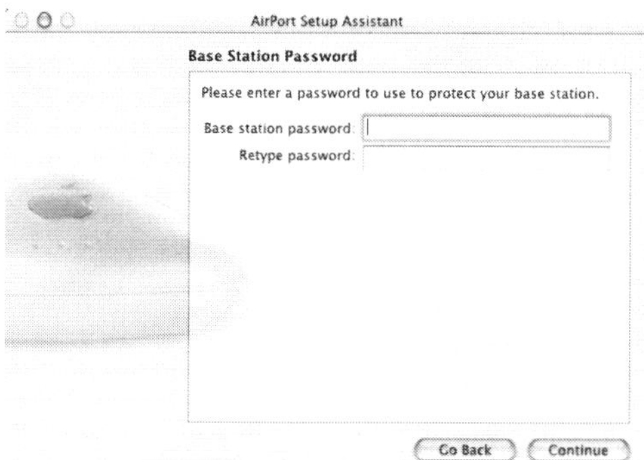

Figure 36 If you want the base station to have a different password, enter it twice here.

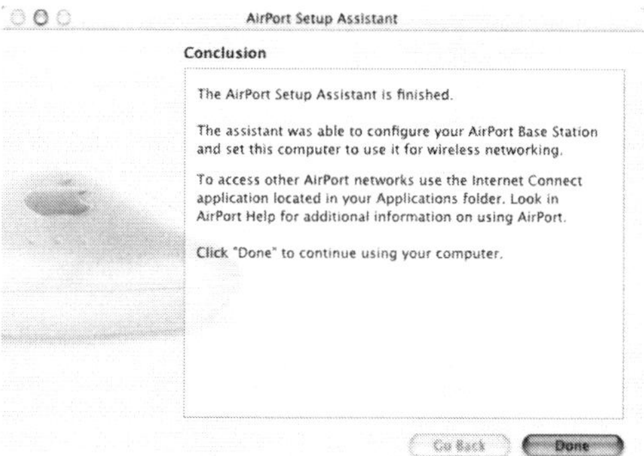

Figure 37 The Conclusion window tells you what has been done.

✔ Tips

- You can only use the AirPort Setup Assistant on a computer with an AirPort card installed. If a card is not installed, the Assistant will tell you (**Figure 38**).
- If your base station has already been configured, after step 2, the Enter Network Password window appears (**Figure 39**). Enter the correct network password and click Continue. A similar window for the Base Station Password appears next. Enter the correct base station password and click Continue. Then continue with step 3.
- In step 4, you can get the access information you need from your ISP or network administrator.
- If you are the only user of your AirPort network, it's okay to have the same password for the network as the base station. But if multiple users will be using the network, you should assign a different password to the base station to prevent other users from changing base station settings.

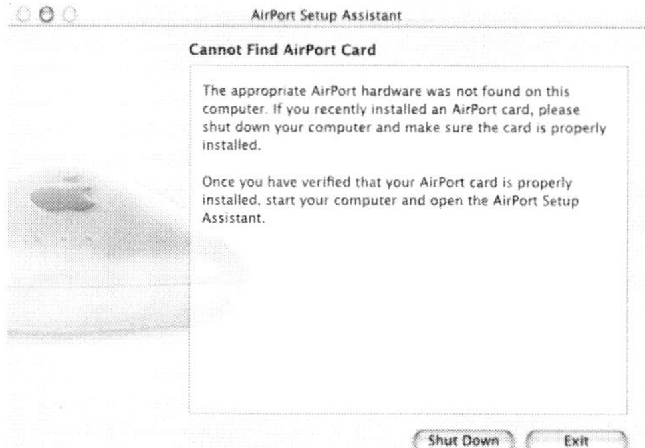

Figure 38 You must use the AirPort Setup Assistant on a computer that has an AirPort card installed.

Figure 39 If the base station has already been set up, you'll have to enter network and base station passwords to access it.

To set up an AirPort-equipped computer to access an AirPort network

1. Open the AirPort Setup Assistant icon in the Utilities folder (**Figure 28**) inside the Applications folder.
2. The AirPort Setup Assistant uses the computer's AirPort card to scan for base stations. It then displays the Introduction window (**Figure 29**). Select the Set up your computer to join an existing AirPort network radio button and click Continue.
3. The Enter Network Password window appears next (**Figure 39**). Enter the password for the AirPort network and click Continue.
4. In the Conclusion window that appears, click Continue.
5. The Assistant sets your computer to access the network and reports its results in the Conclusion window (**Figure 40**). Click Done.

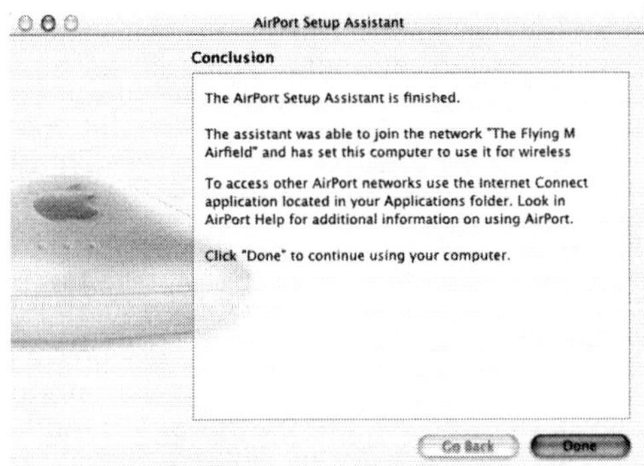

Figure 40 At the end of the setup process, the Assistant tells you what it has done.

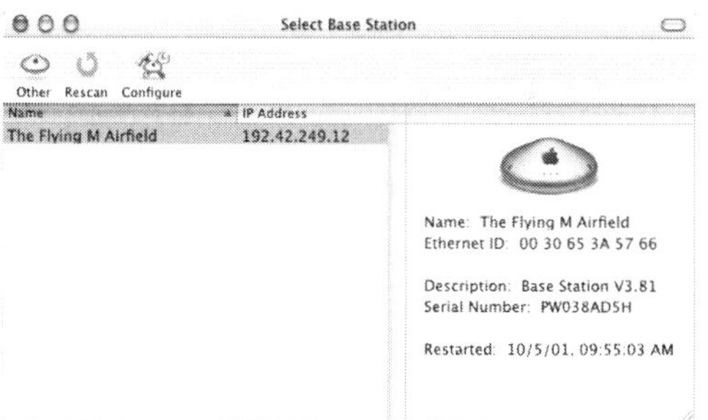

Figure 41 This window lists all of the base stations connected to the Ethernet network.

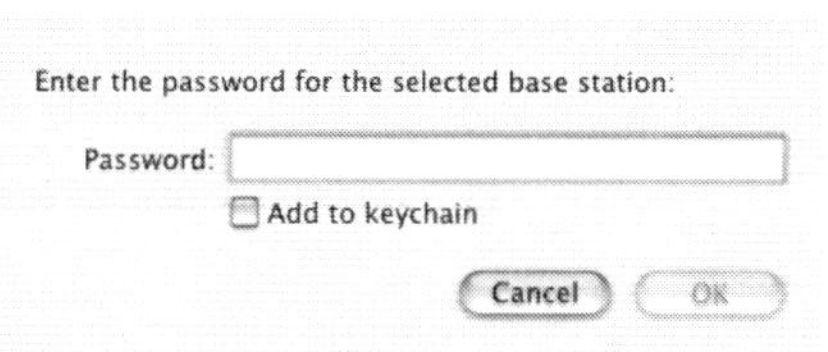

Figure 42 Enter the base station password.

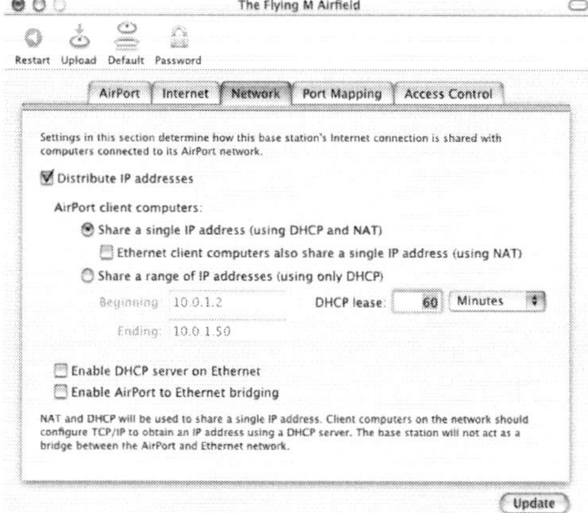

Figure 43 The Network tab of the AirPort Admin Utility's configuration window.

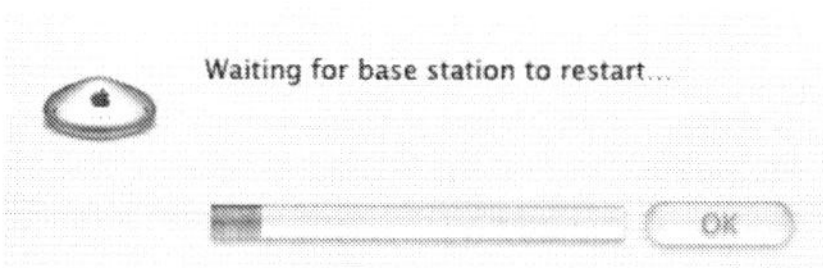

Figure 44 Wait while the base station is restarted.

To set up an AirPort base station as a bridge between AirPort & Ethernet networks

1. Open the AirPort Admin Utility icon in the Utilities folder (**Figure 28**) inside the Applications folder.
2. The AirPort Admin Utility scans the network for base stations and displays a list in the Select Base Station window (**Figure 41**).
3. Select the name of the base station you want to configure as a bridge.
4. Click Configure.
5. In the dialog sheet that appears (**Figure 42**), enter the password for the base station and click OK.
6. A configuration window with the base station name appears. Click the Network tab to display its options (**Figure 43**).
7. Turn off the Distribute IP Addresses check box. All options in the tab turn gray and the Enable AirPort to Ethernet bridging check box is turned on.
8. Click Update.
9. Wait while the base station restarts (**Figure 44**). When it is finished, click OK.

✔ Tips

- You can only use the AirPort Admin Utility on a computer that is connected to the AirPort base station via network. If the base station is not available on the network, the Select Base Station window will be empty.
- If a warning dialog sheet appears after step 8, click OK to dismiss it.
- When you use the base station as a bridge, it no longer provides Internet sharing services. However, Internet services available via the Ethernet network will become available to the AirPort network users.

To connect to an Ethernet network from an AirPort-equipped computer

1. Choose Apple > System Preferences (**Figure 2**), or click the System Preferences icon in the Dock (**Figure 3**).
2. In the System Preferences window that appears (**Figure 1**), click the Network icon in the toolbar or in the Internet & Network row.
3. In the Network preferences pane that appears, choose AirPort from the Show pop-up menu (**Figure 45**).
4. If necessary, click the AppleTalk tab to display its options (**Figure 5**).
5. Turn on the Make AppleTalk Active check box.
6. Click the AirPort tab to display its options (**Figure 46**).
7. Choose an AirPort network from the pop-up menu (there may only be one choice).
8. Enter a password for the AirPort.
9. If necessary, click Apply Now.
10. Choose System Prefs > Quit System Prefs, or press [Apple ⌘][Q].

✔ Tips

- For this to work, your AirPort base station must be configured as a bridge as instructed on the previous page.
- If you turn on the Show AirPort status in menu bar option in the AirPort tab of the Network preferences pane (**Figure 46**), a menu that displays the AirPort signal strength and offers options appears in the menu bar (**Figure 47**).
- To access other computers on the network, follow the instructions in the section titled "To connect to another computer for file sharing" earlier in this chapter.

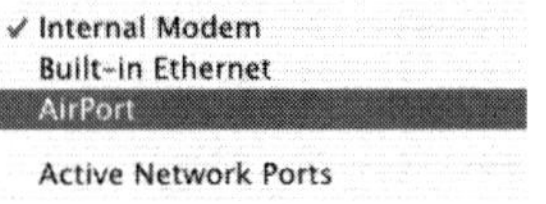

Figure 45 Choose AirPort from the Show pop-up menu.

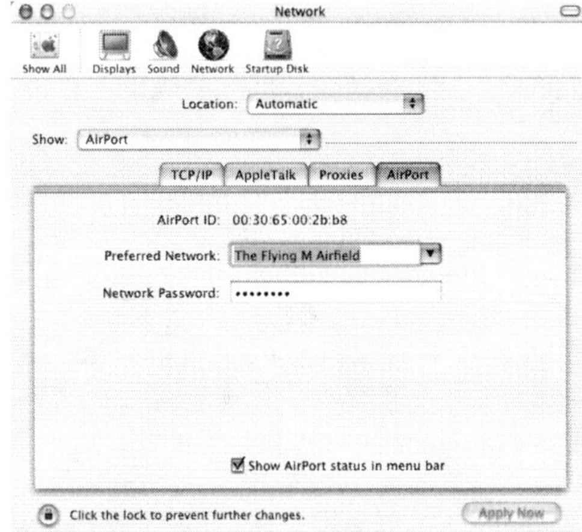

Figure 46 The AirPort tab of the Network preferences pane.

Figure 47 The AirPort menu in the menu bar shows signal strength (in the menu bar icon) and offers options for working with AirPort networks.

Figure 48 NetInfo Manager's main window.

Advanced Network Administration Tools

The Utilities folder inside the Applications folder includes two powerful utilities you can use to modify and monitor a network (**Figure 28**): NetInfo Manager and Network Utility. Although a complete discussion of these utilities is beyond the scope of this book, here's an overview so you know what they do.

NetInfo Manager

NetInfo Manager (**Figure 48**) enables you to explore and, if you have administrative access, modify the network setup of your computer. With it, you can create and modify network users, groups, and domains and manage other network resources.

NetInfo Manager works by opening the NetInfo data hidden away within Mac OS X's configuration files. Although these files can also be explored and modified with command-line interface tools, NetInfo Manager's interface is a bit easier to use.

NetInfo Manager is a network administrator tool that should not be used by the average user.

✖ Caution!

- Making changes with NetInfo Manager when you don' t know what you're doing is a good way to damage NetInfo data files. If you do enough damage, you could make it impossible to use your computer.

✔ Tip

- If you want to learn more about NetInfo data and NetInfo Manager, look for the document titled "Understanding and Using NetInfo," which is available on Apple's Mac OS X Server Web site, www.apple.com/macosxserver/.

Network Utility

Network Utility is an information-gathering tool to help you learn more about and troubleshoot a network. Its features are made available in eight tabs:

- **Info** (**Figure 49**) provides general information about the network interfaces.
- **Netstat** (**Figure 50**) enables you to review network performance statistics.
- **Ping** (**Figure 51**) enables you to test your computer's access to specific domains or IP addresses.
- **Lookup** (**Figure 52**) uses a domain name server to convert between IP addresses and domain names.
- **Traceroute** (**Figure 53**) traces the route from your computer to another IP address or domain.
- **Whois** (**Figure 54**) uses a whois server to get information about the owner and IP address of a specific domain name.
- **Finger** (**Figure 55**) gets information about a person based on his e-mail address.
- **Port Scan** (**Figure 56**) scans a specific IP address for active ports.

✔ Tip

- Many of these utilities are designed to work with the Internet and require Internet access.

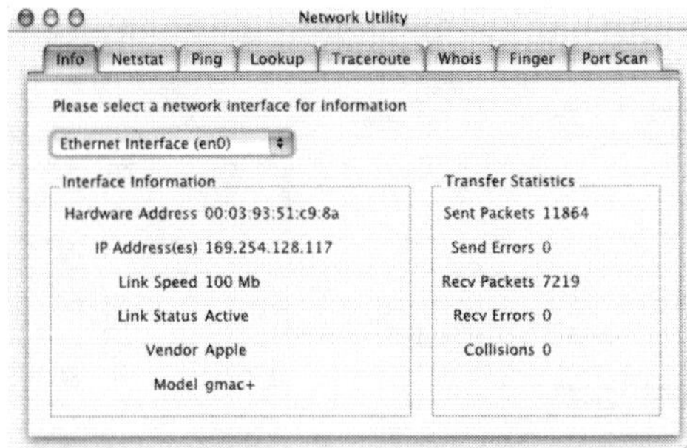

Figure 49 Use the Info tab to get information about a network interface.

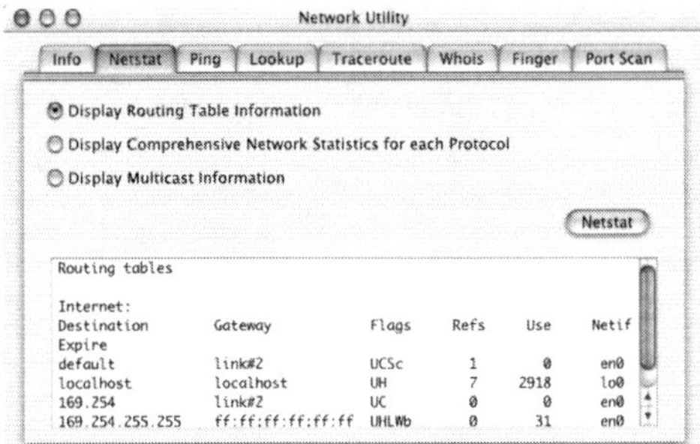

Figure 50 Use the Netstat tab to get network performance statistics.

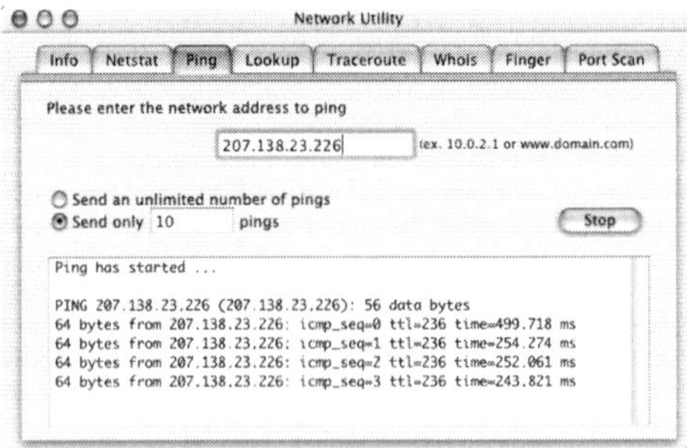

Figure 51 Use the Ping tab to "ping" another computer on the network or Internet.

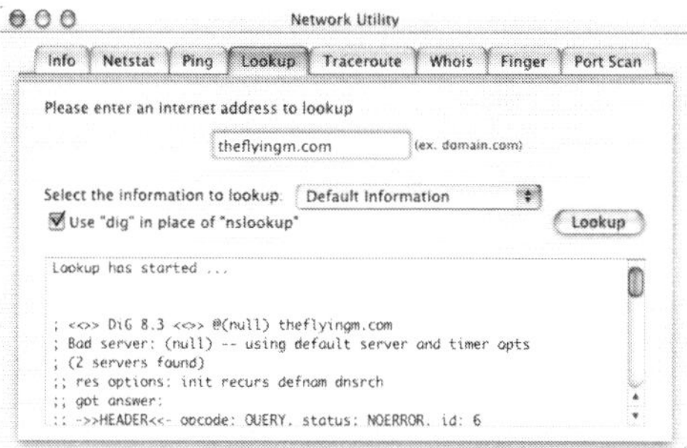

Figure 52 Use the Lookup tab to get the IP address for a specific domain name.

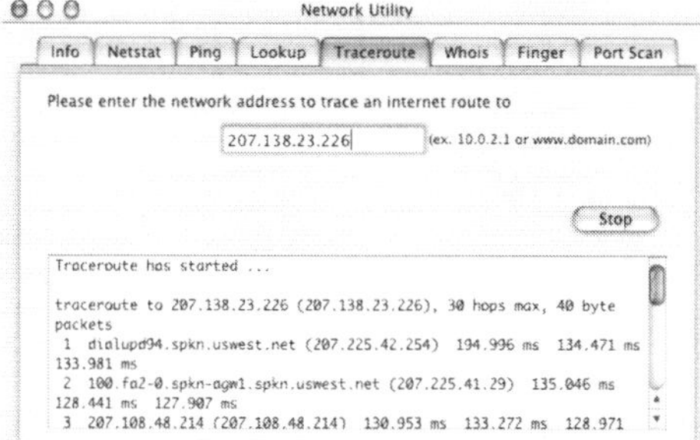

Figure 53 Use the Traceroute tab to trace the routing between your computer another IP address.

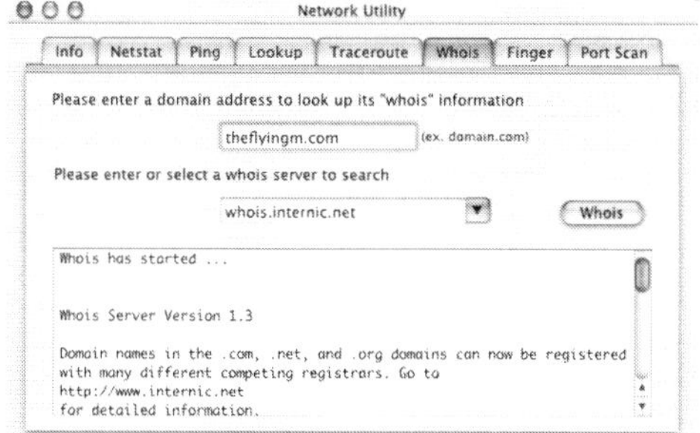

Figure 54 Use the Whois tab to look up information about a domain name.

Figure 55 Use the Finger tab to look up information about a person based on his e-mail address.

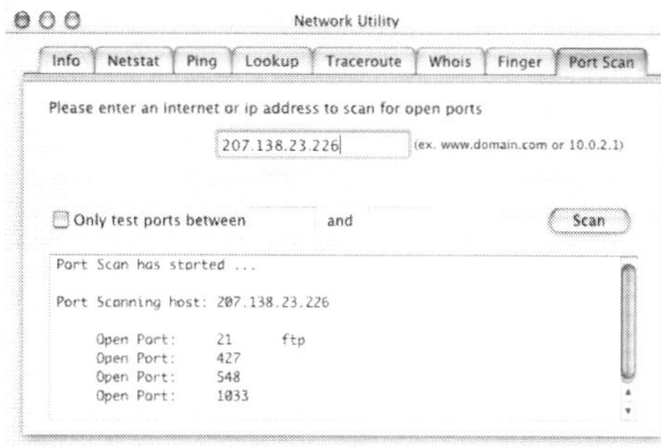

Figure 56 Use the Port Scan tab to check for active ports on another IP address or domain name.

Multiple Users & Security

Multiple Users & Security

Unlike previous versions of Mac OS, Mac OS X is designed to be a multiple-user system. This means that different individuals can log in and use a Mac OS X computer. Each user can install his own applications, configure his own desktop, and save his own documents. User files and setup is kept private. When each user logs in to the computer with his account, he can access only the files that belong to him or are shared.

In addition to passwords to protect each user's private files, each user can take advantage of the keychain access feature, which enables him or her to store passwords for accessing data online or on a network.

In this chapter, I discuss both the multiple-user and keychain access features of Mac OS X.

✔ Tips

- Using a multiple-user operating system doesn't mean that you can't keep your computer all to yourself. You can set up just one user—you. But the multiple-user feature does change the way Mac OS sets up directories on your hard disk and stores documents and applications.
- **Chapter 1** provides some additional information about how Mac OS X's directory structure is set up to account for multiple users. If you're the Admin user for your computer, you may want to consult that chapter to learn more about where shared and private files are installed and saved.

Configuring Mac OS X for Multiple Users

In order to take advantage of the multiple users feature of Mac OS X, you need to set up users.

The Mac OS X Setup Assistant does part of the setup for you. Immediately after you install Mac OS X, the Setup Assistant prompts you for information to set up the Admin user. If you are your computer's only user, you're finished setting up users. But if additional people—coworkers, friends, or family members—will be using your computer, it's in your best interest to set up a separate user account for each one.

In this section, I explain how to add, modify, and delete user accounts.

✔ Tip

- I tell you more about accessing another user's folders and files later in this chapter.

To add a new user

1. Choose Apple > System Preferences (**Figure 1**).

   or

   Click the System Preferences icon on the Dock (**Figure 2**).
2. In the System Preferences window that appears, click the Users icon (in the System area) to display the Users preferences pane (**Figure 3**).
3. Click the New User button to display the New User dialog.
4. If necessary, click the Identity tab (**Figure 4**).
5. Enter the name of the user in the Name edit box.
6. Enter an abbreviated name for the user in the Short Name edit box. This name should be no longer than 8 lowercase characters with no spaces.

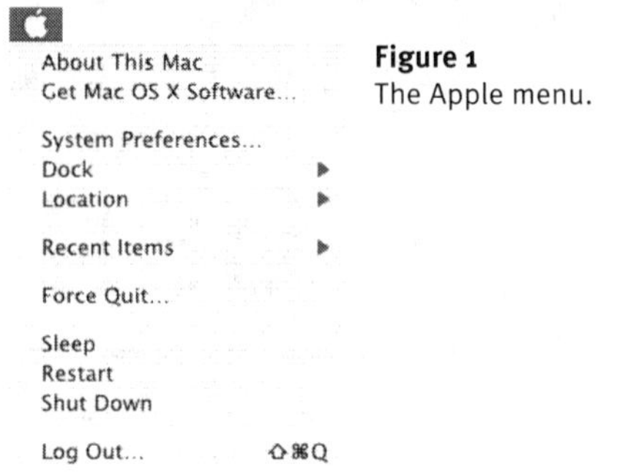

Figure 1 The Apple menu.

Figure 2 The System Preferences icon on the Dock.

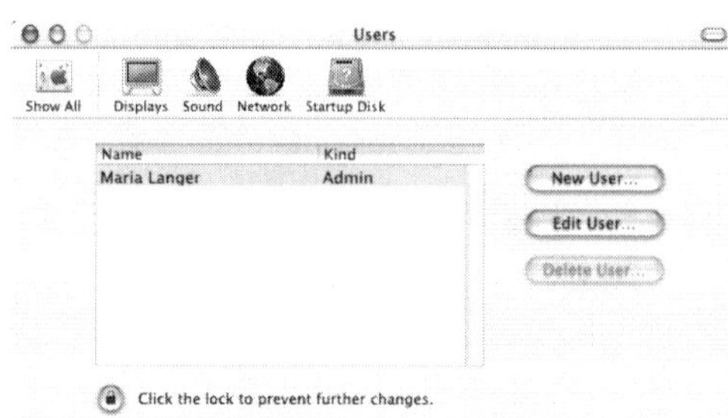

Figure 3 The Users preferences pane with just one user defined.

Figure 4 The Identify tab of the New User dialog.

Figure 5 The Password tab of the New User dialog.

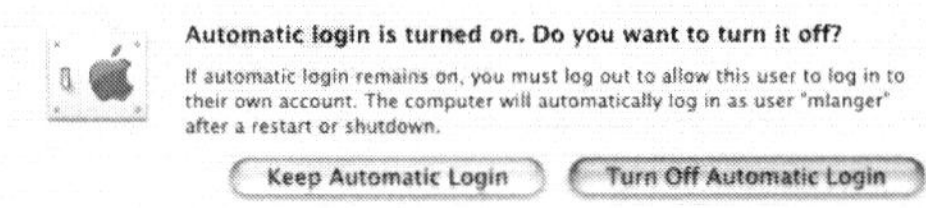

Figure 6 A dialog like this may appear when you add a new user and automatic login is enabled.

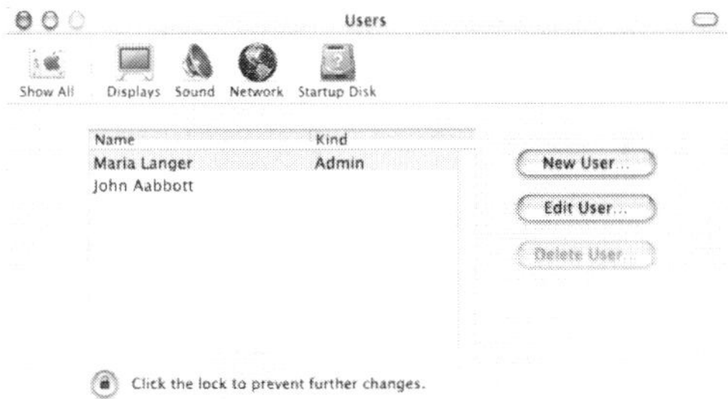

Figure 7 The new user is added to the Users preferences pane.

7. Click to select one of the pictures in the scrolling list to represent the user.

   or

   Drag an image file from a Finder window onto the Login Picture well.

   or

   Click the Choose button and use the Open dialog that appears to locate, select, and open a picture.
8. Click the Password tab (**Figure 5**).
9. Enter a password for the user in the Password and Verify edit boxes. The password must be at least four characters long.
10. If desired, enter a hint for the password in the Password Hint box.
11. If the user should have administrator privileges, turn on the Allow user to administer this computer check box.
12. Click Save.
13. A dialog like the one in **Figure 6** may appear. Click a button:
    - ▲ **Keep Automatic Login** will continue to automatically log in to the computer at startup using the information in the Login preferences pane.
    - ▲ **Turn Off Automatic Login** will require you to manually log in to the computer every time it starts up.

    The new user is listed in the Users preferences pane (**Figure 7**) and a folder for the new user appears in the Users folder (**Figure 9**).

✔ Tip

- I tell you more about setting Login preferences later in this chapter.

To modify a user

1. In the Users preferences pane (**Figure 7**), click to select the name of the user you want to modify.
2. Click the Edit User button.
3. A dialog with the name of the user appears. It has the same two tabs as the New User dialog (**Figures 4** and **5**). Make changes as desired to the user's settings.
4. Click OK to save your changes and return to the User preferences pane.

To remove a user

1. In the Users preferences pane (**Figure 7**), click to select the name of the user you want to remove.
2. Click the Delete User button.
3. A dialog sheet like the one in **Figure 8** appears. Select the name of the user with Admin privileges that you want to assign the user's home folder to.
4. Click Delete to remove the user.

✔ Tip

- When you remove a user, his home folder is renamed with his short name followed by the word *Deleted* (**Figure 9**). This folder can only be moved to the Trash by the system administrator, who has root access.

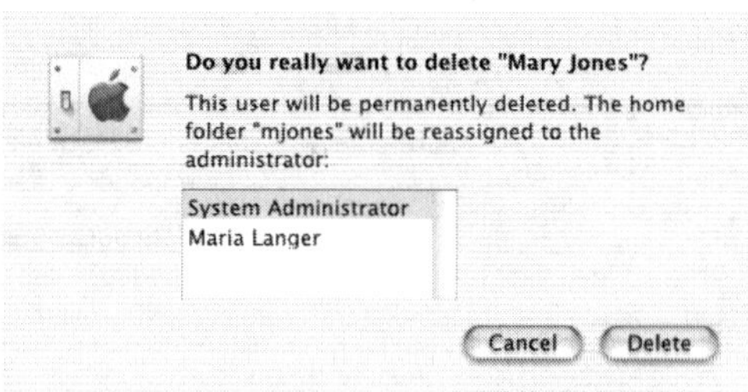

Figure 8 When you delete a user, his Home folder must be assigned to a user with administrative access.

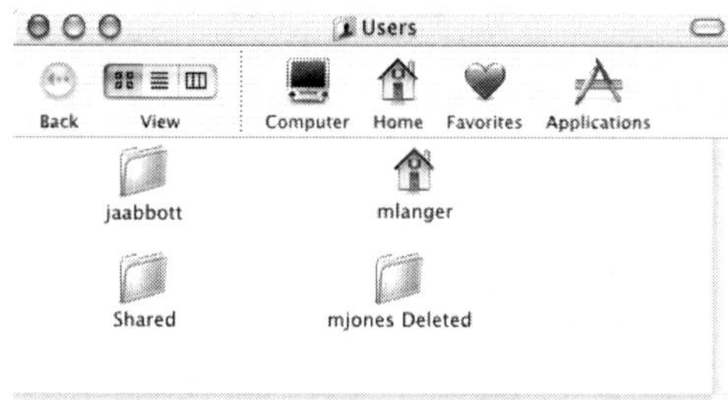

Figure 9 The Users folder contains Home folders for each current and deleted user, as well as a Shared folder that all users can access.

Figure 10 The Login Window tab of the Login preferences pane.

Figure 11 You can display the Login window with name and password fields...

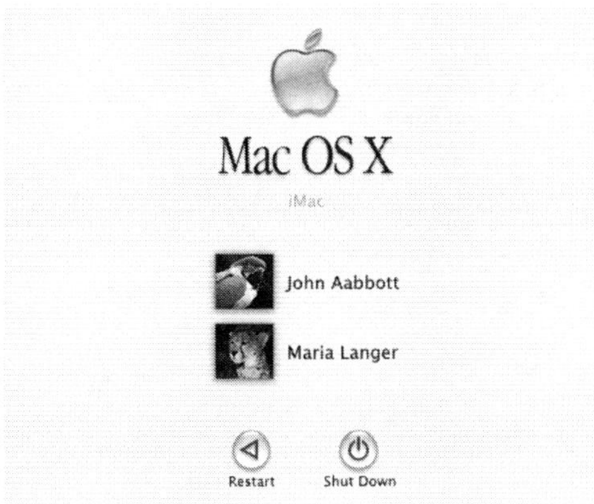

Figure 12 ...or with a list of users.

Setting Login Options

When a system is set up for multiple users, Mac OS X can display the Login window (**Figure 11** or **12**) at startup or after another user has logged off. This enables a user to log in to the computer, thus identifying himself and making his private files available.

You use the Login preferences pane to set options for the Login window, as well as to identify items that should automatically open when a user logs in.

To set Login window preferences

1. Choose Apple > System Preferences (**Figure 1**).

   or

   Click the System Preferences icon on the Dock (**Figure 2**).

2. In the System Preferences window that appears, click the Login icon (in the Personal area) to display the Login preferences pane.
3. Click the Login Window tab (**Figure 10**).
4. Set options in the bottom half of the window as desired:

   ▲ **Display Login Window as** determines how the Login window will appear. **Name and password entry fields** displays edit boxes for the user name and password (**Figure 11**). **List of users with accounts on this computer** displays the name of each user except the System Administrator (or root) user (**Figure 12**).

   ▲ **Show "Other User" in list for network users** makes it possible for users who are not on the user list to connect to the computer if they are set up as network users.

Continued on next page...

Continued from previous page.

- ▲ **Disable Restart and Shut Down buttons** disables these two buttons in the Login window.
- ▲ **Show password hint after 3 attempts to enter a password** displays the user's password hint if he fails to correctly enter his password three times (**Figure 13**).

Figure 13 You can set up the Login window so it helps you remember your password.

✔ Tip

- You can click the Lock button at the bottom of the Login Window tab to prevent other users from making changes to the settings there. Once locked, you'll need an administrator's name and password (**Figure 14**) to unlock and change the settings.

Figure 14 If you click the lock button to prevent changes, you'll have to enter an administrator name and password to unlock the options.

To enable or disable the automatic login feature

1. Display the Login window tab of the Login preferences pane (**Figure 10**).
2. To enable automatic login, turn on the Automatically log in check box. Then enter the user name and password you want to use to log in (**Figure 15**) and click the Save button.

   or

   To disable automatic login, turn off the Automatically log in check box.

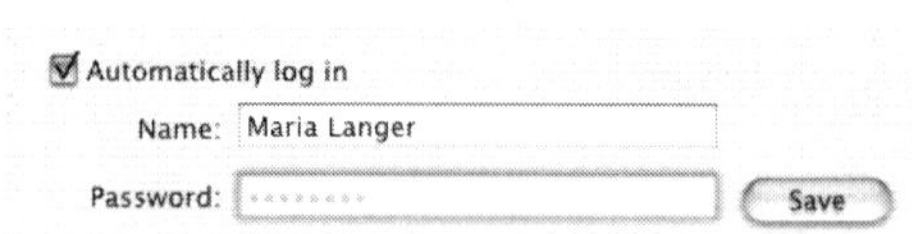

Figure 15 To enable automatic login, turn on the check box and enter the user name and password you want to automatically log in with.

✔ Tips

- Automatic login is especially useful if you're the only person who ever uses your computer and it's in a secure location.
- With the automatic login feature enabled, the only way to display the Login window is to log out.

Figure 16 The Login Items tab of the Login preferences pane.

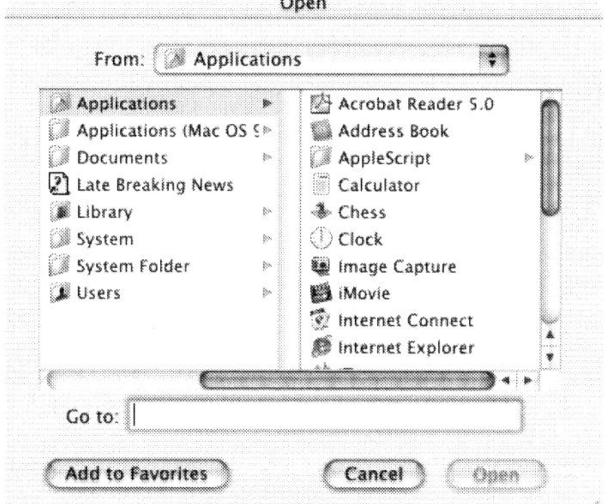

Figure 17 You can use an Open dialog to locate, select, and open the item you want to open automatically at startup.

To specify Login Items

1. Choose Apple > System Preferences (**Figure 1**).

   or

   Click the System Preferences icon on the Dock (**Figure 2**).
2. In the System Preferences window that appears, click the Login icon (in the Personal area) to display the Login preferences pane.
3. Click the Login Items tab (**Figure 16**).
4. To add an item to be opened each time you log in, drag its icon into the list or click the Add button and use the Open dialog that appears (**Figure 17**) to locate, select, and open the item. The item you dragged or selected appears with a check box beside it, as shown in **Figure 16**.

   or

   To remove an item from the list, click to select it and then click the Remove button. The item disappears from the list.
5. To automatically hide an item when it launches, turn on the Hide check box beside it.

✔ Tips

- The items listed in the Login Items tab of the Login preferences pane will only open when the person who set them up logs in. For example, if I set up items for my account, those items would not open when another user logged in.
- This feature can be used like the Startup Items feature in Mac OS 9.x and earlier.

Logging In & Out

The Login window (**Figure 11** or **12**) automatically appears:

- ◆ When you start the computer (if the automatic login feature is disabled).
- ◆ After you log off the computer.

This section explains how you can log in and out of a shared Macintosh.

✔ Tip

- I tell you about the automatic login feature earlier in this chapter.

To log in

1. Enter your name and password in the appropriate edit boxes of the Login window (**Figure 11**).

   or

   Click to select your name in the Login window (**Figure 12**). Then enter your password in the edit box that appears beneath it (**Figure 18**).

2. Click the Login button. If your password was entered correctly, you are logged in to the computer.

✔ Tips

- The Login window that appears varies depending on settings in the Login Window tab of the Login preferences pane. I explain those options earlier in this chapter.
- If you do not correctly enter your password, the Login window shakes when you click the Login button. Repeat the above steps to try again.
- If you clicked the wrong name in step 1, you can click the Go Back button in the Login window (**Figure 18**) to return to the previous screen and select the right name.

Figure 18 If the Login window displays a list of users, when you click a user name, the Password edit box appears.

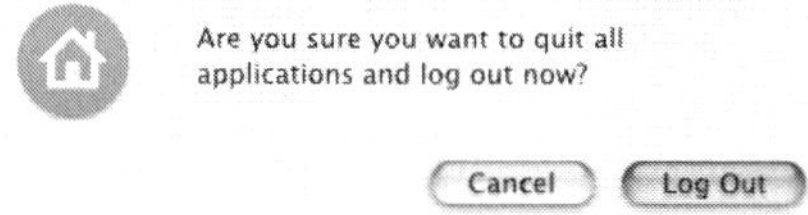

Figure 19 This dialog appears when you use the Log Out command.

To log out

1. Choose Apple > Log Out (**Figure 1**), or press Shift ⌘ Q.
2. A dialog like the one in **Figure 19** appears. Click Log Out, or press Return. You are logged out of the computer and the Login window appears (**Figure 11** or **12**).

✔ Tips

- As the dialog in **Figure 19** warns, logging out of a computer automatically quits all running applications.
- If documents with unsaved changes are open when you log out, you will be prompted to save changes before the log out process is completed.

The Home Folder

When you set up a user, Mac OS X creates a Home folder for the user in the Users folder (**Figure 9**), with the user's short name as the folder name. The icon for the folder appears as a house for the user who is currently logged in and as a regular folder for all other users. Each user's Home folder contains folders for the applications, documents, and settings files for his account (**Figure 20**):

- **Desktop** contains all items (other than mounted disks) on the user's desktop.
- **Documents** is the default file location for document files.
- **Movies**, **Music**, and **Pictures** are for storing video, audio, and image files.
- **Sites** is for the user's Web site, which can be put online with the Personal Web Sharing feature.
- **Library** is for storing various preferences files, as well as fonts.
- **Public** is for storing shared files.
- **Applications**, when present, is for storing applications installed by the user for his private use.

✔ Tips

- You can quickly open your Home folder by clicking the Home icon in the toolbar of any Finder window (**Figure 20**).
- Personal Web Sharing is discussed in **Chapter 5** and fonts are covered in **Chapter 9**.
- Although a user can open another user's Home folder, he can only open the Public and Sites folders within that user's Home folder; all other folders are locked (**Figure 21**). A dialog like the one in **Figure 22** appears if you attempt to open a locked folder.

Figure 20 Each user's Home folder is preconfigured with folders for storing documents and settings files.

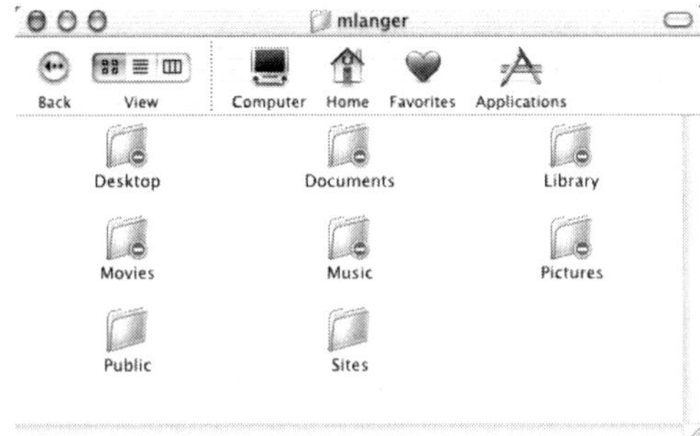

Figure 21 The Home folder in **Figure 20** when viewed by another user.

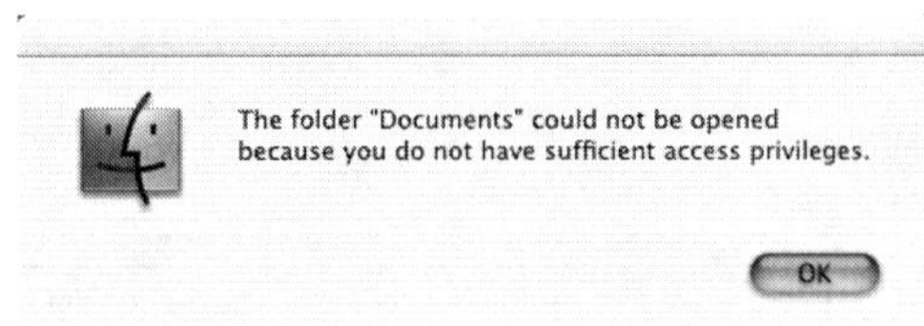

Figure 22 A dialog like this one appears if you try to open another user's private folder.

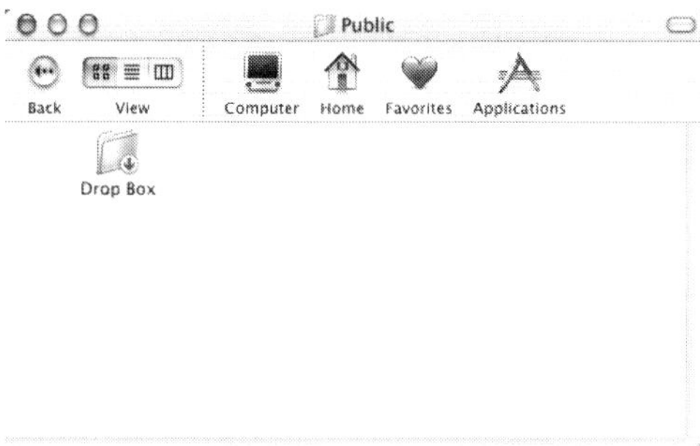

Figure 23 Each user's Public folder contains a Drop Box folder for accepting incoming files.

Sharing Files with Other Users

Mac OS X offers several ways for multiple users of the same computer to share files with each other:

- The **Shared** folder in the Users folder (**Figure 9**) offers read/write access to all users.
- The **Public** folder in each user's home folder (**Figure 20**) offers read access to all users.
- The **Drop Box** folder in each user's Public folder (**Figure 23**) offers write access to all users.

✔ Tips

- *Read* access for a folder enables users to open files in that folder. *Write* access for a folder enables users to save files into that folder.
- File sharing over a network is covered in **Chapter 5**.

To make a file accessible to all other users

Place the file in the Shared folder in the Users folder (**Figure 9**).

or

Place the file in the Public folder in your Home folder (**Figure 20**).

✔ Tip

- If your computer has a system administrator, check to see where the administrator prefers public files to be stored.

To make a file accessible to a specific user

1. Drag the file's icon onto the Drop Box folder icon inside the Public folder in the user's Home folder (**Figure 23**).
2. A dialog like the one in **Figure 24** appears. Click OK. The file moves into the Public folder.

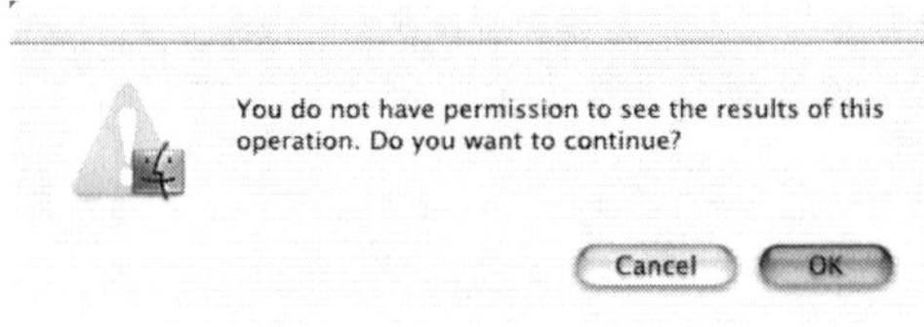

Figure 24 When you drag a file into a Drop Box folder, a dialog like this appears.

✔ Tips

- When you drag a file into a Drop Box folder, the file is moved—not copied—there. You cannot open a Drop Box folder to remove its contents. If you need to access the file, hold down Option while dragging the file into the Drop Box folder to place a copy of the file there. You can then continue working with the original.
- To use the Drop Box, be sure to drag the file icon onto the Drop Box folder icon. If you drag an icon into the Public folder, a dialog like the one in **Figure 25** appears, telling you that you can't modify the Public folder.

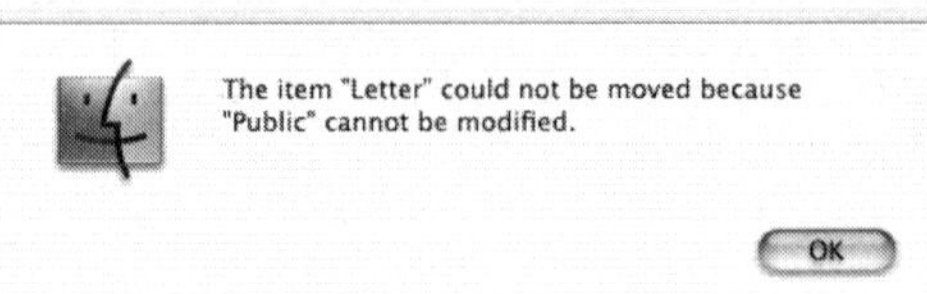

Figure 25 You can't place files into another user's Public folder.

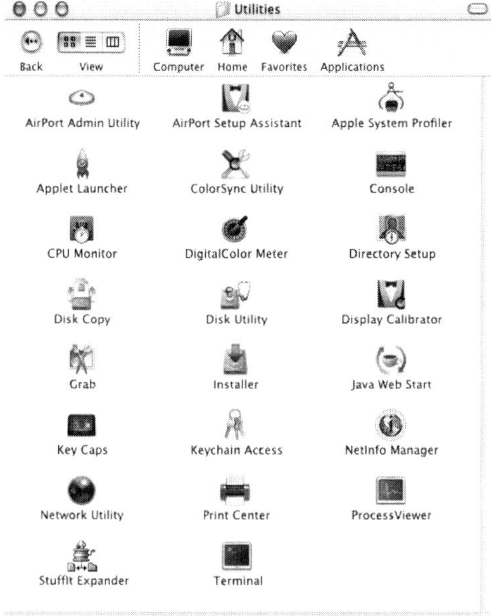

Figure 26 The contents of the Utilities folder inside the Applications folder.

Figure 27 The Keychain window for a default keychain.

Keychain Access

The Keychain Access feature offers users a way to store passwords for accessing password-protected applications, servers, and Internet locations. Each user's keychain is automatically unlocked when he logs into the computer, so the passwords it contains are automatically available when needed to access secured files and sites.

✔ Tips

- Mac OS X automatically creates a keychain for each user, using the user's short name as the keychain name. This is the default keychain.
- Keychain Access only works with applications that are keychain-aware.
- You can also use your keychain to store other private information, such as credit card numbers and bank personal identification numbers (PINs).

To open Keychain Access

Open the Keychain Access icon in the Utilities folder inside the Applications folder (**Figure 26**).

The keychain window for your default keychain appears (**Figure 27**). It lists all the items in your keychain.

To add a keychain item when accessing a secure application, server, or Internet location

1. Follow your normal procedure for accessing the secure item.
2. Enter your password when prompted (**Figure 28**).
3. Turn on the Add Password to Keychain check box. In some applications, you may have to click an Options button to see it (**Figure 29**).
4. Finish accessing the secure item. When you open Keychain Access, you'll see that the password has been added to your keychain (**Figure 30**).

✔ Tip

- The exact steps for adding a keychain when accessing a secure item vary based on the item you are accessing and the software you are using to access it.

To add a keychain item manually

1. Open Keychain Access (**Figures 27** and **30**).
2. Click the Add button to display the New Password Item dialog (**Figure 31**).
3. Enter an identifying name for the item in the Name box.
4. Enter the user ID or account name or number for the item in the Account box.
5. Enter the password for the item in the Password box.

✔ Tip

- If you turn on the Show Typing check box in the New Password Item dialog (**Figure 31**), the password you enter will appear as text rather than as bullets.

Figure 28 This example shows the usual procedure for accessing a secure server. When you click the Options button...

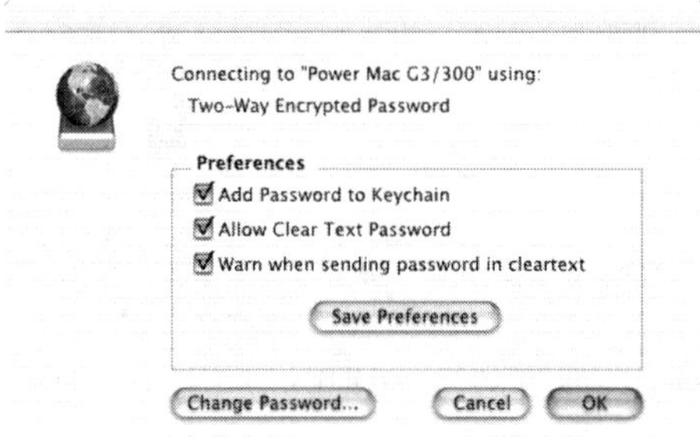

Figure 29 ...a dialog that includes the Add Password to Keychain option appears.

Figure 30 The item is added to your keychain.

Figure 31 Use this dialog to manually enter keychain item information.

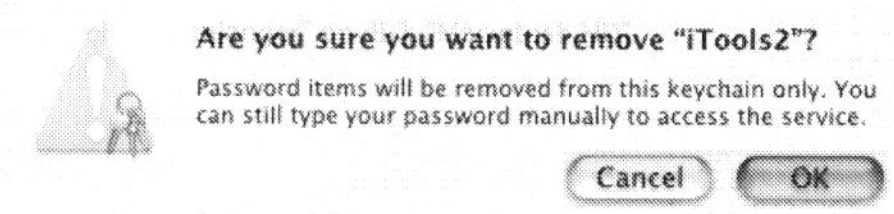

Figure 32 A dialog like this appears when you delete a keychain item.

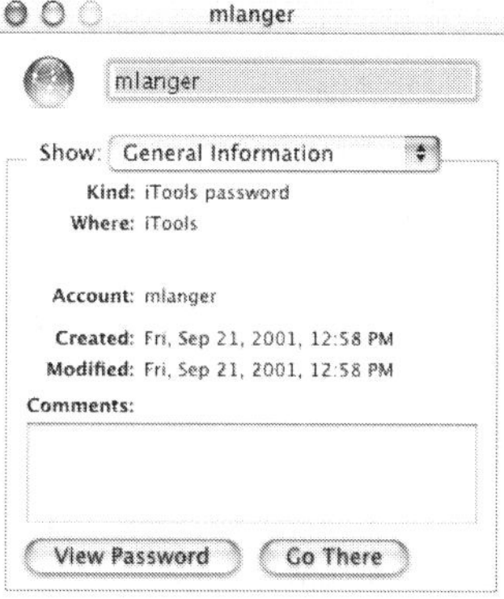

Figure 33 The Info window for a keychain item provides some information and offers one or two options.

Figure 34 Mac OS X whispers the password to you with a tiny dialog like this one.

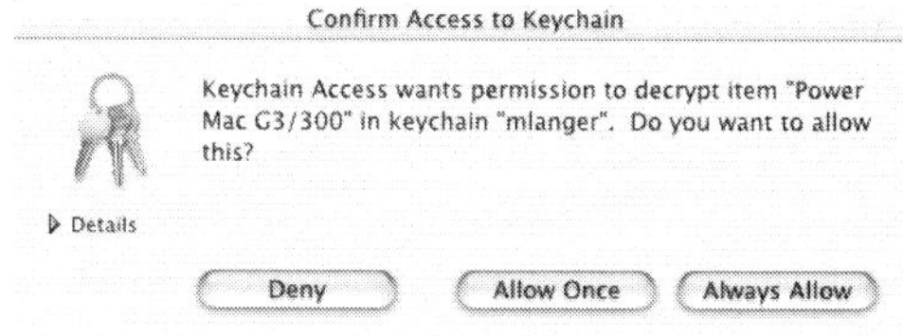

Figure 35 When an application that does not have permission to use a keychain item wants to use it, it displays a dialog like this. You click a button to determine whether to allow access.

To remove a keychain item

1. Open Keychain Access (**Figures 27** and **30**).
2. Select the keychain item you want to remove.
3. Click Remove.
4. A dialog like the one in **Figure 32** appears. Click OK.

✔ Tip

- Removing a keychain item does not prevent you from accessing an item. It just prevents you from accessing it without entering a password.

To get general information about a keychain item

1. Open Keychain Access (**Figures 27** and **30**).
2. Select the keychain item you want to learn about.
3. Click the Get Info button to open the Info window for the item.
4. Choose General Information from the Show pop-up menu **Figure 33**.
5. To see the item password (**Figure 34**), click View Password.

   or

   To open the item's location, click Go There. (This option is not available for application passwords.)
6. Click the Info window's close button to dismiss it.

✔ Tip

- In step 5, if you click the View Password button, a dialog like the one in **Figure 35** may appear. To see the password, you must click the Allow Once or Always Allow button. I tell you more about this dialog later in this chapter.

To set Access Control options

1. Open Keychain Access (**Figures 27** and **30**).
2. Select the keychain item you want to set Access Control options for.
3. Click the Get Info button to open the Info window for the item.
4. Choose Access Control from the Show pop-up menu (**Figure 36**).
5. To allow applications to use the keychain item without displaying a confirmation alert dialog, turn on the Allow access to this item without warning check box. Then select one of the radio buttons beneath it:
   ▲ **Allow access by any application** allows all applications to use the keychain item.
   ▲ **Allow access only by these applications** allows only the applications listed in the window to use the keychain item.
6. In step 5, if you set up access by specific applications, use the Add and Remove button to modify the application list:
   ▲ **Add** displays the Add Trusted Application dialog (**Figure 37**), which you can use to locate and choose an application to add to the list.
   ▲ **Remove**, which is only available when an application in the list is selected, displays a dialog like the one in **Figure 38**. Click OK to remove the application from the list.
7. Click the Info window's close button.
8. If you made changes to the Access Control settings, a dialog like the one in **Figure 39** appears. Click Allow Once to save the change.

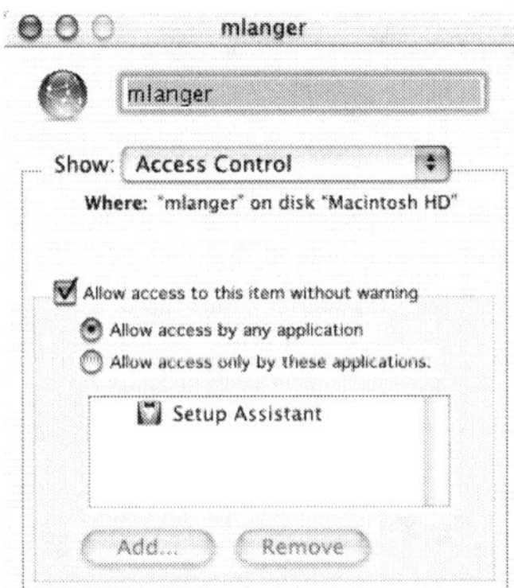

Figure 36 The Access Control information for a keychain item.

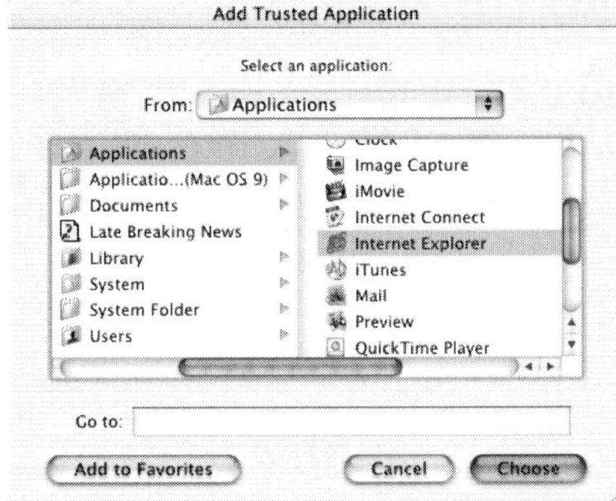

Figure 37 Use the Add Trusted Application dialog to add applications to use with the keychain item.

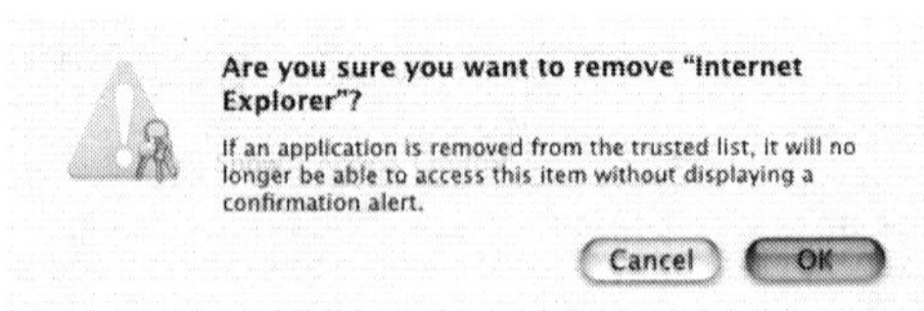

Figure 38 This dialog appears when you remove an application from the application list in the Access Control info window.

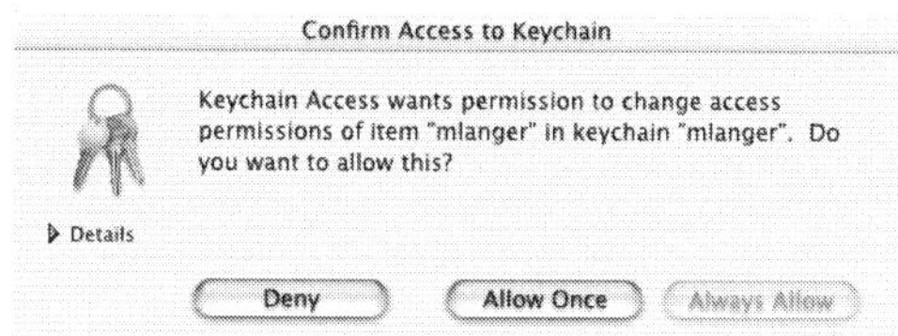

Figure 39 You have to confirm changes to Access Controls before Keychain Access saves them.

Figure 40 This dialog appears if Access Control settings do not allow Finder to use an existing keychain item.

To use a keychain item

1. Follow your normal procedure for accessing the secure item.
2. If Access Control settings are set up to allow access to the item without warning, the item opens without displaying any dialog.

   or

   If Access Control settings are set up to require a warning *or* if Access Control settings are set up to allow access without warning but the application you are using is not included on the application list, a dialog like the one in **Figure 40** appears. Click a button:

   - ▲ Deny prevents use of the keychain item. You will have to manually enter a password to access the secure item.
   - ▲ Allow Once enables the keychain to open the item this time.
   - ▲ Always Allow enables the keychain to open the item and adds the item to the Access Control application list so the dialog does not appear again.

✔ Tips

- The only reason I can think of for denying access with a keychain is if you have another user name and password you want to use.
- If a keychain item does not exist for the secure item, you'll have to go through the usual procedure for accessing the item.

To create a new keychain

1. Open Keychain Access (**Figures 27** and **30**).
2. Choose File > New Keychain (**Figure 41**), or press ⌘N.
3. Use the Save dialog that appears (**Figure 42**) to enter a name for the new keychain and click Save.
4. The New Keychain Passphrase dialog appears (**Figure 43**). Enter the same password or phrase in each edit box and click OK. The new keychain opens in its own window (**Figure 44**).

✔ Tip

- If you're an organization nut, you may want to use multiple keychains to organize passwords for different purposes. Otherwise, one keychain should be enough for you. (It is for me.)

To lock a keychain

1. Open Keychain Access and display the keychain you want to lock (**Figure 30**).
2. Click the Lock button, choose File > Lock "*Keychain Name*", or press ⌘L.

   The keychain window collapses and the phrase "This keychain is locked" appears in the window (**Figure 45**).

✔ Tip

- When a keychain is locked, when you try to open a secure item for which you have a keychain item, a dialog like the one in **Figure 46** appears. You must enter your keychain password or phrase and click OK to unlock the keychain before it can be used.

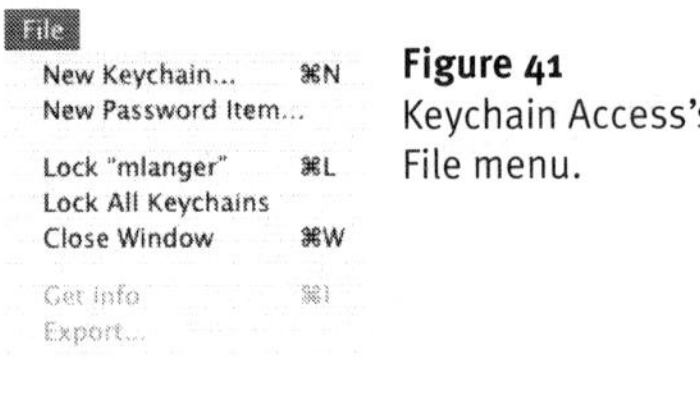

Figure 41 Keychain Access's File menu.

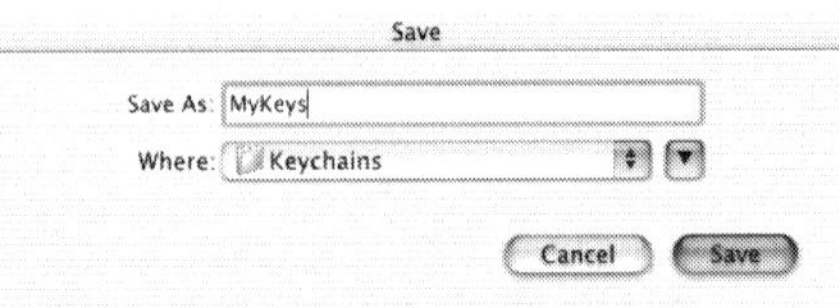

Figure 42 Use this dialog to name and save a new keychain.

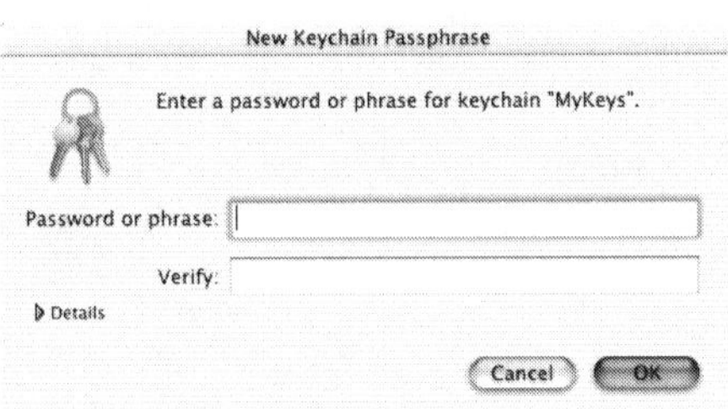

Figure 43 Set the keychain's password by entering the same password or phrase in both edit boxes.

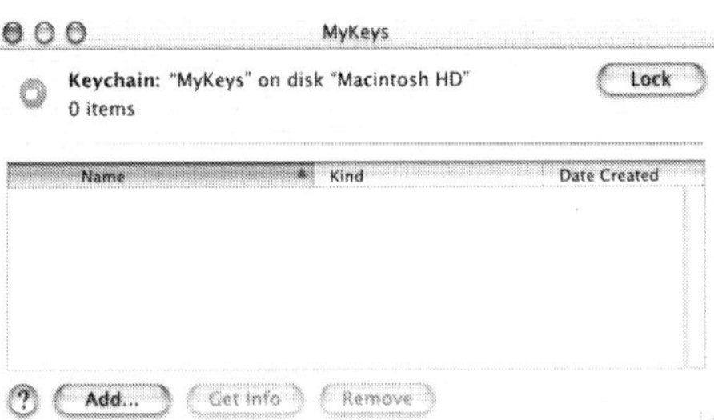

Figure 44 A new keychain, ready for items.

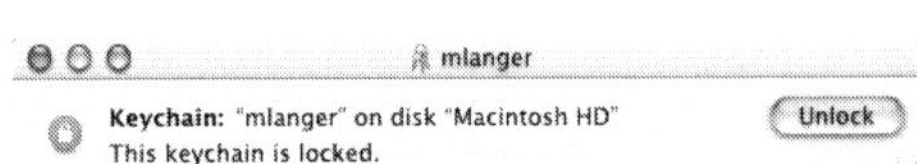

Figure 45 A locked keychain window.

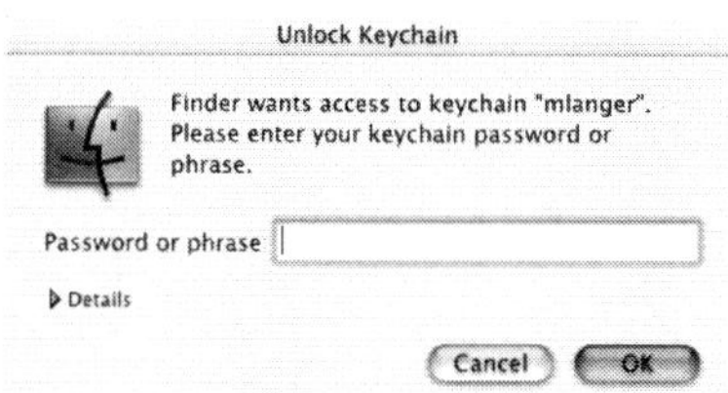

Figure 46 This dialog appears when a keychain is locked and you try to open a secure item for which a keychain item exists.

Keychains
◆ mlanger
MyKeys
Make "MyKeys" Default

Figure 47 The Keychains menu.

Unlock Keychain
Keychain Access wants access to keychain "mlanger". Please enter your keychain password or phrase.
Password or phrase
Details
Cancel
OK

Figure 48 Use this dialog to unlock a keychain.

To unlock a keychain

1. Open or switch to Keychain Access.
2. If the locked keychain window is not showing (**Figure 45**), choose the keychain name from the Keychains menu (**Figure 47**).

   or

   Click the Unlock button on the locked keychain window (**Figure 45**).
3. Enter the keychain's password or phrase in the Unlock Keychain dialog that appears (**Figure 48**) and click OK. The keychain window appears or expands to show its items (**Figure 30**).

✔ Tip

- The password for the keychain Mac OS X automatically creates for you (the one named with your user short name) is the same as your login password.

To make a keychain the default keychain

1. Open Keychain Access.
2. If necessary, use the Keychains menu (**Figure 47**) to open unlock the keychain you want to make the default.
3. Choose Keychains > Make "Keychain Name" Default (**Figure 47**).

✔ Tips

- A diamond appears to the left of the default keychain name on the Keychains menu (**Figure 47**).
- The default keychain is the keychain that new items are added to when you add a keychain item while opening a secure item.
- You can only have one default keychain.

AppleScript & Mac OS X 10.1

BY *Ethan Wilde*

Ethan Wilde bought his first computer, an Apple II, in 1979 after taking a BASIC programming class at San Francisco's Exploratorium. The experience changed his life, and computers have been close to Ethan ever since. Now a principal at Mediatrope, an award-winning multimedia company in San Francisco, Ethan has many Macs to script, when he is not writing books and teaching about AppleScript.

AppleScript & Mac OS X

Mac OS X is different from anything you may know about Mac OS 9, from the Aqua user interface to the System Preferences application. In the midst of this new terrain stands AppleScript 1.7. AppleScript works with Carbon and Cocoa applications developed just for Mac OS X, as well as with older Mac OS 9.x applications and those running in the Classic environment.

Yes, AppleScript is alive and thriving in Mac OS X, and Mac OS X 10.1 offers the functionality you need to get things done. Depending on your coding style, you shouldn't have to change most of your old scripts that control Mac OS 9.x applications for them to run in Mac OS X 10.1. However, none of the scriptable Mac OS 9.x components, such as control panels and extensions, exist in Mac OS X.

As with many of the other Mac operating system components, AppleScript is undergoing a period of transition. Although AppleScript is a core part of both the new and old operating systems, when you move to Mac OS X, you will find that many fundamental things have changed. The Finder in Mac OS X 10.1 does not support labels, for example, so accessing the label index of an item generates an error. Why? In Mac OS X, the Finder does not have responsibility for everything it controlled in Mac OS 9.

This chapter covers the most notable aspects of using AppleScript in Mac OS X, beginning with an overview of what is the same and what has changed.

✔ Tip

- For more information on AppleScript and scripting applications in Mac OS X and Mac OS 9, check out my book, *AppleScript for Applications: Visual QuickStart Guide*, published by Peachpit Press.

An AppleScript Primer

AppleScript is an English-like language; with AppleScript, you can write scripts that can control the actions of your Mac and of your applications.

AppleScript has a host of powerful and flexible features:

- With AppleScript, you can tell scriptable applications to perform tasks, such as open and close.
- In recordable applications, AppleScript can create a script based on a recording of your real-time actions. Only a few applications are recordable, but those few are great demonstrations of the power of recording. Microsoft's Word 2001 is one.
- AppleScript can control many applications over an entire network and control other platforms over the Internet.
- The AppleScript language is dynamically extensible: Each scriptable application has its own dictionary of commands, classes, and properties. However, you don't always need an entire application to add commands to AppleScript. There is another group of language extensions known as scripting additions. Scripting additions are small compiled libraries that also have dictionaries of commands, classes, and properties that extend AppleScript's vocabulary and functionality. In a nutshell, scriptable applications and scripting additions both have dictionaries of additional commands that expand AppleScript.

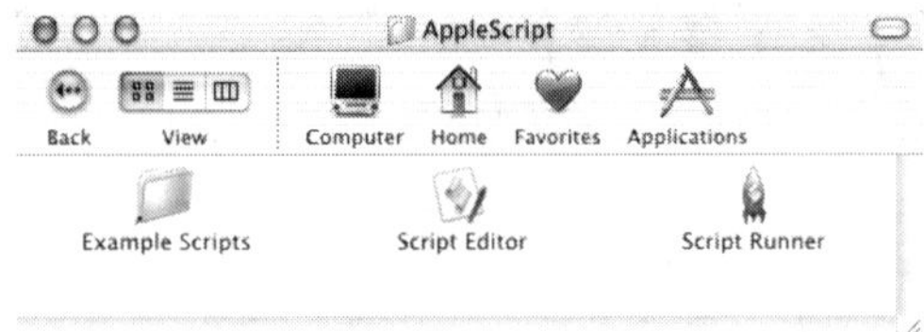

Figure 1 The AppleScript folder inside your Applications folder contains Script Editor and Script Runner, as well as example scripts.

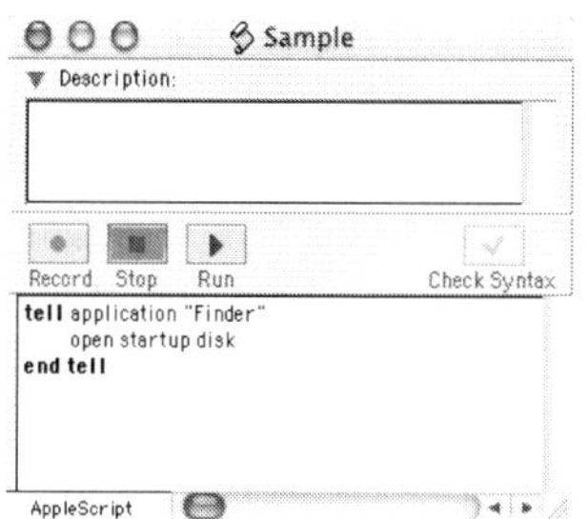

Figure 2 A Script Editor window with a simple script.

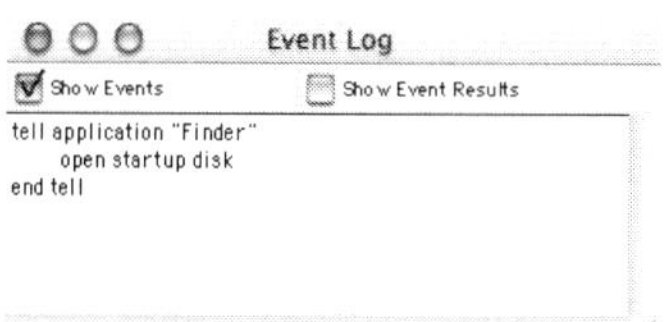

Figure 3 Script Editor's Event Log window.

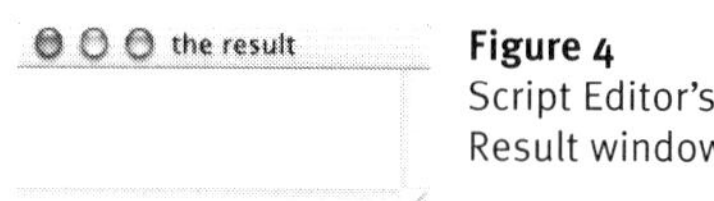

Figure 4 Script Editor's Result window.

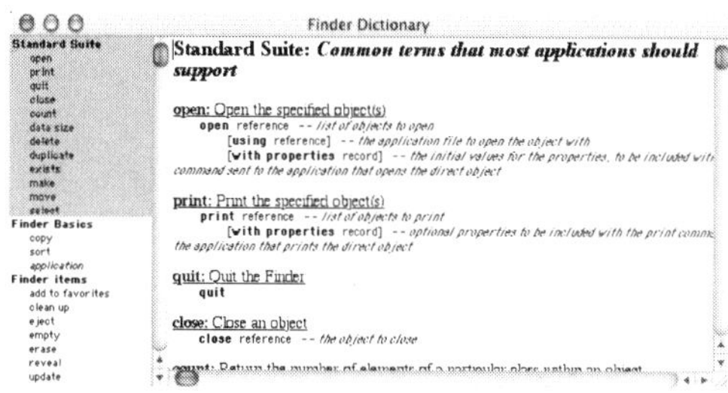

Figure 5 Script Editor's Dictionary window, showing the Finder Dictionary.

The Script Editor

The first chore to undertake when approaching AppleScript in Mac OS X is locating the Script Editor. **Figure 1** shows the AppleScript folder inside the Applications folder, which is where the Script Editor lives. I recommend that you drag the Script Editor icon onto your Dock for permanent easy access; you will use this feature often.

Figures 2 through **5** show the four windows of Script Editor:

- **Script.** The Script window (**Figure 2**) is where you create your script by typing script statements or recording your actions in a recordable application. AppleScript compiles your script and tests for syntax errors whenever you click the Check Syntax button in the Script window. Then click the Run button to execute your script from Script Editor. The Script window also has a description field that you can use to describe your script.
- **Event Log.** Open the Event Log window (**Figure 3**) from the Controls menu. It displays all events and results generated by a running script, which makes it extremely useful for debugging your scripts.
- **Result.** You can also open the Result window (**Figure 4**) from the Controls menu. It displays the results of the last event.
- **Dictionary.** You can open the dictionary of every application or scripting addition in Script Editor. Dictionaries can provide help with proper syntax and teach you an application's script statements, events, and objects (**Figure 5**).

✔ Tip

- Every version of the Mac OS from System 7.1 through Mac OS X (including Mac OS 9.2.1) comes with AppleScript and Script Editor.

AppleScript statements

Every script you write will be made up of a series of statements. A statement is usually just that: a simple English-like sentence with a subject, predicate, and object in the form noun, verb, noun. Here's an example:

```
tell application "Finder" to ¬
open disk "PowerBook G4"
```

As you can probably guess, when this statement is run as part of a script, the Finder opens the disk named *PowerBook G4*.

Statements are made up of *commands* and *objects*. The *target* of a statement should be a specific application program, such as the Finder in this example.

Commands are like verbs; they're words you use to request an action. The action usually points at an object. Objects generally are nouns: They're things you do stuff to.

In the preceding example statement, **tell** is directed at the Finder, which is an object. **open** is a command, or verb, and **disk "PowerBook G4"** is its object.

Each object can have parts, or *elements*. This means that objects such as disks can contain folders and files:

```
tell application "Finder" to ¬
open folder "Applications (Mac OS 9)" of ¬
disk "PowerBook G4"
```

In this example statement, the folder named *Applications* is an element of the disk object named *PowerBook G4*. This statement tells the Finder to open the folder named *Applications (Mac OS 9)*, which is on the disk named *Power-Book G4*.

You may have intuitively understood what the example script did. That's AppleScript syntax at its best.

Targets & tell blocks

In AppleScript, you need to specify the target of the commands in your script. You do this targeting with the **tell** command. Commands that appear outside **tell** blocks must be part of AppleScript's built-in set of commands instead of belonging to any specific application. You can think of the concept of using **tell** to target your commands as setting the context for your commands.

Variables

Variables are where you put values that you are using in your script:

```
set x to "me"
```

In this example, the command **set** tells Apple-Script to set the variable **x** to the string value **"me"**.

A variable is a kind of object that serves as a placeholder for any information you need to manipulate or share with other applications. AppleScript variable names follow a few rules:

- They must start with a letter.
- They can only contain letters, numbers, and underscores (_).
- They cannot be words that are reserved for commands or objects.

Different scripters have different attitudes about naming variables. Some type short, cryptic variable names in the interest of expe-dience. I suggest using descriptive variable names, even if it means a little extra typing.

✔ Tip

- Variables come in many flavors, including strings, numbers, and Booleans. When you assign a value to a variable, you can tell AppleScript what kind of value it is. This is important, because commands often expect to receive values of particular types.

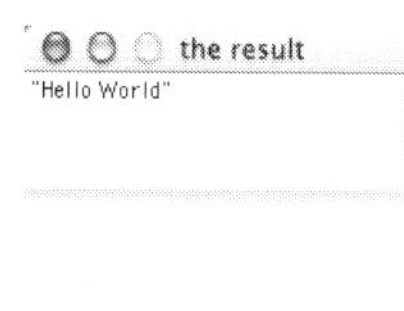

Figure 6 The Result window shows the results of a script that uses the set command, as shown here...

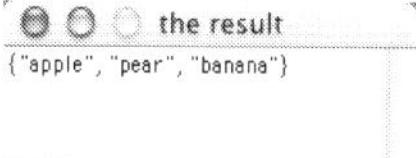

Figure 7 ...and here.

Table 1

Numerical Operators		
Operator	**Meaning**	**Example**
^	Raise to the power of	2^4=16
*	Multiply	1*3=3
+	Add	2+7=9
-	Subtract	5-2=3
/	Divide	8/2=4
div	Divide without remainder	11 div 2=5
mod	Divide, returning remainder	11 mod 2=1

Properties

Your script can define its own properties. A property behaves like a variable that keeps its value across executions. This means that the value in a property will be the same when it stops running as it will be when it runs again. You usually define properties in your script at the beginning of your script, like this:

```
property myUser: "me"
property myDelay: 15
```

Operators

AppleScript lets you perform many operations on values and variables. The type of operator you choose depends on what you are trying to accomplish and the kind of value that your variable holds.

You can combine strings by using the concatenation operator, **&**, as follows:

```
set x to "Hello " & "World"
```

Figure 6 shows the result of the script.

You can also add items to a list by using **&**:

```
set z to {"apple","pear"}& "banana"
```

Figure 7 shows the result of adding an item to a list.

You can use many operators on variables in AppleScript. **Table 1** lists numerical operators.

How to Use This Chapter

In this chapter, we use several presentation styles meant to help you understand and work with AppleScript.

In the instructions that accompany each script, a special typeface indicates actual AppleScript code. For example:

```
tell application "Finder"
  open startup disk
end tell
```

We show all AppleScript scripts in this chapter using the above typeface, with most commands in lowercase letters, making it easy to distinguish between the scripts and the rest of the text in the book. AppleScript itself is case-insensitive (that is, it doesn't distinguish between uppercase and lowercase letters) unless you tell it to behave otherwise.

When a line of AppleScript code is too long to fit on a single line, I have broken it into multiple lines using AppleScript's built-in continuation character: ¬. To generate this character on your keyboard, type Option Return in the Script Editor. Make sure your scripts include continuation characters to tie long lines of code together or you will encounter errors. Here's an example of a line with the continuation character in use:

```
delete word 1 of paragraph 2 ¬
of document "AS and the Internet"
```

In most cases, the instructions for typing AppleScript statements are immediately followed by indented text that explains what the preceding statement(s) mean or do. Don't type these explanations! Just enter the statements presented in the special code font.

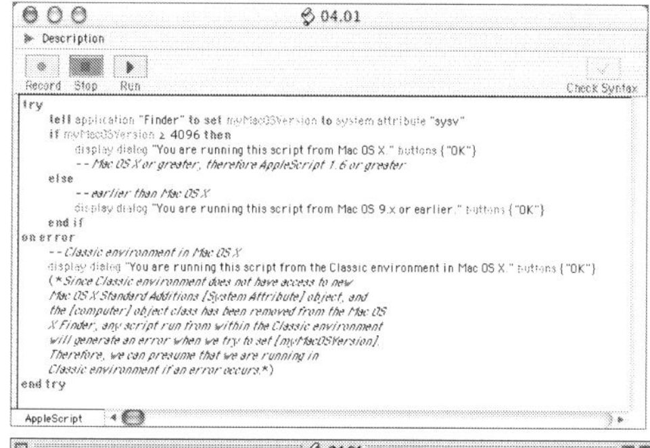

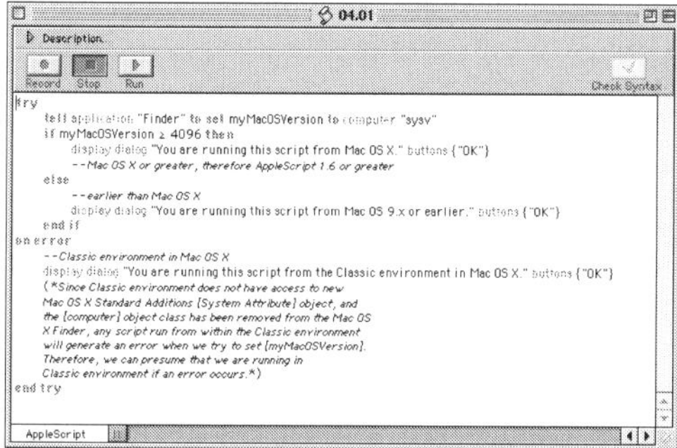

Figure 8 The same script in the Mac OS X Script Editor (top) and the Mac OS 9 Script Editor (bottom) shows that the only difference is the Aqua interface.

Table 2

Standard AppleScript File Extensions in Mac OS X

Extension	File Description
.scpt	Compiled script
.applescript	Uncompiled text-only script
.app	Applets and droplets
.osax	Mac OS X Scripting Addition
.asdictionary	Mac OS X application dictionary file

What Is the Same About AppleScript in Mac OS X

The AppleScript engineering team at Apple has done an amazing job of making AppleScript consistent between Mac OS X and earlier versions of the Mac OS. Generally, any scripts you create should operate the same way whether you run them in Mac OS X 10.1, in Mac OS 9.2.1, or in the Classic environment of Mac OS X.

Apple has done their best to synchronize AppleScript in both Mac OS X 10.1 and Mac OS 9.2.1. This is not to say that the language in both operating systems is identical; many differences exist between the AppleScript language in Mac OS X 10.1 and Mac OS 9.2.1. Here, in detail, are some of the differences:

Script Editor

Apple has kept the functionality of the Mac OS X 10.1 and Mac OS 9.2.1 versions of Script Editor identical. **Figure 8** compares the Mac OS 9 and Mac OS X Script Editor windows, showing that the only difference is the Aqua interface.

Mac OS 9.2.1 Scripting Additions

You can still use older Mac OS 9.2.1-compatible Scripting Additions in Mac OS X 10.1. See "Scripting Additions in Mac OS X" later in this chapter for details on using old additions in your Mac OS X scripts.

Saved script file types

Script Editor in Mac OS X 10.1 saves compiled scripts, text-only scripts, applets, and droplets with traditional Mac OS 9-compatible file types and icons. It also recognizes a new series of file extensions for each kind of script file to operate with Mac OS X's support for file extensions. See **Table 2** for a reference to the standard AppleScript file extensions.

Scriptable applications

In Mac OS X, AppleScript works with applications created for Mac OS X as well as with Classic applications. You can write a single script in Mac OS X that controls applications running in the Classic environment and in Mac OS X applications. Do note that the Mac OS X Finder, although similar to the Mac OS 9 version, has different capabilities and, therefore, has a different AppleScript dictionary.

File paths

In AppleScript 1.7 for both Mac OS X and Mac OS 9.2.1, file paths are delimited by colons (:). This delimiter remains the same for compatibility in Mac OS X, even though true file paths in Mac OS X are delimited by a forward slash (/).

Full Unicode support

AppleScript in both Mac OS X and Mac OS 9.2.1 supports all standard text operations with Unicode data, including comparisons and concatenation.

Bugs squashed

AppleScript in both versions of the Mac OS includes numerous bug fixes. These fixes include the prevention of a crash on **middle of {}**, proper error generation on accessing **item 0** of a list, and proper Keychain support in **mount volume**.

Program linking

Mac OS X 10.1, with its new Internet Services capabilities, supports many forms of program linking, so your scripts can target applications on Mac OS 9, Mac OS X, and even remote machines.

Scripted Internet connections

You can script connecting to the Internet. The Internet-connection functions in Mac OS 9's Network Setup Scripting have been replaced in Mac OS X by the Internet Connect application.

Flattened Script Files Supported in Mac OS X

Mac OS X supports the storage of compiled scripts in the data fork of a file, instead of relying on a resource fork. This feature is beneficial when you're transmitting a script over the Internet for execution locally. Now you can transmit a compiled script without encoding or BinHexing it.

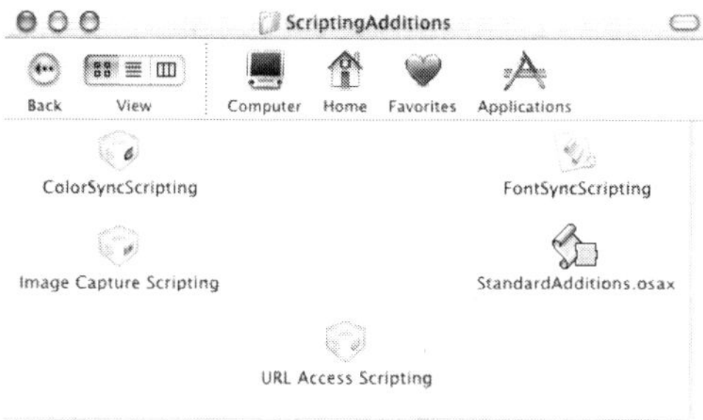

Figure 9 The system's ScriptingAdditions folder contains Apple-installed Scripting Additions.

What Is Different About AppleScript in Mac OS X

Now, for the strong of heart, the news about what has changed in AppleScript 1.7 for Mac OS X. Because Mac OS X is a new operating system with radically different underpinnings from those of Mac OS 9.2.1, AppleScript needed to change in Mac OS X to accommodate the new OS's functionalities and requirements. Because of the differences between AppleScript in Mac OS X and Mac OS 9.2.1, you sometimes will need to include code in your own scripts to check the version of AppleScript. See "Detecting the Current Versions of AppleScript and Mac OS" later in this chapter for a useful version-detection script.

Here are the differences between Mac OS X and Mac OS 9.2.1:

Placement of Scripting Additions in the file system

Mac OS X has changed the way Scripting Additions are stored and accessed. Instead of using a single Scripting Additions folder, Mac OS X has multiple directories where you can place Scripting Additions for access. System-installed additions are placed in /System/Library/ScriptingAdditions/. You cannot add any files to this directory, which is reserved for Apple's use. **Figure 9** shows all the system-installed Scripting Additions in Mac OS 10.1. See "Scripting Additions in Mac OS X" later in this chapter for more information.

Native Mac OS X Scripting Additions

Mac OS 9.2.1 Scripting Additions themselves must be rewritten to work natively in Mac OS X, although a Mac OS X script can access these additions through the Classic environment. See "Scripting Additions in Mac OS X" later in this chapter for more information.

Location of Scripts folder

In Mac OS X, each user can have a Scripts folder located at ~/Library/Scripts/ (~ is the home directory). The Script Runner application gives you access to compiled scripts saved in your Scripts folder. See "Advantages of Script Runner" for more information.

File extensions

Mac OS X supports the use of file extensions to indicate file type. One major impact of this change is that the **info for** command can now return a null value for the **file type** property of a file, because Mac OS 9 file types are optional in Mac OS X. Script Editor supports the file extension convention along with Classic file types for script and Scripting Addition files, so a set of standard file extensions is used for script files. Refer to **Table 2** for a complete list.

The Finder

Yes, Virginia, there is a Finder in Mac OS X 10.1. This Finder does many of the things that the venerable Mac OS 9 Finder did—but not all of them. You may need to change scripts written for the Mac OS 9 Finder to work in Mac OS X. The **computer** class, for example, has been removed from the Finder's dictionary and replaced by the new **System Attribute** command in the Standard Additions OSAX. Some commands remain in the Finder 10.1 dictionary but actually are carried out by other applications. **Figure 10** shows an example of some of the terminology in the new Mac OS X 10.1 Finder Legacy Suite.

Figure 10 The Finder's dictionary in Mac OS X 10.1 includes the Legacy suite.

WHAT'S DIFFERENT

Table 3

Scriptable Mac OS 9 System Components Not in Mac OS X

Component	Comment
AirPort Scripting	Available for Mac OS 9.2.1 in AirPort 1.3 upgrade
Apple Data Detectors	Not available
Apple Menu Options	Not available
Application Switcher	Not available
ColorSync	Provided as ColorSyncScripting application addition
Desktop Printing Manager	Print Center has some scriptability in version 10.1 of Mac OS X
File Exchange	Not available
File Sharing	Not available
FileSharing Commands	File sharing can be started from the command line
Folder Actions	Not available
FontSync Extension	Provided as the FontSynScripting application addition
FontSync	Provided as the FontSynScripting application addition
Keyboard Addition	No scripting access to these functions
Keychain Scripting	No scripting access to these functions
Location Manager	Not available
Memory	Not available
MonitorDepth	Use QuickTime Player for similar functionality
Mouse	Not available
Network Setup Scripting	Some functions can be performed from Internet Connect or the command line
Sound Scripting	No scripting access to these functions
Speech Listener	Not available
Startup Disk	Not available

Scriptable operating system components

Mac OS X has no control panels, extensions, or many other of the scriptable operating-system components you grew used to in Mac OS 9. The new System Preferences application is not scriptable. Network Setup Scripting is not available; neither is the scriptable Desktop Printing Manager. Expect to see more Mac OS X system components gain AppleScript support in coming releases. Until then, you'll need to find other ways of scripting the operating system.

Several Mac OS X Scripting Additions are already available to offer AppleScript scripts access to the Unix command line to execute shell commands. For now, these additions are your only recourse for scripting many OS settings. **Table 3** shows a partial list of scriptable Mac OS 9 system components that are no longer available in Mac OS X.

Launching script applets at startup

The Mac OS 9 Startup Items folder does not exist in Mac OS X. Use the Login pane of the System Preferences application to add your applet to the Login Items tab. **Figure 11** shows the Login Items tab.

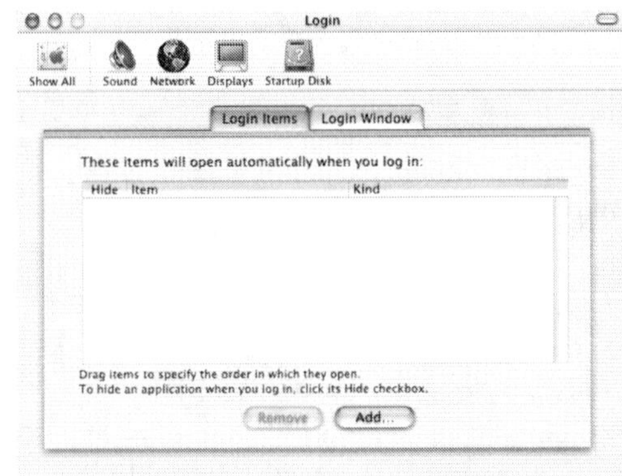

Figure 11 The Login preferences pane includes the Login Items tab. This tab is where you add and remove items that you want to open at startup, including scripts and applications.

Access to Unix from AppleScript (and vice versa)

Mac OS X is based on Unix and gives you a command line from which you can execute many powerful built-in system utility programs. Mac OS X provides a way for you to run scripts from the command line. Third-party developers have already released Mac OS X Scripting Additions that provide the means to access the Unix command line. See "Using a Scripting Addition or Terminal to Access Unix Commands" later in this chapter for more information.

Toolbar scripts instead of folder-action scripts

The Mac OS X 10.1 Finder does not support folder actions, although the Folder Action suite remains in the Standard Additions Scripting Addition. Instead, Finder 10.1 lets you drag script applets and droplets into the toolbar.

Print Center

Desktop Printers are gone, but Print Center supports basic scripting. Printers and their jobs can be accessed via script.

Program linking SOAP and XML-RPC servers with Internet Services

The advanced capabilities of remote Web services are available to your AppleScripts for free in Mac OS X 10.1.

TextEdit

SimpleText stays back in Mac OS 9.2.1, and Mac OS X 10.1 gets a scriptable text editor: TextEdit. Mac OS X comes with a very scriptable text editor that support plain-text and Rich Text (RTF) formats.

AppleScript support in Cocoa

Cocoa applications have built-in AppleScript support. Because this support is standard, scripting behavior and limitations typically are the same across Cocoa applications.

Changes in the item class

The Finder in Mac OS X 10.1 can access invisible Mac OS X system directories only with the **item** class. For example:

```
tell application "Finder" to set myRef to item "etc"¬
of the startup disk as alias
```

More Finder changes

The Finder in Mac OS X 10.1 behaves differently from the Mac OS 9 Finder. The following line will not work in Mac OS X but does in Mac OS 9:

```
tell application "Finder" to set myRef to move ¬
myAlias to Trash
```

Full-power development with AppleScript Studio

With AppleScript Studio, scripters can use AppleScript in Apple's complete development suite: Interface Builder and Project Builder.

Detecting the Current Versions of AppleScript & Mac OS

In the world of Mac OS X, your script may run in several environments:

- AppleScript in Mac OS X
- AppleScript in the Mac OS X Classic environment
- AppleScript in Mac OS 9.2.1 or earlier

Because the dictionaries of the Finder and many system components are different between Mac OS X and Mac OS 9.2.1, your script may need to know which environment it is running in. **Script 1** demonstrates a handler that determines whether it is running in Mac OS X, the Classic environment in Mac OS X, or Mac OS 9.2.1 or earlier.

Figures 12, **13**, and **14** show the dialog box displayed by the script in each environment.

To determine whether a script is running in Mac OS X, Classic or Mac OS 9.2.1

Type the following statements into the Script Editor window, pressing Return after each one. (An explanation appears after each statement that requires one.)

```
try
```

You start with a **try** statement to catch any errors. This statement is particularly useful in this script, because the next line will generate an error in the Classic environment.

```
tell application "Finder" to set ¬
myMacOSVersion to computer "sysv"
```

Now you ask either Mac OS 9.2.1 or Mac OS X 10.1 for the OS version.

Script 1 This script determines whether it is running in Mac OS X, Mac OS 9, or the Classic environment.

script

```
try
  tell application "Finder" to set ¬
  myMacOSVersion to computer "sysv"
  if myMacOSVersion ≥ 4096 then
    display dialog "You are running this script ¬
    from Mac OS X." buttons {"OK"}
  else
    display dialog "You are running this script ¬
    from Mac OS 9.x or earlier." ¬
    buttons {"OK"}
  end if
on error
  display dialog "You are running this script ¬
  from the Classic environment in Mac OS X." ¬
  buttons {"OK"}
end try
```

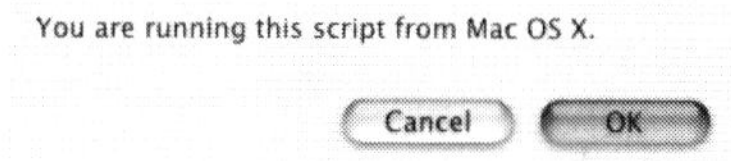
You are running this script from Mac OS X.
Cancel
OK

Figure 12 The script shows this dialog when it detects that it is running in Mac OS X.

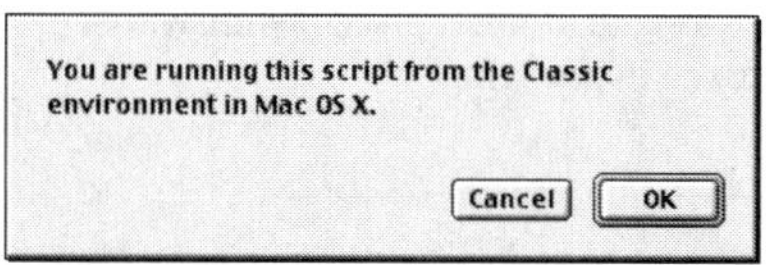
You are running this script from the Classic environment in Mac OS X.
Cancel
OK

Figure 13 The script shows this dialog when it detects that it is running in the Classic environment in Mac OS X.

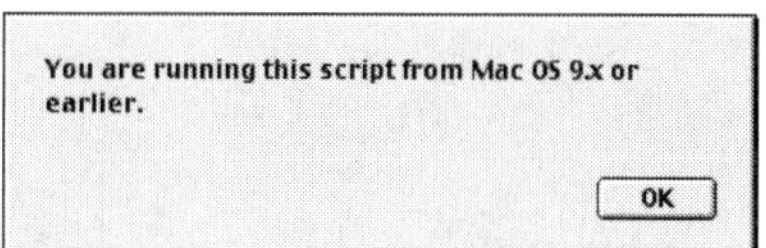
You are running this script from Mac OS 9.x or earlier.
OK

Figure 14 The script shows this dialog when it detects that it is running in Mac OS 9 or earlier.

```
if myMacOSVersion ≥ 4096 then
```

If the value returned is greater than or equal to 4096, you are in Mac OS X. If the value is greater than or equal to 4112, you are in Mac OS X version 10.1 or later.

```
display dialog "You are running this script ¬
from Mac OS X." buttons {"OK"}
```

You let the user know that the script is running in Mac OS X or later and therefore is using AppleScript 1.7 or later.

```
else
```

If the value is less than 4096, you're in Mac OS 9 or earlier.

```
display dialog "You are running this script ¬
from Mac OS 9.x or earlier." buttons {"OK"}
end if
```

A dialog announces the OS used.

```
on error
display dialog "You are running this script ¬
from the Classic environment in Mac OS X." ¬
buttons {"OK"}
end try
```

Because the Classic environment does not have access to the new Mac OS X Standard Additions **System Attribute** object, and because the **computer** object class has been removed from the Mac OS X Finder, any script run from within the Classic environment will generate an error when you try to set **myMacOSVersion**. Therefore, you can presume that you are running in Classic environment if an error occurs.

Scripting Additions in Mac OS X

You should know some basic realities about Scripting Additions in Mac OS X:

- Scripting additions need to be designed to work natively with Mac OS X.
- Scripting additions can be stored in several places on a Mac OS X machine, providing different user access levels.
- Older Scripting Additions will work only through the Classic environment. **Script 2** demonstrates how to use a Classic scripting addition from Mac OS X.

Where you place Scripting Additions determines who can access them:

- Place Scripting Additions that you want to add for all users of a specific machine in /Library/ScriptingAdditions/.
- Place Scripting Additions that you want to add for a single user in that user's own Library folder (~/Library/ScriptingAdditions, in which ~ is the user's home directory inside of /Users/).

Script 3 demonstrates how to access the dictionaries of installed Classic scripting additions. To do so, you need to enclose the Classic Scripting Addition commands inside a tell block targeting a Classic application. You will also use the Classic Script Editor and the Mac OS X Script Editor to complete the scripting as well as the Acme Script Widgets 2.5.2 Scripting Addition.

Script 2 This handler contains the Classic Scripting Addition commands within a tell statement targeting the Classic application Apple Guide. Enter this part in the Classic Script Editor.

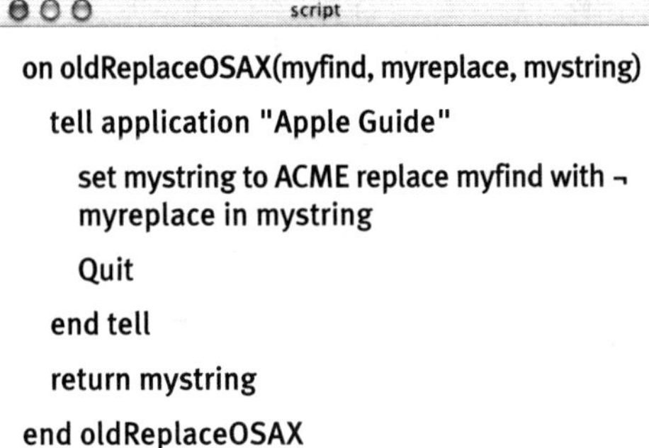


```
on oldReplaceOSAX(myfind, myreplace, mystring)
  tell application "Apple Guide"
    set mystring to ACME replace myfind with ¬
    myreplace in mystring
    Quit
  end tell
  return mystring
end oldReplaceOSAX
```

SCRIPTING ADDITIONS

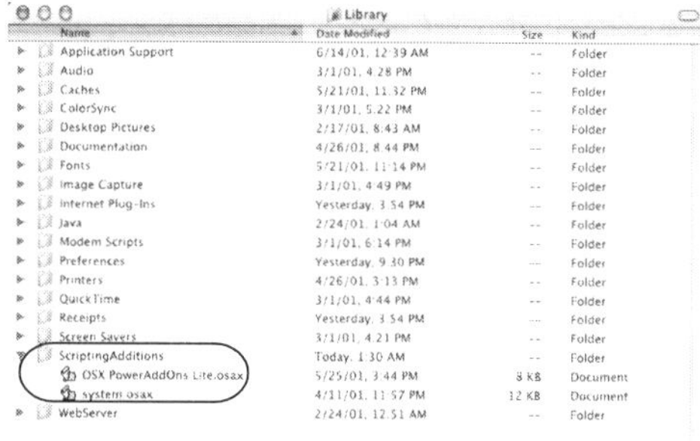

Figure 15 The local machine's ScriptingAdditions folder contains Scripting Additions that are available to all users.

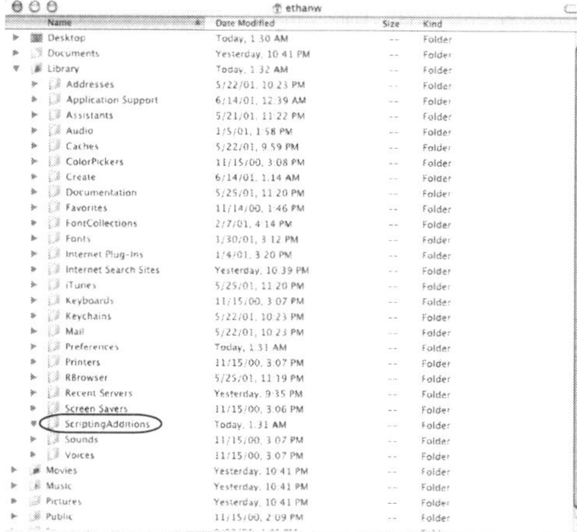

Figure 16 An individual user's ScriptingAdditions folder, shown here without any contents.

To add a Mac OS X Scripting Addition that all users can access

1. Open the Library folder.
2. If a folder named ScriptingAdditions does not exist, create it.
3. Drag the new Mac OS X Scripting Addition into the ScriptingAdditions folder.

   Figure 15 shows the expanded folder with two additions.

To add a Mac OS X Scripting Addition that a single user can access

1. Open the user's home folder.
2. Open the Library folder inside the user's home folder.
3. If a folder named ScriptingAdditions does not exist, create it.
4. Drag one ore more Mac OS X Scripting Additions into the folder.

   Figure 16 shows the expanded folder with no Scripting Additions in it.

To use Classic Scripting Addition commands from a Mac OS X script

1. Type the following statements into the Classic Script Editor, pressing Return after each one. (An explanation appears after each statement that requires one.)

```
on oldReplaceOSAX(myfind, myreplace, ¬
mystring)
```

Start the handler in the Classic Script Editor while running Mac OS X or Mac OS 9 to get access to the Scripting Addition's dictionary terminology. If you omit this step, you'll have to write raw Apple Event codes (**Figure 17**), because the Mac OS X Script Editor does not have ready access to the terminology of Classic additions.

This handler has three values passed to it. In this case, this handler receives a string to search for, a string to replace the search string with, and the full string to search and return modified.

```
tell application "Apple Guide"
```

You need to put your Scripting Addition command inside a **tell** block that addresses a Classic application to get access to the Classic addition's command. I use Apple Guide because it is a faceless Classic application that launches quickly. Be sure to launch the Classic environment before using any scripts that call Classic applications or additions.

```
set mystring to ACME replace myfind with ¬
myreplace in mystring
```

Now the **mystring** variable is assigned to the result of the Acme Script Widgets Scripting Addition command **ACME replace**, which does the work for you.

```
Quit
end tell
```

You quit Apple Guide.

Script 3 Uses handler written to call Classic Scripting Addition from Mac OS X. Add the main part of the script in the Mac OS X Script Editor and run it from there.

```
set myInput to text returned of ¬
(display dialog "Input string" default answer ¬
"A's become B's")
set myOutput to oldReplaceOSAX("A", "B", ¬
myInput)
display dialog myOutput
on oldReplaceOSAX(myfind, myreplace, ¬
mystring)
  tell application "Apple Guide"
    set mystring to ACME replace myfind with ¬
    myreplace in mystring
    Quit
  end tell
return mystring
end oldReplaceOSAX
```

Using Acme Script Widgets

This script requires the Scripting Addition Acme Script Widgets (Acme Technologies; www.acmetech.com). You must have Acme Script Widgets installed in your Scripting-Additions folder for this script to work.

Acme Script Widgets is shareware and costs $29 for a single-user license.

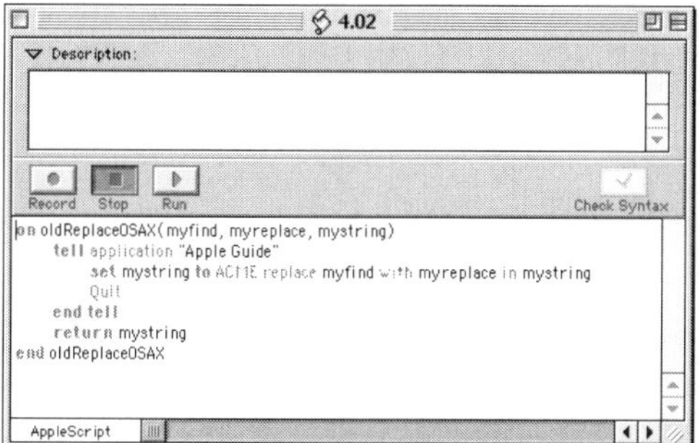

Figure 17 The handler shown in this window, written in the Classic Script Editor, calls a Classic Scripting Addition command, ACME replace.

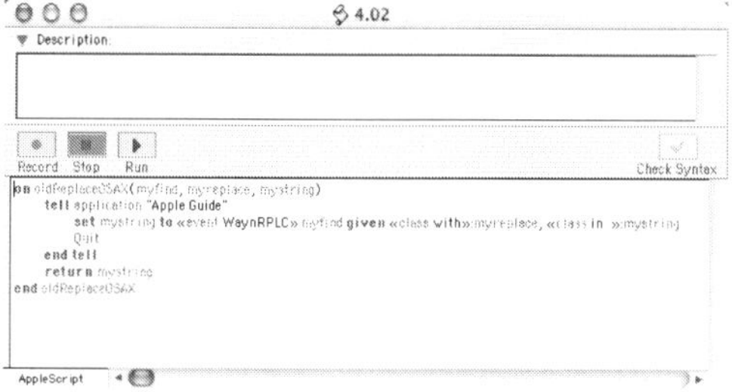

Figure 18 The Classic Scripting Addition command, ACME replace, is displayed as Apple Event codes in the Mac OS X Script Editor because it cannot access the terminology of Classic additions.

Figure 19 The Mac OS X script prints the user to enter a string to be modified by the Classic addition's string replacement command.

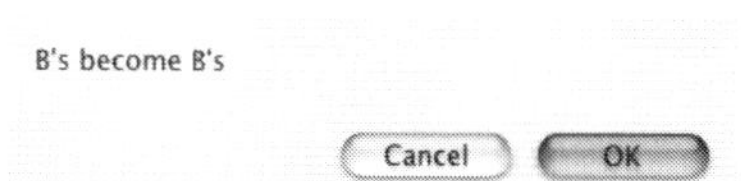

Figure 20 The Mac OS X script shows the result of the ACME replace command from the Classic Scripting Addition ACME Script Widgets.

return mystring

end oldReplaceOSAX

The handler returns the updated string value in the **mystring** variable before ending.

2. When you are done, your script should look like the one in **Figure 18**. Save the script in the Classic Script Editor and close it before opening it the Mac OS X Script Editor and continuing. (Notice in the script window that the Mac OS X Script Editor displays the raw Apple Event codes for the Classic Scripting Addition command.)

set myInput to text returned of ¬
(display dialog "Input string" default answer ¬
"A's become B's")

You add some code in the Mac OS X Script Editor. In this example, prompt the user for a string to be modified.

set myOutput to oldReplaceOSAX("A", "B", ¬
myInput)

Next, the handler that invokes the Classic Scripting Addition is called. The returned value is stored in the **myOutput** variable.

display dialog myOutput

A dialog box displays the updated text.

3. Run this script from the Mac OS X Script Editor to see screens like **Figures 19** and **20**.

Life with File Suffixes & Path Delimiters

The file system itself has changed in Mac OS X. The concept of domains relates to the file system and user permissions. The **path to** command has been updated to include a new **from** modifier that lets you request paths to special folders based on the domain, so that you can get file paths for the ScriptingAdditions folder for a user, for the whole machine, or for the system. **Figure 21** shows the dictionary entry for the Standard Additions **path to** command.

The new world of Mac OS X includes a different kind of file path from the one you've all grown used to: the Unix, or *Posix*, file path with forward slash (/) delimiters (for example, /System/Library). In AppleScript, however, the new file paths are not used; the traditional Macintosh file paths with colon (:) delimiters are still used for aliases and file specifications. **Script 4** shows how to get Posix file paths for a file by using the system Scripting Addition for Mac OS X.

Script 4 The Posix and Mac file paths to a user-selected file. Requires the free third-party System Scripting Addition for Mac OS X.

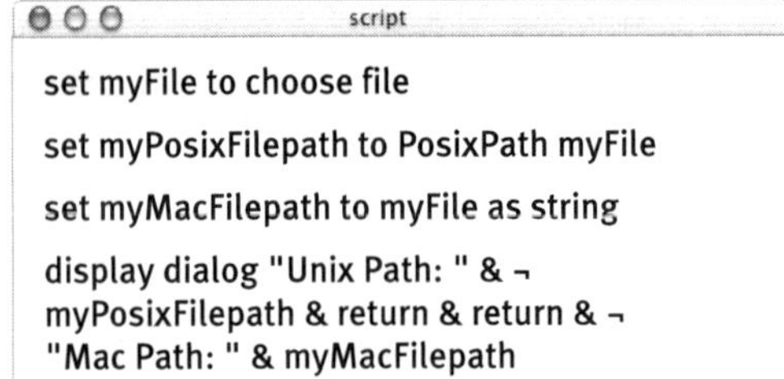

```
set myFile to choose file
set myPosixFilepath to PosixPath myFile
set myMacFilepath to myFile as string
display dialog "Unix Path: " & ¬
myPosixFilepath & return & return & ¬
"Mac Path: " & myMacFilepath
```

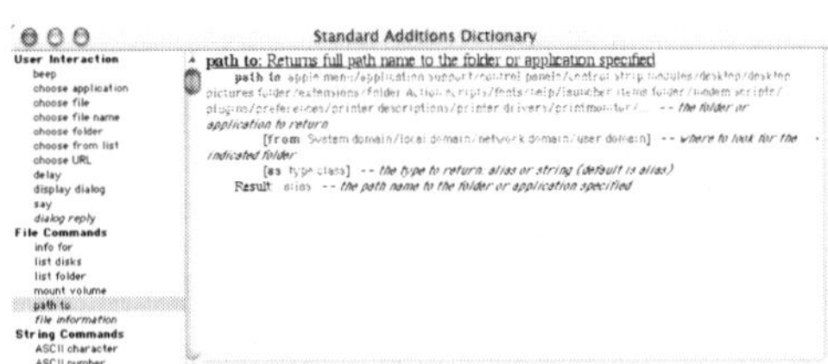

Figure 21 The Mac OS X Standard Additions path to command's terminology includes a from modifier to allow you to access the paths of special folders in different user domains.

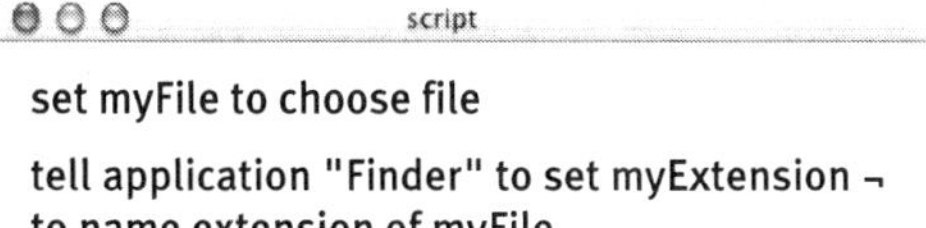

Figure 22 The script displays this dialog, showing the Posix file path and the Mac file path for the file chosen by the user.

Script 5 This script shows how easy it is to access the file extension of a file from the Finder.

```
set myFile to choose file
tell application "Finder" to set myExtension ¬
to name extension of myFile
display dialog myExtension
```

Using the System Scripting Addition

The freeware System Scripting Addition was created by Hideaki Iimori (www.bekkoame.ne.jp/~iimori/).

To get the Posix file path for a file selected by the user

Type the following statements into the Script Editor window, pressing Return after each one. (An explanation appears after each statement that requires one.)

set myFile to choose file

Start by prompting the user to select a file, and store a reference to the file in the **myFile** variable.

set myPosixFilepath to PosixPath myFile

Next, use the system Scripting Addition command **PosixPath** to convert the alias reference stored in the **myFile** variable.You need to have installed the system.osax Scripting Addition file in ~/Library/ScriptingAdditions/ or /Library/ScriptingAdditions/ before starting.

set myMacFilepath to myFile as string

Now convert the file alias to a string.

display dialog "Unix Path: " & ¬
myPosixFilepath & return & return & ¬
"Mac Path: " & myMacFilepath
Finally, show both Posix and Mac file paths to the same file in a dialog. Figure 22 shows a sample.

✔ Tips

- When using the **info for** command, your scripts need to be ready to encounter missing file types, because Mac OS X doesn't require each file to have a creator and file type. File extensions such as .jpg and .txt are used in Mac OS X in place of file types and creator codes.
- In Finder 10.1, you can access file extension attributes by using the **name extension** property of an item. **Script 5** demonstrates how easy it is to access the file extension of a file from the Finder.

Scripting Addition Global Context Supported in Mac OS X 10.1

In versions of Mac OS X before 10.1, terms that belonged to scripting additions were not handled within **tell** blocks as expected. In Mac OS X 10.1, terms that belong to Scripting Additions are once again handled by most applications inside **tell** blocks, so simple behaviors such as displaying a dialog within a scriptable application will work in Mac OS X 10.1 as it does in Mac OS 9. Because of this, you should upgrade to Mac OS X version 10.1.

Script 6 provides a simple demonstration of how user interaction dialog boxes are shown in the script's window layer, not the frontmost application in versions of Mac OS X before 10.1.

Script 6 This simple script demonstrates how Scripting Addition commands are run in the context of the script itself and not in applications when run in Mac OS X versions before 10.1

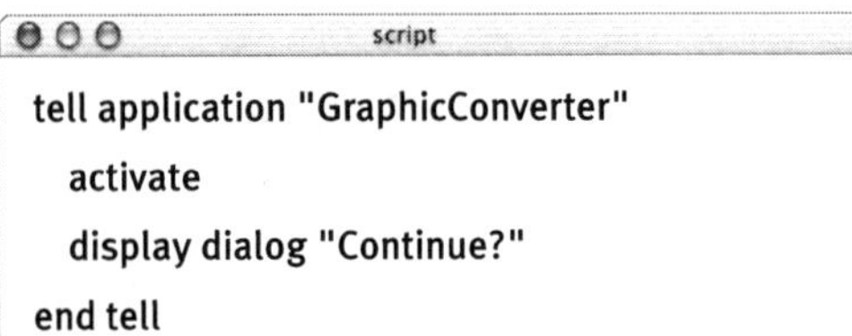
script
tell application "GraphicConverter"
activate
display dialog "Continue?"
end tell

To see user-interaction dialogs behind the frontmost application in versions of Mac OS X before 10.1

1. Type the following statements into the Script Editor window, pressing Return after each one. (An explanation appears after the statements.)

   ```
   tell application "GraphicConverter"
   activate
   display dialog "Continue?"
   end tell
   ```

   This script launches an application and brings it to the front before invoking the display dialog command, which will show up behind the application's windows.

2. Run this script from the Mac OS X Script Editor in a version of Mac OS X prior to 10.1 to see how the dialog comes up in the Script Editor behind the GraphicConverter program (**Figure 23**).

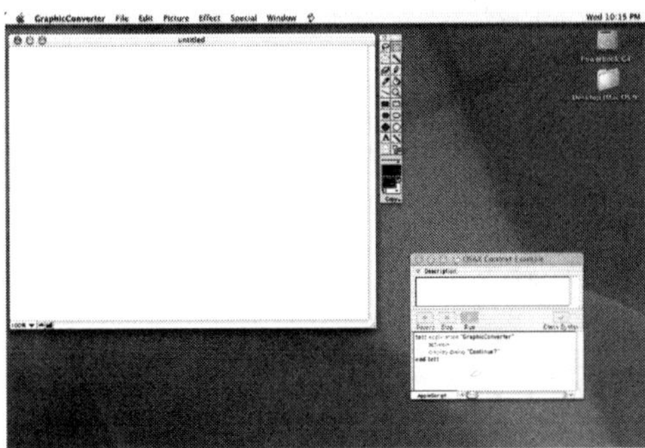

Figure 23 The script is running from Script Editor and waiting to be brought to the front by the user so that the dialog can be shown.

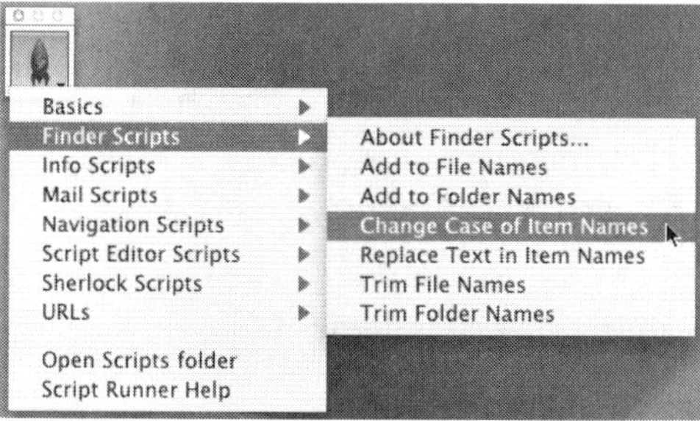

Figure 24 The Script Runner palette with a script selected from the menu.

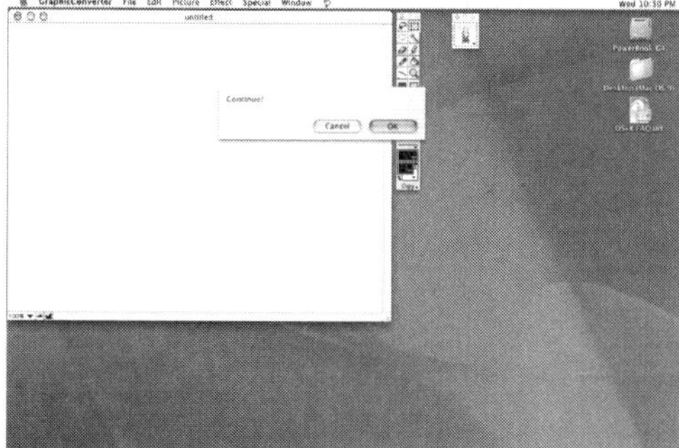

Figure 25 A script launched from Script Runner runs in front of all applications.

Using Script Runner & ScriptMenu

Mac OS X 10.1 provides two useful AppleScript user interface enhancements: Script Runner and ScriptMenu. **Figure 24** shows the Script Runner palette opened by the user. Script Runner has permanent frontmost status in Mac OS X, so any script run from Script Runner runs front of whatever application is currently frontmost. **Figure 25** shows a script's dialog floating on top of the GraphicConverter application, thanks to Script Runner. Script Runner can be found in the AppleScript folder inside your Applications folder (**Figure 1**).

In addition to Script Runner's palette, Mac OS X 10.1 gives you the ScriptMenu, which replaces the functionality provided in Mac OS 9 by Leonard Rosenthol's OSA Menu extension. To use ScriptMenu, download it from Apple's AppleScript site at www.apple.com/applescript. Installing ScriptMenu is easy: Simply drag the ScriptMenu.menu file onto your menu bar in the Finder. The Script Menu icon will appear immediately. It shows all the scripts contained in both the /Library/Scripts folder and the user's ~/Library/Script folder. ScriptMenu displays and runs AppleScript scripts, as well as Perl and shell scripts.

Using a Scripting Addition or Terminal to Access Unix Commands

Several free and shareware Scripting Additions for Mac OS X give your scripts access to the Unix command line. In this section, you will explore one the System scripting addition (**system.osax**) and look at some basic uses of the special **system** command that the Scripting Addition provides. This command provides interactive access to Unix command-line commands, with Unix-command-generated output returned to the script.

Script 7 uses the Unix **uptime** command to display interesting status information about the local machine. **Script 8** uses the Unix **nslookup** command to provide domain name service information for machine host names, such as www.apple.com.

To display system statistics from the Unix uptime command

Type the following statements into the Script Editor window, pressing Return after each one. (An explanation appears after each statement that requires one.)

set mySystemOnStats to system "uptime"

Start by assigning the output of the Unix **uptime** command to your AppleScript variable **mySystemOnStats**.

say mySystemOnStats

Next, have the system speak the output text from **uptime**.

display dialog mySystemOnStats

Finish by displaying the output in a dialog. **Figure 26** shows an example.

Script 7 This script uses the System OSAX to get system statistics from the Unix uptime command, speak them, and display them to the user.

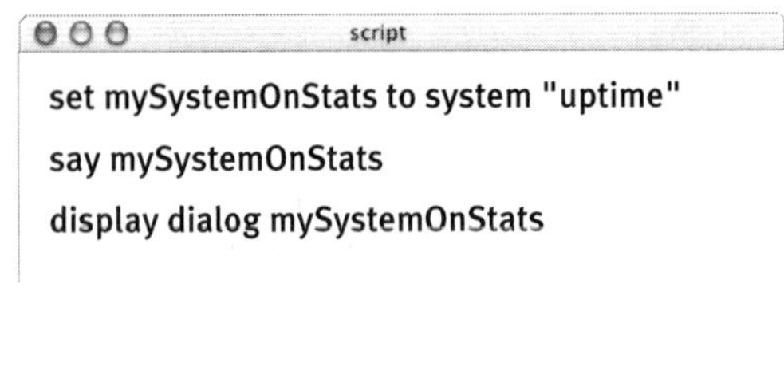

```
set mySystemOnStats to system "uptime"
say mySystemOnStats
display dialog mySystemOnStats
```

10:36PM up 11:23, 1 user, load averages: 0.05, 0.17, 0.14

Cancel OK

Figure 26 The result of the Unix uptime command.

Script 8 The System OSAX resolves host names with the Unix nslookup command.

```
script

set myHostname to text returned of ¬
(display dialog "Enter hostname to lookup:" ¬
default answer "www.apple.com")
if myHostname ≠ "" then
    set myDNSResults to ¬
    (system "nslookup " & myHostname)
    display dialog paragraph 5 of ¬
    myDNSResults & return & paragraph 6 ¬
    of myDNSResults
end if
```

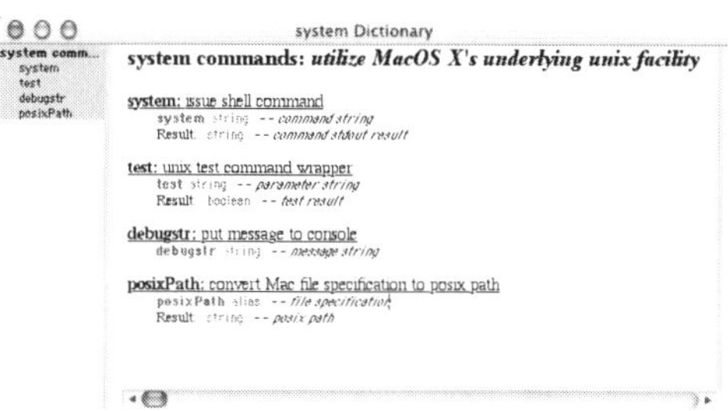

Figure 27 The System command's definition.

Scripting the Terminal Application in Mac OS X 10.1

The Terminal application, located in your Utilities folder, supports basic scripting in version 10.1 of Mac OS X. Try this sample script:

```
tell application "Terminal" to do script with ¬
command "date"
```

To resolve the IP address of a host name with the Unix nslookup command

Type the following statements into the Script Editor window, pressing Return after each one. (An explanation appears after each statement that requires one.)

```
set myHostname to text returned of ¬
(display dialog "Enter hostname to lookup:" ¬
default answer "www.apple.com")
```

Start by prompting the user to enter a host name to look up. A default value is shown.

```
if myHostname ≠ "" then
```

If the user has entered anything, the script continues execution.

```
set myDNSResults to ¬
(system "nslookup " & myHostname)
```

Using the **system** command from the System Scripting Addition, you invoke the Unix **nslookup** command, passing it the host name entered by the user. The result of the command is returned in the **myDNSResults** variable. **Figure 27** shows the **system** command's definition in the AppleScript dictionary of the System Scripting Addition.

```
display dialog paragraph 5 of ¬
myDNSResults & return & paragraph 6 ¬
of myDNSResults
end if
```

The IP address and host name of the response typically are in the fifth and sixth lines of the output returned from **nslookup**, so the script displays these two lines.

Scheduling Scripts with cron and osascript

Now that you have the power of Unix inside your operating system, you can take advantage of it. Mac OS X features some basic, but useful, Unix command-line commands that provide access to AppleScript from Unix. The commands include:

- **osascript** executes a compiled AppleScript file from the command line or **cron**.
- **osacompile** lets you create compiled scripts from text.
- **osalang** prints information about OSA languages.

You can run any of these commands directly from the Terminal application, or you can schedule the running of your own scripts by using the Unix **cron** utility and the **osascript** command.

✔ Tips

- The **osascript** command doesn't allow all compiled scripts to run without flaw. Scripts with user-interaction commands have context problems, such as dialogs staying behind all other open windows.
- While you're using the Terminal program, you can find out more about osascript, osacompile, osalang, and **cron** by typing **man** followed by the name of the command (for example, **man osascript**) and pressing Return (**Figure 28**).

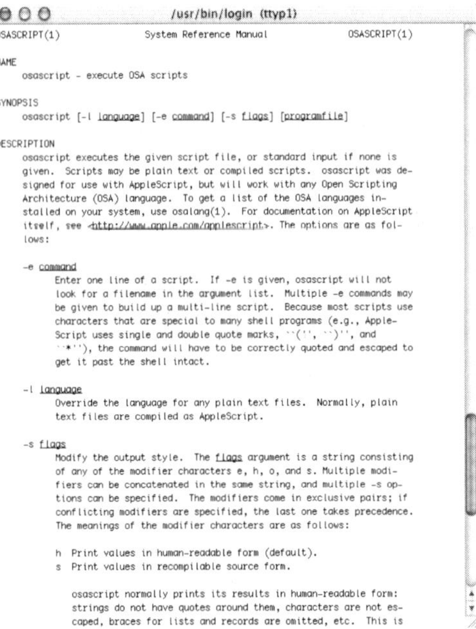

Figure 28 The man page entry for the Unix osascript command.

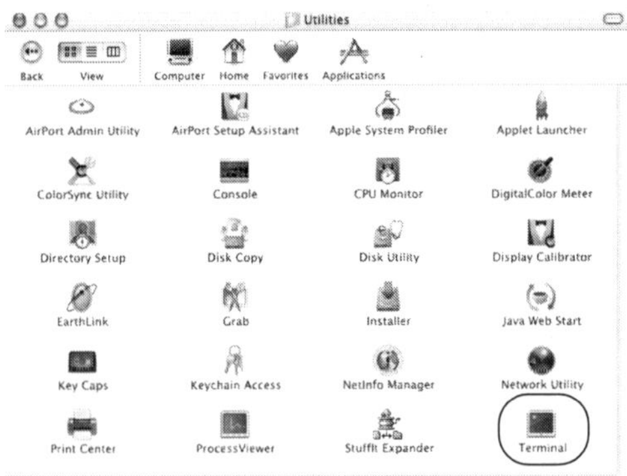

Figure 29 The Terminal application is inside the Utilities folder.

Figure 30 When you enter the first command into the Terminal window, it displays a Password prompt.

Figure 31 The pico editing session with the unedited /etc/crontab file displayed.

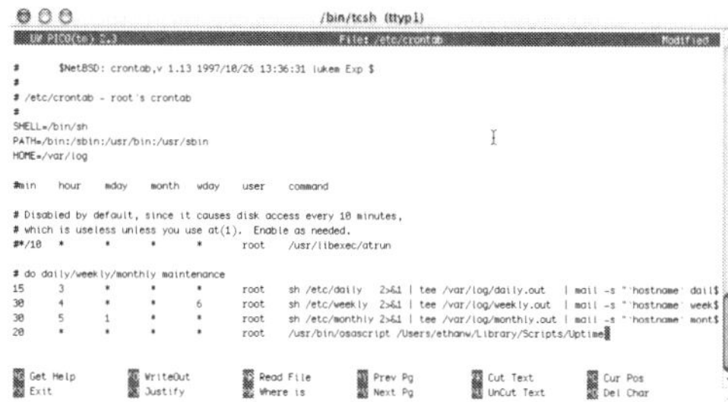

Figure 32 After editing the /etc/crontab file, it may look something like this.

To schedule a saved compiled script to run automatically every hour

1. Open the Terminal application. Terminal is located in the Utilities folder inside your Applications folder (**Figure 29**).
2. At the prompt in the open Terminal window, type **sudo pico /etc/crontab** and press Return. The system will prompt you to enter your password (**Figure 30**).
3. Enter the password, and press Return. The Terminal window should look like **Figure 31**. The **cron** configuration file, /etc/crontab, is open.
4. Use arrow keys to move the insertion point below the last line of the file.
5. Type the following to make your script run at 20 minutes past the hour, every hour:
   20Tab*****Tab*****Tab*****Tab*****Tab**root**Tab**/usr/bin/osascript**Tab
6. Enter the Posix path to the compiled script file that you want to run. In the example in **Figure 32**, this path is **/Users/ethanw/Library/Scripts/Uptime**.
7. Press Control X to exit.
8. When prompted, type **y** and press Return to save the modified /etc/crontab file.
9. Quit the Terminal program.

✖ Warning

- Modifying Unix system files such as /etc/crontab is serious business. Be careful that you don't delete any portion of the existing configuration file when you modify it.

Adding Scripts to the Finder's Toolbar

The Finder in Mac OS X 10.1 supports an innovative new user-interface feature for accessing AppleScript applets and droplets. This feature is called Toolbar Scripts by Apple. The name sums it up. You can drag any applet or droplet onto your Finder's toolbar to place it there and remove it by holding [⌘] and dragging it off the toolbar.

The functionality of Toolbar Scripts helps make up for Mac OS X's lack of folder action script support. Script 9 shows a sample Toolbar Script that archives the frontmost Finder folder, adding the user name and date.

✔ Tip

- I recommend that you keep all your Toolbar Scripts files in a common folder. I put mine in my Scripts folder. **Figure 33** shows an applet file in my Scripts folder and on my toolbar, ready to use. **Figure 34** shows what happens when the Finder can't find a Toolbar Script's original file.

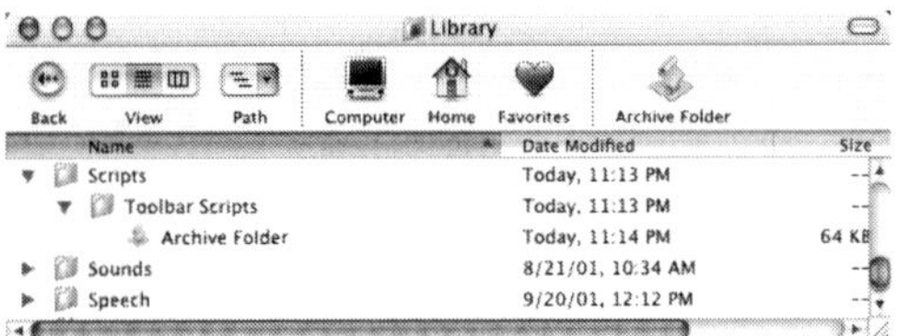

Figure 33 The Toolbar Scripts applet file Archive Folder appears in Scripts folder and on the toolbar, ready to use.

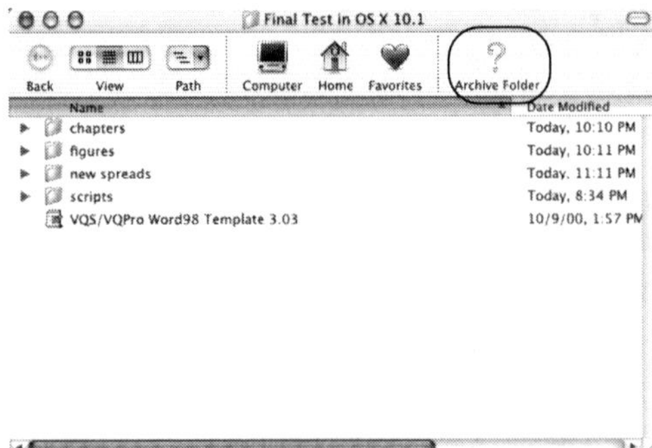

Figure 34 The Finder toolbar shows a question mark icon when a Toolbar Script's original file cannot be found.

Script 9 This script archives the frontmost Finder window in another folder.

```
script
on run
  set {myname, mypath} to frontWindowPath()
  if button returned of (display dialog ¬
  "Archive '" & myname & "'?") is "OK" then
    set myarchive to (choose folder with ¬
    prompt "Select folder to archive into")
    set myuser to characters 1 thru -2 of ¬
    (system "whoami") as string
    set mydate to year of (current date) & "-" ¬
    & getMonthNumber(current date) & "-" ¬
    & day of (current date) as string
    set mynewname to myname & "_" ¬
    & mydate & "_" & myuser
    tell application "Finder"
      set mynewarchive to duplicate alias ¬
      mypath to folder myarchive
      set name of mynewarchive to mynewname
    end tell
  end if
end run
on getMonthNumber(anydate)
  set mymonthnum to 0
  repeat with mymonth in {January, February, ¬
  March, April, May, June, July, August, ¬
  September, October, November, December}
    set mymonthnum to mymonthnum + 1
    if month of anydate is mymonth then ¬
    exit repeat
  end repeat
  return mymonthnum
end getMonthNumber
on frontWindowPath()
  tell application "Finder"
    set myfolderpath to target of ¬
    front Finder window as alias
    set myfoldername to name of myfolderpath
  end tell
  return {myfoldername, myfolderpath as string}
end frontWindowPath
```

To archive the frontmost Finder window's folder

Type the following statements into the Script Editor window, pressing Return after each one. (An explanation appears after each statement that requires one.)

```
on run
```

```
set {myname, mypath} to frontWindowPath()
```

The script starts by getting the name and path of the folder in the frontmost Finder window.

```
if button returned of (display dialog ¬
"Archive '" & myname & "'?") is "OK" then
```

The user is prompted to decide whether to archive the folder. If the user clicks the OK button, the following steps are executed.

```
set myarchive to (choose folder with ¬
prompt "Select folder to archive into")
```

Now the user chooses a folder in which to save the archived folder.

```
set myuser to characters 1 thru -2 of ¬
(system "whoami") as string
```

The script uses the System Scripting Additions **system** command to issue a Unix **whoami** command and return the current short user name.

```
set mydate to year of (current date) & "-" ¬
& getMonthNumber(current date) & "-" ¬
& day of (current date) as string
```

Now it is time to format a date string, using the **getMonthNumber** handler.

```
set mynewname to myname & "_" ¬
& mydate & "_" & myuser
```

Next, a new file name is assembled in the **mynewname** variable.

Continued on next page...

Continued from previous page.

```
tell application "Finder"
set mynewarchive to duplicate alias ¬
mypath to folder myarchive
set name of mynewarchive to mynewname
end tell
```

It's time to talk to the Finder and have it duplicate the frontmost Finder folder in the archive folder and rename the new folder.

```
end if
end run
```

The if statement is closed and the run handler ended.

```
on getMonthNumber(anydate)
set mymonthnum to 0
repeat with mymonth in {January, February, ¬
March, April, May, June, July, August, ¬
September, October, November, December}
set mymonthnum to mymonthnum + 1
if month of anydate is mymonth then ¬
exit repeat
end repeat
return mymonthnum
end getMonthNumber
```

This handler receives a date value and returns an integer matching the month of the date (3 for March, for example).

```
on frontWindowPath()
tell application "Finder"
set myfolderpath to target of ¬
front Finder window as alias
set myfoldername to name of myfolderpath
end tell
return {myfoldername, myfolderpath as string}
end frontWindowPath
```

This handler gets the path to the frontmost Finder window's folder and returns the name and path of the folder in a list.

Setting the Default Printer with Print Center

Mac OS X 10.1's Print Center provides access to all printers and jobs, including the default printer, known as current printer in Print Center's dictionary. **Script 10** lets the user choose a new default printer from a list of installed printers.

Figure 35 shows how Print Center's Printer List window looks on the Mac running the script. **Figure 36** shows the list displayed by **Script 10** when it prompts the user to select a new default printer.

Script 10 This script lets the user choose a new default printer from a list of installed printers.

```
tell application "Print Center"
  set myprinternames to name of every printer
  set mydefaultprinter to current printer
  set mydefaultprintername to ¬
  name of mydefaultprinter
end tell
set myprinter to (choose from list myprinternames ¬
with prompt "Set new default printer" default ¬
items {mydefaultprintername}) as string
try
  tell application "Print Center"
    repeat with i from 1 to count of items in ¬
    myprinternames
      if name of printer i = myprinter then
        set current printer to printer i
        exit repeat
      end if
    end repeat
    quit
  end tell
end try
```

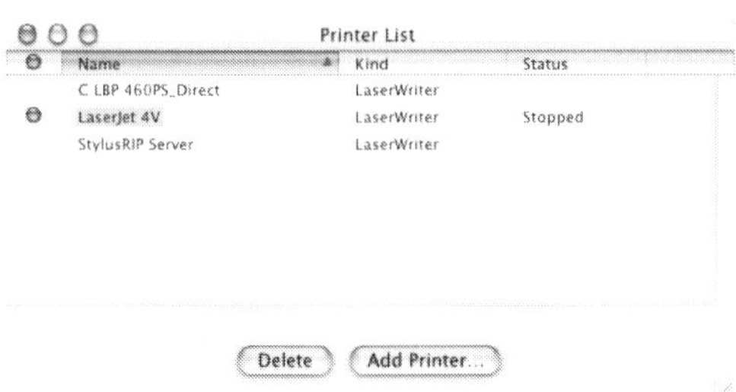

Figure 35 The Printer List window of Print Center displays all installed printers.

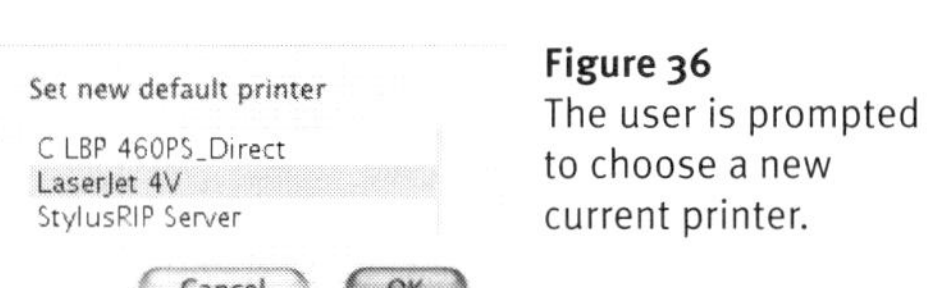

Figure 36 The user is prompted to choose a new current printer.

To change the current printer with Print Center

Type the following Statements into the Script Editor window, pressing Return after each one. (An explanation appears after each statement that requires one.)

tell application "Print Center"

set myprinternames to name of every printer

The script starts by getting a list that contains the name of every printer installed in Print Center.

set mydefaultprinter to current printer

Next, the default printer object is stored in **mydefaultprinter** for later use.

set mydefaultprintername to ¬
name of mydefaultprinter

end tell

The script retrieves the name of the default printer, using the printer object in **mydefaultprinter**.

Continued on next page...

Continued from previous page.

```
set myprinter to (choose from list myprinternames ¬
with prompt "Set new default printer" default ¬
items {mydefaultprintername}) as string
```

Prompt the user with a list of available printer names (**Figure 36**). The script preselects the current printer name with default items.

```
try
tell application "Print Center"
repeat with i from 1 to count of items in ¬
myprinternames
if name of printer i = myprinter then
set current printer to printer i
exit repeat
end if
end repeat
quit
end tell
end try
```

The script loops through all available printer names until the name matching the user selection is found. When the desired name is found, that printer is made the current printer by an index reference. Print Center quits when everything else finishes.

Accessing the World with Internet Services

Starting with AppleScript 1.7 in Mac OS X 10.1, scripts have access to the growing world of Web-based services on the Internet. Two new functions, **call soap** and **call xmlrpc**, give AppleScript scripts the capability to access Perl scripts and database CGIs that provide XML-RPC or SOAP gateways.

XML-RPC is a protocol that uses XML to make remote procedure HTTP calls over the Internet. *SOAP* (Simple Object Access Protocol) is a protocol designed for exchanging information in a distributed environment, in which a server may consist of a hierarchy of objects with methods and properties.

To begin using these new functions, you should be familiar with XML-RPC and SOAP. The XML-RPC specification is described at www.xmlrpc.com/spec. The SOAP specification is available at www.w3.org/TR. Additional references can be found in **Table 4**.

Script 11 demonstrates a spelling check using a Web-based spelling checker. **Script 12** performs an English-to-Spanish translation using a Web-based translation utility.

Table 4

Web Sites About XML-RPC and SOAP

Site	URL
Apple's Internet Services Site	http://developer.apple.com/techpubs/macosx/Carbon/interapplicationcomm/soapXMLRPC/
Apache SOAP Site	http://xml.apache.org/soap/
IBM Web Services	http://xml.apache.org/soap/
UserLand's XML-RPC Site	http://www.xmlrpc.com/
W3C SOAP 1.1 Definition	http://www.w3.org/TR/SOAP/
WebServices.org	http://www.webservices.org/
XMethods SOAP Service List	http://www.xmethods.com/

To check the spelling of a phrase with an Internet-based spelling CGI

Type the following statements into the Script Editor window, pressing Return after each one. (An explanation appears after each statement that requires one.)

```
set myphrase to text returned of ¬
(display dialog "Spell check this phrase" ¬
default answer "Orangees and Aples")
```

First, the user is prompted to enter a phrase to spelling check (**Figure 37**).

```
set mycorrectphrase to ""
```

A variable is initialized to hold the correctly spelled phrase.

```
repeat with myword in every word of myphrase
```

A loop is started to cycle through every word in the phrase to spell-check.

```
set myfinalword to spelledright(myword)
```

The **spelledright** handler is called to get the correct spelling for the current word.

```
if myfinalword = "" then
set mycorrectphrase to mycorrectphrase ¬
& myword & " "
```

If a null string is returned, the word was spelled correctly, and **myword** is appended to the **mycorrectphrase** variable.

```
else
set mycorrectphrase to mycorrectphrase ¬
& myfinalword & " "
end if
end repeat
```

Otherwise, the word was spelled incorrectly, and **myfinalword** is appended to the **mycorrectphrase** variable.

```
display dialog mycorrectphrase
```

The correctly spelled phrase is shown in a dialog.

Script 11 This script uses the simple XML-RPC protocol to call a publicly available spelling-checker CGI that has a XML-RPC gateway.

```
set myphrase to text returned of ¬
(display dialog "Spell check this phrase" ¬
default answer "Orangees and Aples")
set mycorrectphrase to ""
repeat with myword in every word of myphrase
  set myfinalword to spelledright(myword)
  if myfinalword = "" then
    set mycorrectphrase to mycorrectphrase ¬
    & myword & " "
  else
    set mycorrectphrase to mycorrectphrase ¬
    & myfinalword & " "
  end if
end repeat
display dialog mycorrectphrase
on spelledright(anyword)
  set myChoice to ""
  tell application "http://www.stuffeddog.com/¬
  speller/speller-rpc.cgi"
    set mySpellCheckResults to call xmlrpc ¬
    {method name:"speller.spellCheck", ¬
    parameters:{anyword, {}}}
  end tell
  if mySpellCheckResults ≠ "" then
    set myChoice to (choose from list ¬
    (suggestions of item 1 of ¬
    mySpellCheckResults) with prompt ¬
    "Spelling for '" & anyword & "'")
    if class of myChoice is not list then set ¬
    myChoice to ""
  end if
  return myChoice
end spelledright
```

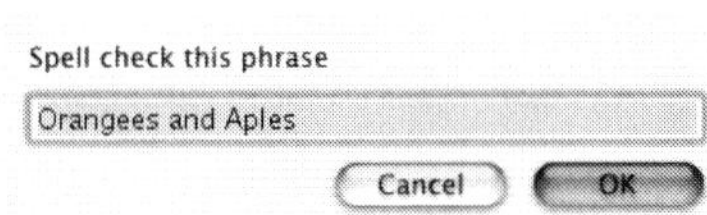

Figure 37 The script prompts the user to enter a phrase to check.

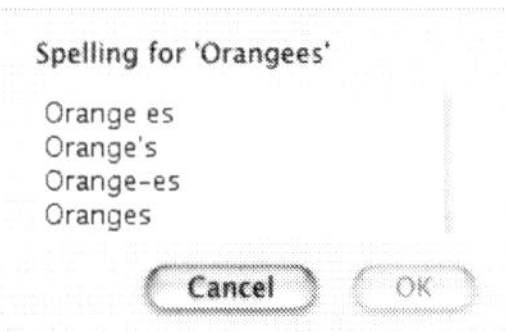

Figure 38 The script displays a list of possible correct spellings provided by the spelling checker CGI.

on spelledright(anyword)

The **spelledright** handler takes one string argument.

set myChoice to ""

This handler returns the **myChoice** variable.

tell application "http://www.stuffeddog.com/¬ speller/speller-rpc.cgi"

set mySpellCheckResults to call xmlrpc ¬ {method name:"speller.spellCheck", ¬ parameters:{anyword, {}}}

end tell

The spelling checker CGI is called at www.stuffeddog.com. A method and parameter are passed to the CGI with the call xmlrpc function. The parameter is the word to check.

if mySpellCheckResults ≠ "" then

set myChoice to (choose from list ¬ (suggestions of item 1 of ¬ mySpellCheckResults) with prompt ¬ "Spelling for '" & anyword & "'")

if class of myChoice is not list then set ¬ myChoice to ""

end if

If the result is a null string, the word is spelled correctly. Otherwise, the user is prompted to choose a word from a list of suggested words (**Figure 38**).

return myChoice

end spelledright

The handler returns the new spelling.

To translate an English phrase to Spanish using BabelFish via SOAP

Type the following statements into the Script Editor window, pressing Return after each one. (An explanation appears after each statement that requires one.)

```
property mySOAPmethod : "BabelFish"
property mySOAPnamespace : ¬
"urn:xmethodsBabelFish"
property mySOAPaction : ¬
"urn:xmethodsBabelFish#BabelFish"
property myTranslationMode : "en_es"
```

This script starts by defining all the necessary SOAP values for proper operation of the BabelFish translation engine at services.xmethods.net.

```
set myTranslationText to text returned of ¬
(display dialog "English to translate to ¬
Spanish" default answer "")
```

The user is prompted for a English phrase to translate (**Figure 39**).

```
set errFlag to false
```

An error flag variable is set up for later testing.

```
try
tell application "http://¬
services.xmethods.net:80/perl/soaplite.cgi"
set mySOAPresult to call soap ¬
{method name:mySOAPmethod, method ¬
namespace uri:mySOAPnamespace, ¬
parameters: {translationmode:¬
myTranslationMode, ¬
sourcedata:myTranslationText}, ¬
SOAPAction:mySOAPaction}
end tell
```

In a **try** block to intercept errors, the script talks to the remote Perl CGI at services.xmethods.net with the **call soap** function. The **call soap** function requires a **method name**, **method namespace uri**, **parameters** unique to each Web application, and a **SOAPaction**.

Script 12 This script uses the powerful SOAP protocol to call the BabelFish translation engine on the xMethods site.

```
property mySOAPmethod : "BabelFish"
property mySOAPnamespace : ¬
"urn:xmethodsBabelFish"
property mySOAPaction : ¬
"urn:xmethodsBabelFish#BabelFish"
property myTranslationMode : "en_es"
set myTranslationText to text returned of ¬
(display dialog "English to translate to ¬
Spanish" default answer "")
set errFlag to false
try
  tell application "http://¬
  services.xmethods.net:80/perl/soaplite.cgi"
    set mySOAPresult to call soap ¬
    {method name:mySOAPmethod, method ¬
    namespace uri:mySOAPnamespace, ¬
    parameters:{translationmode:¬
    myTranslationMode, ¬
    sourcedata:myTranslationText}, ¬
    SOAPAction:mySOAPaction}
  end tell
  on error errMessage number errNumber
  set errFlag to true
  if errNumber is -916 then display dialog ¬
  "Could not connect to service."
end try
if not errFlag then display dialog "English: ¬
" & myTranslationText & return & return & ¬
"Spanish: " & mySOAPresult
```

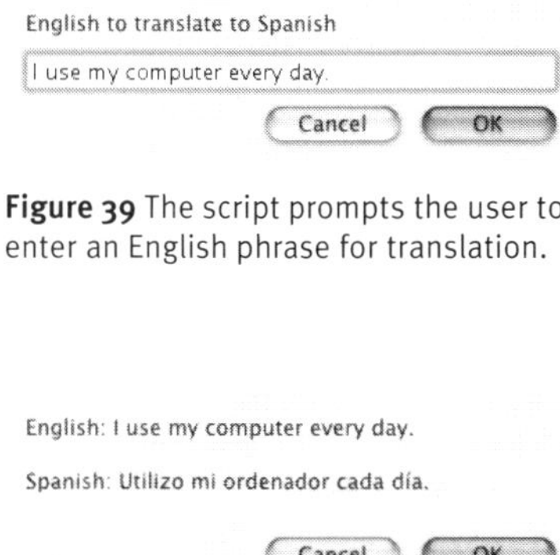
English to translate to Spanish
I use my computer every day.
Cancel
OK
English: I use my computer every day.
Spanish: Utilizo mi ordenador cada día.
Cancel
OK

Figure 39 The script prompts the user to enter an English phrase for translation.

Figure 40 After getting results via SOAP from BabelFish, the script displays the phrase in both languages.

```
on error errMessage number errNumber
set errFlag to true
if errNumber is -916 then display dialog ¬
"Could not connect to service."
end try
```

If an error happens, the script checks the error number. If a connection error took place, the number matches -916, and a dialog is displayed.

```
if not errFlag then display dialog "English: " ¬
& myTranslationText & return & return & ¬
"Spanish: " & mySOAPresult
```

If no error happened, a dialog shows the phrase in both languages (**Figure 40**).

Connecting with Internet Connect

Although the Network Setup Scripting application of Mac OS 9 does not have a complete counterpart in Mac OS X 10.1, the Internet Connect application provides scriptable access to TCP/PPP and Remote Access connections. **Script 13** demonstrates how to use Internet Connect to make a dial-up connection to a phone number.

To make a connection with Internet Connect

Type the following statements into the Script Editor window, pressing Return after each one. (An explanation appears after each statement that requires one.)

```
property mynumber : "415-555-1212"
property myuser : "Ethan"
```

These properties set the phone number and user name to use in the dial-up connection attempt.

```
set mypassword to text returned of ¬
(display dialog "Password" default answer "")
```

The script prompts the user for a password (**Figure 41**).

```
tell application "Internet Connect"
connect to telephone number mynumber ¬
as user myuser with password mypassword
quit
end tell
```

Finally, the connect command of Internet Connect makes a connection before the application quits.

Script 13 This script uses the Internet Connect application to make a dial-up connection.

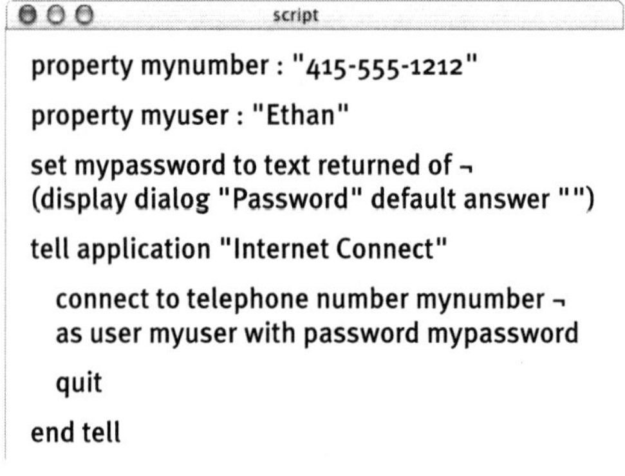

```
property mynumber : "415-555-1212"
property myuser : "Ethan"
set mypassword to text returned of ¬
(display dialog "Password" default answer "")
tell application "Internet Connect"
	connect to telephone number mynumber ¬
	as user myuser with password mypassword
	quit
end tell
```

Figure 41 The script prompts the user for a password.

Script 14 This script uses the scriptable Cocoa application TextEdit to randomize the font size of each character in the current document.

```
tell application "TextEdit"
  if (count of documents) > 0 then
    set mycharcount to count of ¬
    every character of text of document 1
    repeat with mycharnum from ¬
    1 to mycharcount
      set size of character mycharnum of ¬
      text of document 1 to random number ¬
      from 9 to 48
    end repeat
  end if
end tell
```

resizing text example.rtf

You are a special friend!

Figure 42 The current TextEdit window after **Script 14** has run.

Scripting TextEdit for Fun

The Mac OS X application TextEdit demonstrates how Cocoa applications get AppleScript support free. The dictionary of TextEdit includes access to all documents and text in the application.

Script 14 modifies the font size of all text in the current document. **Figure 42** shows the TextEdit window after the script has run.

To randomize the font sizes of all characters in the current TextEdit document

Type the following statements into the Script Editor window, pressing Return after each one. (An explanation appears after each statement that requires one.)

```
tell application "TextEdit"
```

```
if (count of documents) > 0 then
```

The script tests to ensure that at least one document is open in TextEdit.

```
set mycharcount to count of ¬
every character of text of document 1
```

The number of characters in the current document is stored in **mycharcount**.

```
repeat with mycharnum from 1 to mycharcount
```

```
set size of character mycharnum of ¬
text of document 1 to random number ¬
from 9 to 48
```

```
end repeat
```

```
end if
```

```
end tell
```

A repeat loop traverses the integers from 1 to **mycharcount**, setting the font size of each character at the index position **mycharnum** to a random number.

Full-Power Development with AppleScript Studio

The true power of AppleScript in Mac OS X 10.1 will be unleashed when Apple ships the new AppleScript Studio development environment. Based on Apple's sophisticated Project Builder and Interface Builder applications, AppleScript Studio integrates AppleScript development into these tools. AppleScript now becomes a development language on par with Java and Objective-C in Mac OS X.

Each AppleScript Studio compiled application contains at least one compiled script in its bundle, where all the AppleScript you could ever write can respond to a complete set of events for all the Cocoa interface elements, including menus, windows, and all window controls. The compiled project from AppleScript Studio is a full Cocoa application.

Figure 43 shows the main windows for the enhanced Interface Builder that is part of AppleScript Studio-notice how events appear in a checklist. Scripters can attach script handlers to any of the numerous events available for most Cocoa user interface elements.

Figure 44 shows the script editing environment of Project Builder in AppleScript Studio. Now AppleScript developers can use the tools of Project Builder, previously reserved for Java and Objective-C programmers.

Figure 45 shows the AppleScript dictionary view of Project Builder in AppleScript Studio. AppleScript Studio's version of Project Builder includes enhancements to aid AppleScript creation, including debugging support.

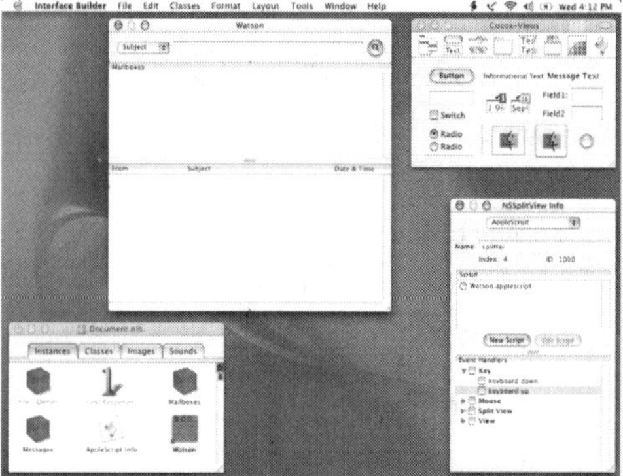

Figure 43 The Interface Builder portion of AppleScript Studio shows how easy it is to assemble a complete Cocoa application built with AppleScript.

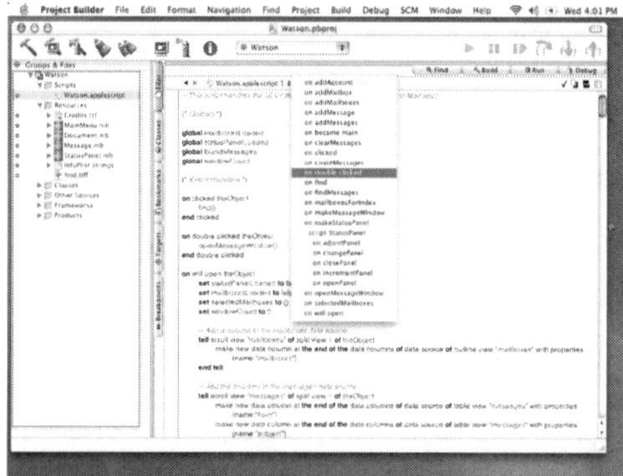

Figure 44 One of Interface Builder's palettes shows some of the AppleScript-enabled Cocoa user interface options.

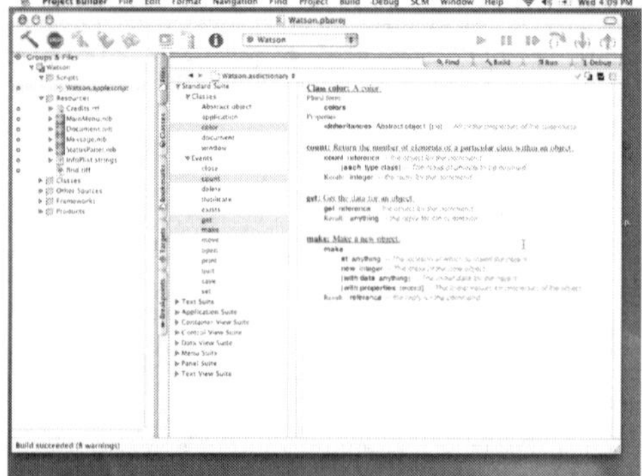

Figure 45 Another Project Builder feature in AppleScript Studio is the AppleScript dictionary viewer.

AppleScript Studio

System Preferences

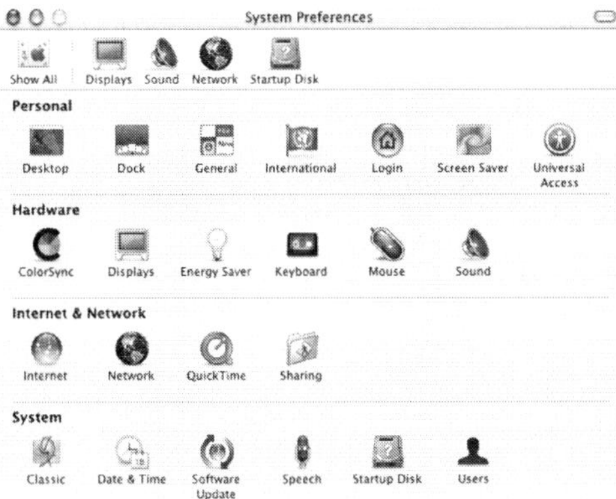

Figure 1 The System Preferences window, with icons for all panes displayed.

System Preferences

One of the great things about Mac OS is the way it can be customized to look and work the way you want it to. Many customization options can be set within the System Preferences application (**Figure 1**). That's where you'll find a variety of preference panes, each containing settings for a part of Mac OS.

In Mac OS X 10.1, System Preferences panes are organized into four categories:

- **Personal** preference panes enable you to set options to customize various Mac OS X appearance and operation options for personal tastes. This chapter covers Desktop, Dock, General, International, Screen Saver, and Universal Access; Login is covered in **Chapter 6**.
- **Hardware** preference panes control settings for various hardware devices. This chapter covers Displays, Energy Saver, Keyboard, Mouse, and Sound; ColorSync is covered in **Chapter 10**.
- **Internet & Network** preference panes enable you to set options related to Internet and network connections. This chapter covers Internet and QuickTime; Network and Sharing are covered in **Chapter 5**.
- **System** preference panes control various aspects of your computer's operation. This chapter covers Date & Time, Software Update, and Startup Disk. Classic is covered in **Chapter 2**, Speech is covered in **Chapter 11**, and Users is covered in **Chapter 6**.

To open System Preferences

Choose Apple > System Preferences (**Figure 2**).

or

Click the System Preferences icon in the Dock (**Figure 3**).

The System Preferences window appears (**Figure 1**).

To open a preferences pane

Click the icon for the pane you want to display.

or

Choose the name of the pane you want to display from the View menu (**Figure 4**).

✔ Tips

- To display icons for all System Preferences panes, click the Show All button in the toolbar of the System Preferences window.
- You can customize the System Preferences window's toolbar. Simply drag an icon for a preferences pane into the toolbar. You can then access that pane no matter what pane is displayed in the window.

To quit System Preferences

When you are finished setting Preference options, choose System Prefs > Quit System Prefs (**Figure 5**), or press ⌘Q.

✔ Tip

- Clicking the Preferences window's close box does not quit System Preferences. To quit, you must use the Quit command or its shortcut key.

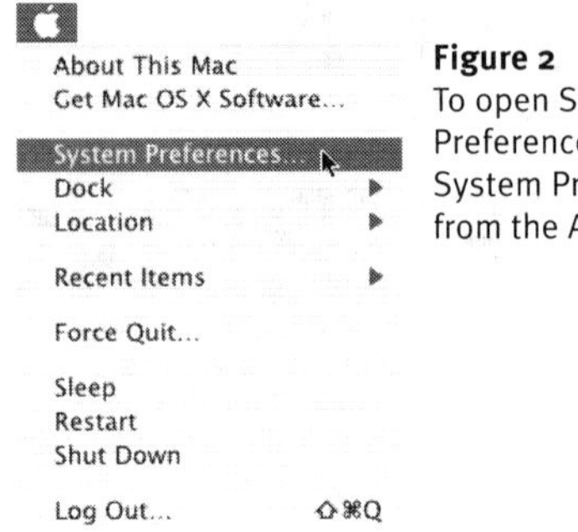

Figure 2 To open System Preferences, choose System Preferences from the Apple menu...

Figure 3 ...or click the System Preferences icon in the Dock.

Figure 4 The View menu lists all of the System Preferences panes.

System Prefs
About System Prefs
Services
Hide System Prefs ⌘H
Hide Others
Show All
Quit System Prefs ⌘Q

Figure 5 The System Prefs menu.

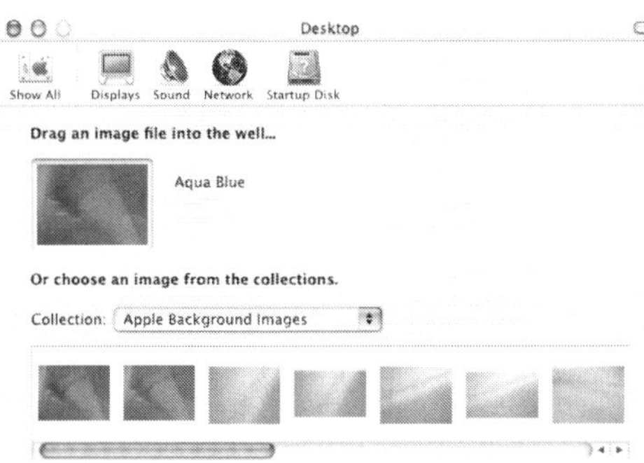

Figure 6 The Desktop preference pane, showing the default settings.

Figure 7 The Collection pop-up menu.

Figure 8 You can also select from the pictures in your Pictures folder.

Figure 9 Use this dialog to location, select, and open a folder containing pictures.

Desktop

The Desktop preference pane (**Figure 6**), which is new in Mac OS X 10.1, enables you to set the background picture for the Mac OS X Desktop.

To select a preinstalled image for the background

1. In the Desktop preference pane (**Figure 6**), choose the name of an image collection from the Collection pop-up menu (**Figure 7**). The images in the collection appear in the bottom of the window.
2. Click to select the image you want. It appears in the image well in the middle of the window and the Desktop's background picture changes.

To use your own image file for the background

1. In the Desktop preference pane (**Figure 6**), choose Pictures Folder from the Collection pop-up menu (**Figure 7**). The images in the Pictures Folder appear in the bottom of the window (**Figure 8**).

   or

   In the Desktop preference pane (**Figure 6**), choose Choose Folder from the Collection pop-up menu (**Figure 7**). Then use the dialog sheet that appears (**Figure 9**) to locate, select, and open the folder containing the picture you want to use.
2. Click to select the image you want.

or

Drag the icon for the image file you want to use into the image well in the middle of the Desktop preferences pane (**Figure 6**).

The image you clicked or dragged appears in the image well and the Desktop's background picture changes.

Dock

The Dock preference pane (**Figure 10**), which was revised for Mac OS X 10.1, offers several options for customizing the Dock's appearance and functionality.

To customize the Dock

In the Dock preference pane (**Figure 10**), set options as desired:

- To set the size of the Dock and its icons, drag the Dock Size slider to the left or right.
- To enable Dock icon magnification (**Figure 11**), turn on the Magnification check box and drag the slider to the left or right to specify how large the magnified icons should become when you point to them.
- To hide the Dock until you need it, turn on the Automatically hide and show the Dock check box. With this feature enabled, the Dock disappears until you move the mouse pointer to the edge of the screen where the Dock is positioned.
- To change the Dock's position on the screen select one of the Position on screen options: Left (**Figure 12**), Bottom (the default), or Right.
- To set the special effect Mac OS X uses to minimize a window to an icon in the Dock and maximize an icon from the Dock to a window, choose an option from the Minimize using pop-up menu:
  - ▲ Genie Effect, the default option, shrinks the window into the Dock like a genie slipping into a magic lamp. (Well, how else could you describe it?)
  - ▲ Scale Effect simply shrinks the icon into the Dock.
- To display the "bouncing icon" animation while a program is launching, turn on the Animate opening applications check box.

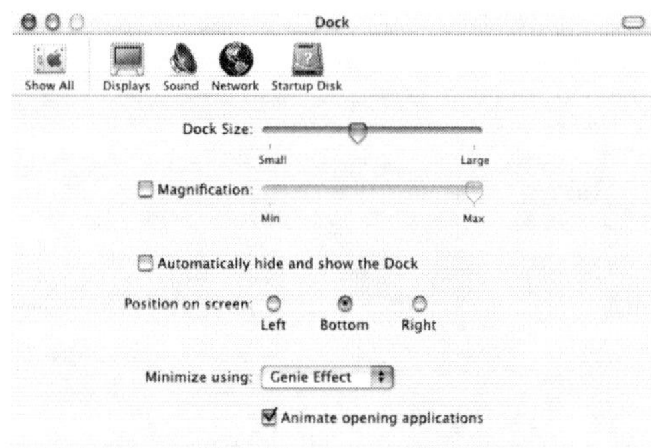

Figure 10 The Dock preferences pane.

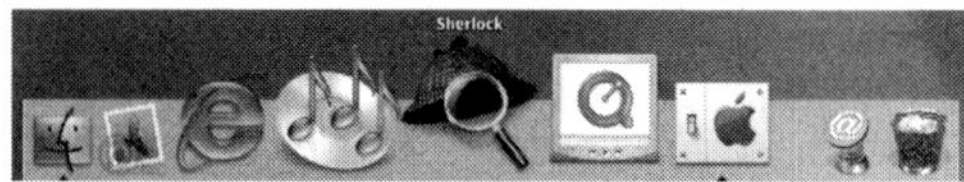

Figure 11 With magnification enabled, when you point to an icon in the Dock, it grows so you can see it better.

Figure 12 When you set the Dock's position to Left, it appears as a vertical bar of icons on the left side of the screen, below the Apple menu.

Figure 13 Use the Dock submenu under the Apple menu to set some Dock options.

✔ Tips

- You can use the Dock submenu under the Apple menu (**Figure 13**) to set some Dock options without opening the Dock preferences pane. (You can also use this submenu to open the Dock preferences pane.)
- If you think the Dock takes up too much valuable real estate on your screen, try one of these options:
  - Set the Dock size smaller, then enable magnification so the icons enlarge when you point to them.
  - Position the Dock on the right. In most cases, document and Finder windows won't need to cover that area of the screen.
  - Turn on the Automatically hide and show the Dock check box. (This is what I do and it works like a charm.)
- Although the Genie Effect is pretty cool, the Scale Effect requires less system resources and may improve performance when minimizing and maximizing windows and icons.
- You can add, remove, or rearrange icons on the Dock by dragging them, as discussed in *Mac OS X: Visual QuickStart Guide.*

General

The General preferences pane (**Figure 14**), which was revised for Mac OS X 10.1, enables you to set options for color, scroll bar functionality, recent items, and text smoothing.

To set General preferences

In the General preferences pane (**Figure 14**), set options as desired:

- Use the Appearance pop-up menu to choose a color for buttons, menus, and windows throughout Mac OS X and Mac OS X applications.
- Use the Highlight color pop-up menu to choose a highlight color for text in documents, fields, and lists.
- Select one of the Place scroll arrow options to specify where scroll arrows should appear in windows and scrolling lists:
  - ▲ **At top and bottom** places a scroll arrow at each end of the scroll bar (**Figure 15**).
  - ▲ **Together** places both scroll arrows together at the bottom or right end of the scroll bar (**Figure 16**).
- Select one of the Click in the scroll bar to options to specify what happens when you click in the scroll track of a scroll bar.
  - ▲ **Jump to next page** scrolls to the next window or page of the document.
  - ▲ **Scroll to here** scrolls to the relative location in the document. For example, if you click in the scroll track two-thirds of the way between the top and bottom, you'll scroll two-thirds of the way through the document. (This is the same as dragging the scroller to that position.)

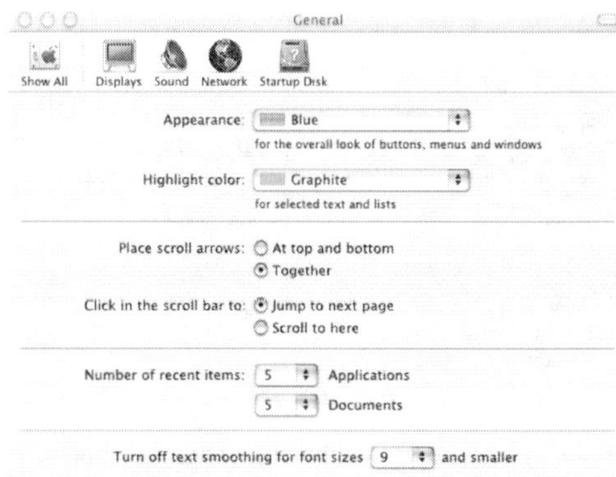

Figure 14 The General preferences pane.

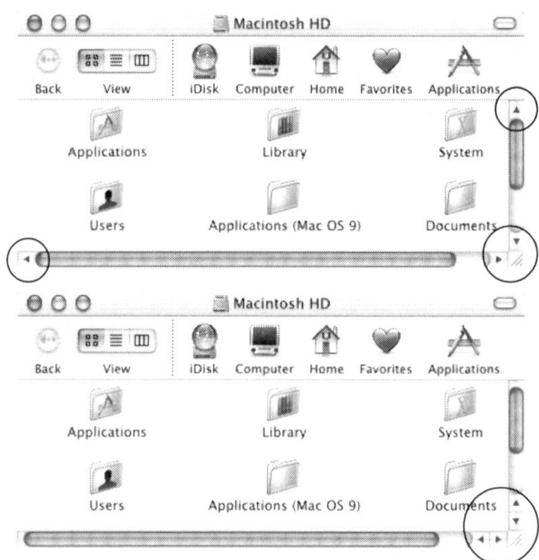

Figures 15 & 16 A window with scroll bars at top and bottom (top) and the same window with scroll bars together (bottom).

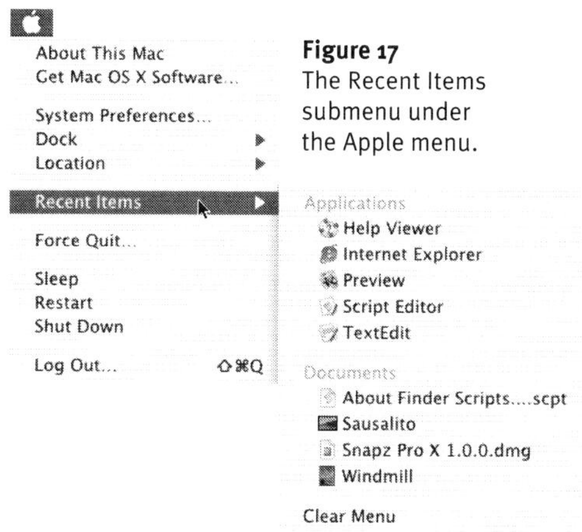

Figure 17 The Recent Items submenu under the Apple menu.

12-point text with text smoothing turned on.

12-point text with text smoothing turned off.

Figure 18 As these example show, text smoothing can change the appearance of text on screen.

- Choose the number of items you want Mac OS X to consider "recent" from the Applications and Documents pop-up menus. Options range from 5 to 50.
- Choose a text smoothing font size option from the pop-up menu. The smaller the size, the more font smoothing is on screen. Your options are 8, 9, 10, and 12.

✔ Tips

- Recent items appear on the Recent Items submenu under the Apple menu (**Figure 17**).
- You can clear the Recent Items submenu by choosing Apple > Recent Items > Clear Menu (**Figure 17**).
- Text smoothing uses a process called *antialiasing* to make text more legible onscreen. Antialiasing creates gray pixels between black ones and white ones to eliminate sharp edges. **Figure 18** shows what text looks like with text smoothing turned on and off.

International

The International preferences pane enables you to set options that control how Mac OS X works in an environment where U.S. English is not the primary language or multiple languages are used.

International preferences are broken down into five different categories, each with its own screen in the pane: Language (**Figure 19**), Date (**Figure 24**), Time (**Figure 26**), Numbers (**Figure 27**), and Keyboard Menu (**Figure 28**).

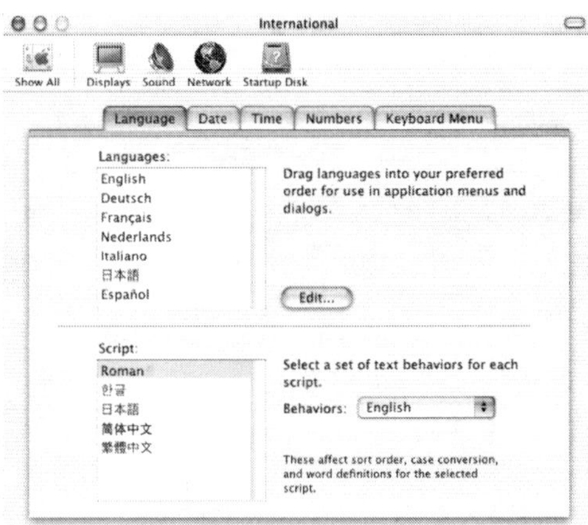

Figure 19 The Language tab of the International preference pane.

To set the preferred language & behaviors

1. In the International Preferences pane, click the Language tab (**Figure 19**).
2. To set the preferred order for languages to appear in application menus and dialogs, drag languages up or down in the Languages list (**Figure 20**).
3. To set sort order, case conversion, and word definition behaviors for text, click to select a script in the Script menu, and then choose an option from the Behaviors pop-up menu (**Figure 21**).

Figure 20 You can change the preferred language order by dragging a language up or down in the list.

Figure 21 The Behaviors pop-up menu lists language behaviors for the selected Script.

Figure 22 Turn on check boxes for the language you want to include in the Languages list.

✔ Tips

- You can edit the Languages list. Click the Edit button in the top half of the Language tab (**Figure 19**) to display a dialog sheet like the one in **Figure 22**. Turn on the check boxes beside each language you want to include in the list and click OK to save your changes.
- The changes you make to the Languages list in step 2 take effect in the Finder the next time you restart or log in. Changes take effect in applications (**Figure 23**) the next time you open them.
- A *script* is a writing system or alphabet.

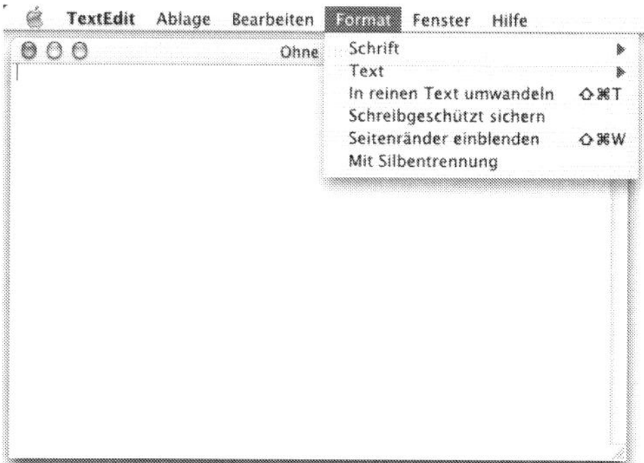

Figure 23 Changing the language of an application's menus and dialogs is as easy as dragging the language to the top of the Languages list (**Figure 20**). Here's TextEdit in German (Deutch).

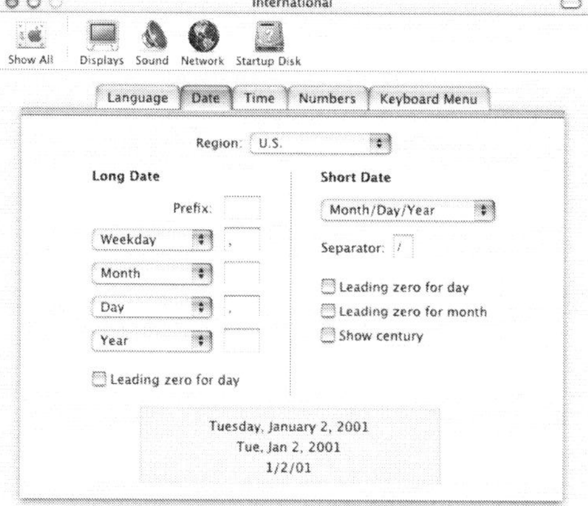

Figure 24 The Date tab of the International preferences pane.

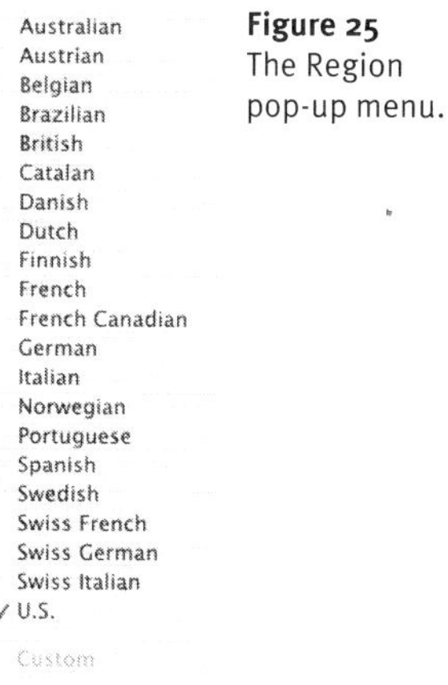

Figure 25 The Region pop-up menu.

To set the date format

1. In the International Preferences pane, click the Date tab (**Figure 24**).
2. Choose an option from the Region pop-up menu (**Figure 25**).
3. Set options in the Long Date side of the window by choosing options from pop-up menus and entering prefix or separator characters in edit boxes.
4. Set options in the Short Date side of the window by choosing an option from the pop-up menu and entering a separator character in the edit box.
5. Fine tune your settings by turning on check boxes as desired:
   - ▲ **Leading zero for day** includes a zero as the first digit of day numbers less than 10.
   - ▲ **Leading zero for month** includes a zero as the first digit of month numbers less than 10.
   - ▲ **Show century** displays years as four digits.

✔ Tips

- Changes in this tab affect how dates are displayed throughout Mac OS X and its applications.
- The long date can display the weekday, month, day, and year. The weekday and month are displayed in words. The short date displays only the month, day, and year.
- The sample dates at the bottom of the window show the effect of each of your changes.

To set the time format

1. In the International Preferences pane, click the Time tab (**Figure 26**).
2. Choose an option from the Region pop-up menu (**Figure 25**).
3. Select a clock option:
   - ▲ **24-hour clock** numbers hours to 24 and does not need abbreviations to indicate whether the time is in the morning or afternoon/evening.
   - ▲ **12-hour clock** numbers hours to 12 and needs abbreviations to indicate whether the time is in the morning or afternoon/evening. If you select this option, you can also choose one of the options beneath it to specify how midnight and noon should appear, as 0:00 or 12:00.
4. If you selected 12-hour clock in step 2, enter abbreviations to be used for times before and after noon.
5. To display a zero as the first digit of times before the hour of 10, turn on the Use leading zero for hour check box.

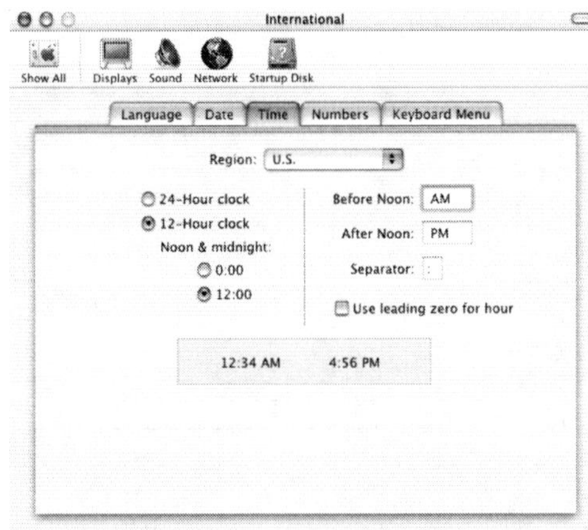

Figure 26 The Time tab of the International preferences pane.

✔ Tips

- Changes in this tab affect how times are displayed throughout Mac OS X and its applications, including the menu bar clock. I explain how to customize the menu bar clock later in this chapter.
- The sample times at the bottom of the window show the effect of each of your changes.

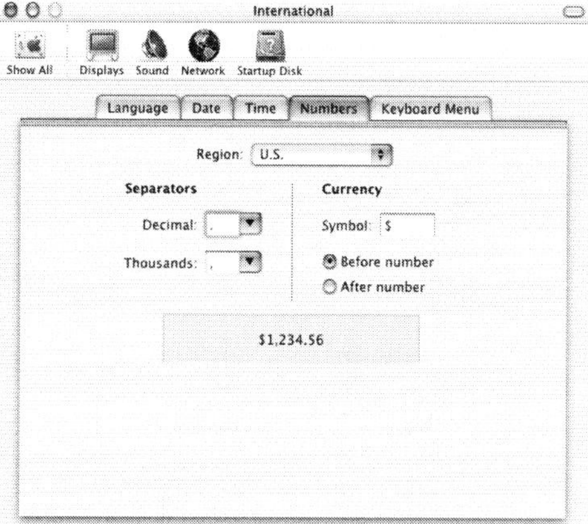

Figure 27 The Numbers tab of the International preferences pane.

To set the number format

1. In the International Preferences pane, click the Numbers tab (**Figure 27**).
2. Choose an option from the Region pop-up menu (**Figure 25**).
3. Choose or enter separators for numbers:
   - ▲ **Decimal** is the character that appears between whole numbers and decimals (like dollars and cents).
   - ▲ **Thousands** is the character that appears between hundreds and thousands digits. It separates groups of three digits in numbers larger than 999.
4. Enter a currency symbol in the Symbol edit box.
5. Select a radio button to specify whether the currency symbol should appear before the number or after it.

✔ Tips

- Changes in this tab affect how numbers are displayed throughout Mac OS X and its applications.
- The sample number at the bottom of the window shows the effect of each of your changes.

To create & customize a keyboard menu

1. In the International Preferences pane, click the Keyboard Menu tab (**Figure 28**).
2. Turn on the check boxes beside each keyboard layout you may want to use with Mac OS X. If more than one keyboard is selected, a Keyboard menu appears to the right of the Help menu on the menu bar (**Figure 29**).
3. To customize the way the keyboard menu feature works, click the Options button. A dialog sheet like the one in **Figure 30** appears. Toggle check marks beside options as desired and click OK:
   - ▲ **Keyboard Menu Shortcuts** enables you to switch from one keyboard layout to the next by pressing ⌘ Option Spacebar. (The ⌘ Spacebar shortcut to switch to the default keyboard layout cannot be disabled.)
   - ▲ **Font and keyboard synchronization** automatically switches to the keyboard layout a font is synchronized to. The switch occurs when you click in or select text formatted with that font.

✔ Tip

- Font and keyboard synchronization is handled internally by international bundle resources included in font files. You cannot change synchronization options; you can only disable this feature.

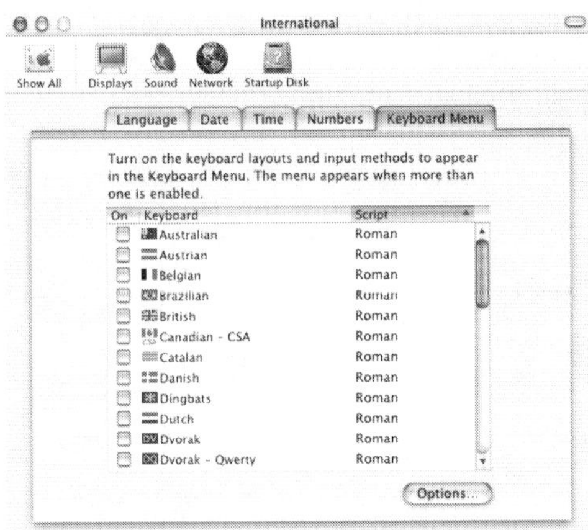

Figure 28 The Keyboard Menu tab of the International preferences pane.

Figure 29 An icon for the Keyboard menu appears to the right of the Help menu in all applications.

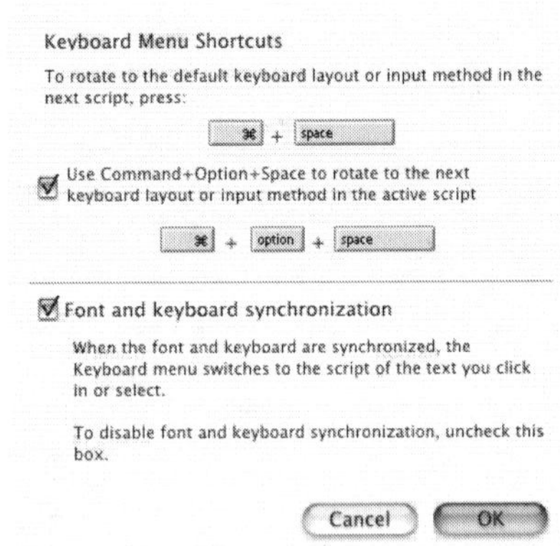

Figure 30 Use this dialog sheet to customize the way the keyboard menu feature works.

To switch keyboard layouts

Choose a different keyboard layout from the Keyboard menu (**Figure 31**).

or

Press ⌘ Option Spacebar until the flag or icon for the layout you want to use appears in the menu bar (**Figure 29**).

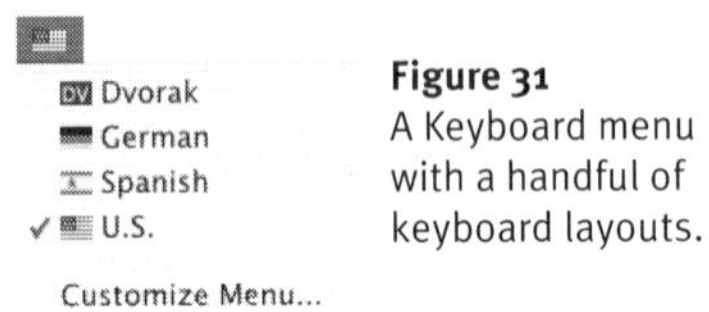

Figure 31 A Keyboard menu with a handful of keyboard layouts.

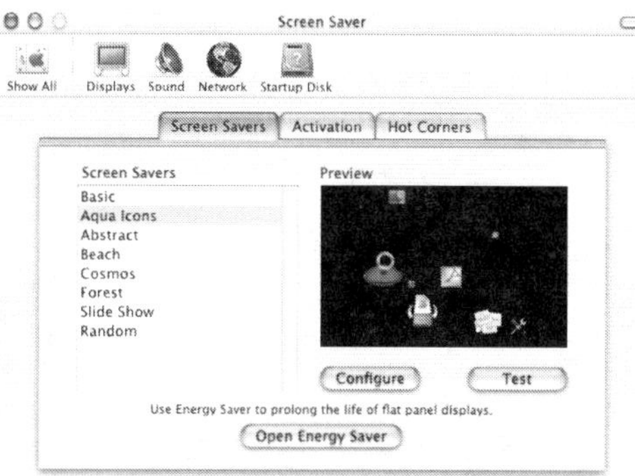

Figure 32 The Screen Savers panel of the System Preferences Screen Saver pane.

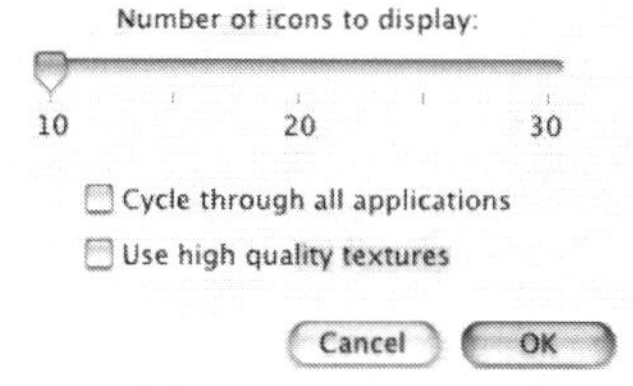

Figure 33 The configuration dialog sheet for the Aqua Icons screen saver.

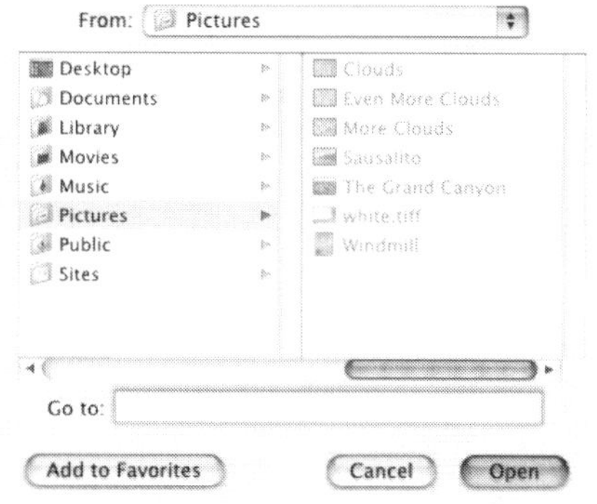

Figure 34 To configure the Slide Show screen saver, choose a folder containing the pictures you want to display.

Screen Saver

The Screen Saver preference pane enables you to activate and configure Mac OS X's built-in screen saver.

The Screen Saver pane includes three tabs: Screen Savers (**Figure 32**), Activation (**Figure 35**), and Hot Corners (**Figure 36**).

To select & configure a screen saver

1. In the Screen Saver preferences pane, click the Screen Savers tab (**Figure 32**).
2. Select one of the options in the Screen Savers list. A preview of the screen saver you selected appears in the Preview area.
3. To set options for the screen saver, click Configure. Not all screen savers can be configured and the options that are available vary depending on the screen saver you selected in Step 2:
   - **Aqua Icons** (**Figure 33**) enables you to set the number of icons to display, whether all application icons should be displayed, and whether icons should be displayed with high quality textures.
   - **Slide Show** (**Figure 34**) enables you to select a different folder containing images to display in the slide show. The default folder is your Pictures folder.
4. To see what the screen saver looks like on your screen, click Test. The screen goes black and the screen saver kicks in. To go back to work, move your mouse.

✔ Tip

- The Energy Saver preferences pane offers more protection for flat panel, PowerBook, and iBook displays than Screen Saver. Energy Saver is covered later in this chapter.

To set screen saver automatic activation options

1. In the Screen Saver preferences pane, click the Activation tab (**Figure 35**).
2. Drag the slider to the right or left to set the amount of idle time before the screen saver automatically activates.
3. Select one of the password protection radio buttons:
   - ▲ **Do not ask for a password** enables you to clear the screen saver and view the screen without entering a password.
   - ▲ **Use my user account password** requires you to enter your user password to clear the screen saver and view the screen. (This can prevent busybodies from viewing your screen or accessing your computer while you're away from your desk.)

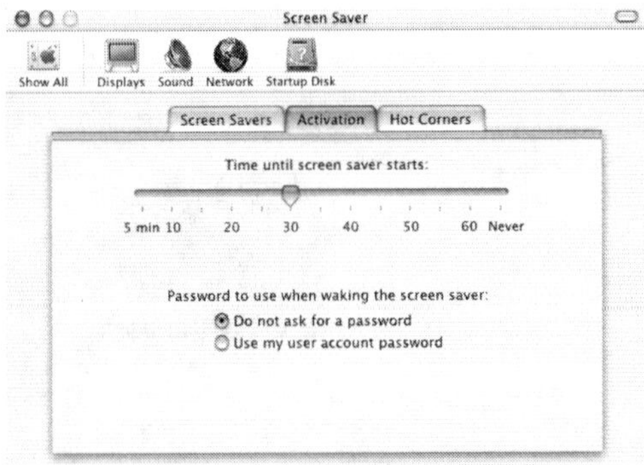

Figure 35 The Activation tab of the Screen Saver preferences pane.

✔ Tip

- Don't confuse the Screen Saver's password feature with system security. Password-protecting your computer for security purposes is covered in **Chapter 6**.

To set hot corner activation options

1. In the Screen Saver preferences pane, click the Hot Corners tab (**Figure 36**).
2. Click in a corner to select that corner as a hot corner:
   - ▲ One click places a check mark in the corner. A check tells Screen Saver to activate when you position your mouse pointer in that corner of the screen.
   - ▲ Two clicks places a minus sign in the corner. A minus sign tells Screen Saver never to activate when the mouse pointer is positioned in that corner of the screen.

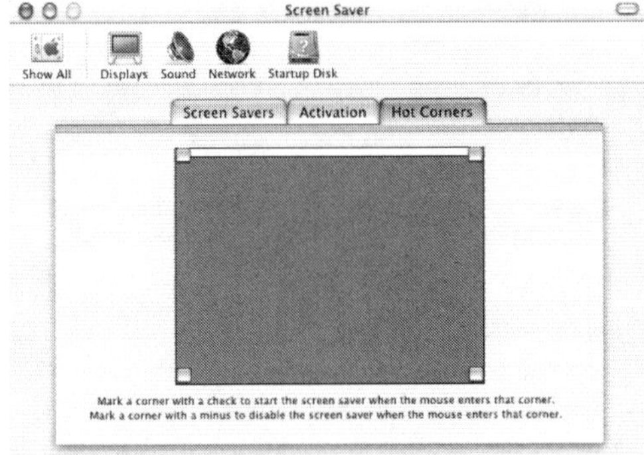

Figure 36 The Hot Corners tab of the Screen Saver preferences pane.

✔ Tip

- You can place check marks and minus signs in any combination in the screen corners.

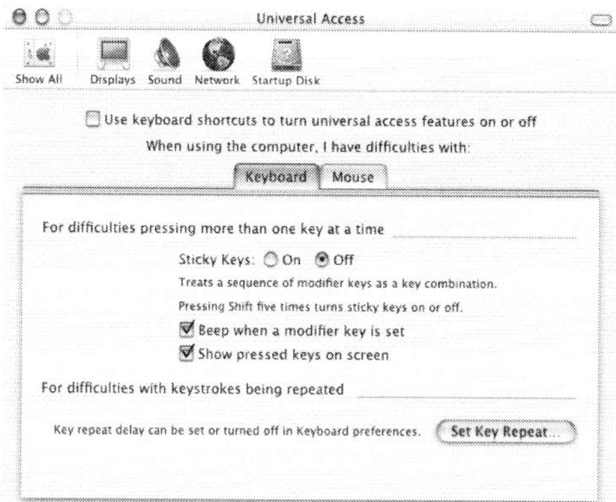

Figure 37 The Keyboard tab of the Universal Access preferences pane.

Figure 38 Universal Access can show you which keys you pressed—in this example, ⌘ and Shift.

✔ Tip

- Clicking the Set Key Repeat button displays the Keyboard preferences pane, which is discussed later in this chapter, so you can set options for making the keyboard easier to use.

Universal Access

The Universal Access Preference pane, which is new in Mac OS X 10.1, enables you to set options for making your computer's keyboard or mouse easier to use.

Universal Access consists of two features:

- **Sticky keys** enables you to press a sequence of keys as a key combination. This is useful if you have trouble pressing more than one key at a time.
- **Mouse keys** enables you to move the mouse pointer using keypad keys. This is useful if you have trouble moving the mouse.

Universal Access features are enabled and configured in two tabs of the preferences pane: Keyboard (**Figure 37**) and Mouse (**Figure 39**).

✔ Tips

- To use keyboard shortcuts to toggle Universal Access features on or off, turn on the check box near the top of the Universal Access pane (**Figures 37** and **39**). Then:
  - Press Shift five times to toggle sticky keys on or off.
  - Press Option five times to toggle mouse keys on or off.

To enable & configure sticky keys

1. In the Universal Access preferences pane, click the Keyboard tab (**Figure 37**).
2. To enable sticky keys, select On.
3. Set options as desired:
   - **Beep when a modifier key is set** plays a sound when a modifier key you press is recognized by the system.
   - **Show pressed keys on screen** displays the image of the modifier key on screen when it is recognized by the system (**Figure 38**).

To enable & configure mouse keys

1. In the Universal Access preferences pane, click the Mouse tab (**Figure 39**).
2. To enable mouse keys, select On.
3. Set options as desired:
   - ▲ **Initial Delay** determines how long you must hold down the key before the mouse pointer moves.
   - ▲ **Maximum Speed** determines how fast the mouse pointer moves.

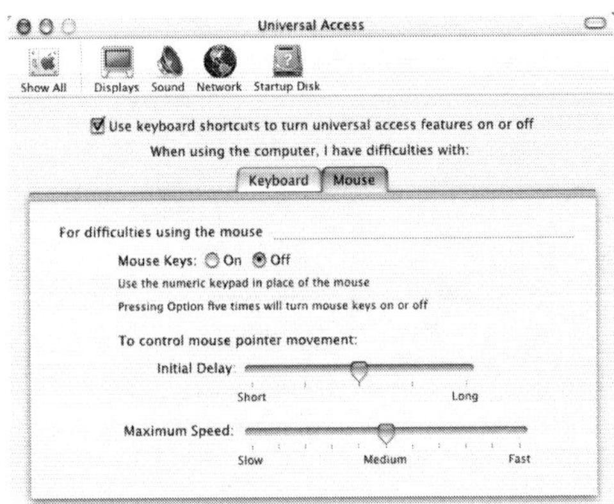

Figure 39 The Mouse tab of the Universal Access preferences pane.

✔ Tips

- To move the mouse with mouse keys enabled, hold down a key on the numeric keypad.
- Mouse keys does not enable you to "click" the mouse button with a keyboard key.

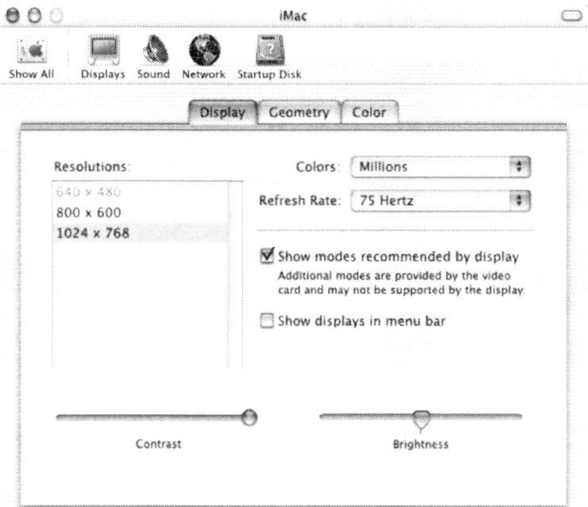

Figure 40 The Display tab of the Displays preferences pane.

Figure 41 An iMac display set to 800 x 600 resolution...

Figure 42 ...and the same display set to 1024 x 768 resolution.

Displays

The Displays preferences pane enables you to set the resolution, colors, geometry, and other settings for your monitor. Settings are organized into tabs; this section covers the Display (**Figure 40**), Geometry (**Figure 44**), and Color (**Figure 45**) tabs.

✔ Tip

- The options that are available in the Displays preference pane vary depending on your computer and monitor. The options shown in this chapter are for an iMac.

To set basic display options

1. In the Displays preference pane, click the Display tab (**Figure 40**).
2. Set options as desired:
   - ▲ **Resolutions** control the number of pixels that appear on screen. The higher the resolution, the more pixels appear on screen. This makes the screen contents smaller, but shows more onscreen, as shown in **Figures 41** and **42**.
   - ▲ **Colors** controls the number of colors that appear on screen. The more colors, the better the screen image appears.
   - ▲ **Refresh Rate** controls the screen refresh rate, in hertz. The higher the number, the steadier the image.
   - ▲ **Show modes recommended by display** shows only options recommended for the display in the Resolutions list and Colors and Refresh Rate pop-up menus. Turning this option off makes it possible to choose from among more options, but not all options may be supported by your monitor.

Continued on next page...

Continued from previous page.

- ▲ **Show displays in menu bar** places a displays menu in the menu bar, to the left of the menu bar clock and Sound menu (if displayed; see **Figure 43**).
- ▲ **Contrast** adjusts the screen's contrast—the difference between light and dark areas.
- ▲ **Brightness** adjusts the brightness of the screen's image.

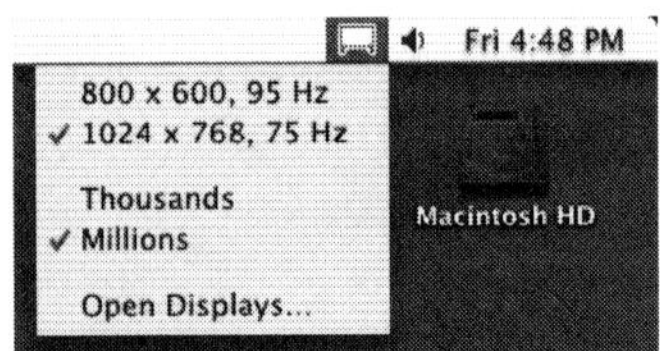

Figure 43 In Mac OS X 10.1, You can add a Displays menu to the menu bar.

To set display geometry

1. In the Displays preference pane, click the Geometry tab (**Figure 44**).
2. Select a setting radio button. The buttons around the monitor picture on the right side of the window change to illustrate what they control.
3. Click buttons around the monitor picture to change the display's geometry. As you click, the borders of the screen will change and move.
4. Repeat steps 2 and 3 for each setting you want to adjust.

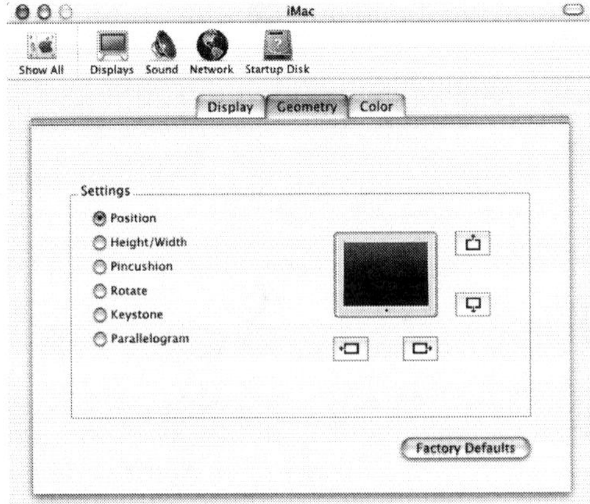

Figure 44 The Geometry tab of the Displays preferences pane.

✔ Tips

- ■ To undo any changes in the Geometry tab, click the Factory Defaults button.
- ■ The Geometry tab appears only on machines with built-in monitors, like an iMac.

To set display color profile

1. In the Displays preference pane, click the Color tab (**Figure 45**).
2. Select one of the Display Profiles.

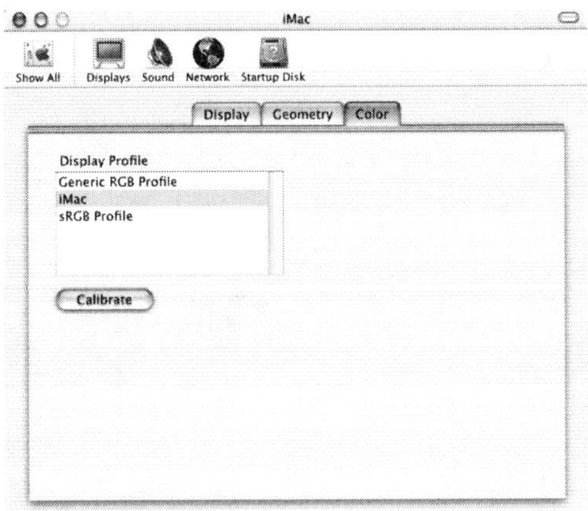

Figure 45 The Color tab of the Displays preferences pane.

✔ Tips

- ■ Color profiles is an advanced feature of Mac OS that enables you to display colors onscreen as they will appear when printed.
- ■ Clicking the Calibrate button in the Color tab of the Displays preference pane opens the Display Calibrator Assistant, which I discuss in **Chapter 10**.

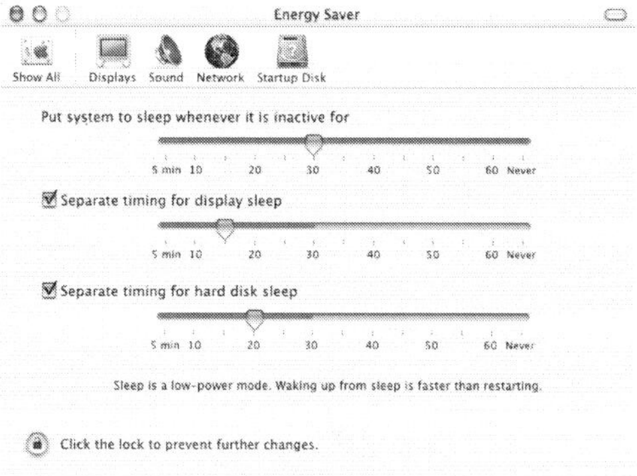

Figure 46 The Energy Saver preferences pane.

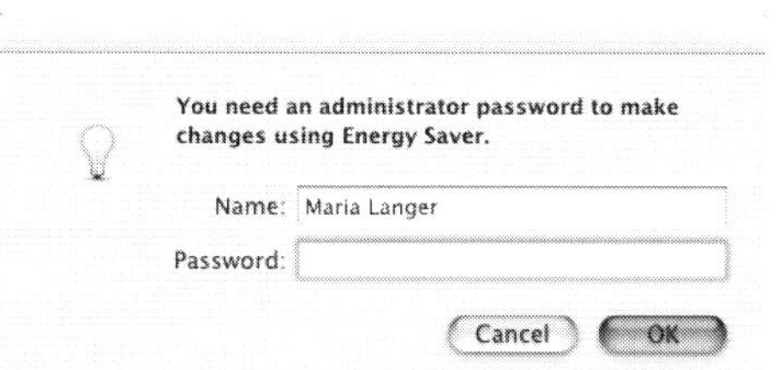

Figure 47 If you lock the Energy Saver settings, you'll need an administrator password to unlock them.

✔ Tips

- You cannot set display sleep or hard disk sleep for longer than system sleep.
- If you lock the Energy Saver settings, when you click the lock to unlock them, a password dialog like the one in **Figure 47** appears. You must enter administrator login information to unlock the Energy Saver settings and make changes.

Energy Saver

The Energy Saver pane (**Figure 46**) enables you to specify settings for automatic system, display, and hard disk sleep. These settings can reduce the amount of power your computer uses when idle.

✔ Tips

- Energy Saver settings are especially important for PowerBook and iBook users running on battery power.
- To wake a sleeping display, press any key.
- Display sleep is a better way to protect flat panel displays and displays on PowerBooks and iBooks than a screen saver. The Mac OS X Screen Saver is covered earlier in this chapter.
- A sleeping hard disk wakes automatically when it needs to.

To set Energy Saver options

1. Display the Energy Saver preferences pane (**Figure 46**).
2. Set options as desired:
   - ▲ To set the system sleep timing, drag the top slider to the left or right.
   - ▲ To set display sleep timing, turn on the check box beside Separate timing for display sleep and drag its slider to the left or right.
   - ▲ To set hard disk sleep timing, turn on the check box beside Separate timing for hard disk sleep and drag its slider to the left or right.
   - ▲ To prevent unauthorized changes to the Energy Saver settings, click the lock button.

Keyboard

The Keyboard preferences pane enables you to customize the way the keyboard works. Options can be set under two tabs:

- **Repeat Rate** (**Figure 48**) enables you to set key repeat rate options for keyboard operation.
- **Full Keyboard Access** (**Figure 49**), which is new in Mac OS X 10.1, enables you to access menus, dialog controls, and other interface elements with the keyboard.

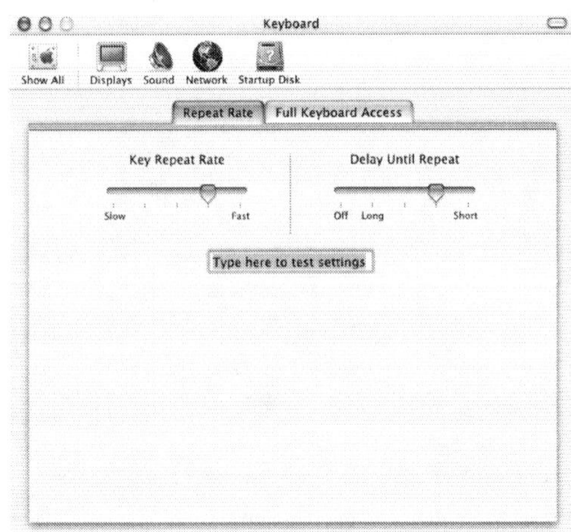

Figure 48 The Key Repeat tab of the Keyboard preferences pane.

To set key repeat options

1. In the Keyboard preferences pane, click the Key Repeat tab (**Figure 48**).
2. Set options as desired:
   - ▲ **Key Repeat Rate** sets how fast a key repeats when held down.
   - ▲ **Delay Until Repeat** sets how long a key must be pressed before it starts to repeat.
3. Test your settings by typing in the test field at the bottom of the pane. If necessary, repeat step 2 to fine-tune your settings for the way you type.

✔ Tip

- Key Repeat settings are especially useful for heavy-handed typists.

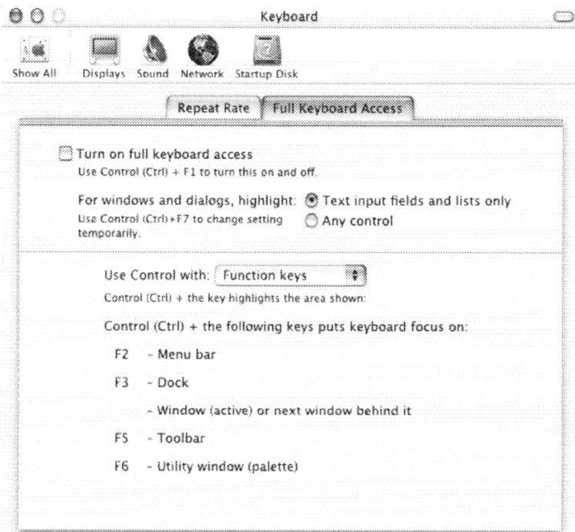

Figure 49 The Full Keyboard Access tab of the Keyboard preferences pane with Function key settings displayed.

Figure 50 The Letter keys settings for Full Keyboard Access.

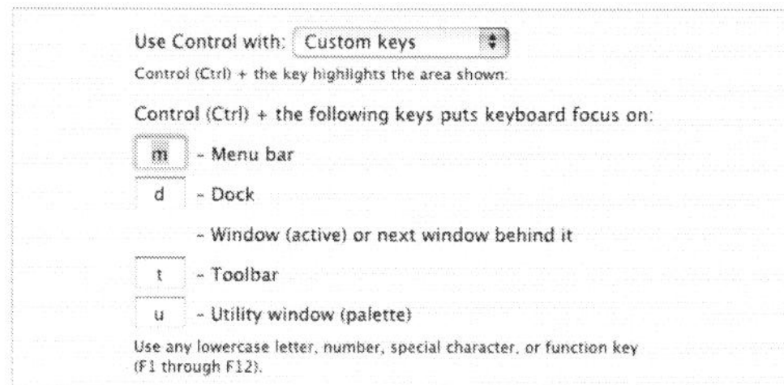

Figure 51 The default Custom keys settings for Full Keyboard Access.

To enable & configure full keyboard access

1. In the Keyboard preferences pane, click the Full Keyboard Access tab (**Figure 49**).
2. To enable full keyboard access, turn on the check box labeled Turn on full keyboard access.
3. Select one of the window and dialog highlighting options:
   - ▲ **Text input fields and lists only** enables you to use the keyboard to access edit boxes and scrolling lists only.
   - ▲ **Any control** enables you to use the keyboard to access any control within a window or dialog box.
4. Choose an option from the Use Control with pop-up menu. Choosing a different option will change the bottom half of the window:
   - ▲ **Function keys** (**Figure 49**) displays function keys to operate full keyboard access.
   - ▲ **Letter keys** (**Figure 50**) displays alphabetic characters to operate full keyboard access.
   - ▲ **Custom keys** (**Figure 51**) displays edit boxes containing default keys to operate full keyboard access. You can enter any lowercase letter or function key from F1 through F12 in each edit box to customize the entries.

✔ Tips

- To enable or disable full keyboard access without opening System Preferences, press Control F1.
- To temporarily change the windows and dialogs highlight option set in step 3 without opening System Preferences, press Control F7.

To use full keyboard access

Hold down Control and press the key for the item you want to access (**Table 1**). The item becomes highlighted. Then:

- Press Tab or Shift Tab (or use the arrow keys) to highlight the next or previous option.
- Press Return to select an item or open an icon.

Here's an example. To open an item on the Dock with Function keys selected (**Table 1** and **Figure 49**):

1. Press Control F4 to highlight an icon on the Dock (**Figure 52**).
2. Press Tab to highlight the item you want.
3. Press Return to open the highlighted icon.

Here's another example. To select a menu option with Letter keys selected (**Table 1** and **Figure 50**):

1. Press Control M to activate the menu bar and display a menu (**Figure 53**).
2. Press ← or → to display the menu you want.
3. Press ↓ until the command you want is highlighted.
4. Press Return to choose the highlighted command.

Table 1

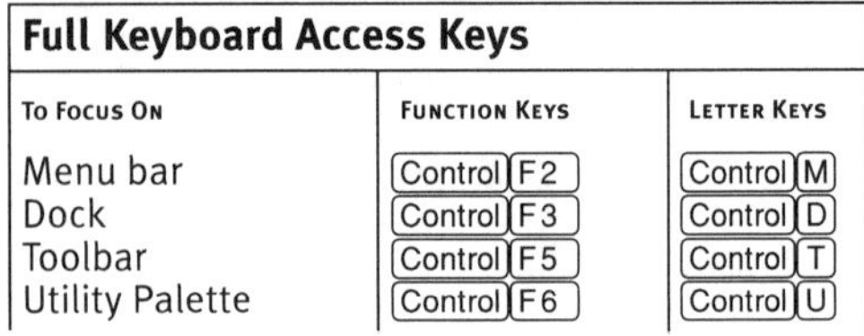

Full Keyboard Access Keys

To Focus On	Function Keys	Letter Keys
Menu bar	Control F2	Control M
Dock	Control F3	Control D
Toolbar	Control F5	Control T
Utility Palette	Control F6	Control U

Figure 52 With full keyboard access enabled, you can use a keystroke to select an icon in the Dock...

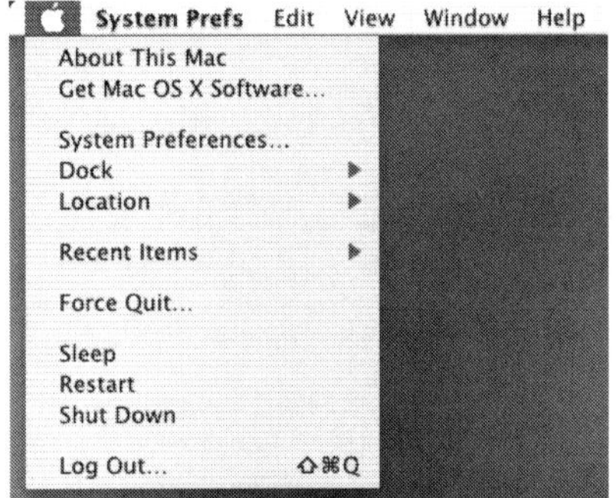

Figure 53 ...or display and choose a command from a menu.

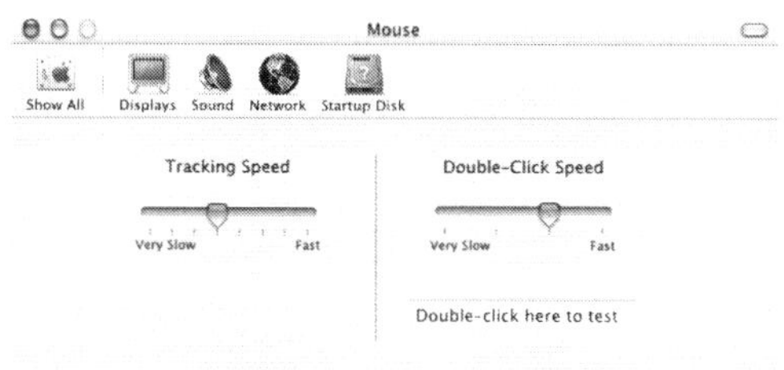

Figure 54 The Mouse preferences pane.

Mouse

The Mouse preferences pane (**Figure 54**) enables you to set options that control the way the mouse works, including the tracking and double-click speed.

To set mouse speeds

1. Display the Mouse preferences pane (**Figure 54**).
2. Set options as desired:
   - ▲ **Tracking Speed** enables you to set the speed of the mouse movement on your screen.
   - ▲ **Double-Click Speed** enables you to set the amount of time between each click of a double-click. You can test the double-click speed by double-clicking in the test area; make changes as necessary to fine-tune the speed.

✔ Tip

- If you're just learning to use a mouse, try setting the tracking and double-click speeds to slower than the default settings.

Sound

The Sound preferences pane enables you to set options to control the system and alert sounds and output device. The settings are broken down into two tabs: Alerts (**Figure 55**) and Output (**Figure 57**).

✔ Tip

- The options that appear in the Sound preferences pane vary depending on your computer and the output devices connected to it. The figures on these pages show options on an iMac.

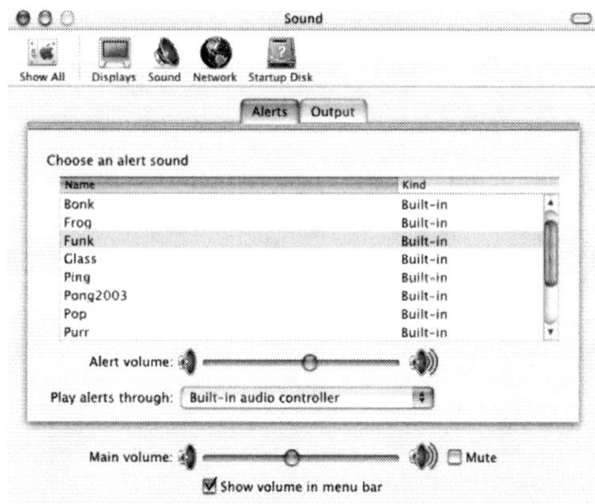

Figure 55 The Alerts tab of the Sound preferences pane.

To set system volume

1. Display the Sound preferences pane (**Figure 55** or **57**).
2. Set options as desired:
   - ▲ To set the system volume, drag the Main Volume slider to the left or right.
   - ▲ To keep your computer quiet, turn on the Mute check box.
   - ▲ To display a Sound volume menu in the menu bar (**Figure 56**), turn on the Show volume in menu bar check box.

Figure 56 The Sound volume menu appears in the menu bar beside the menu bar clock.

✔ Tips

- The main volume is the maximum volume for all sounds, including alerts, games, QuickTime movies, and iTunes music.
- Each time you move and release the Main volume slider in step 2, an alert sounds so you can hear a sample of your change.
- The Sound volume menu, which is a new feature of Mac OS X 10.1, appears on the right end of the menu bar, just to the left of the menu bar clock (**Figure 56**). To use the menu, click to display the slider and drag it up or down. You can rearrange the menus on the right end of the menu bar by holding down [⌘] while dragging them.

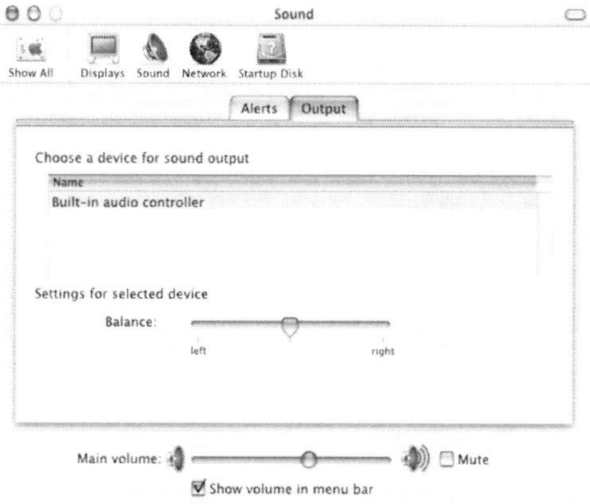

Figure 57 The Output tab of the Sound preferences pane.

To set alert sound options

1. In the Sound preferences pane, click the Alerts tab (**Figure 55**).
2. Set options as desired:
   - ▲ To set the alert sound, select one of the options in the scrolling list.
   - ▲ To set the alert volume, drag the Alert volume slider to the left or right.
   - ▲ To set the output device for alert sounds, choose an option from the Play alerts through pop-up menu.

✔ Tips

- Each time you move and release the slider or select a different alert sound, an alert sounds so you can hear a sample of your change.
- Alert volume depends partly on the main volume setting, which is discussed on the previous page. An alert sound cannot be louder than the main sound.

To set output device options

1. In the Sound preferences pane, click the Output tab (**Figure 57**).
2. Set options as desired:
   - ▲ To set the output device, select one of the options in the scrolling list.
   - ▲ To set the speaker balance for the selected device, drag the Balance slider to the left or right.

✔ Tip

- Each time you move and release the slider, an alert sounds so you can hear a sample of your change.

Internet

The Internet preferences pane enables you to set options for accessing Internet features. Option are broken down into four tabs:

- **iTools** (**Figure 58**) enables you to set your member name and password for using iTools.
- **Email** (**Figure 59**) enables you to set your default e-mail reader application, e-mail address, and e-mail server information.
- **Web** (**Figure 62**) enables you to set your default Web browser, home page, search page, and file download location.
- **News** (**Figure 64**) enables you to set your default news reader application, news server information, and connection information.

✔ Tip

- Connecting to and using the Internet is covered in detail in *Mac OS X: Visual QuickStart Guide.*

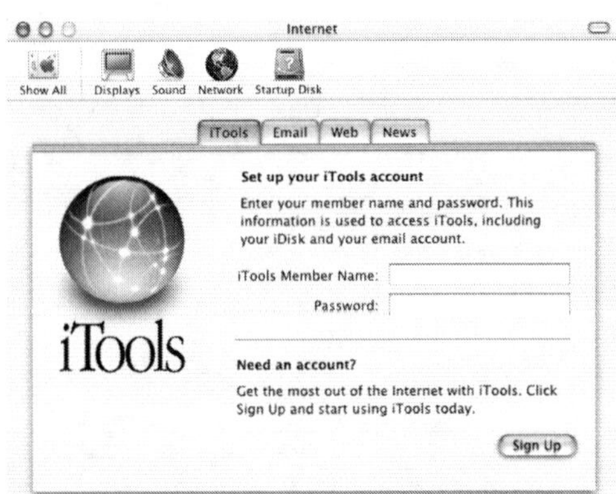

Figure 58 The iTools tab of the Internet preferences pane.

To set iTools options

1. In the Internet preferences pane, click the iTools tab (**Figure 58**).
2. Enter your user ID in the iTools Member Name edit box.
3. Enter your password in the Password edit box.

✔ Tips

- If you do not yet have an iTools account, you can click the Sign Up button to connect to the Internet and create one.
- Using iDisk, a part of iTools, is covered in detail in **Chapter 12**.
- Using iTools is covered in *Mac OS X: Visual QuickStart Guide.*

Figure 59 The Email tab of the Internet preferences pane.

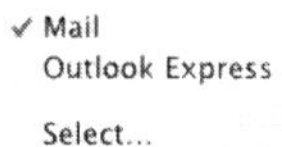

Figure 60 Use this pop-up menu to select your preferred e-mail program.

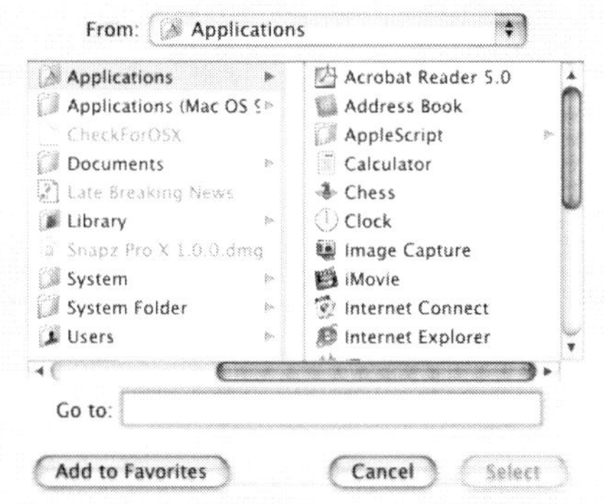

Figure 61 You can use a standard Open dialog to locate and select an e-mail application if it does not appear on the Default Email Reader pop-up menu (**Figure 60**).

To set Email options

1. In the Internet preferences pane, click the Email tab (**Figure 59**).
2. To specify your e-mail application, choose an option from the Default Email Reader pop-up menu (**Figure 60**). The default selection is Mail, but you can choose any e-mail program that is listed or choose Select to use an Open dialog sheet (**Figure 61**) to locate and select the program you want to use.
3. Fill in the fields with address and connection information for your e-mail address. This information should have been provided by your ISP or network administrator.

✔ Tips

- If you turn on the Use iTools Email account check box, all other options are filled in and you can skip step 3.
- Using Mail is covered in *Mac OS X: Visual QuickStart Guide.*

To set Web options

1. In the Internet preferences pane, click the Web tab (**Figure 62**).
2. To specify your Web browser application, choose an option from the Default Web Browser pop-up menu (**Figure 63**). The default option is Internet Explorer, but you can choose any Web browser that is listed or choose Select to use an Open dialog (**Figure 61**) to locate and select the program you want to use.
3. Enter URLs for your preferred Web pages:
   - ▲ **Home Page** is the Web page that opens when you launch your Web browser.
   - ▲ **Search Page** is the Web page that appears when you click the Search button or tab in your Web browser.
4. To specify a folder into which downloaded files should be saved, enter a pathname in the Download Files To edit box. If you prefer, you can click the Select button to display a standard Open dialog similar to the one in **Figure 61** to locate and select a download location.

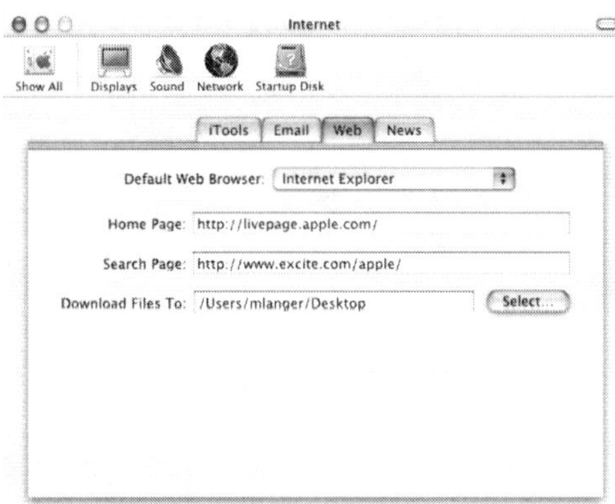

Figure 62 The Web tab of the Internet preferences pane.

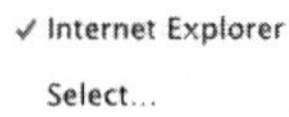

Figure 63 The Default Web Browser pop-up menu.

To set News options

1. In the Internet preferences pane, click the News tab (**Figure 64**).
2. To specify your news reader application, choose an option from the Default News Reader pop-up menu (**Figure 65**). The default option is Outlook Express, a Classic application that comes with Mac OS 9.1 and later, but you can choose any news reader application that is listed or choose Select to use an Open dialog (**Figure 61**) to locate and select the program you want to use.
3. Fill in the fields with server and connection information to access news groups. This information should have been provided by your ISP or network administrator.

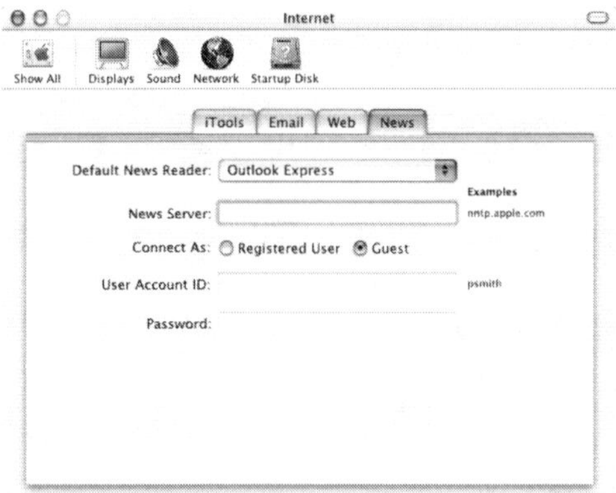

Figure 64 The News tab of the Internet preferences pane.

✓ Outlook Express
Select...

Figure 65 The Default News Reader pop-up menu.

QuickTime

The QuickTime preferences pane enables you to set options that control the way QuickTime works. The pane's options are broken down into five tabs:

- **Plug-In** (**Figure 66**) controls the way the QuickTime Plug-in works with your Web browser.
- **Connection** (**Figure 68**) enables you to specify a connection speed for downloading and playing QuickTime content.
- **Music** (**Figure 71**) enables you to specify a music synthesizer to play QuickTime music and MIDI files.
- **Media Keys** (**Figure 72**) enables you to add, modify, or remove keys for accessing secured QuickTime media files.
- **Update** (**Figure 75**) enables you to update or install Apple or third-party QuickTime software.

✔ Tips

- For the most part, these options affect how QuickTime works within your Web browser. You can customize the way the QuickTime Player application works by setting options in its General Preferences dialog; choose QuickTime Player > Preferences > Player Preferences while the QuickTime Player application is active.
- Using the QuickTime Player is covered in *Mac OS X: Visual QuickStart Guide*.

To set QuickTime Plug-In Options

1. In the QuickTime preferences pane, click the Plug-In tab (**Figure 66**).
2. Set options as desired:
   - ▲ **Play movies automatically** plays QuickTime movies automatically as they are downloaded to your Web browser. With this option turned on, the movie will begin to play as it downloads to your computer. With this option turned off, you'll have to click the Play button on the QuickTime controller to play the movie after it has begun to download.
   - ▲ **Save movies in disk cache** saves a copy of downloaded movies in your Web browser's disk cache whenever possible. This makes it possible to replay the movie at another time without reloading it. This feature is limited by the size of your Web browser's disk cache; as soon as the cache is full, old movies are deleted to make room for new downloaded pages, images, and other media.
   - ▲ **Enable kiosk mode** hides the options to save movies and to change QuickTime settings from within your Web browser. With this option turned off, you can hold down Control and click a QuickTime movie to display a contextual menu with commands for working with the movie or QuickTime settings.
   - ▲ **MIME settings** displays a dialog like the one in **Figure 67** that you can use to select document types you want the QuickTime Plug-in to handle. Click a triangle to display options beneath it. Click a check box to toggle the setting on or off. When you're finished, click OK.

Figure 66 The Plug-In tab of the QuickTime preferences pane.

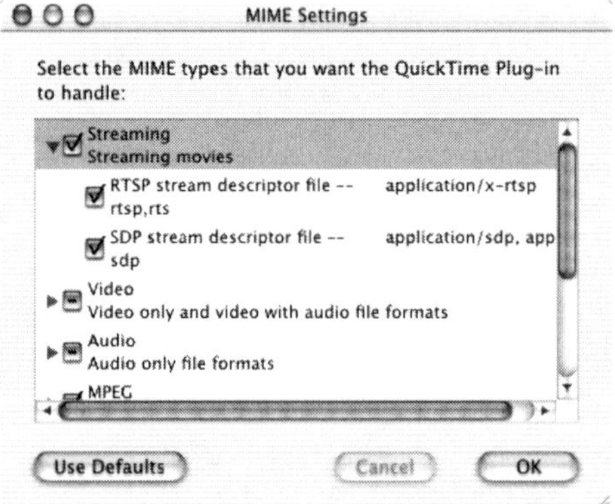

Figure 67 Use the MIME Settings dialog to specify the types of documents that should be handled by the QuickTime Plug-In.

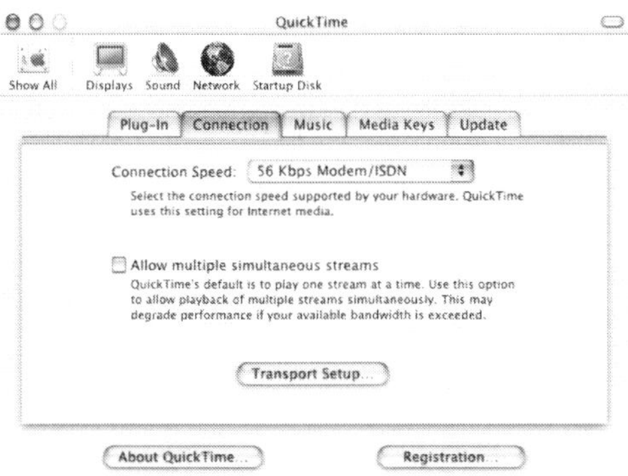

Figure 68 The Connection tab of the QuickTime preferences pane.

28.8/33.6 Kbps Modem
✓ 56 Kbps Modem/ISDN
112 Kbps Dual ISDN/DSL
256 Kbps DSL/Cable
384 Kbps DSL/Cable
512 Kbps DSL/Cable
768 Kbps DSL/Cable
1 Mbps Cable
1.5 Mbps T1/Intranet/LAN
Intranet/LAN

Figure 69 The Connection Speed pop-up menu.

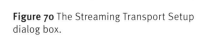

Streaming Transport Setup

Select a transport protocol and port ID, or click Auto Configure to have QuickTime make the selection for you.

Transport Protocol: UDP

RTSP Port ID: 554
7070
Other

Auto Configure

Figure 70 The Streaming Transport Setup dialog box.

To set QuickTime connection options

1. In the QuickTime preferences pane, click the Connection tab (**Figure 68**).
2. Choose the speed at which you connect to the Internet from the Connection Speed pop-up menu (**Figure 69**).
3. To play multiple data streams at the same time, turn on the Allow multiple simultaneous streams check box.
4. To select a streaming video transport protocol and port number, click the Transport Setup button. Then set options in the Streaming Transport Setup dialog that appears (**Figure 70**) and click the close button.

✓ Tips

- Because of performance issues, the simultaneous streams feature should only be enabled if your connection speed exceeds 112 Kbps. (In fact, it is turned on by default at 112 Kbps or higher.) When used with slower connection speeds, QuickTime media may not play back smoothly.
- If you're not sure what to set in the Streaming Transport Setup dialog (**Figure 70**) in step 4, click the Auto Configure button, wait for QuickTime to set the options for you, and click the close button to dismiss the dialog.

To set the QuickTime music synthesizer

1. In the QuickTime preferences pane, click the Music tab (**Figure 71**).
2. Select one of the options in the list.
3. Click Make Default.

✔ Tip

- The options that appear in the list vary depending on the synthesizers installed in your computer.

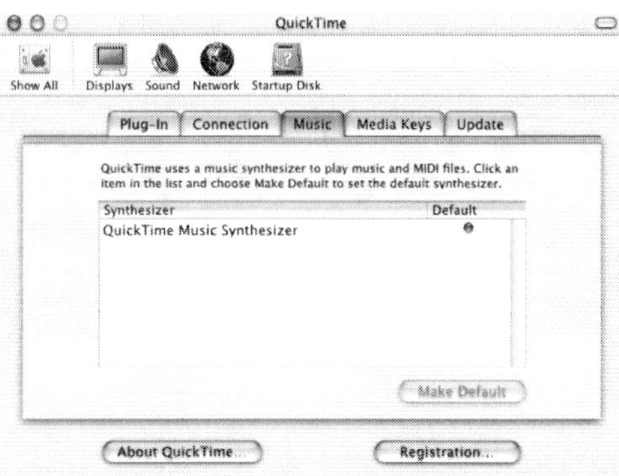

Figure 71 The Music tab of the QuickTime preferences pane.

To add, remove, or modify QuickTime media keys

1. In the QuickTime preferences pane, click the Media Keys tab (**Figure 72**).
2. Modify the list of media keys as desired:
   - ▲ To add a media key, click Add. Then use the dialog sheet that appears (**Figure 73**) to enter the category and key and click OK.
   - ▲ To modify a media key, select the key in the list and click Edit. Then use the dialog sheet that appears (**Figure 73**) to modify the key's information.
   - ▲ To remove a media key, select the key in the list and click Delete. Then click Delete in the confirmation dialog that appears (**Figure 74**).

✔ Tip

- You must have a media key set up to access secured QuickTime media.

Figure 72 The Media Keys tab of the QuickTime preferences pane.

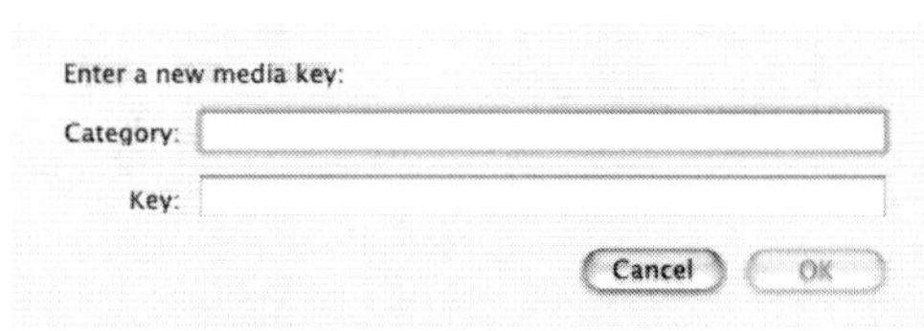

Figure 73 Use this dialog sheet to enter media key information.

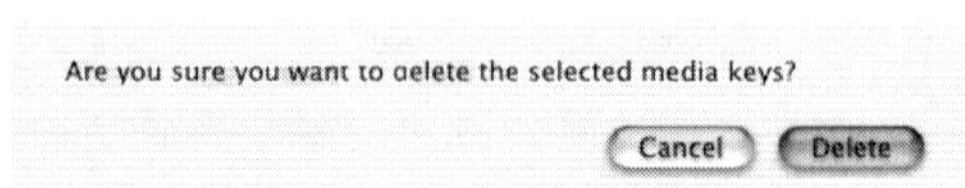

Figure 74 This dialog box appears when you delete a media key.

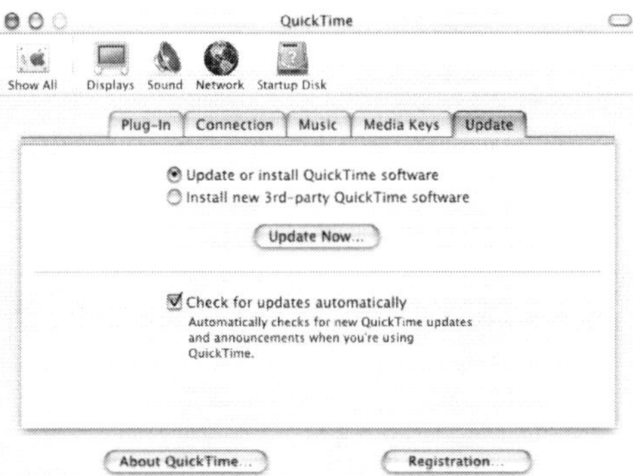

Figure 75 The Update tab of the QuickTime preferences pane.

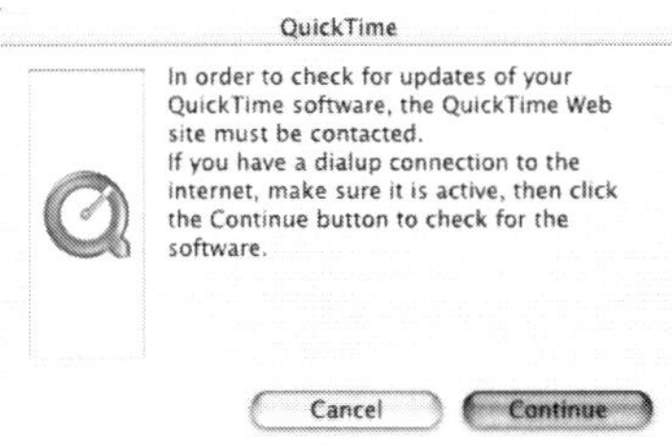

Figure 76 If this dialog appears, make sure you're connected to the Internet and click Continue.

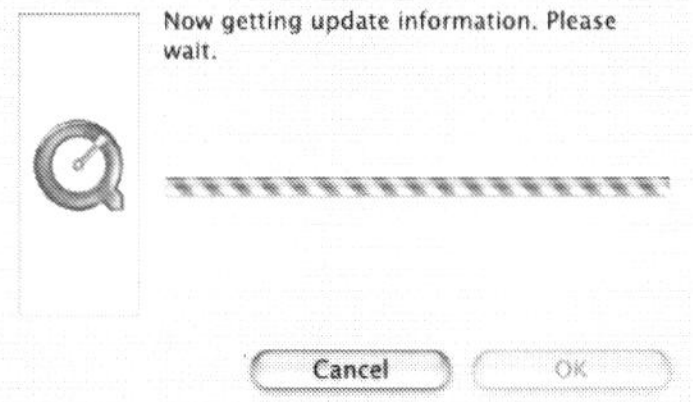

Figure 77 A status dialog like this may appear while your computer searches for updates.

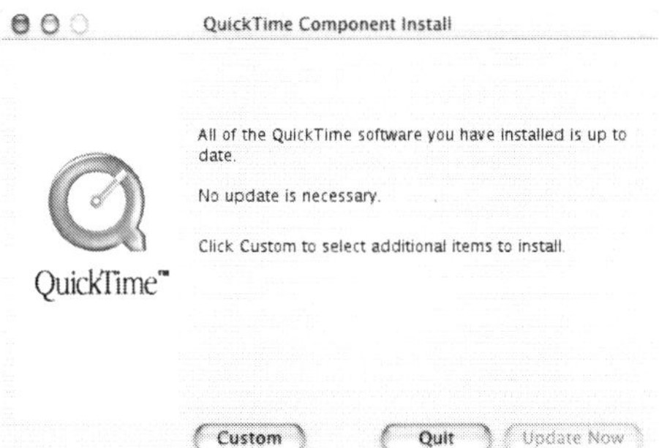

Figure 78 The QuickTime Component Install dialog tells you whether an update is necessary.

To update QuickTime software

1. In the QuickTime preferences pane, click the Update tab (**Figure 75**).
2. Select one of the update/install options:
   - ▲ **Update or install QuickTime software** searches the QuickTime Web site for QuickTime software published by Apple.
   - ▲ **Install new 3rd-party QuickTime software** searches the QuickTime Web site for third-party software that works with QuickTime.
3. Click Update Now to launch the Software Update or QuickTime Updater application.
4. A dialog like the one in **Figure 76** may appear. If you have a dialup Internet connection, connect to the Internet and click Continue.
5. A progress dialog like the one in **Figure 77** may appear while your computer searches for update information. When it's finished, the QuickTime Component Install dialog (**Figure 78**) appears to tell you whether you need to update.
   - ▲ If an update is available, click Update Now and follow the instructions that appear onscreen.
   - ▲ If no update is necessary, click Quit.

✔ Tips

- You must have an Internet connection to update QuickTime with this feature.
- If an update is available in step 5, you can click the Custom button to pick and choose among the updates to install.
- If you turn on the Check for Updates automatically check box in the Update tab of the Quicken preferences pane (**Figure 75**), your computer will automatically check for updates and display the Quick-Time Component Install dialog (**Figure 78**) when an update is available.

To upgrade to QuickTime Pro

1. Display any tab of the QuickTime preferences pane (**Figure 66**, **68**, **71**, **72**, or **75**).
2. Click the Registration button.
3. In the registration information dialog sheet that appears (**Figure 79**), click Register Online.

   or

   If you already have a QuickTime Pro key, skip ahead to step 5.
4. Your Web browser launches, connects to Apple's Web site, and displays the Get QuickTime Pro page. Follow the instructions that appear onscreen to purchase a QuickTime Pro key. Then switch back to System Preferences.
5. In the registration information dialog sheet (**Figure 79**), click Edit Registration.
6. Enter your registration information in the edit boxes and click OK.

✔ Tips

- A QuickTime Pro upgrade adds features to the QuickTime Player software, including the ability to edit and save QuickTime files.
- You can confirm that your registration information has been properly entered by clicking the Registration button in any tab of the QuickTime preferences pane (**Figure 66**, **68**, **71**, **72**, or **75**). The QuickTime version information should appear right above the buttons in the registration information dialog that appears.

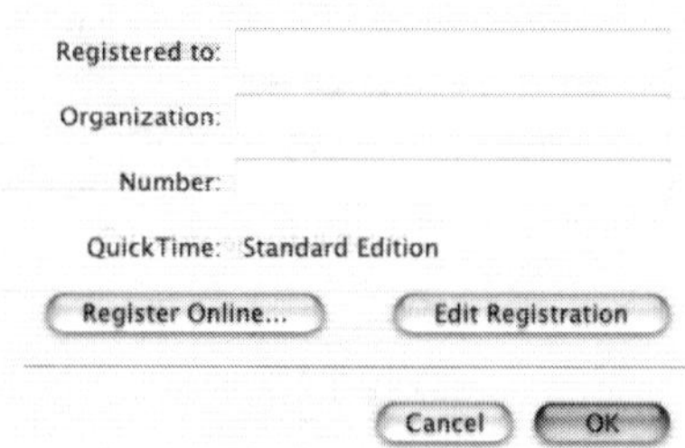

Figure 79 Use this dialog to enter, edit, and check registration information.

Date & Time

The Date & Time preferences pane (**Figures 80**, **82**, **83**, and **84**) includes four panels for setting the system time and clock options:

- **Date & Time** (**Figure 5**) enables you to manually set the date and time.
- **Time Zone** (**Figure 7**) enables you to set your time zone.
- **Network Time** (**Figure 8**) enables you to synchronize your system clock with a network time server.
- **Menu Bar Clock** (**Figure 9**) enables you to set options for the appearance of the digital clock in the menu bar.

✔ Tips

- If you have an Internet connection, the Network Time feature ensures that your computer's clock is always correct.
- To prevent unauthorized changes to the Date & Time settings, click the lock button. Later, if you click the lock to unlock them, a password dialog similar to the one in **Figure 47** appears. You must enter administrator login information to unlock the Date & Time settings and make changes.

To manually set the date & time

1. In the Date & Time preferences pane, click the Date & Time tab (**Figure 80**).
2. Make changes as follows:
   - ▲ To change the date, click the arrow buttons beside the month and year to set the month and year. Then click the current date on the calendar to set the date.
   - ▲ To change the current time, click the part of the time that you want to change (**Figure 81**) and type a new value or use the arrow keys beside the time to change the value.
3. Click Save.

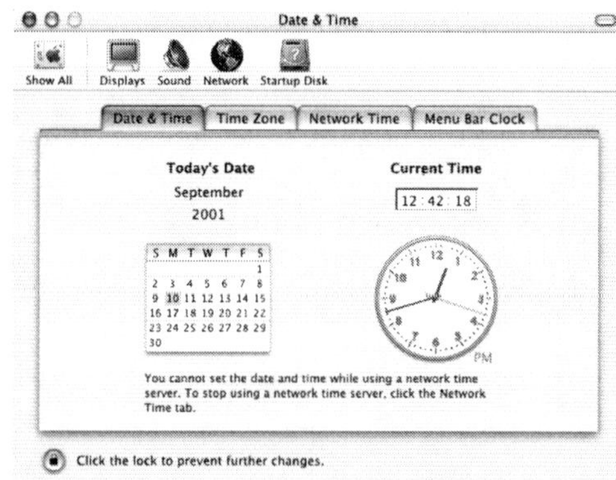

Figure 80 The Date & Time tab of the Date & Time preferences pane.

Current Time

12 : 42 : 56

Figure 81 Click a time value and enter a new value to change it.

✔ Tips

- Another way to change the time in step 2 is to drag the hands of the analog clock so they display the correct time. (This is kind of cool, but it's tough to be accurate.)
- You can't manually change the date or time if you have enabled the network time server feature; I tell you more about that on the next page.

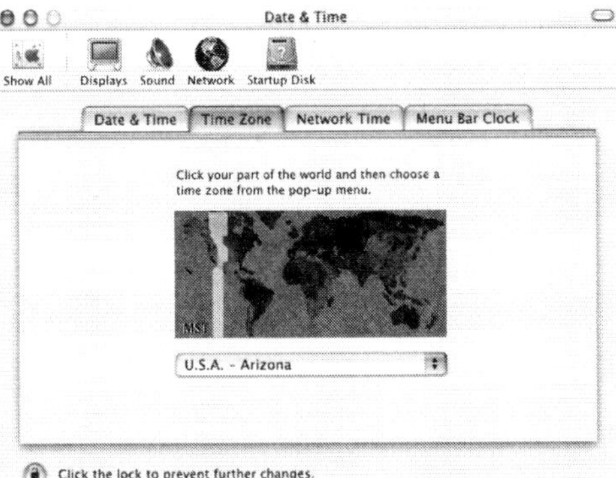

Figure 82 The Time Zone tab of the Date & Time preferences pane.

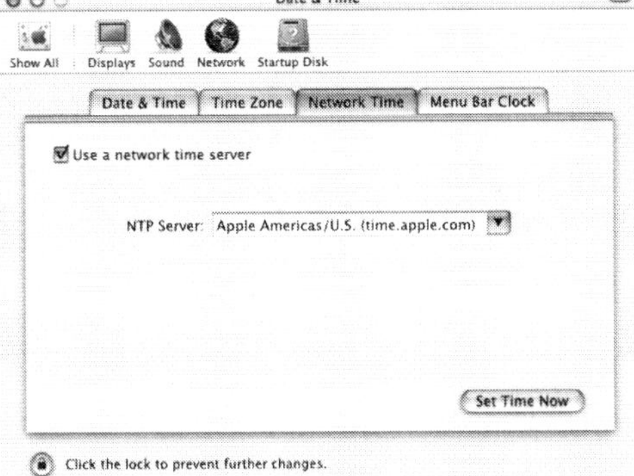

Figure 83 The Network Time tab of the Date & Time preferences pane.

To set the time zone

1. In the Date & Time preferences pane, click the Time Zone tab (**Figure 82**).
2. Click your approximate location on the map. A white bar indicates the time zone area.
3. If necessary, hoose the name of your time zone from the pop-up menu beneath the map.

✔ Tips

- In step 3, only those time zones that apply to the white bar on the map are listed in the pop-up menu. If your time zone does not appear in the menu, make sure you clicked the correct area in the map in step 2.
- It's a good idea to choose the correct time zone, since Mac OS uses this information with the network time server (if utilized) and to properly change the clock for daylight saving time.

To use a network time server

1. In the Date & Time preferences pane, click the Network Time tab (**Figure 83**).
2. Turn on the Use a network time server check box.
3. Choose the closest time server from the NTP Server pop-up menu.
4. To set the time immediately, click the Set Time Now button.

✔ Tips

- With the network time server feature enabled, your computer will use its network or Internet connection to periodically get the date and time from a time server and update the system clock automatically.
- You must have a network or Internet connection capable of accessing a time server to use this feature.

To set menu bar clock options

1. In the Date & Time preferences pane, click the Menu Bar Clock tab (**Figure 84**).
2. To enable the menu bar clock, turn on the Show the clock in the menu bar check box.
3. Toggle check boxes to specify how the menu bar clock looks:
   - ▲ **Display the time with seconds** displays the seconds as part of the time.
   - ▲ **Append AM/PM to the time** displays AM or PM after the time.
   - ▲ **Show the day of the week** displays the three-letter abbreviation for the day of the week before the time.
   - ▲ **Flash the time separators** blinks the colon(s) in the time every second. (Talk about a potentially annoying distraction!)

   The clock changes immediately to reflect your settings.

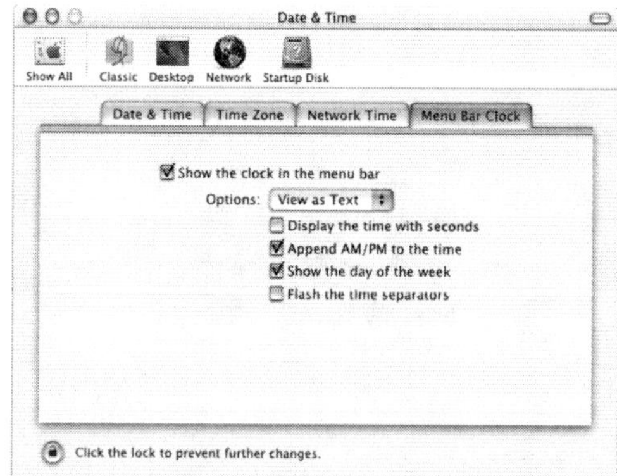

Figure 84 The Menu Bar Clock panel of the System Preferences Date & Time pane. These are the default settings.

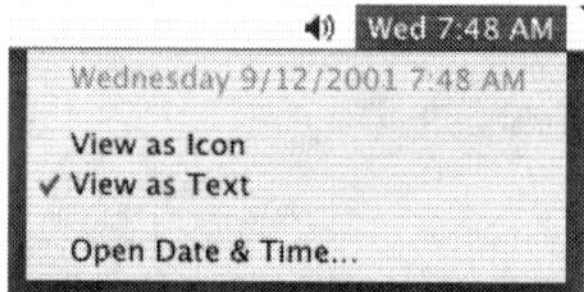

Figure 85 The menu bar clock is also a menu.

✔ Tips

- You can switch between a 12-hour clock and a 24-hour clock. Use settings in the Time tab of the International preferences pane, which I discuss earlier in this chapter.
- The menu bar clock is also a menu that displays the full date and time and offers options for changing the clock display (**Figure 85**).
- Choosing View as Icon from the menu bar clock menu (**Figure 85**) converts the digital clock to a tiny analog clock.
- The menu bar clock settings have nothing to do with the Clock application, which can place a clock in the Dock or onscreen as a floating window. The Clock application is covered in *Mac OS X: Visual QuickStart Guide*.

Figure 86 The Software Update preferences pane.

Software Update

The Software Update preferences pane (**Figure 86**) enables you to configure the Mac OS software update feature. This program checks Apple's Internet servers for updates to your Mac OS X software and enables you to download and install them.

✔ Tip

- You must have an Internet connection to update Mac OS X software with this feature.

To set software update options

1. Display the Software Update preferences pane (**Figure 86**).
2. Select one of the two Update Software options:
   - ▲ **Manually** checks for software updates only when you initiate an update.
   - ▲ **Automatically** checks for software periodically without manually initiating an update. If you select this option, choose one of the options from the Check for updates pop-up menu: Daily, Weekly, or Monthly.

✔ Tip

- If you select the Automatically option, in step 2, your computer will display a Software Update window like the one in **Figure 88** if any updates are available after a check. Follow the instructions in step 2 to install software and/or dismiss the window.

To update software

1. In the Software Update preferences pane (**Figure 86**), click Update Now.

   Your computer connects to the Internet and checks Apple's servers for update information. A status bar appears in the bottom of the Software Update preferences pane as it works (**Figure 87**).

2. When the check is complete, the Software Update window appears (**Figure 88**). It contains information about whether any updates are available.

   ▲ To install updates, turn on the check mark beside each update you want to install. Then click Install. Follow any additional instructions that appear onscreen.

   ▲ To quit Software Update without installing any software, choose Software Update > Quit Software Update or press ⌘Q.

✔ Tips

- Some software updates may require that you provide an administrator password before installation. If so, an Authenticate dialog like the one in **Figure 89** will appear. Enter administrator login information in the appropriate edit boxes and click OK to continue.

- You can click the Show Log button to display a dialog sheet containing recent update information (**Figure 90**). Click Close Log to dismiss the sheet when you are finished with it.

Figure 87 A status bar appears in the bottom of the Software Update preference panel while your computer checks for updates.

Figure 88 A list of software updates appears in the Software Update window. (How nice of Apple to put a Test Update online so I could take this screen shot!)

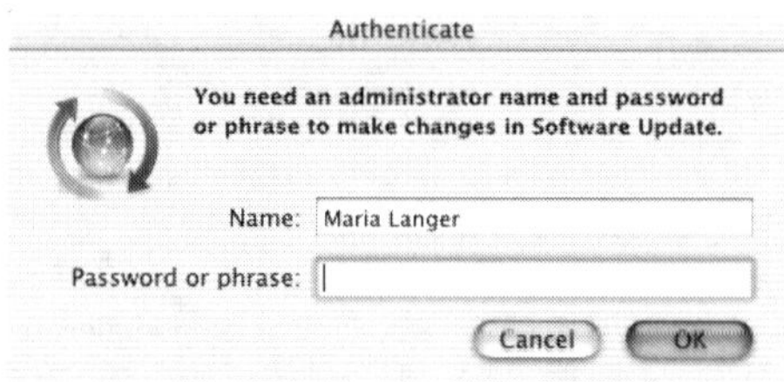

Figure 89 Some software updates may require administrator login information to process.

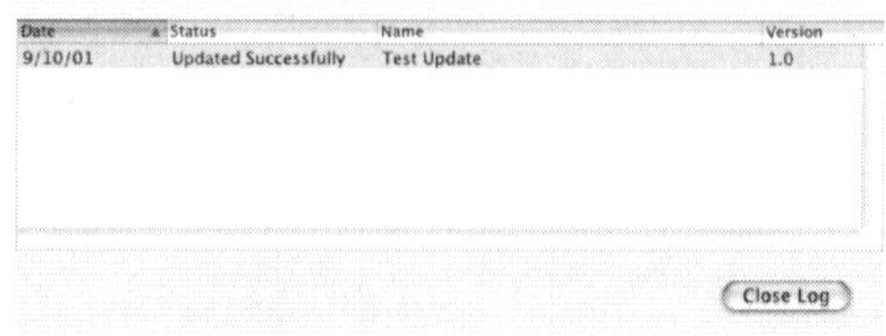

Figure 90 The Show Log button displays a log of your software updates.

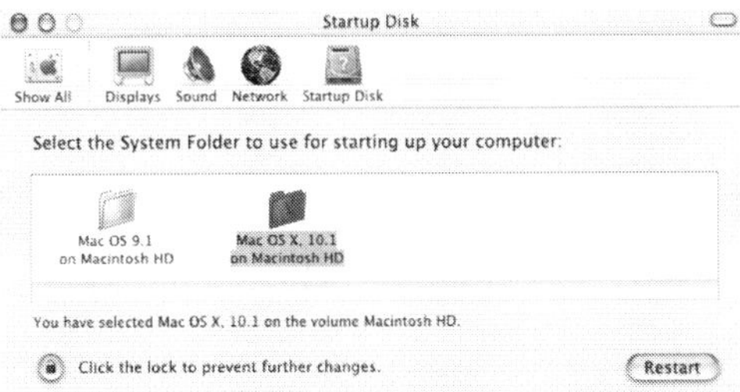

Figure 91 The Startup Disk preferences pane.

Startup Disk

The Startup Disk preferences pane (**Figure 91**) enables you to select a startup disk and, if desired, restart your computer. You might find this helpful if you want to start your computer under Mac OS 9.1 or 9.2 or from a bootable CD-ROM disc, such as a Mac OS installer disc.

✔ Tips

- Starting your computer under Mac OS 9.x is discussed in **Chapter 2**.
- Mac OS X enables you to have multiple System Folders on a single disk or partition. Startup Disk is the tool you use to select which System Folder should be used at startup.

To select a startup disk

1. Display the Startup Disk preferences pane (**Figure 91**).
2. Click the icon for the startup folder or disk you want to use.
3. To immediately restart your computer, click the Restart button.

✔ Tip

- To prevent unauthorized changes to the Startup Disk settings, click the lock button. Later, if you click the lock to unlock them, a password dialog similar to the one in **Figure 47** appears. You must enter administrator login information to unlock the Startup Disk settings and make changes.

Fonts

Fonts & Font Formats

Fonts are typefaces that appear on screen and in printed documents. When they're properly installed, they appear on all Font menus and in font lists.

Mac OS X supports several types of fonts:

- **Data fork TrueType format** (.dfont) stores all information in the data fork of the file, including resources used by Mac OS drawing routines.
- **Microsoft Windows font formats** are Windows format font files. These include TrueType fonts (.ttf) and TrueType collections (.ttc).
- **OpenType font technology** (.otf) was developed by Adobe Systems, Inc. and Microsoft Corporation. Designed to be cross-platform, the same font files work on both Mac OS and Windows computers.
- **PostScript fonts in Mac OS or Windows format** are used primarily for printing. These fonts must be accompanied by corresponding bitmapped font files.
- **Mac OS 9.x and earlier font formats** include Mac OS TrueType fonts and bitmapped fonts.

✔ Tips

- Traditionally, Mac OS files could contain two parts or *forks*: a *resource fork* and a *data fork*. This causes incompatibility problems with non-Mac OS systems, which do not support a file's resource fork. Data fork suitcase format fonts don't have resource forks, so they can work on a variety of computer platforms.
- PostScript font technology was developed by Adobe Systems, Inc.

Installing Fonts

On a typical Mac OS X system, fonts can be installed in four or more places (**Table 1**). Where a font is installed determines who can use it.

- **User fonts** are installed in a user's Fonts folder (**Figure 1**). Each user can install, control, and access his or her own fonts. Fonts installed in a user's Fonts folder are available only to that user.
- **Local fonts** are installed in the Fonts folder for the startup disk (**Figure 2**). These fonts are accessible to all local users of the computer. Only an Admin user can modify the contents of this Fonts folder.
- **System fonts** are installed in the Fonts folder for the system (**Figure 3**). These fonts are installed by the Mac OS X installer and are used by the system. The contents of this Fonts folder should not be modified.
- **Classic fonts** are installed in the Fonts folder within the Mac OS 9.x System Folder (**Figure 4**). These are the only fonts accessible by the Classic environment, although Mac OS X can use these fonts, even when the Classic environment is not running.
- **Network fonts** are installed in the Fonts folder for the network. These fonts are accessible to all local area network users. This feature is normally used on network file servers, not the average user's computer. Only a network administrator can modify the contents of this Fonts folder.

✔ Tips

- Duplicate fonts are resolved based on where they are installed, in the following order: User, Local, Network, System, and

Table 1

Font Installation Locations

Font Use	Font Folder
User	HD/Users/UserName/Library/Fonts/
Local	HD/Library/Fonts/
System	HD/System/Library/Fonts/
Classic	HD/System Folder/Fonts
Network	Network/Library/Fonts/

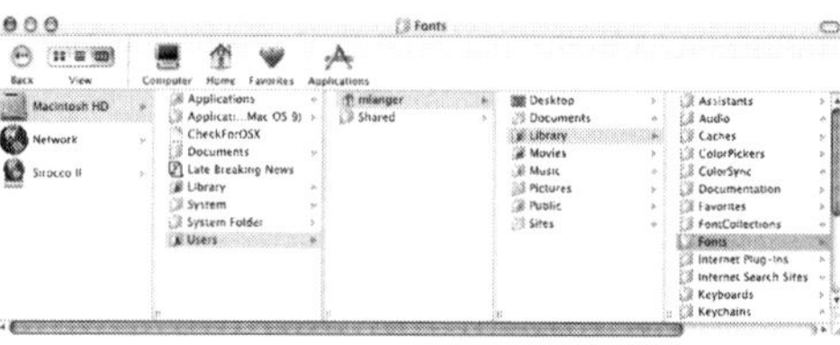

Figure 1 User fonts are installed in the Fonts folder within the user's Library folder.

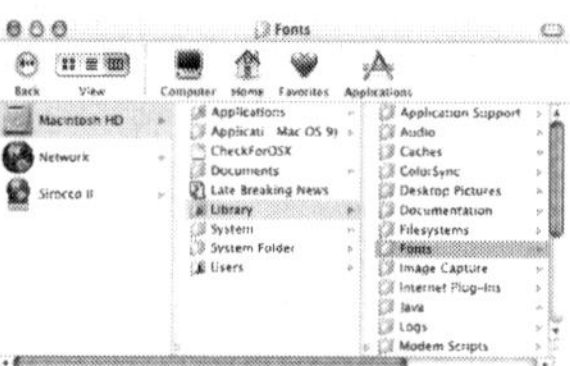

Figure 2 Local fonts are installed in the Fonts folder within the startup disk's Library folder.

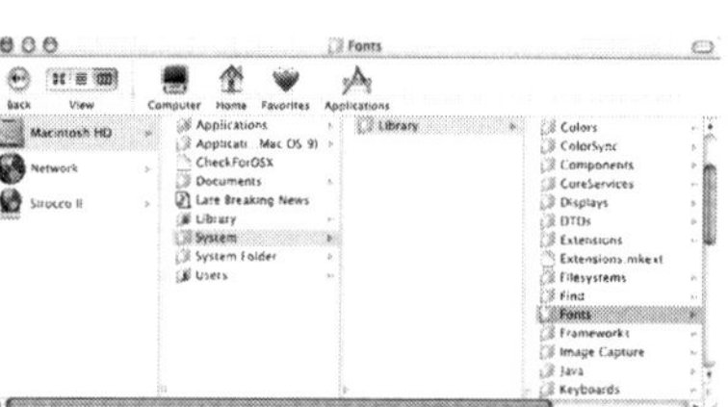

Figure 3 System fonts are installed in the Fonts folder within the System's Library folder.

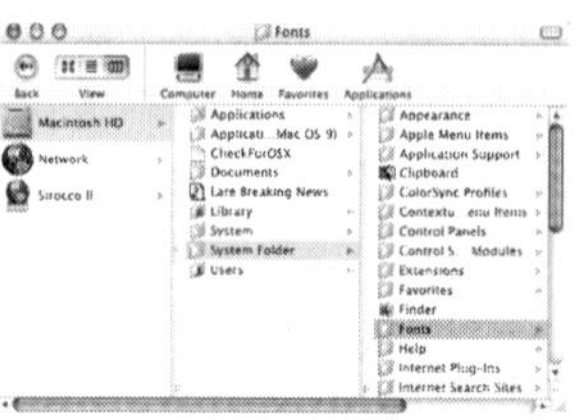

Figure 4 Classic fonts are installed in the Fonts folder within the Mac OS 9.x System Folder.

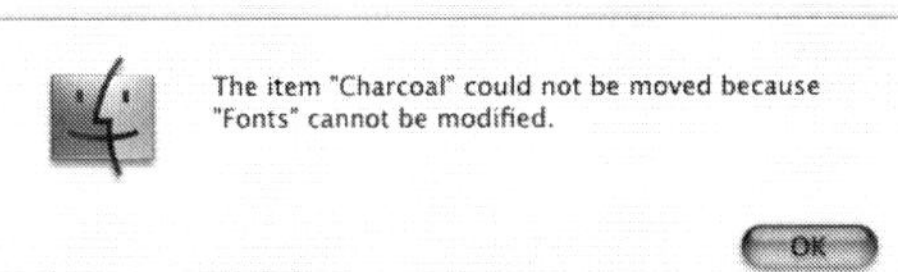

Figure 5 A dialog like this appears if you try to change a Fonts folder and do not have enough privileges.

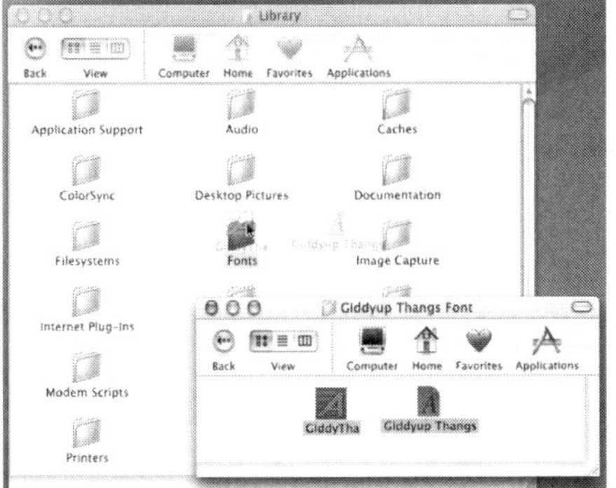

Figure 6 To install a font, drag it into (or onto) the appropriate Fonts folder. This illustration shows a PostScript font file with its accompanying bitmap font file being installed.

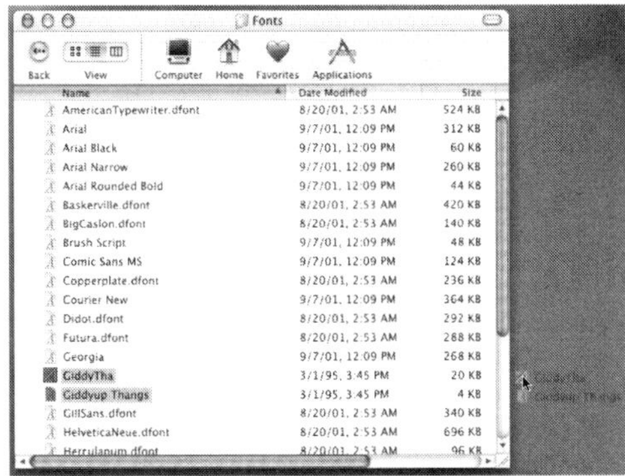

Figure 7 To uninstall a font, drag it out of the Fonts folder. This illustration shows the font installed in **Figure 5** being uninstalled.

Classic. For example, if the same font existed as both a User and System font, the User font would be used.

- Changes to the Fonts folder take effect when an application is opened.
- If you do not have the correct privileges to change a Fonts folder, a dialog like the one in **Figure 5** will appear. Click OK. If you need to make changes to that Fonts folder, ask a user with Admin privileges to do it for you.

To install a font

Drag all files that are part of the font into the appropriate Fonts folder (**Figure 6**).

To uninstall a font

Drag all files that are part of the font out of the Fonts folder they were installed in (**Figure 7**).

Key Caps

Key Caps enables you to see and locate the characters in your fonts.

To use Key Caps

1. Open the Key Caps icon in the Utilities folder inside the Applications folder (**Figure 8**). The Key Caps window appears (**Figure 9**).
2. Set options as desired and view results in the Key Caps window:
   - ▲ To see what the characters of a different font look like, choose the font name from the Font menu (**Figure 10**).
   - ▲ To see what characters look like with a modifier key (such as Shift or Option) pressed, press the modifier key (**Figure 11**).

✔ Tips

- You can type in the Key Caps window to see what a string of text looks like in a specific font.
- You can use Key Caps to learn special characters. For example, hold down Option while looking at the Key Caps window (**Figure 11**) to see a bullet (•), registered trademark symbol (®), and copyright symbol (©). To type one of these characters, hold Option while pressing the appropriate keyboard key: Option 8 for •, Option R for ®, and Option G for ©.
- Accented characters (for example é, ñ, and ü) require two keystrokes to type. First type the keystroke for the accent, then type the character that you want the accent to appear over. For example, to type á, press Option E and then A. The two-stroke characters appear in Key Caps with a white box around them when you hold down Option (**Figure 11**).

Figure 8 The Key Caps icon.

Figure 9 The Key Caps window, displaying characters from the Lucida Grand Regular font. (The keyboard in this illustration is a standard iMac keyboard; your keyboard layout may be different.)

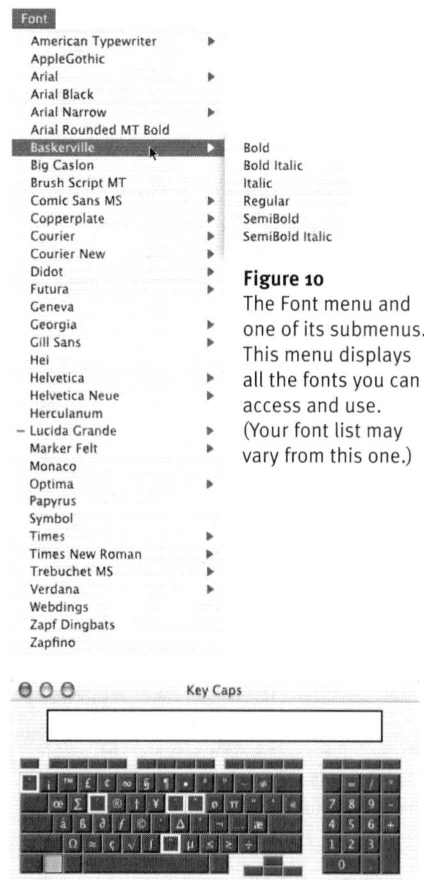

Figure 10 The Font menu and one of its submenus. This menu displays all the fonts you can access and use. (Your font list may vary from this one.)

Figure 11 In this example, holding down Option displays additional characters in the font.

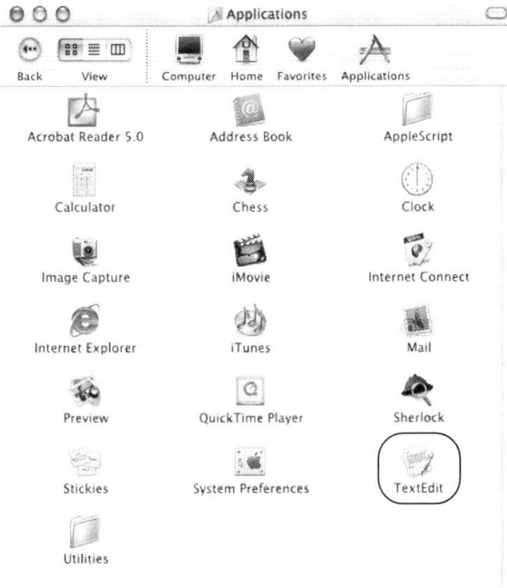

Figure 12 You can find TextEdit in the Applications folder.

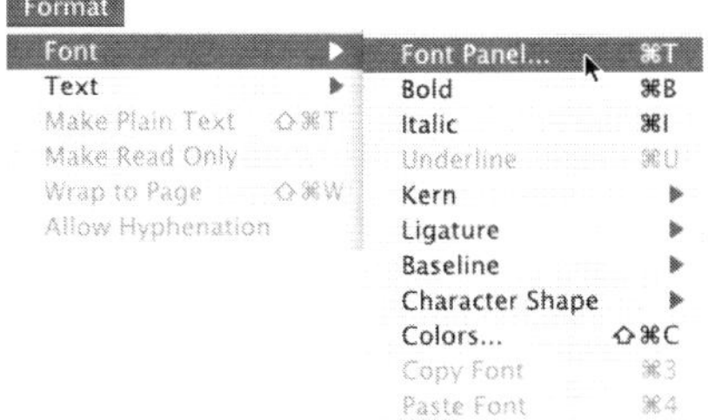

Figure 13 Choose Font Panel from the Font submenu under TextEdit's Format menu.

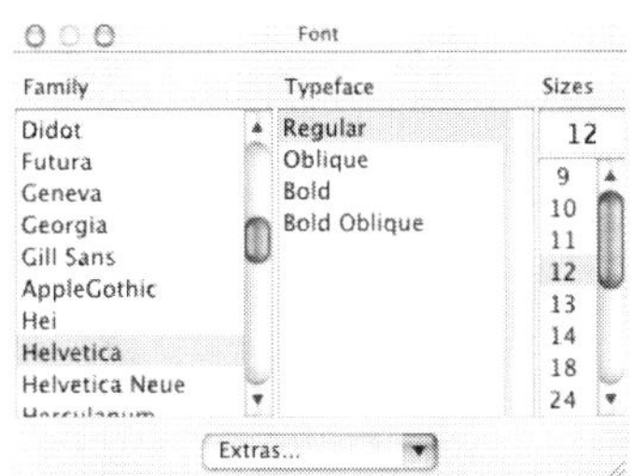

Figure 14 TextEdit's Font panel.

The Font Panel

The Font panel offers a standard interface for formatting font characters in a document. It also offers access to additional options for organizing and obtaining fonts.

✔ Tips

- This part of the chapter looks at the Font panel as it appears in TextEdit, the text editor that comes with Mac OS X. You can find TextEdit in the Applications folder on the Mac OS X startup disk (**Figure 12**).
- The Font panel is only available in Cocoa applications and not Carbon applications., To learn more about Carbon and Cocoa, consult **Chapter 1**.

To open TextEdit's Font panel

With TextEdit active, choose Format > Font > Font Panel (**Figure 13**) or press ⌘T. The Font panel appears (**Figure 14**).

To apply font formatting

1. Open the Font panel (**Figure 14**).
2. Select a font family from the Family list.
3. Select a style from the Typeface list.
4. Select a size from the Sizes list.

   or

   Enter the size you want in the Sizes edit box.

   The changes you make are applied to selected text or to text typed at the insertion point.

Continued on next page...

Continued from previous page.

✔ Tips

- The styles that appear in the Typeface list vary depending on the font selected in the Family list. Some font families offer more styles than others.
- *Oblique* is similar to italic. *Light, regular, medium, bold,* and *black* refer to font weights or boldness.
- If the Sizes area in step 4 displays a slider as shown in **Figure 23**, drag the slider to change the size.

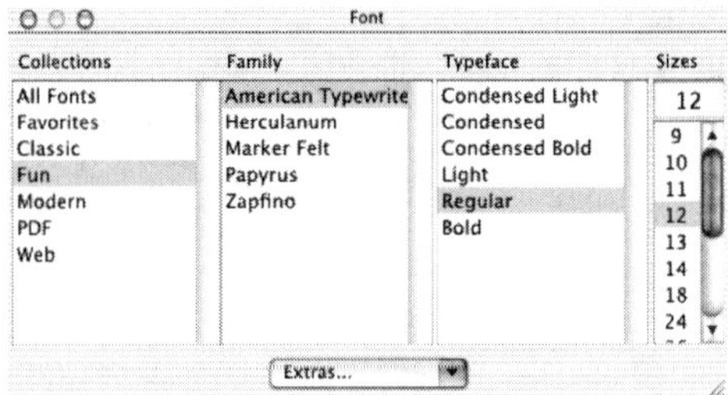

Figure 15 The Font panel, expanded to show the Collections list.

To view font collections

Drag the resize control in the lower-right corner of the Font panel to the right to make the window wider. Release the mouse button when a Collections list appears in the panel to the left of the Family list (**Figure 15**).

✔ Tips

- The Font panel includes a number of predefined collections: Classic, Fun, Modern, PDF, and Web. It also includes the Favorites collection, which is empty until you add favorite fonts.
- Font collections make it easier to find the fonts you use most, especially when there are many fonts installed on your computer.

To see only fonts within a specific collection

In the Collections list, select the name of the collection you want to see. The Family list changes to show only fonts within the collection (**Figure 15**).

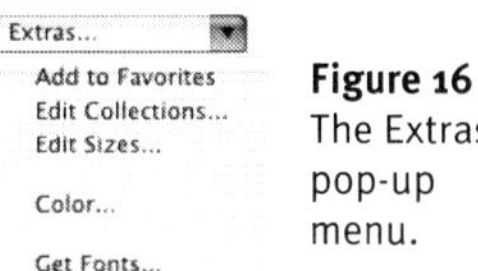

Figure 16 The Extras pop-up menu.

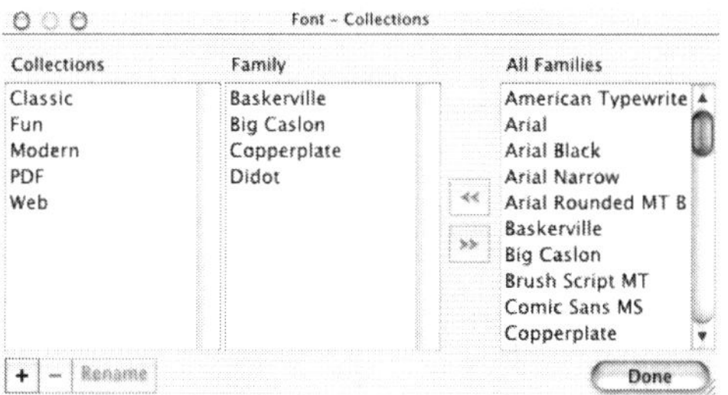

Figure 17 Use the Font – Collections panel to modify collections.

Figure 18 When you add a collection, you can edit its name before adding fonts to it.

To modify collections

1. Choose Edit Collections from the Extras pop-up menu (**Figure 16**). The Font panel changes to the Font – Collections panel (**Figure 17**).
2. In the Collections list, select the name of the collection you want to modify.
3. To remove a font from the collection, select the font in the Family list and click the >> button.

   or

   To add a font to the collection, select the font in the All Families list and click the << button.
4. Repeat step 3 until the collection includes the fonts you want.
5. Repeat steps 2 through 4 to edit other collections.
6. Click Done. Your changes are saved and the Font – Collections panel is replaced by the Font panel.

✔ Tips

- To add a new collection, click the + button in step 2. A collection named New-1 appears (**Figure 18**). Use standard editing techniques to change the name of the collection and press Return. Then follow steps 3 and 4 to add fonts to the new collection.
- To remove a collection, click the – button after step 2. The collection disappears.
- To rename a collection, click the Rename button after step 2. Use standard editing techniques to change the name of the collection and press Return.
- Removing a font or a collection does not delete fonts from your computer.

To add a font to the Favorites collection

1. In the Font panel (**Figure 14**), select the Family, Typeface, and Size of the font you want to add to the Favorites collection.
2. Choose Add to Favorites from the Extras pop-up menu (**Figure 16**).

   When you select the Favorites collection in the Font panel, you can see that the font was added to the collection (**Figure 19**).

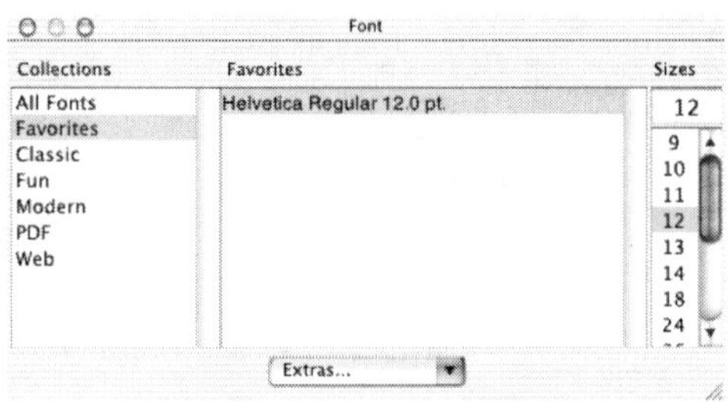

Figure 19 A font in the Favorites collection appears in its typeface.

✔ Tip

- Fonts added to the Favorites collection appear in their typeface style (**Figure 19**).

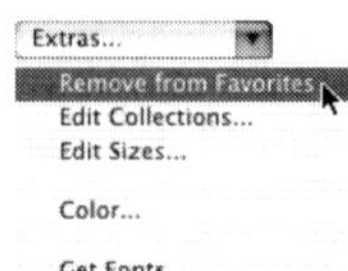

Figure 20 Choose Remove from Favorites from the Extras pop-up menu.

To remove a font from the Favorites collection

1. In the Font panel, select Favorites in the Collections list (**Figure 19**).
2. In the Favorites list, select the favorite font that you want to remove.
3. Choose Remove from Favorites from the Extras pop-up menu (**Figure 20**).

   The font is removed from the Favorites list.

✔ Tip

- Removing a font from the Favorites collection does not delete the font from your computer.

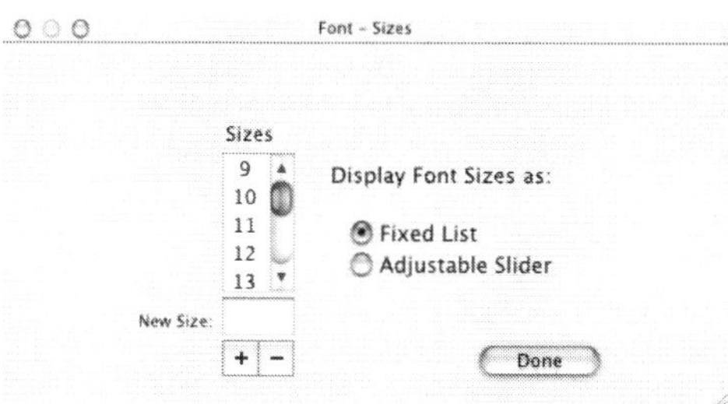

Figure 21 The Font – Sizes panel with Fixed List selected...

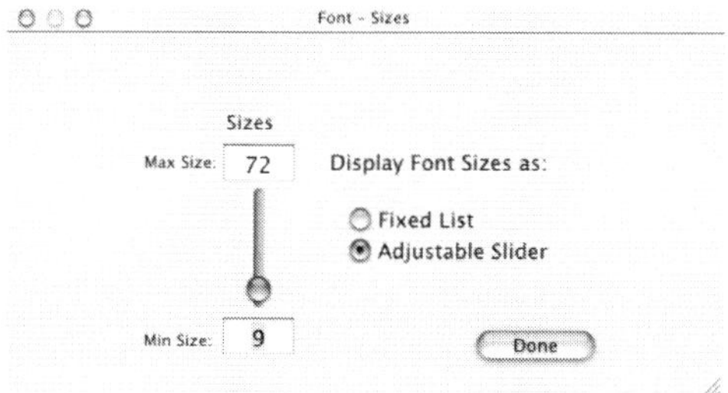

Figure 22 ...and with Adjustable Slider selected.

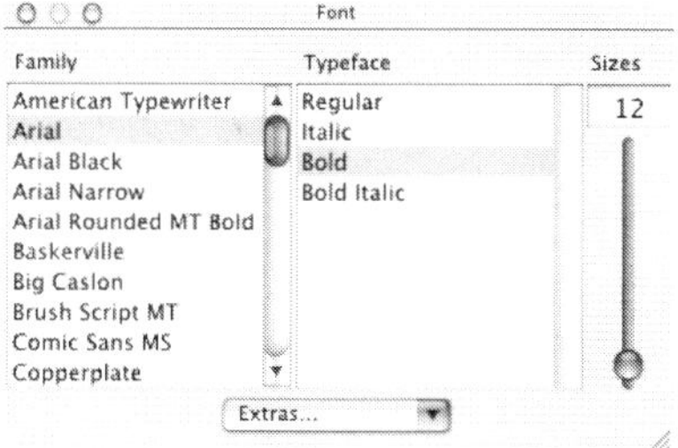

Figure 23 Here's what the Font panel looks like with a Sizes slider instead of a Sizes list.

To modify the Sizes list

1. In the Font panel (**Figure 14** or **16**), choose Edit Sizes from the Extras pop-up menu (**Figure 16**). The Font panel changes to the Font – Sizes panel (**Figure 21**).
2. Select the Fixed List radio button.
3. To add a size to the list, enter a size in the New Size edit box and click the + button. The size is added to the list.

   or

   To remove a size from the list, select the size you want to remove and click the – button. The size is removed from the list.
4. Click Done. The Font – Sizes panel is replaced by the modified Font panel.

✔ Tip

- Sizes measurements can be expressed in 10ths of an inch. For example, 10.5 and 16.7 are both valid sizes.

To replace the Sizes list with a slider

1. In the Font panel (**Figure 14** or **17**), choose Edit Sizes from the Extras pop-up menu (**Figure 16**). The Font panel changes to the Font – Sizes panel (**Figure 21**).
2. Select the Adjustable Slider radio button. The dialog changes (**Figure 22**).
3. Exter the maximum font size in the Max Size edit box.
4. Enter the minimum font size in the Min Size edit box.
5. Click Done. The Font – Sizes panel is replaced by the Font panel, which now has a Sizes slider (**Figure 23**).

✔ Tip

- In my opinion, a Sizes list (**Figures 14** and **16**) is a lot easier to use that a Sizes slider (**Figure 23**).

To change the font color

1. In the Font panel (**Figure 14**, **17**, or **23**), choose Color from the Extras pop-up menu (**Figure 16**).
2. In the Colors panel that appears (**Figure 24**), click to select the color you want.
3. Click Apply. The color you selected is applied to selected text or text typed at the insertion point.
4. To dismiss the Colors panel, click its close button.

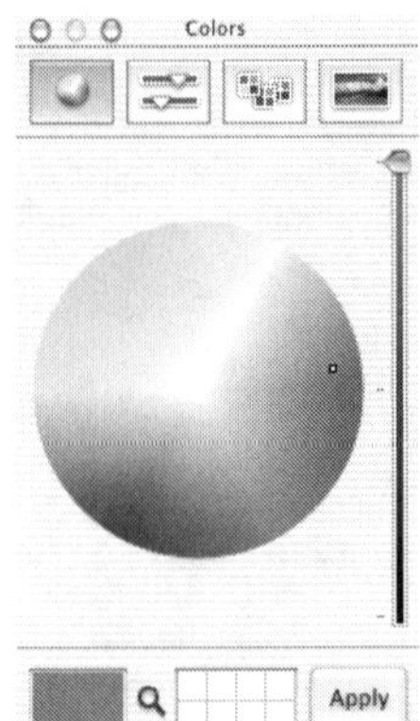

Figure 24
Use the Colors panel to select a color to apply to selected text or text typed at the insertion point.

✔ Tips

- TextEdit enables you to change the color of text without opening the Font panel. Choose Format > Font > Colors (**Figure 13**) to display the Colors panel.
- You can click buttons at the top of the Colors panel (**Figure 24**) to change the type of color picker. Explore this option to see which picker you like best.

To obtain additional fonts

1. In the Font panel (**Figure 14**, **17**, or **23**), choose Get Fonts from the Extras pop-up menu (**Figure 16**).

   Your computer launches the default Web browser, connects to the Internet, and displays the Apple – Fonts – Buy page on Apple's Web site.
2. Follow the instructions that appear in the browser window to look at, purchase, and download fonts.

✔ Tip

- Fonts are also available from commercial font developers such as Adobe Systems and International Typeface Corporation (ITC) and from shareware developers.

Mac OS Utilities

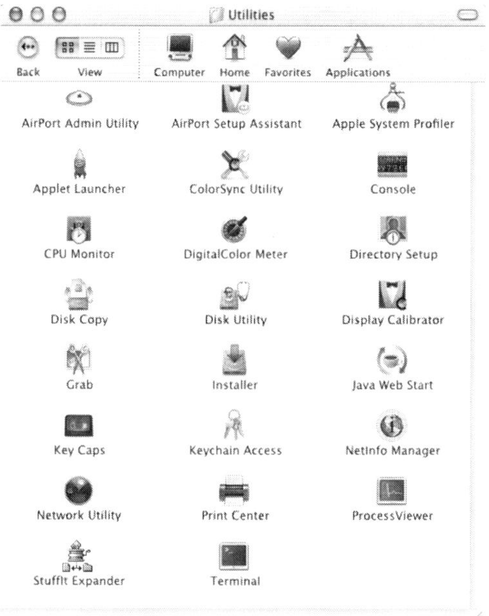

Figure 1 The Utilities folder contains a bunch of utility applications for working with your computer and files.

Mac OS Utilities

The Utilities folder inside the Applications folder (**Figure 1**) includes a number of utility applications you can use to work with your computer and its files.

This chapter covers the following utilities that are installed as part of Mac OS X 10.1:

- **Apple System Profiler** provides information about your Mac's installed software and hardware.
- **Applet Launcher** enables you to run Java applets without opening a Web browser.
- **ColorSync Utility** enables you to check and repair ColorSync profiles and to assign profiles to hardware devices.
- **Console** displays technical messages from the system software and applications.
- **CPU Monitor** displays information about your computer CPU's workload.
- **Digital Color Meter** enables you to measure and translate colors on your display.
- **Disk Copy** enables you to create and open disk image files.
- **Disk Utility** enables you to check, format, partition, and get information about disks.
- **Display Calibrator** is an assistant to help you calibrate your display and create a ColorSync profile for it.

Continued on next page...

Continued from previous page.

- **Grab** enables you to capture screen images and save them as image files.
- **Installer** enables you to install software.
- **Java Web Start** enables you to run Java applications on the Web by simply clicking a link in a Web browser window.
- **Print Center** enables you to maintain a printer list and check the status of documents sent to printers.
- **Process Viewer** displays a list of the processes running on your computer.
- **StuffIt Expander** opens compressed or archived files in a variety of formats.

✔ Tips

- Disk Utility combines the features of the Disk First Aid and Drive Setup utilities in Mac OS 9.x and earlier.
- This chapter does not cover the following utilities, which are discussed elsewhere in this book:
  - Terminal, in **Chapters 3** and **4**.
  - Airport Admin Utility, Airport Setup Assistant, Directory Setup, Net Info Manager, and Network Utility, in **Chapter 5**.
  - Keychain Access, in **Chapter 6**.
  - Key Caps, in **Chapter 9**.

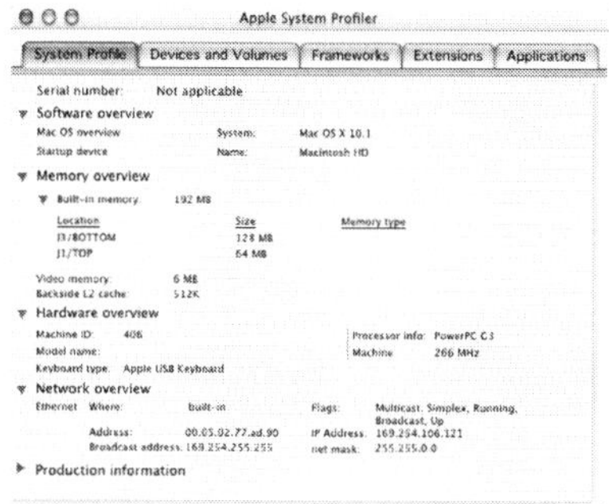

Figure 2 The System Profile tab of Apple System Profiler shows general system information.

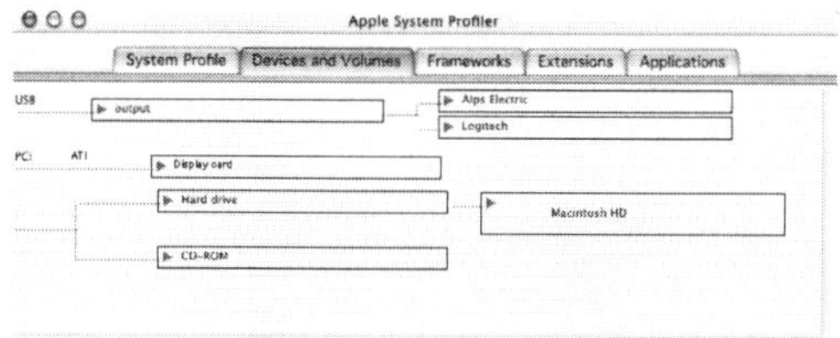

Figure 3 The Devices and Volumes tab of Apple System Profiler shows hardware and network devices.

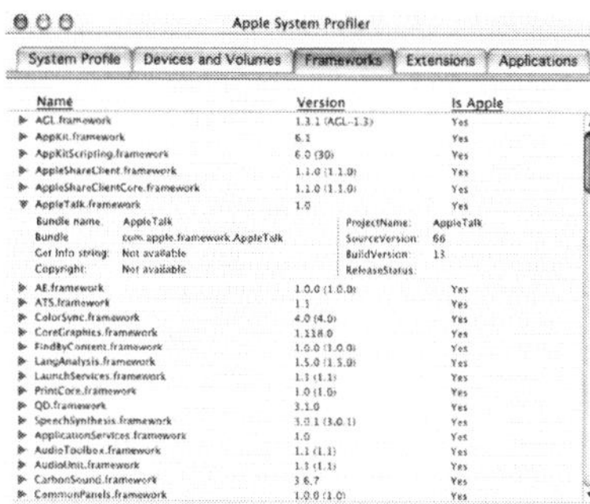

Figure 4 The Frameworks tab of the Apple System Profiler shows installed frameworks.

Apple System Profiler

The Apple System Profiler application provides information about your computer's hardware and software. This information can come in handy when you are troubleshooting problems or just need to know more about the hardware and software installed on your computer.

Apple System Profiler's main window is broken into five tabs of information:

- **System Profile** (**Figure 2**) provides general information about your computer system, including the operating system, memory, processor, keyboard, and network.
- **Devices and Volumes** (**Figure 3**) displays a diagram showing the hardware and network devices accessible to the computer.
- **Frameworks** (**Figure 4**) displays a list of installed frameworks.
- **Extensions** (**Figure 5**) displays a list of installed extensions or device drivers.
- **Applications** (**Figure 6**) displays a list of all installed software applications.

✔ Tips

- *Frameworks* are "bundles" of programming code—specifically, shared libraries and resources—that work with the Mac OS X system software and various applications. Frameworks, shared libraries, and resources are of interest primarily to programmers; most Mac OS X users do not need to know about or understand them.
- A *device driver* is special software that enables your computer to control a hardware device.

To get system information

1. Open the Apple System Profiler icon in the Utilities folder (**Figure 1**).
2. In the Apple System Profiler window that appears, click the tab for the type of information you want (**Figures 2** through **6**).

   or

   Choose the type of information you want from the Commands menu (**Figure 7**).
3. Wait while your computer gathers the information. This may take a few moments. When it is finished, the requested appears in the window.

✔ Tips

- As shown in **Figure 7**, you can also use the (⌘ 1) through (⌘ 5) shortcut keys to select the type of information you want to display.
- You can click a triangle to the left of an item in any Apple System Profiler window to display or hide detailed information. This is shown in **Figures 2**, **4**, **5**, and **6**.
- You can use other commands on the Commands menu (**Figure 7**) and shortcut keys to update Apple System Profiler information:
  - ▲ **Gather remaining information** ((⌘ G)) gathers information that has not yet been gathered.
  - ▲ **Update all information** ((⌘ U)) updates the information in all five tabs.
  - ▲ **Update *Tab Name*** ((⌘ R)) updates the information in the currently displayed tab. The name of this command changes depending on which tab is displayed.

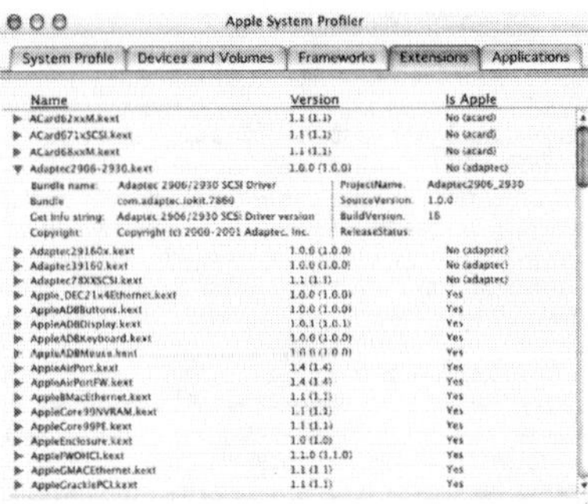

Figure 5 The Extensions tab of Apple System Profiler shows installed extensions.

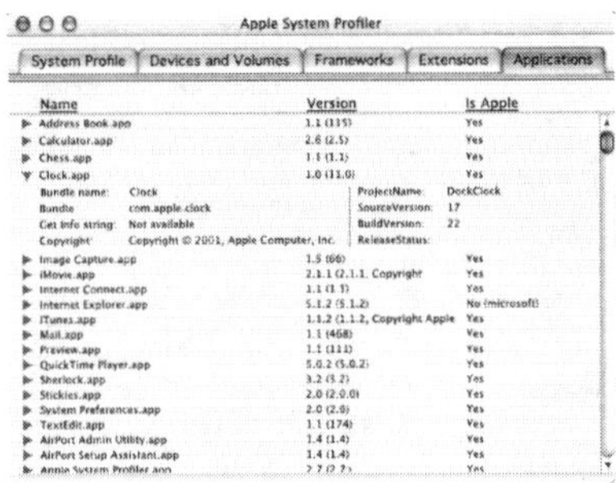

Figure 6 The Applications tab of Apple System Profiler lists all installed applications.

Figure 7 Apple System Profiler's Commands menu.

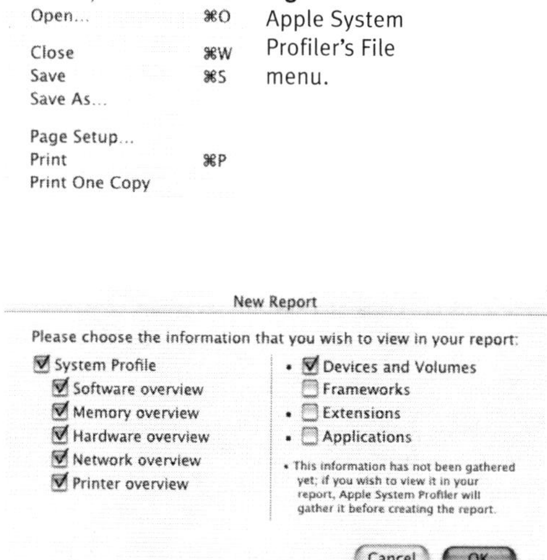

Figure 8 Apple System Profiler's File menu.

Figure 9 Use this dialog to select the information you want to include in the report.

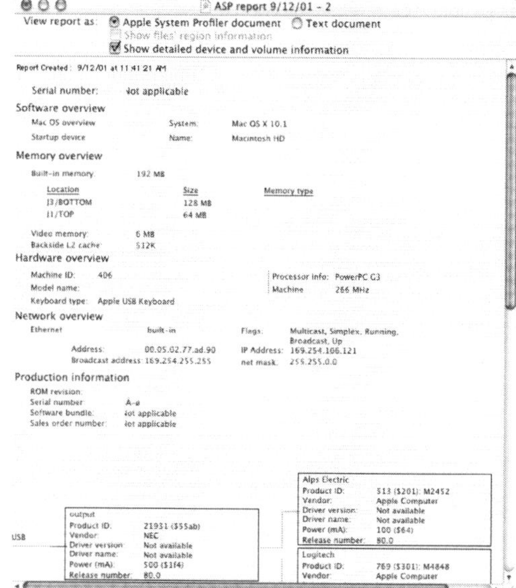

Figure 10 Here's a report generated with the selections shown in **Figure 9**.

To create an Apple System Profiler report

1. In Apple System Profiler, choose File > New Report (**Figure 8**), or press ⌘N.
2. In the New Report dialog that appears (**Figure 9**), turn on the check boxes for the information you want to include in the report.
3. Click OK. Your computer gathers the information it needs to complete the report and displays it onscreen in a report window. **Figure 10** shows an example of what a report with the settings shown in **Figure 9** might look like.

✔ Tips

- You can change the way the report looks by setting options at the top of the report window (**Figure 10**).
- Commands under the File menu (**Figure 8**) enable you to save, print, and close reports, as well as open reports already saved on disk.

To set volume searching options

1. In Apple System Profiler, choose Commands > Search Options (**Figure 7**), or press [⌘ ⌘][F] to display the Search Options dialog (**Figure 11**).
2. Click the tab for the category of information you want to set search options for.
3. Turn on the check box beside each disk or volume you want to search for information.
4. Repeat steps 2 and 3 for each category of information you want to check or change.
5. Click OK.

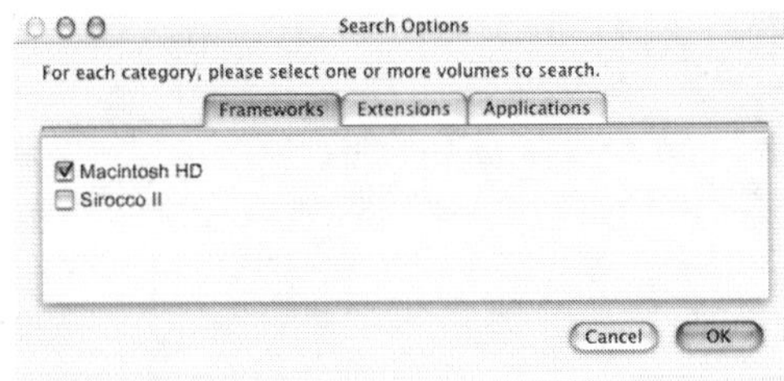

Figure 11 Use the Search Options dialog to specify which volumes your computer should search for frameworks, extensions, and applications.

To set Apple System Profiler preferences

1. Choose Apple System Profiler > Preferences (**Figure 12**).
2. Set options in the Preferences dialog that appears (**Figure 13**).
   - ▲ To specify the default items to appear checked off in the New Report dialog (**Figure 9**), toggle check boxes on the left side of the dialog.
   - ▲ To specify the information that should be gathered when Apple System Profiler is launched, toggle check boxes in the top-right of the dialog.
   - ▲ To remember the Apple System Profiler window location and size, turn on the Save window location and size check box.
   - ▲ To set the default format for newly created reports, select one of the options in the bottom-right of the dialog. If you select Apple System Profiler document, you can also toggle a check box to display or hide the expanded information; this option is always turned on for Text documents.
3. Click OK to save your settings.

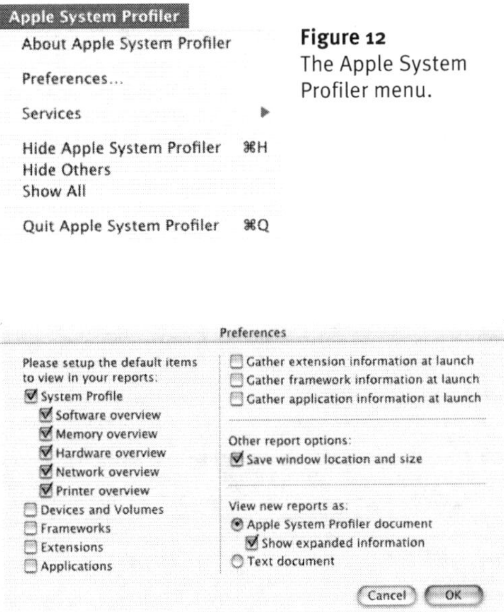

Figure 12 The Apple System Profiler menu.

Figure 13 Apple System Profiler's Preferences dialog.

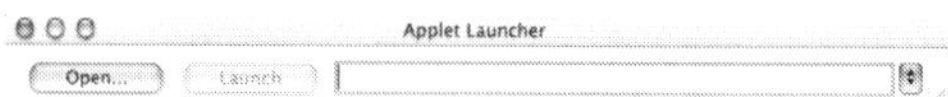

Figure 14 The Applet Launcher window.

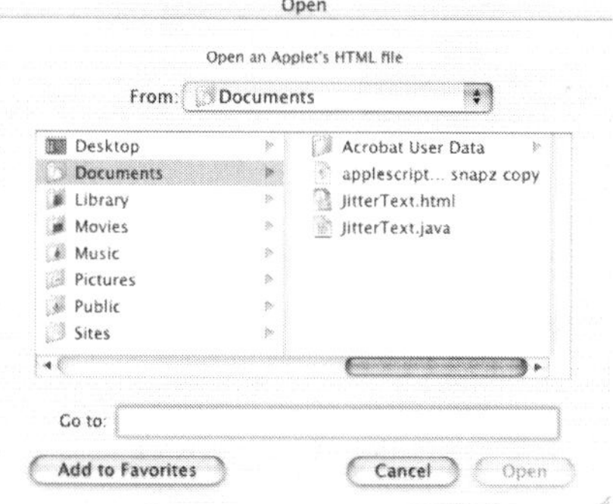

Figure 15 You can use a standard Open dialog to locate, select, and open an HTML file containing a Java applet...

Figure 16 ...or enter the complete URL for the HTML file in the edit box.

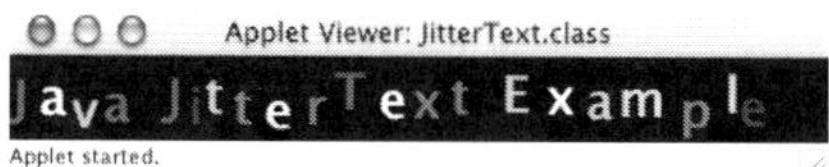

Figure 17 The applet's interface appears in the Applet Viewer window.

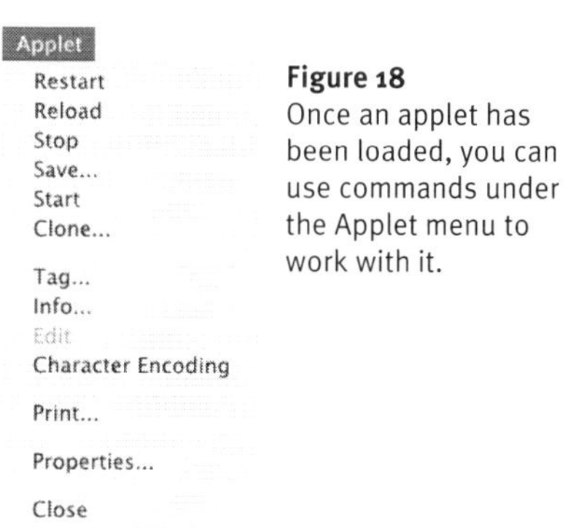

Figure 18 Once an applet has been loaded, you can use commands under the Applet menu to work with it.

Applet Launcher

Applet Launcher is an application that enables you to run a Java applet in an HTML file without using a Web browser.

To open a Java applet with Applet Launcher

1. Open the Applet Viewer icon in the Utilities folder (**Figure 1**) to display the Applet Launcher window (**Figure 14**).
2. Click the Open button and use the dialog that appears (**Figure 15**) to locate, select, and open an HTML file containing a Java applet.

   or

   Enter the complete URL for an HTML file containing a Java applet in the edit box (**Figure 16**) and then click Launch.

   The applet loads and starts. Its interface appears in the Applet Viewer window (**Figure 17**).

✔ Tip

- Once an applet has been loaded, you can use commands under the Applet menu (**Figure 18**) to work with it. (The Applet Viewer window must be active to use this menu.)

ColorSync Preferences & the ColorSync Utility

ColorSync is an industry-standard technology that helps designers match the colors they see onscreen to those in devices such as scanners, printers, and imagesetters. For the average user, color matching may not be very important, but for a designer who works with color, correct reproduction makes it possible to complete complex projects on time and within budget.

To use ColorSync, you must set it up and then instruct your software to use it. In this section, I explain how to set ColorSync preferences and how to use the ColorSync utility to work with ColorSync profiles and devices.

✔ Tip

- A complete discussion of ColorSync is far beyond the scope of this book. To learn more about ColorSync features and settings, visit **www.apple.com/colorsync**.

To set ColorSync preferences

1. Choose Apple > System Preferences or click the System Preferences icon in the Dock.
2. In the System Preferences dialog that appears, click the ColorSync icon to display the ColorSync preferences pane.
3. Click the Device Profiles tab to display its options (**Figure 19**).
4. Choose the desired option from the pop-up menu for each type of device:
   - ▲ **Input** includes scanners and digital cameras.
   - ▲ **Display** is the computer's monitor.
   - ▲ **Output** includes color printers and video recorders.
   - ▲ **Proof** includes high-end proofing devices.

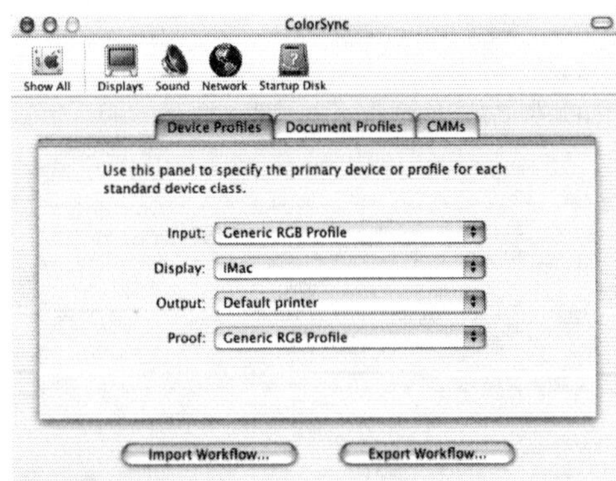

Figure 19 The Device Profiles tab of the ColorSync preferences pane.

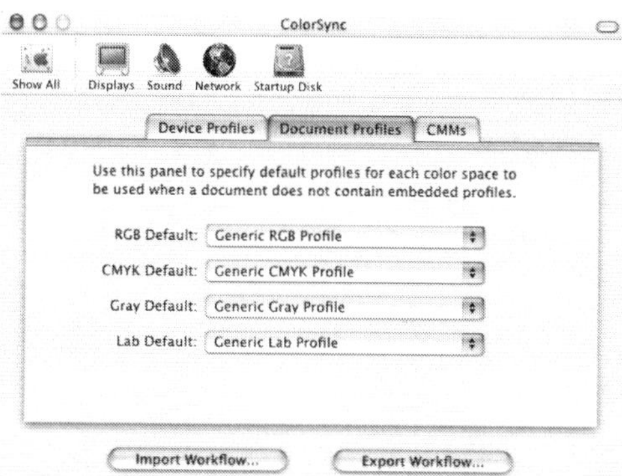

Figure 20 The Document Profiles tab of the ColorSync preferences pane.

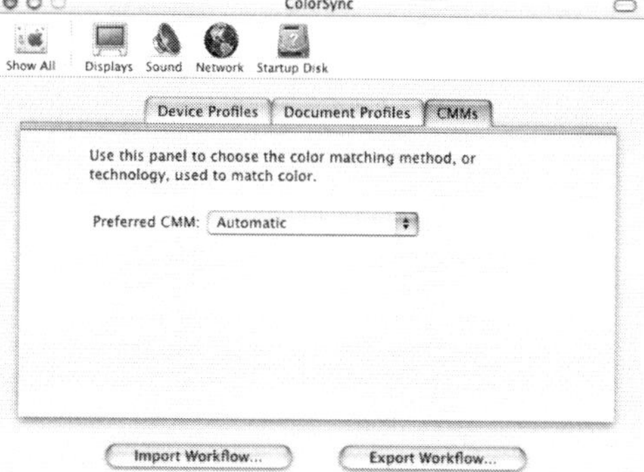

Figure 21 The CMMs tab of the ColorSync preferences pane.

5. Click the Document Profiles tab to display its options (**Figure 20**).
6. Choose the desired option from the pop-up menu for each type of color space.
7. Click the CMMs tab to display its options (**Figure 21**).
8. Select a color matching method from the Preferred CMM pop-up menu.

✔ Tips

- A ColorSync or ICC *profile* is a standard file format that provides output color information for a device based on a specific input.
- *ICC* stands for *International Color Consortium*, a group that sets standards for color profiles.
- A *color space* is a range of color coordinates that defines the hues and shades a device can print or display.
- If an application that utilizes ColorSync enables you to set profile information within the application, those selections will override the ones set in the ColorSync preferences pane.
- You can save a group of color ColorSync preference settings—known as a *workflow*—by clicking the Export Workflow button in the ColorSync preferences pane (**Figures 19** through **21**) and using the Save dialog that appears to name and save the workflow file. Likewise, you can import a saved workflow by clicking the Import Workflow button and using the Open dialog that appears to locate, select, and open the workflow file. This makes it possible to share workflow files with other Mac OS users.

To verify and/or repair ColorSync profiles

1. Open the ColorSync Utility icon in the Utilities folder (**Figure 1**).
2. In the ColorSync Utility window that appears, click the Profile First Aid icon (**Figure 22**).
3. Click Verify to check all installed profiles for errors.

   or

   Click Repair to repair any errors in installed profiles.
4. Wait while ColorSync Utility checks or repairs installed profiles. When it's finished, it displays results in its window (**Figure 23**).

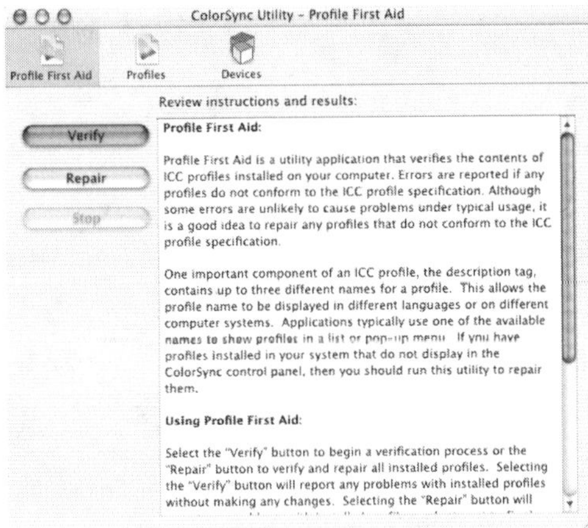

Figure 22 When you first display the Profile First Aid section of the ColorSync Utility, a window full of instructions appears.

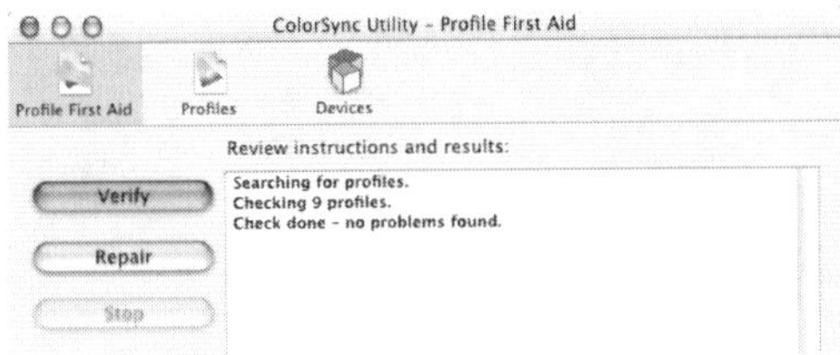

Figure 23 Here's what the results of a profile verification might look like.

To view a list of installed profiles

1. Open the ColorSync Utility icon in the Utilities folder (**Figure 1**).
2. In the ColorSync Utility window that appears, click the Profiles icon (**Figure 24**).
3. If necessary, click triangles beside a folder pathname to view a list of the items in the folder.

✔ Tip

- Clicking an item displays information about it in the right side of the window, as shown in **Figure 24**, including the file's disk location (path) and contents.

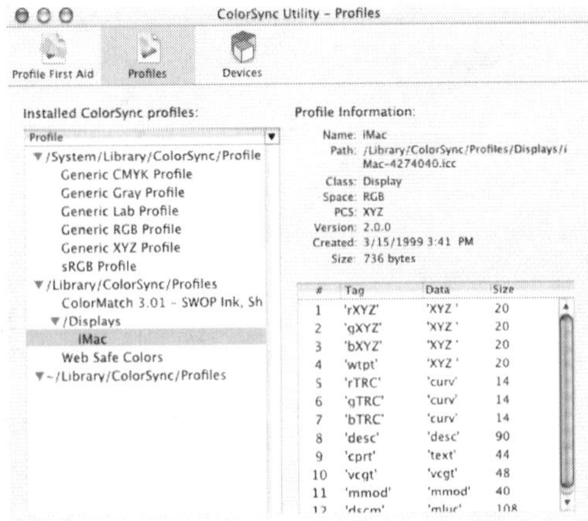

Figure 24 The Profiles section of the ColorSync utility displays a list of all installed profiles. Click a profile to learn more about it.

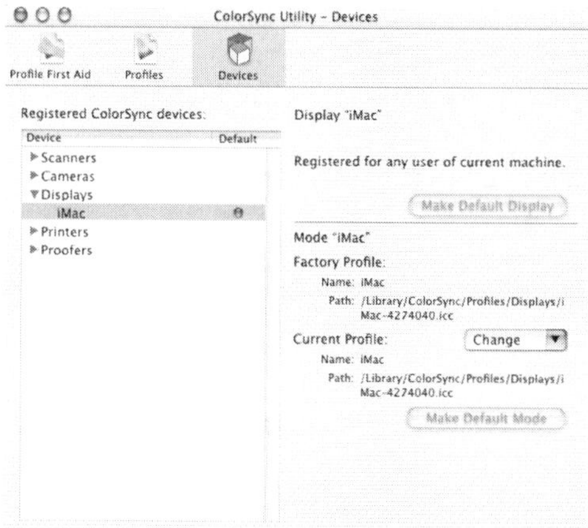

Figure 25 The Devices section of the ColorSync utility displays a list of all registered devices. Click a device to learn more about it.

To view a list of registered devices

1. Open the ColorSync Utility icon in the Utilities folder (**Figure 1**).
2. In the ColorSync Utility window that appears, click the Devices icon (**Figure 25**).
3. If necessary, click the triangle beside a device type to view a list of the devices of that type.

✔ Tips

- A registered device is one that is recognized by the system software and has a ColorSync profile assigned to it.
- Clicking an item displays information about it in the right side of the window, as shown in **Figure 25**, including the profile.
- You can change an item's profile by choosing an option from the Current Profile pop-up menu when the item is displayed.
- If there is more that one device for a type of device, you can make one of the devices the default. Simply select it in the list (**Figure 25**) and click the Make Default *Type* button. (The exact label on the button varies depending on what type of item is selected.)

Console

The Console application enables you to read messages from the Mac OS X system software and applications. You might find this useful if you are a programmer or are troubleshooting a problem. (If not, you'll probably think it looks like a bunch of gibberish.)

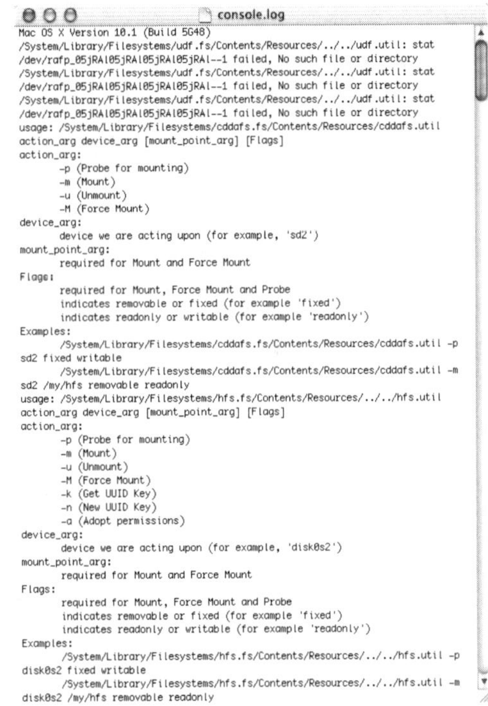

Figure 26 The console.log window records messages sent by Mac OS and its applications. (What may look like a bunch of gibberish to you and me can help a programmer or troubleshooter debug a Mac.)

To view system messages

1. Open the Console icon in the Utilities folder (**Figure 1**).
2. The console.log window appears (**Figure 26**). Scroll through its contents to read messages.

✓ Tips

- The most recent console.log entries appear at the end of the document.
- You can use commands under the Format menu and its Font submenu (**Figure 27**) to change the appearance of text in the window.

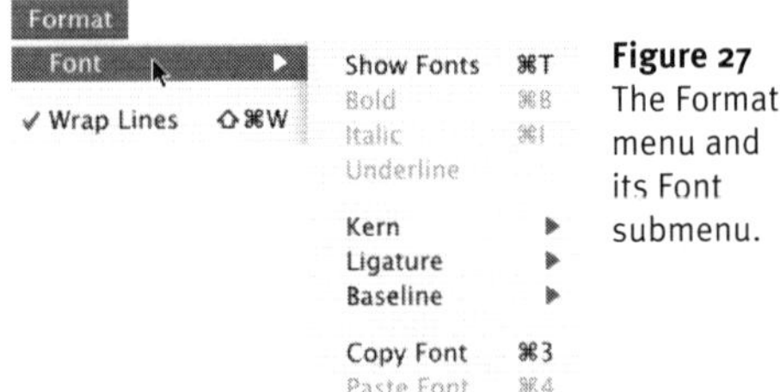

Figure 27 The Format menu and its Font submenu.

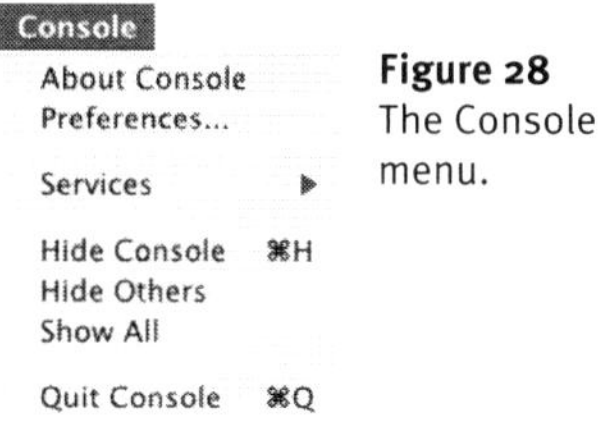

Figure 28 The Console menu.

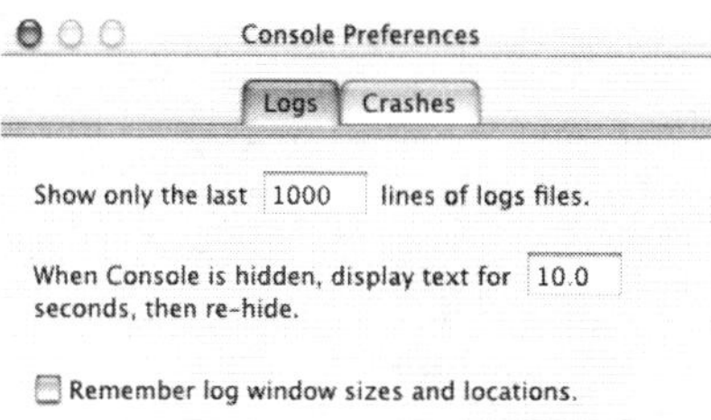

Figure 29 The Logs tab of the Console Preferences window.

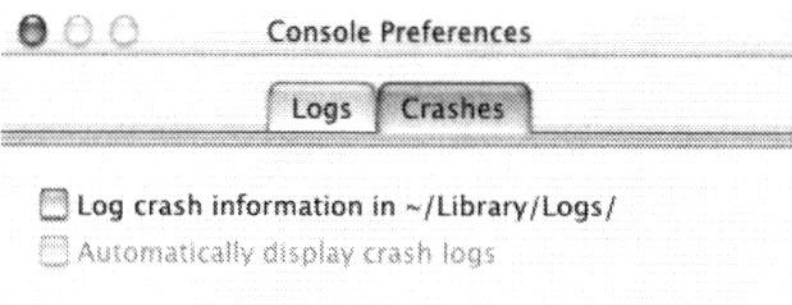

Figure 30 The Crashes tab of the Console Preferences window.

To set Console preferences

1. Choose Console > Preferences (**Figure 28**) to display the Console Preferences window.
2. Click the Logs tab (**Figure 29**) and set options as desired:
   - ▲ **Show only the last *n* lines of log files** enables you to specify the maximum number of lines that should appear in the log.
   - ▲ **When Console is hidden, display text for *n* seconds, then rehide** enables you to specify the amount of time Console should reappear when it has a message to display if it is hidden.
   - ▲ **Remember Log window sizes and locations** tells Console to display windows at the same size and in the same location they last appeared.
3. Click the Crashes tab (**Figure 30**) and set options as desired:
   - ▲ **Log crash information in ~/Library/ Logs/** creates a separate log of crash-related information and saves it in the Logs folder inside the Library folder.
   - ▲ **Automatically display crash logs** automatically displays crash-related information when you launch Console. This option can only be turned on if the option above it is enabled.
4. Click the close button to save your preference settings.

CPU Monitor

CPU Monitor is an application that provides information about CPU (central processing unit) activity, in graphical format. This information may be helpful when performing intensive operations that require a great deal of CPU resources, such as rendering graphics and compressing video.

To monitor your CPU's activity

1. Open the CPU Monitor icon in the Utilities folder (**Figure 1**).
2. One or more of the three CPU Monitor windows (**Figures 31** through **33**) should appear; if not, choose the one you want from the Processes menu (**Figure 34**).

✔ Tips

- You can move any of CPU Monitor's windows anywhere you like onscreen.
- All of CPU Monitor's windows (**Figures 31** through **33**) appear atop any other open windows, even if CPU Monitor is not active.
- To clear the contents of the expanded window (**Figure 33**), choose Processes > Clear Expanded window or press [Ć ⌘][K].
- Commands on the Processes menu (**Figure 34**) also enable you to open related applications, including Process Viewer (discussed later in this chapter) and Terminal (referred to as "Top" on the menu; discussed in **Chapters 3** and **4**).

To set CPU Monitor preferences

1. Choose CPU Monitor > Preferences (**Figure 35**) to display the Console Preferences window.
2. Click the Floating View tab (**Figure 36**) and set options as desired to customize the floating view display:

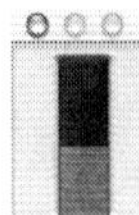

Figure 31 CPU Monitor's standard window displays a blue graphic to indicate CPU activity.

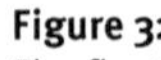

Figure 32 The floating window first appears in the lower-left corner of the screen, but can be moved. It displays CPU activity with a green graphic.

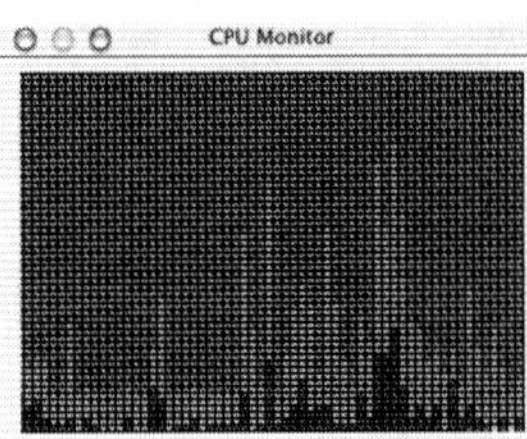

Figure 33 The expanded window uses multiple colors to display CPU activity.

Processes
Display Standard Window ⌘S
Toggle Floating Window ⌘F
Display Expanded Window ⌘E
Clear Expanded Window ⌘K
Open Process Viewer ... ⌘P
Open Top ... ⌘T

Figure 34 Use commands under the Processes menu to show or hide windows and open related applications.

CPU Monitor
About CPU Monitor
Preferences...
Services ▸
Hide CPU Monitor ⌘H
Hide Others
Show All
Quit CPU Monitor ⌘Q

Figure 35 The CPU Monitor menu.

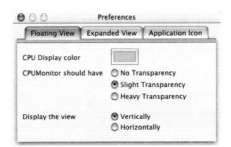

Preferences
Floating View | Expanded View | Application Icon
CPU Display color
CPUMonitor should have: No Transparency / Slight Transparency / Heavy Transparency
Display the view: Vertically / Horizontally

Figure 36 The Floating View tab of the Preferences window.

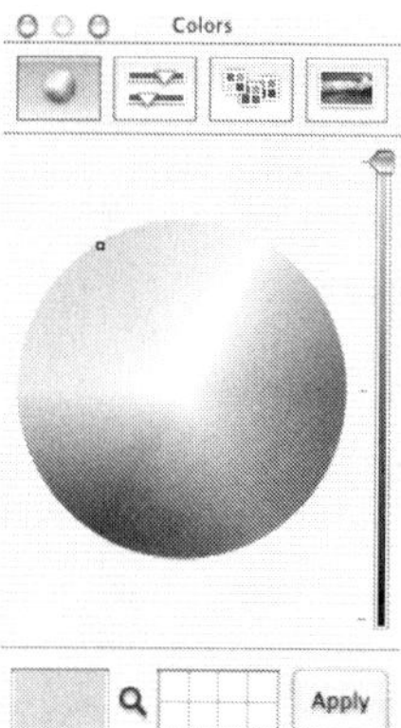

Figure 37 Use a standard Colors palette to select a new color.

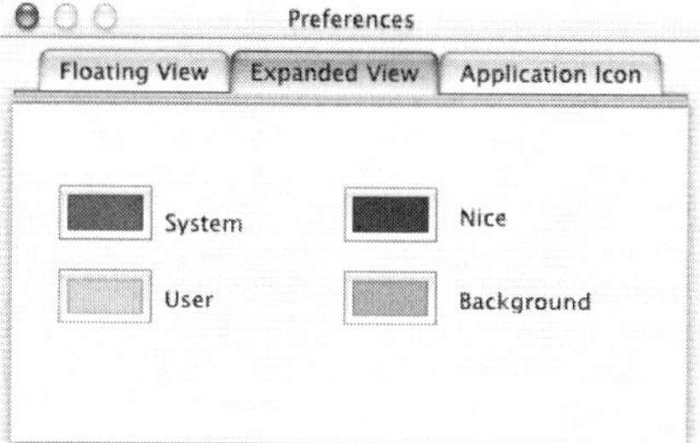

Figure 38 The Expanded View tab of the Preferences window.

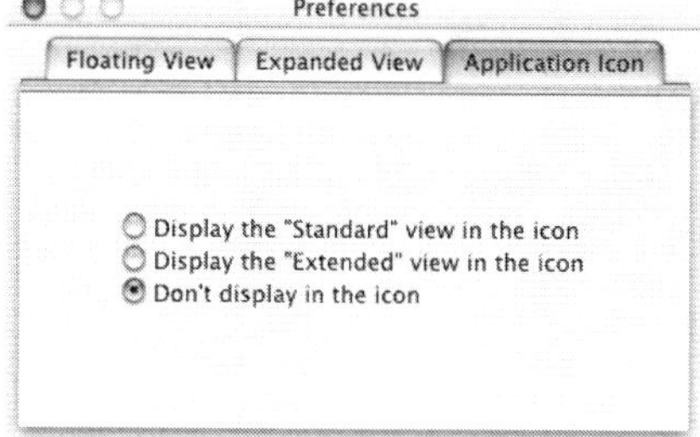

Figure 39 The Application Icon tab of the Preferences window.

Figures 40 & 41 CPU Monitor's standard view (above) and extended view (below) can be reduced to icon size and displayed in the Dock.

- ▲ **CPU Display color** enables you to set the color for the activity graphic display. Click the color sample to display a Colors palette (**Figure 37**), then choose the color you want and click Apply. Click the Colors palette's close button to dismiss it.
- ▲ **CPU Monitor transparency** enables you to specify how transparent the window should be. Select one of the radio buttons.
- ▲ **Display the view** enables you to specify whether the window should display vertically or horizontally. Select one of the radio buttons.

3. Click the Expanded View tab (**Figure 38**) to set colors for each part of the expanded window view. Click a color sample to display a Colors palette (**Figure 37**), then choose the color you want and click Apply. When you are finished, click the Colors palette's close button to dismiss it.
4. Click the Application Icon tab (**Figure 39**) and select an option to determine whether one of the views should appear in the CPU Monitor icon in the Dock.
   - ▲ **Display the "Standard" view in the icon** displays the standard window's view in the Dock icon (**Figure 40**).
   - ▲ **Display the "Extended" view in the icon** displays a miniaturized version of the extended window's view in the Dock icon (**Figure 41**).
   - ▲ **Don't display the icon** does not display any window's view in the Dock.

✔ Tip

- ■ If you display one of the window's views as an icon in the Dock, that view cannot be displayed as a window on your Desktop.

Digital Color Meter

The Digital Color Meter (**Figure 42**) enables you to measure colors that appear on your display as RGB, CIE, or Tristimulus values. This enables you to precisely record or duplicate colors that appear onscreen.

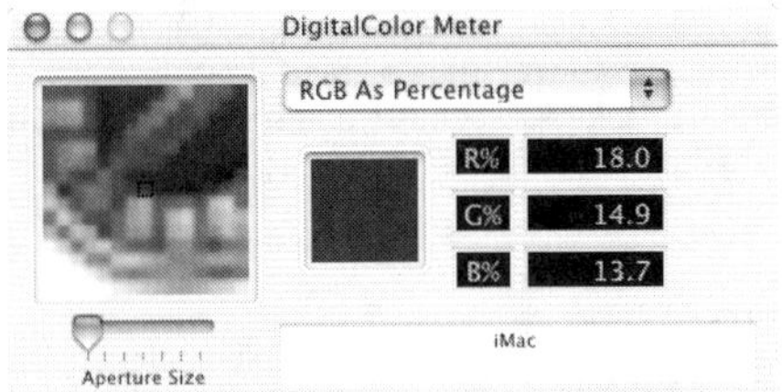

Figure 42 The Digital Color Meter can tell you the color of any area onscreen—in this case, one of the pixels in its icon.

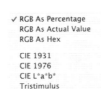

✔ Tip

- A discussion of color technology is far beyond the scope of this book. To learn more about how your Mac can work with colors, visit the ColorSync page on Apple's Web site, www.apple.com/colorsync/.

To measure color values

1. Open the Digital Color Meter icon in the Utilities folder (**Figure 1**) to display the Digital Color Meter window (**Figure 42**).
2. Point to the color onscreen that you want to measure. Its values appear in the right side of the Digital Color Meter window (**Figure 42**).
3. If desired, choose a different option from the pop-up menu above the measurements (**Figure 43**). The value display changes to convert values to that measuring system.

✓ RGB As Percentage
RGB As Actual Value
RGB As Hex
CIE 1931
CIE 1976
CIE L*a*b*
Tristimulus

Figure 43 Choose an option to determine the system or units of the color measurement.

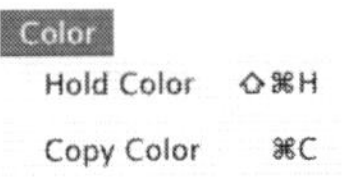

Figure 44 Use the Color menu to work with sampled colors.

✔ Tips

- You can use commands under the Color menu (**Figure 44**) to work with a selected color. (It's best to use the shortcut keys for these commands, since moving the mouse pointer will also change the sampled color.):
  - ▲ **Hold Color** (Shift ⌘ H) saves the color in the sample well until you choose the Hold Color command again.
  - ▲ **Copy Color** (⌘ C) copies the color information to the clipboard, where it can be pasted into other applications.

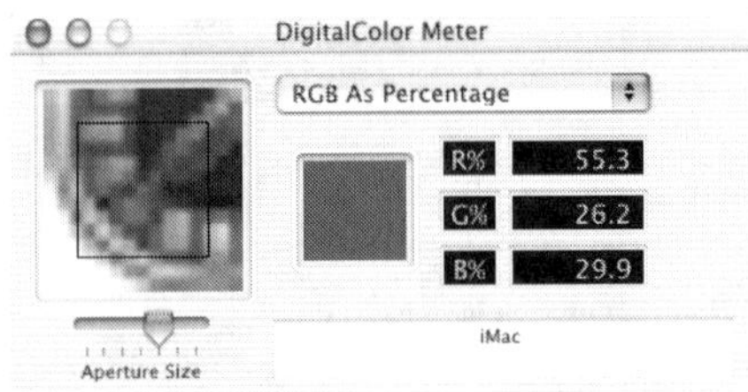

Figure 45 By changing the aperture setting, you can sample more pixels. Digital Color Meter automatically computes the average.

- You can change the amount of color that is sampled by dragging the Aperture Size slider to the right or left (**Figure 45**). A large aperture size will average the colors within it.

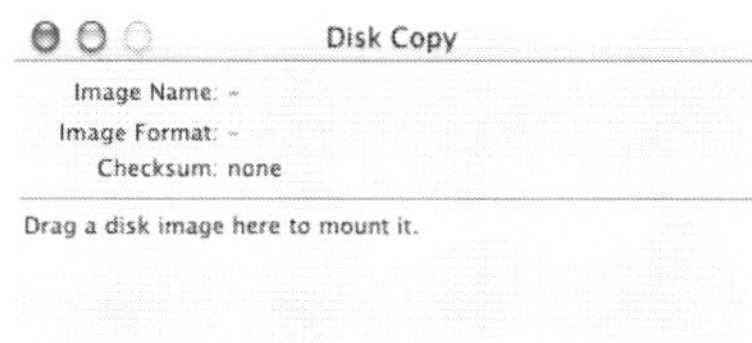

Figure 46 Disk Copy's main window includes instructions for mounting a disk image file.

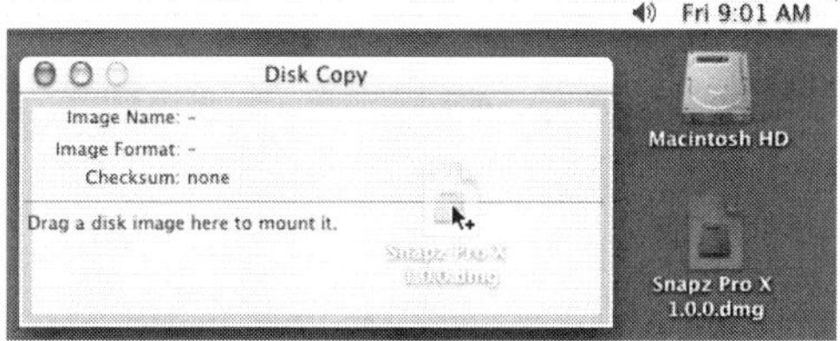

Figure 47 Drag a disk image file's icon into the Disk Copy window.

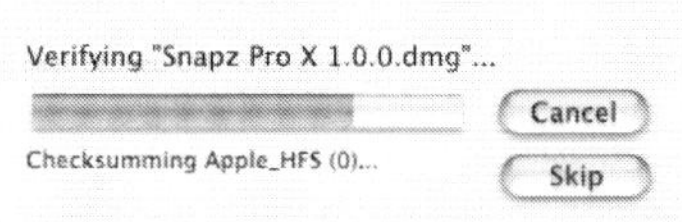

Figure 48 Disk Copy displays a progress dialog sheet as it works.

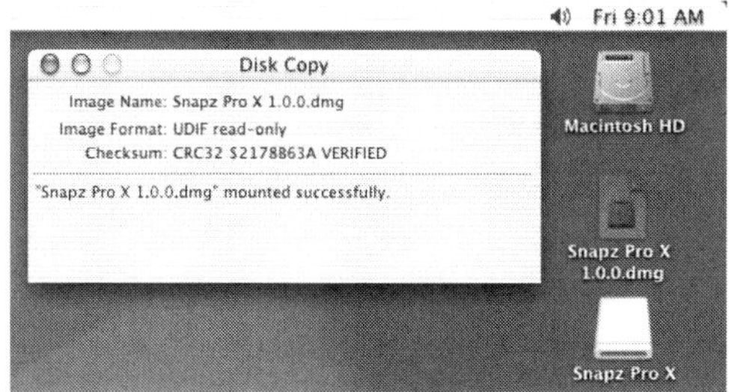

Figure 49 When Disk Copy is finished, an icon representing the disk image's contents appears on the desktop.

Disk Copy

Disk Copy is a utility that you can use to create and mount disk images. A *disk image* is a single file that contains everything on a disk. You can mount a disk image on your desktop just like any other disk. You can also use Disk Copy to burn a CD-R disc from a disk image.

✔ Tips

- Disk images are often used to distribute software updates or drivers on the Internet.
- Disk image files often include *.img* or *.dmg* filename extensions.
- Mounting disks is discussed in *Mac OS X: Visual QuickStart Guide.*

To mount a disk image

1. Open the Disk Copy icon in the Utilities folder (**Figure 1**). Disk Copy's main window should appear (**Figure 46**).
2. Drag the icon for disk image file into the Disk Image window (**Figure 47**).

   Disk Copy displays a progress dialog sheet as it works (**Figure 48**). When it's finished, a disk icon representing the disk image's contents appears on the desktop and Disk Copy's window displays information about the disk image file (**Figure 49**).

✔ Tip

- You can also mount a disk image by dragging its file icon onto the Disk Copy icon.

To unmount a disk image

Drag the mounted disk icon to the Trash.

or

Select the disk icon and choose File > Eject Disk or press ⌘ E.

Although the icon disappears from the desktop, all of its contents remain on the disk image file.

To create a disk image file

1. Open the Disk Copy icon in the Utilities folder (**Figure 1**).
2. Choose Image > New Blank Image (**Figure 50**), or press ⌘N, to display the New Blank Image dialog (**Figure 51**).
3. In the top part of the dialog, enter a name and specify a disk location in which to save the disk image file.
4. In the bottom part of the dialog, set options as desired:
   - ▲ **Volume Name** is the name of the disk.
   - ▲ **Size** is the size of the disk. Choose an option from the pop-up menu (**Figure 52**). If you choose Custom, use the dialog sheet that appears (**Figure 53**) to set the size in sectors, KB, or MB.
   - ▲ **Format** is the format of the disk. Choose an option from the pop-up menu: MS-DOS, Mac OS Extended, Mac OS Standard, or UNIX File System.
   - ▲ **Encryption** is file encryption to apply to the disk image file. Choose an option from the menu. The selections are none and AES-128.
5. Click Create. Disk Copy creates a disk image file to your specifications and mounts it on the desktop (**Figure 54**).
6. Copy items to the disk or its open window just as if it were a regular disk. The items you copy to the disk are automatically copied into the disk image file.

✔ Tips

- The size of a disk image file is determined by the size specified in step 4 above.
- Copying files to disk is discussed in *Mac OS X: Visual QuickStart Guide.*
- A disk image can be opened by any Mac OS user running a recent version of Disk Copy.

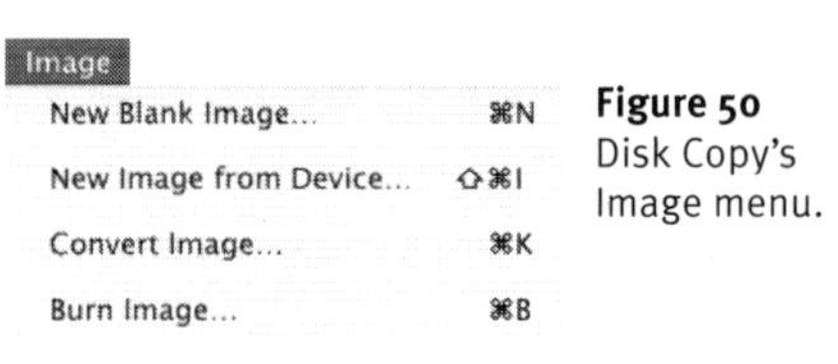

Figure 50 Disk Copy's Image menu.

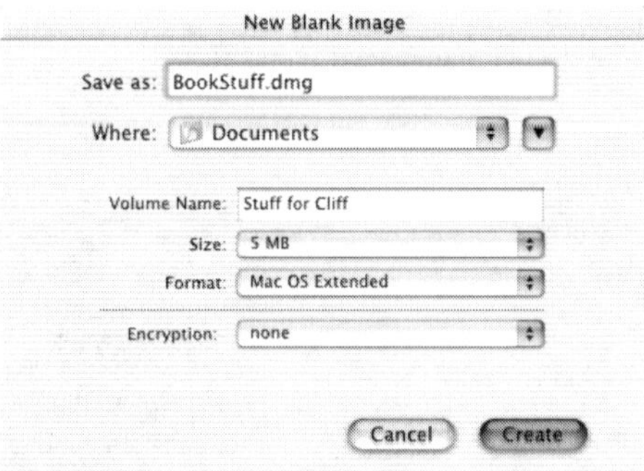

Figure 51 Use the New Blank Image dialog to set options for a new disk image.

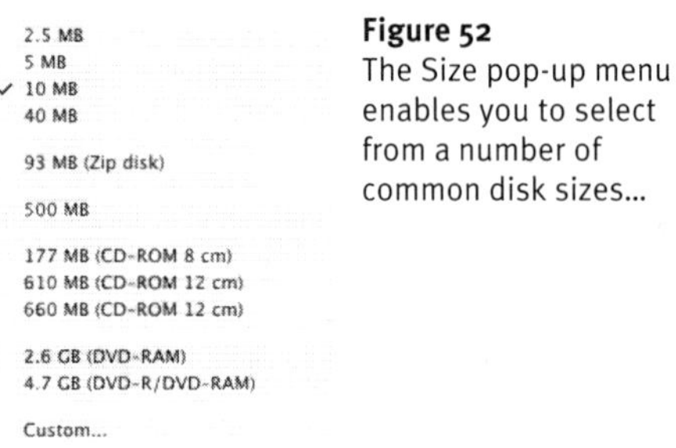

Figure 52 The Size pop-up menu enables you to select from a number of common disk sizes...

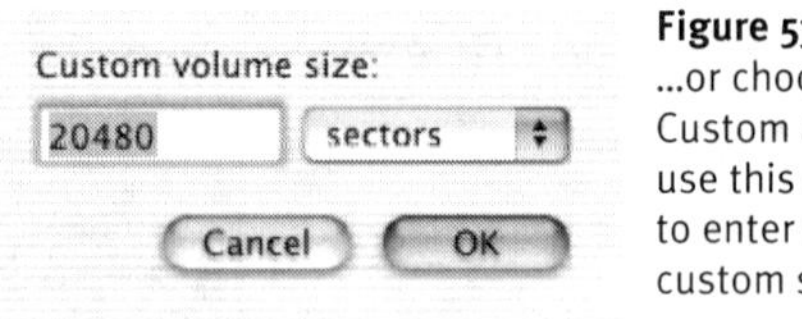

Figure 53 ...or choose Custom and use this dialog to enter a custom size.

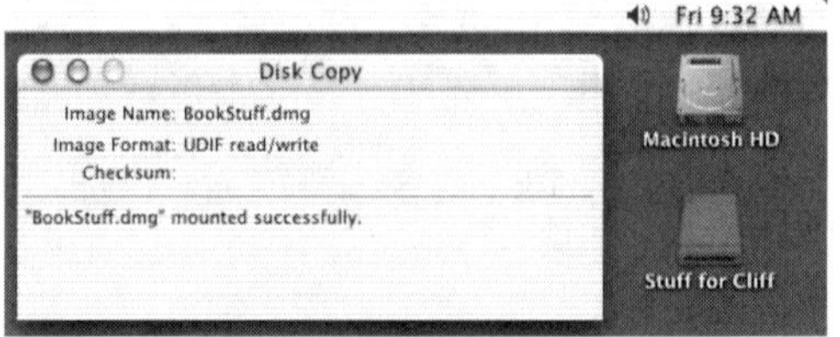

Figure 54 After creating the disk image, Disk Copy mounts it as a disk on your desktop. Here's the disk image created with the settings in **Figure 51**.

Creating a Disk Image File

Figure 55 Use the Burn Image dialog to locate and select a disk image to burn onto CD-ROM.

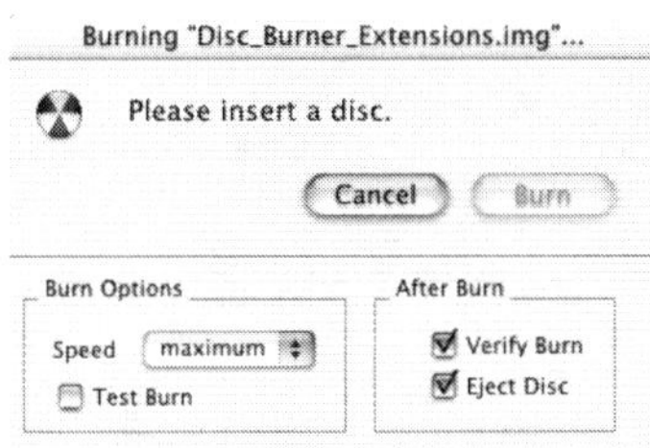

Figure 56 The Burning dialog prompts you to insert a disc and set options for the burn.

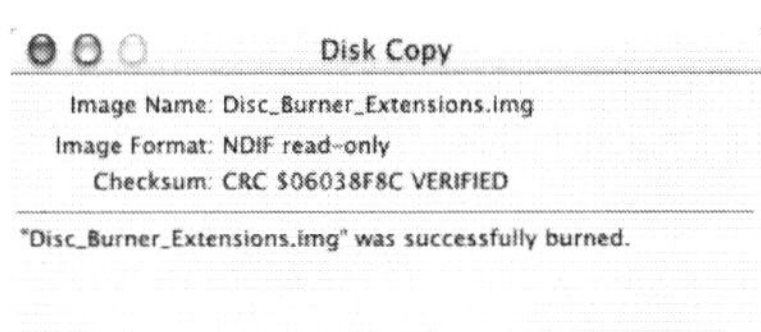

Figure 57 The Disk Copy window provides information about the completed process.

To burn a CD from a disk image

1. Open the Disk Copy icon in the Utilities folder (**Figure 1**).
2. Choose Image > Burn Image (**Figure 50**), or press [Apple ⌘][B].
3. A dialog like the one in **Figure 55** appears. Use it to locate and select a disk image file. Then click Burn.
4. The Burning dialog appears next (**Figure 56**). It prompts you to insert a CD-R disc and offers options for burning it:
   - ▲ **Speed** enables you to set the burn speed. Your options range from 1x to 40x; select maximum to use the maximum speed your CD-R device can handle.
   - ▲ **Test Burn** enables you to simulate the disc burning process. This does not actually write to the CD.
   - ▲ **Verify Burn** tells Disk Copy to check the CD for errors after it has written to it.
   - ▲ **Eject Disc** tells Disk Copy to eject the CD when it is finished working with it.
5. Insert a CD-R disc and click Burn.
6. Wait while Disk Copy writes to the CD. When it is finished, the main Disk Copy window provides information about the completed process (**Figure 57**).

✔ Tip

- You must have CD-R to create or "burn" CD-ROM discs.

BURNING CDS

To set Disk Copy preferences

1. Choose Disk Copy > Preferences (**Figure 58**) to display the Disk Copy Preferences window.

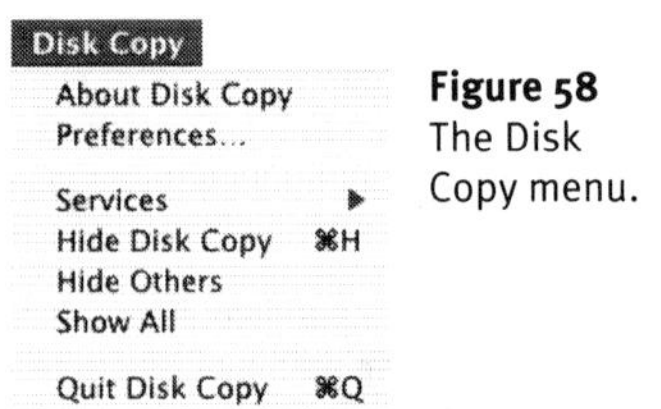

Figure 58 The Disk Copy menu.

2. Click the Verifying tab (**Figure 59**) to set options for verifying disk images:
   - ▲ **Verify Checksums** tells Disk Copy to check the checksums in disk image files before mounting them.
   - ▲ **Ignore invalid checksums** tells Disk Copy to ignore incorrect checksums when found and mount disks anyway.
   - ▲ **Don't verify images** enables you to specify two groups of disk image files that should not be verified: **On remote volumes** are disk images on network disks and **on locked media** are disk images on CD-ROM discs and other media that cannot be written on.

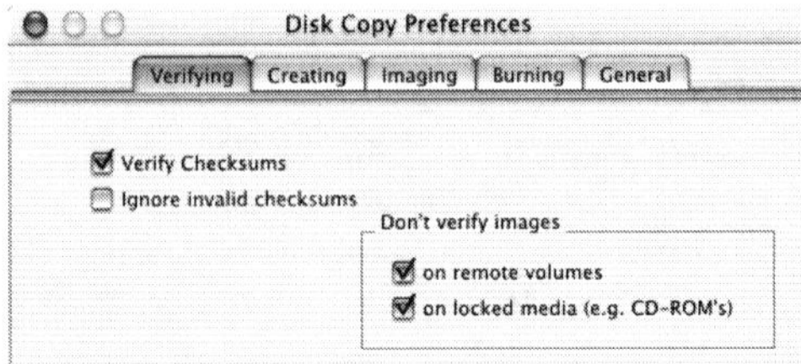

Figure 59 The Verifying tab of the Disk Copy Preferences window.

3. Click the Creating tab (**Figure 60**) to set the default values in the New Blank Image dialog (**Figure 51**):
   - ▲ **Volume Format** is the disk format.
   - ▲ **Volume Size** is the disk size.
   - ▲ **Encryption** is the encryption method.

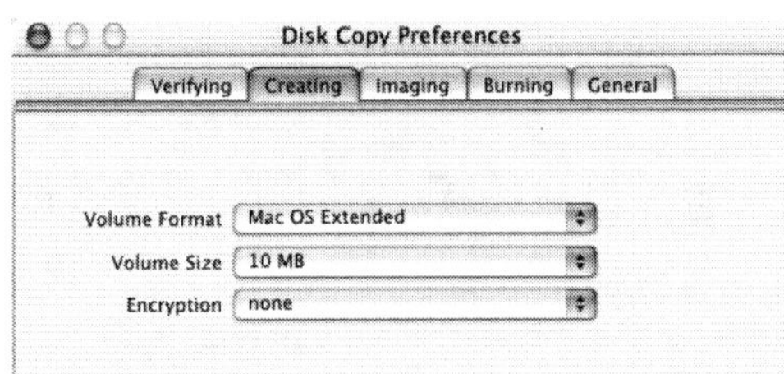

Figure 60 The Creating tab of the Disk Copy Preferences window.

4. Click the Imaging tab (**Figure 61**) to set options for creating disk images:
   - ▲ **Image Type** is the type of image; your choices are: read/write, read/only, compressed, and DVD/CD master.
   - ▲ **Segment Size** is the size of disk segments; your choices are: unlimited, 90 MB, 630 MB, 1 GB, and 2 GB.
   - ▲ **Encryption** is the encryption method.
   - ▲ **Mount afterwards** tells Disk Copy to mount disk images after it creates them.

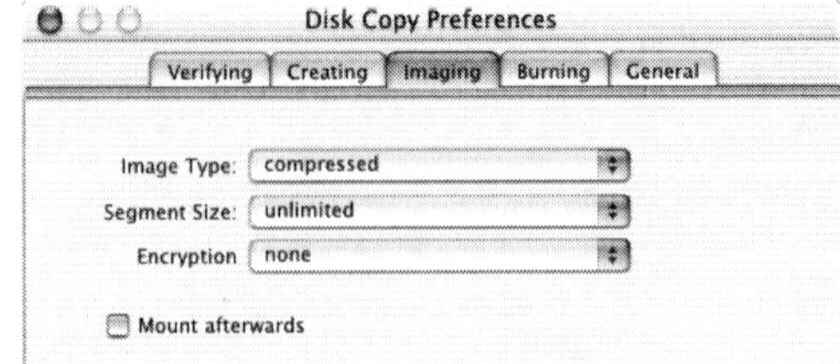

Figure 61 The Imaging tab of the Disk Copy Preferences window.

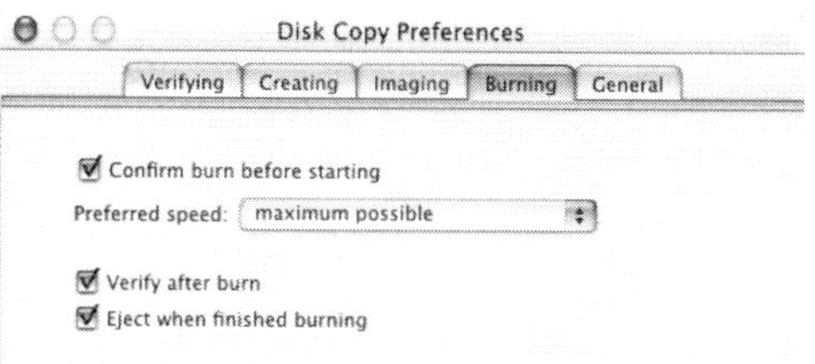

Figure 62 The Burning tab of the Disk Copy Preferences window.

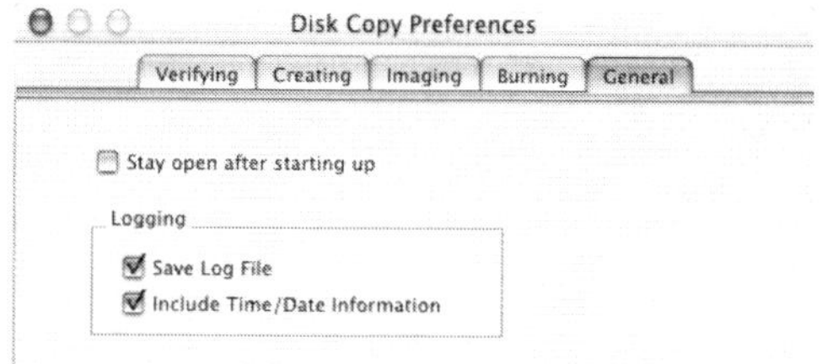

Figure 63 The General tab of the Disk Copy Preferences window.

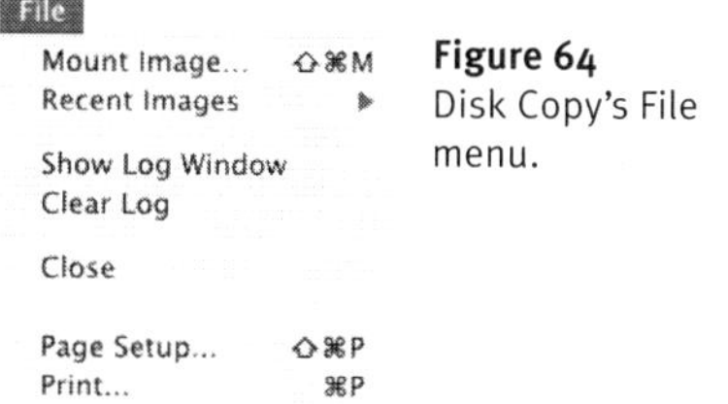

Figure 64 Disk Copy's File menu.

Figure 65 The Disk Copy Log keeps track of everything Disk Copy does.

5. Click the Burning tab (**Figure 62**) to set options for burning CD-Rs:
   - ▲ **Confirm burn before starting** displays a confirmation dialog before Disk Copy begins writing to the CD.
   - ▲ **Preferred speed** is the write speed you would prefer the CD-R to write at. Your choices range from 1x to 40x, but you can choose maximum possible to let the CD-R device pick the appropriate speed.
   - ▲ **Verify after burn** checks the CD for errors after it has been created.
   - ▲ **Eject when finished burning** ejects the CD after it has been created (and, if applicable, verified).
6. Click the General tab (**Figure 63**) to set general Disk Copy options:
   - ▲ **Stay open after starting up** tells Disk Copy to remain open after it has been started by dragging a disk image icon onto the Disk Copy icon.
   - ▲ **Save Log File** saves a log of all Disk Copy activity.
   - ▲ **Include Date/Time Information** includes the date and time in log entries.
7. Click the window's close button to dismiss it and save your settings.

✔ Tips

- A checksum is a mathematical calculation used to verify that a disk image file does not have file corruption.
- To view Disk Copy's log, choose File > Show Log Window (**Figure 64**). The log appears in the Disk Copy Log window (**Figure 65**).
- To clear the Disk Copy Log, choose File > Clear Log (**Figure 64**).

Disk Utility

Disk Utility, as the name implies, is a utility for working with disks. Its features and options are accessible through five tabs:

- **Information** provides general information about the selected disk or volume (**Figures 66** and **67**).
- **First Aid** (**Figure 68**) enables you to verify and repair a disk or volume.
- **Erase** (**Figure 70**) enables you to erase a selected disk or volume.
- **Partition** (**Figure 72**) enables you to divide a disk into several volumes or partitions.
- **RAID** enables you to set up a RAID disk.

✔ Tips

- Disk Utility combines the features of the Disk First Aid and Drive Setup utilities in Mac OS 9.x and earlier.
- A *disk* is a storage device. A *volume* is a portion of a disk formatted for storing files.
- Disk Utility's RAID tab is not covered in this book. To learn more about this feature, enter a search phrase of RAID in Mac Help and follow links that appear for specific instructions.

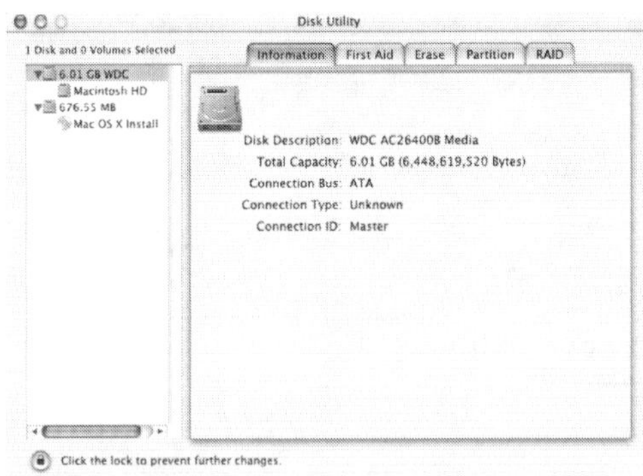

Figure 66 Disk Utility's Information tab can display information about a selected disk...

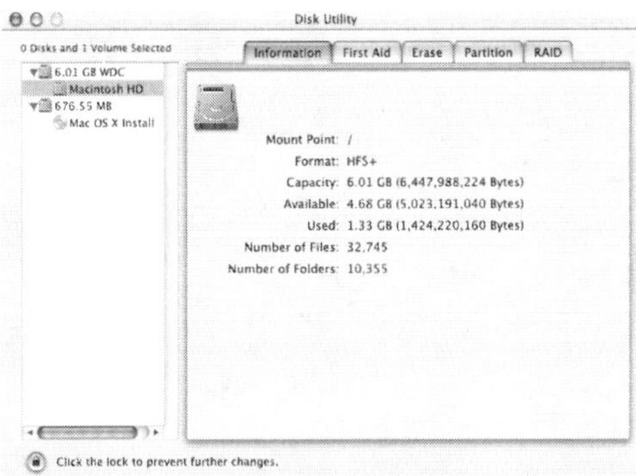

Figure 67 ...or volume.

To get information about a disk or volume

1. Open the Disk Utility icon in the Utilities folder (**Figure 1**).
2. In the Disk Utility window that appears, click the Information tab.
3. On the left side of the window, click the name of the disk or volume that you want to get information about. The information appears in the right side of the window, as shown in **Figures 66** and **67**.

✔ Tip

- In step 3, you may have to click the triangle to the left of a disk name to view a list of volumes on it.

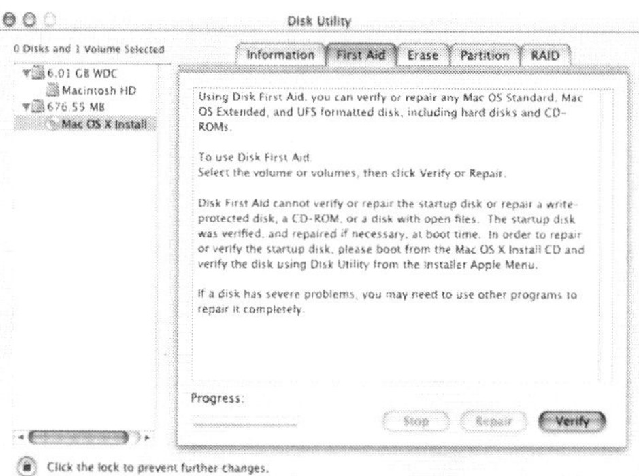

Figure 68 The First Aid tab enables you to verify and repair disks or volumes.

Figure 69 At the end of the verification (or repair) process, Disk Utility's First Aid feature reports results.

To verify or repair a disk or volume

1. Open the Disk Utility icon in the Utilities folder (**Figure 1**).
2. In the Disk Utility window that appears, click the First Aid tab.
3. On the left side of the window, select the disk(s) or volume(s) you want to verify or repair (**Figure 68**).
4. Click Verify or Repair.
5. Wait while your computer checks and/or repairs the selected disk. When it's done, it reports its results on the right side of the window (**Figure 69**).

✔ Tips

- You cannot verify or repair the startup disk or volume. You cannot repair read-only media, such as a CD-ROM disc. (This is why the Repair button is not available in **Figure 68**.)
- To verify or repair your startup disk or volume, start your computer from another disk, such as the Mac OS X install disk.
- To select more than one disk or volume in step 3, hold down [⌘] while clicking each item.
- Disk Utility's First Aid feature cannot repair all disk problems. For severely damaged disks, you may need to acquire third-party utilities, such as Norton Disk Doctor or Disk Warrior.
- It's a good idea to periodically use Disk Utility's First Aid feature to verify and/or repair your disks. Repairing small disk problems as they occur can prevent them from snowballing into big problems.

To erase a disk or volume

1. Open the Disk Utility icon in the Utilities folder (**Figure 1**).
2. In the Disk Utility window that appears, click the Erase tab.
3. On the left side of the window, select the disk or volume you want to erase (**Figure 70**).
4. Set options for the volume:
   - ▲ **Volume Format** is the format applied to the volume: Mac OS Extended (the default selection), Mac OS Standard, or UNIX File System.
   - ▲ **Name** is the name of the volume.
   - ▲ **Install Mac OS 9 Drivers** installs drivers on the disk so it can be read by computers running Mac OS 9.x. (This option is only available if you select a disk to erase.)
5. Click Erase.
6. A dialog sheet like the one in **Figure 71** appears. Click Erase.
7. Wait while your computer erases the disk or volume. A progress dialog appears as it works. When it's finished, an icon for the erased disk or volume reappears on the desktop.

✖ Caution!

- Erasing a disk or volume permanently removes all data. Do not erase a disk if you think you will need any of the data it contains.

✔ Tip

- When you erase a disk, you replace all volumes on the disk with one blank volume. When you erase a volume, you replace that volume with a blank volume.

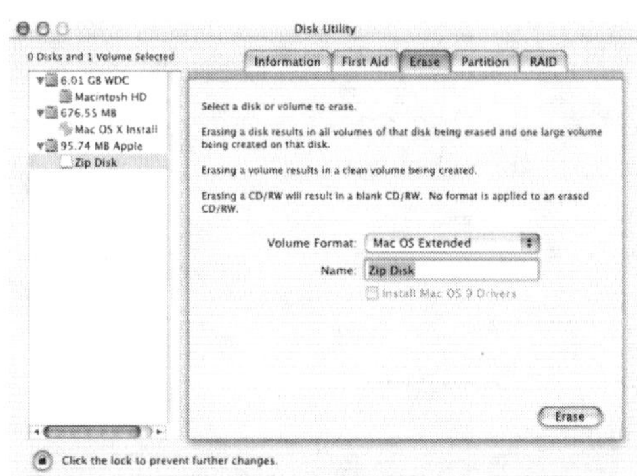

Figure 70 Use Disk Utility's Erase tab to erase a disk or volume.

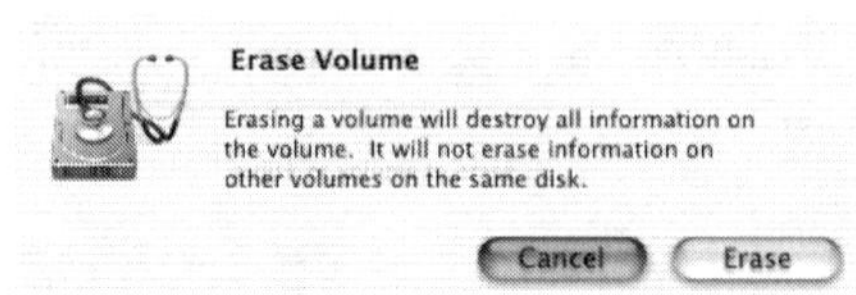

Figure 71 A dialog like this appears to confirm that you really do want to erase the volume or disk.

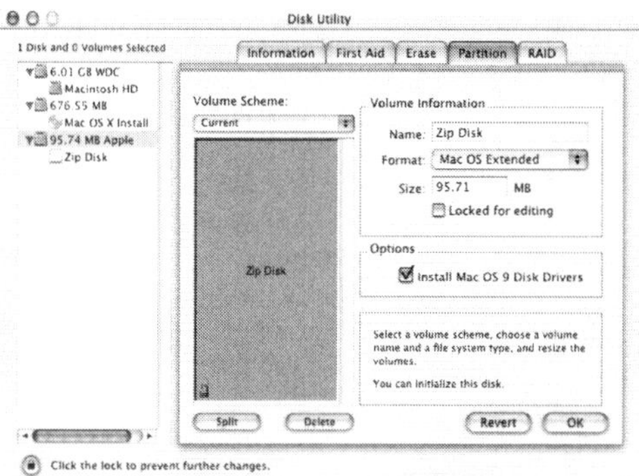

Figure 72 Use Disk Utility's Partition tab to set up partitions on a disk.

✓ Current
1 Partition
2 Partitions
3 Partitions
4 Partitions
5 Partitions
6 Partitions
7 Partitions
8 Partitions

Figure 73
The Volume Scheme pop-up menu.

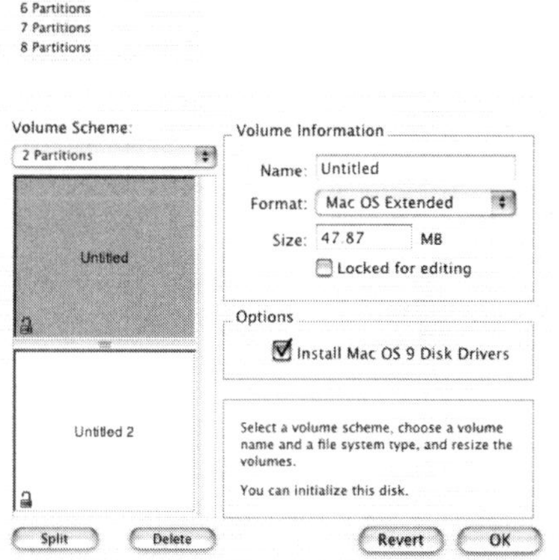

Figure 74 When the volume scheme is set for multiple volumes, you can set options for each one.

Warning!
Saving the new volumes will erase all existing volumes. This can NOT be undone. Are you sure you want to do that?
Cancel
Partition

Figure 75 If you're sure you want to change the volume scheme, click Partition.

✖ Caution!

- As warned in **Figure 75**, saving new volumes will erase all existing volumes, thus erasing data.

To partition a disk

1. Open the Disk Utility icon in the Utilities folder (**Figure 1**).
2. In the Disk Utility window that appears, click the Partition tab.
3. On the left side of the window, select the disk you want to partition (**Figure 72**).
4. Choose an option from the Volume Scheme pop-up menu (**Figure 73**). The area beneath the pop-up menu changes (**Figure 74**).
5. In the Volume Scheme area, select a volume. Then set options as desired:
   - ▲ **Name** is the name of the volume.
   - ▲ **Format** is the volume format: Mac OS Extended (the default option), Mac OS Standard, UNIX File System, or Free Space.
   - ▲ **Size** is the amount of disk space allocated to that partition.
   - ▲ **Locked for editing** prevents changes to the partition's settings.
   - ▲ **Install Mac OS 9 Disk Drivers** enables the disk's partitions to be read by computers running Mac OS 9.x.
6. Repeat step 5 for each partition.
7. Click OK.
8. A warning dialog like the one in **Figure 75** appears. Click Partition.
9. Wait while your computer erases the disk and creates the new partitions. When it's finished, icons for each formatted partition appear on the desktop.

✔ Tips

- If you select Free Space as the format for any partition in step 5, that partition cannot be used to store files.
- You can also change the partition size in step 5 by dragging the divider between partitions in the Volume Scheme area.

To unmount a volume

1. On the left side of the Disk Utility window, select the volume you want to unmount.
2. Choose Options > Unmount (**Figure 76**), or press ⌘ U. The volume's icon disappears from the desktop. The volume name appears in gray on the left side of the Disk Utility window (**Figure 77**).

✔ Tip

- You cannot unmount the startup volume.

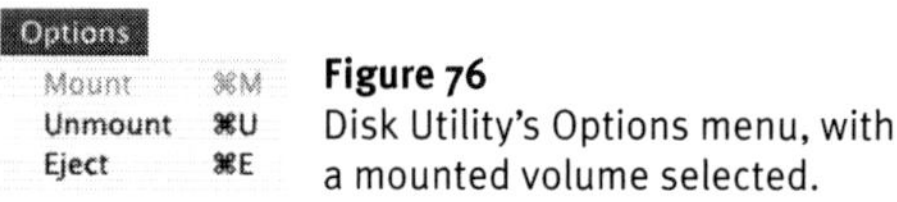

Figure 76
Disk Utility's Options menu, with a mounted volume selected.

Figure 77
When a volume has been unmounted, its name appears in gray in the Disk Utility window.

To mount a volume

1. On the left side of the Disk Utility window, select the volume you want to mount.
2. Choose Options > Mount (**Figure 78**), or press ⌘ M. The volume's icon appears on the desktop. The volume name appears in black on the left side of the Disk Utility window.

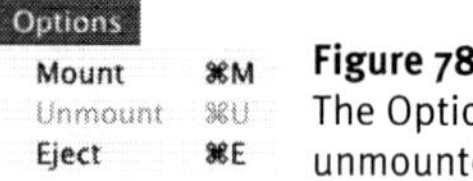

Figure 78
The Options menu, with an unmounted volume selected.

To eject a disk or volume

1. On the left side of the Disk Utility window, select the disk or volume you want to eject.
2. Choose Options > Eject (**Figure 76** or **78**), or press ⌘ E. The disk or volume icon disappears from the desktop and its name is removed from the left side of the Disk Utility window. If you ejected removable media (such as a CD-ROM disc or Zip disk), the disk is ejected from its drive.

✔ Tip

- You cannot eject the startup disk or volume.

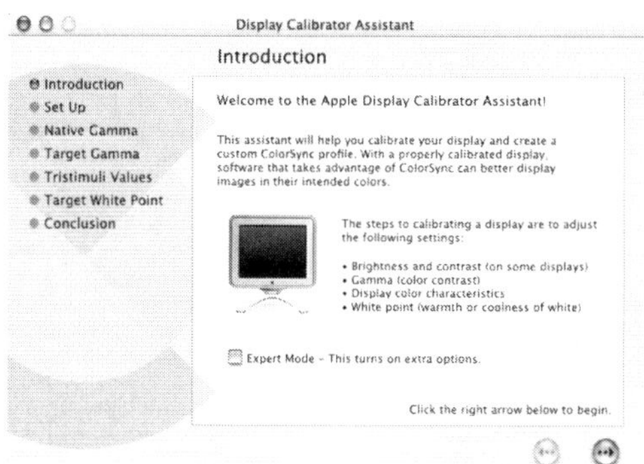

Figure 79 The Introduction screen of the Display Calibrator Assistant explains what the assistant does.

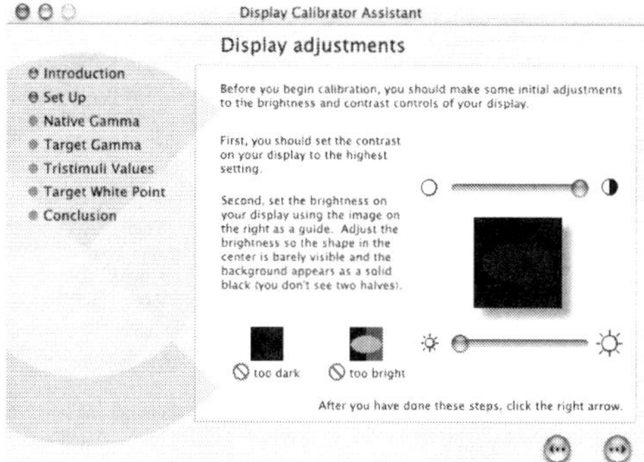

Figure 80 Use the Display adjustments screen to adjust the contrast and brightness of the display.

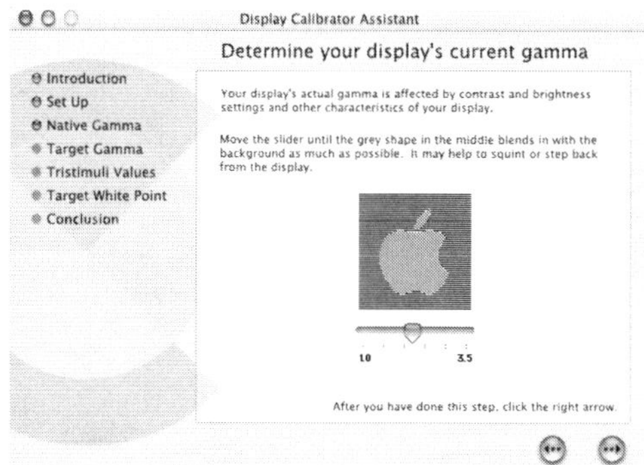

Figure 81 The Determine your display's current gamma enables you to adjust the image display to set gamma values.

Display Calibrator

The Display Calibrator utility enables you to adjust the settings of your monitor so that it properly displays colors. It utilizes an assistant that steps you through the process of making adjustments. When it's finished, a custom ColorSync profile is created and saved for your monitor.

Calibrating a monitor only needs to be done once; your computer and monitor will remember the settings by referencing the ColorSync profile. Although having perfect color display isn't very important for average users, it's vital for graphics professionals who work with color.

✔ Tip

- Your monitor should be properly calibrated if you plan to use ColorSync, which is covered earlier in this chapter.

To calibrate your monitor

1. Open the Display Calibrator icon in the Utilities folder (**Figure 1**).
2. The Introduction screen of the Display Calibrator Assistant window appears (**Figure 79**). Read the information in the window and click the right-pointing arrow to continue.
3. Read and follow the instructions that appear in the Display adjustments screen (**Figure 80**) to set the contrast and brightness. Then click the right arrow.
4. Read and follow the instructions that appear in the Determine your display's current gamma screen (**Figure 81**) to set the gamma values. Then click the right arrow.

Continued on next page...

Continued from previous page.

5. Read and follow the instructions that appear in the Select a target gamma screen (**Figure 82**) to choose a desired gamma setting. Each time you select a different option, the color picture on the right side of the screen changes. Select the one you like best. Then click the right arrow.
6. Read and follow the instructions that appear in the Select your display's color characteristics screen (**Figure 83**). You should be able to select an option that describes your display. Then click the right arrow.
7. Read and follow the instructions that appear in the Select a target white point screen (**Figure 84**) to determine how white should appear on screen. Each time you select a different option, the screen changes. Select the one you prefer or that best meets your needs. Then click the right arrow.
8. Enter a name for your profile in the edit box on the Conclusion screen (**Figure 85**). Then click Create. Display Calibrator creates the new profile and then quits.

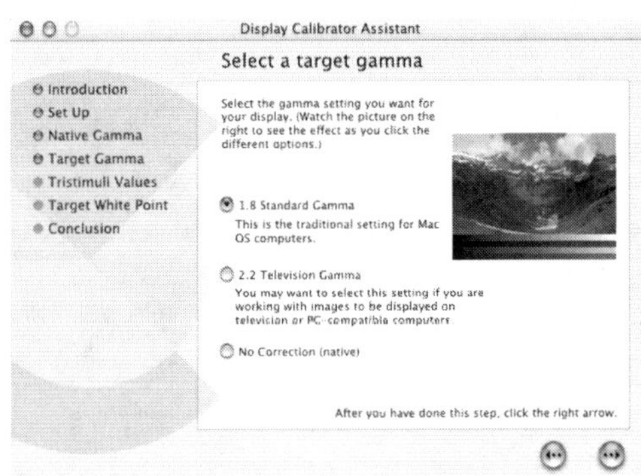

Figure 82 Use the Select a target gamma screen to select your preferred gamma setting.

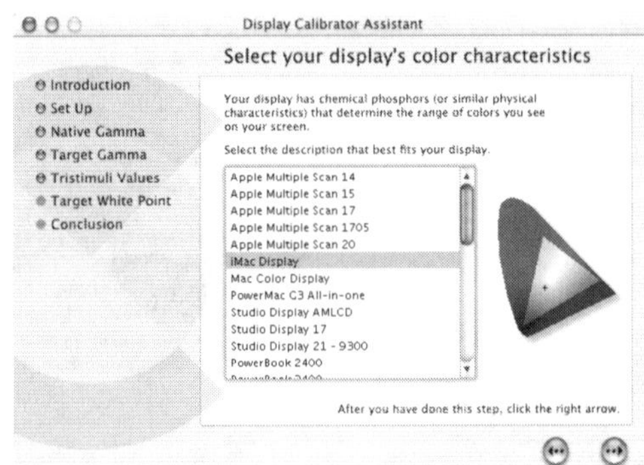

Figure 83 In the Select your display's color characteristics screen, you can select an option that describes your display.

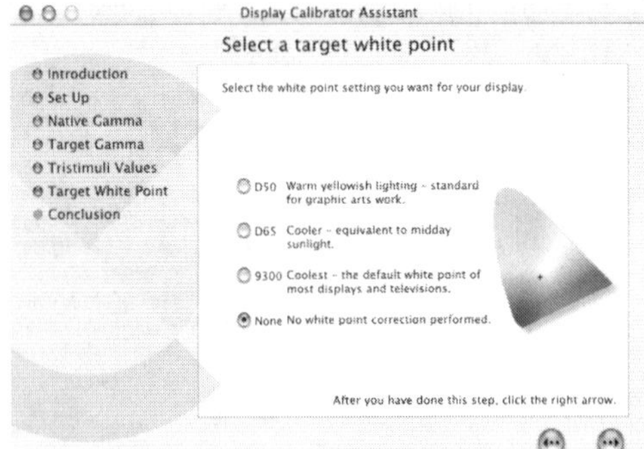

Figure 84 Use the Select a target white point to specify how white should appear onscreen.

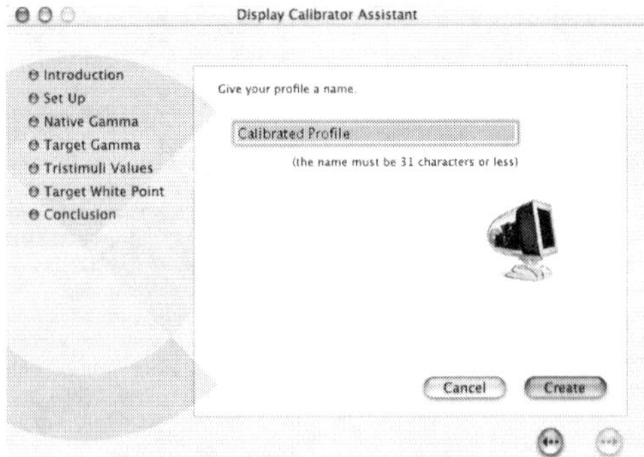

Figure 85 In the last assistant step, enter a name for the profile the Display Calibrator Assistant creates.

Figure 86 If Grab is already running, click its icon in the Dock to make it active.

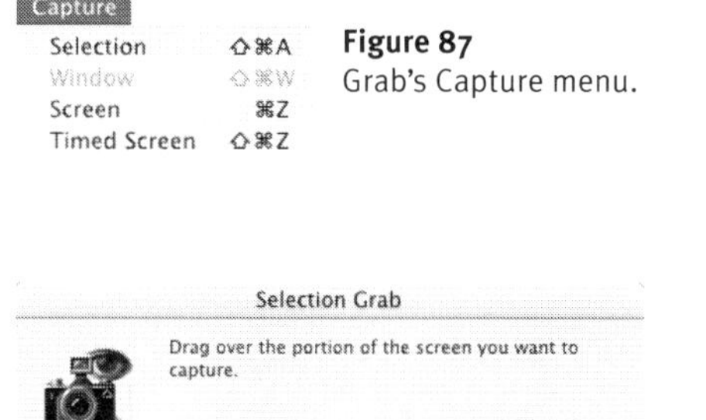

Figure 87 Grab's Capture menu.

Figure 88 The Selection Grab dialog includes instructions for selecting a portion of the screen.

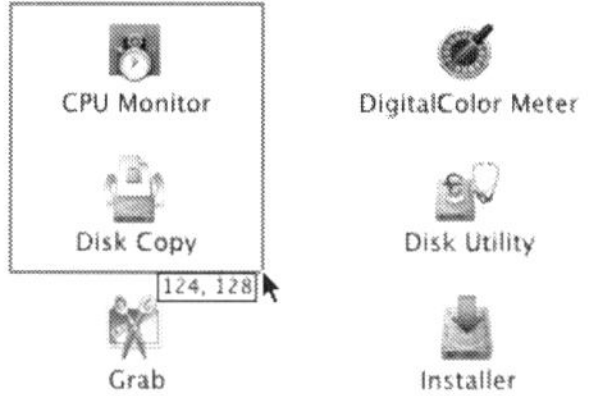

Figure 89 Use the mouse to drag a red rectangle around the portion of the screen you want to capture.

Grab

Grab is an application that can capture screen shots of Mac OS X and its applications. You tell Grab to capture what appears on your screen or on a portion of it and it creates a TIFF file. You can then view the TIFF file with Preview or any software package capable of opening TIFFs.

✔ Tips

- You might find screen shots useful for documenting software—or for writing books like this one!
- Although Grab is a useful—and free—screen shot utility, it isn't the best available for Mac OS X. Snapz Pro X, a shareware program from Ambrosia Software, is a far better option. If you take a lot of screen shots, be sure to check out this program at www.ambrosiasw.com.

To create a screen shot

1. Set up the screen so it shows what you want to capture.
2. Open the Grab icon in the Utilities folder (**Figure 1**).

   or

   If Grab is already running, click its icon on the Dock (**Figure 86**) to make it active.
3. Choose an option from the Capture menu (**Figure 87**) or press its corresponding shortcut key:
   - ▲ **Selection** (Shift ⌘ A) enables you to capture a portion of the screen. When you choose this option, the Selection Grab dialog (**Figure 88**) appears. Use the mouse pointer to drag a box around the portion of the screen you want to capture (**Figure 89**). Release the mouse button to capture the screen.

Continued on next page...

Continued from previous page.

- ▲ **Screen** (⌘ Z) enables you to capture the entire screen. When you choose this option, the Screen Grab dialog (**Figure 90**) appears. Click outside the dialog to capture the screen.
- ▲ **Timed Screen** (Shift ⌘ Z) enables you to capture the entire screen after a ten-second delay. When you choose this option, the Timed Screen Grab dialog (**Figure 91**) appears. Click the Start Timer button, then activate the program you want to capture and arrange on-screen elements as desired. After ten seconds, the screen is captured.

4. Grab makes a camera shutter sound as it captures the screen. A moment later, the image appears in an untitled document window (**Figure 92**).
5. If you are satisfied with the screen shot, choose File > Save (**Figure 93**) or press ⌘ S and use the Save As dialog sheet that appears to save it as a file on disk.

   or

   If you are not satisfied with the screen shot, choose File > Close (**Figure 93**) or press ⌘ W to close the window. In the Close dialog sheet that appears, click Don't Save.

✔ Tips

- Although the Capture menu (**Figure 87**) includes a Window option, it cannot be selected. To capture a window, use the Timed Screen option as discussed in step 3 above.
- In Mac OS X 10.1 and later, you can create screen shots without Grab. Press Shift ⌘ 3 to capture the entire screen or Shift ⌘ 4 to capture a portion of the screen. The screen shot is automatically saved on the desktop. This feature is available in Mac OS 9.x and earlier but was not available in the initial release of Mac OS X.

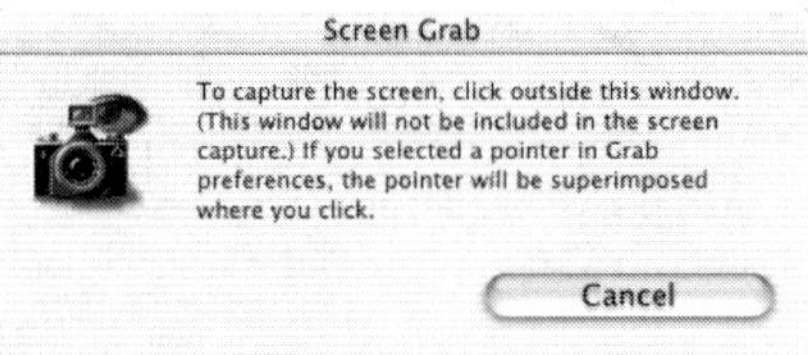

Figure 90 The Screen Grab dialog provides instructions for capturing the entire screen.

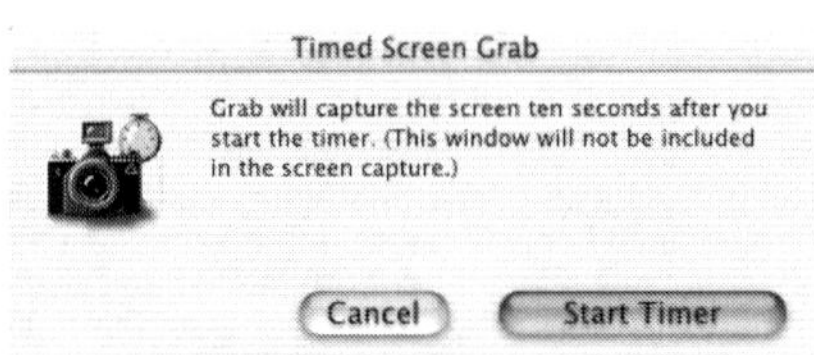

Figure 91 The Timed Screen Grab dialog includes a button to start the 10-second screen grab timer.

Figure 92 The image you capture—in this case, the entire screen—appears in a document window.

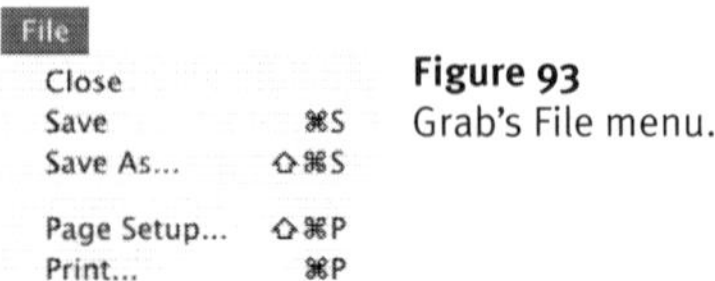

Figure 93 Grab's File menu.

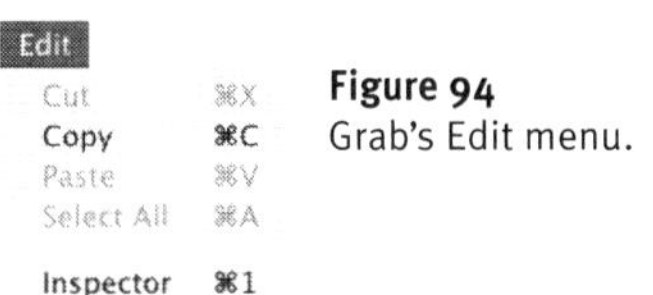

Figure 94
Grab's Edit menu.

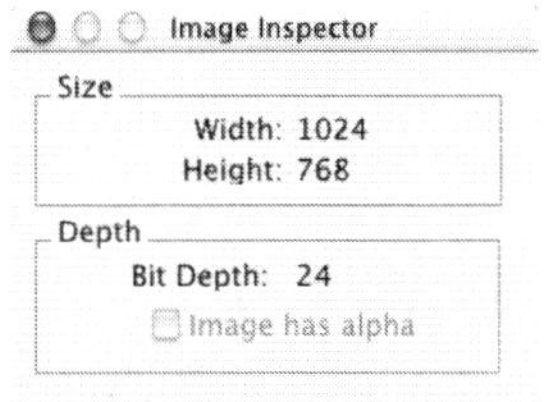

Figure 95
The Image Inspector provides information about the image in the active Grab window.

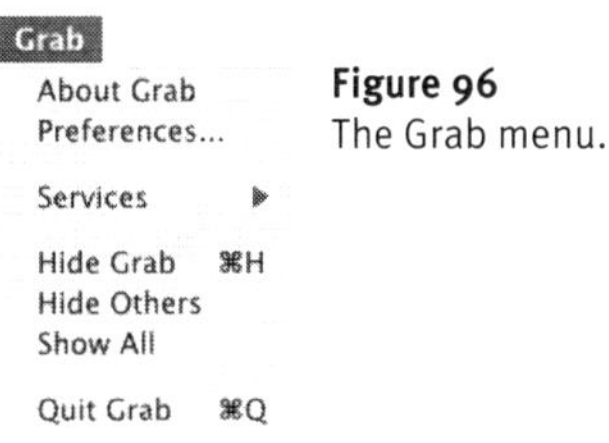

Figure 96
The Grab menu.

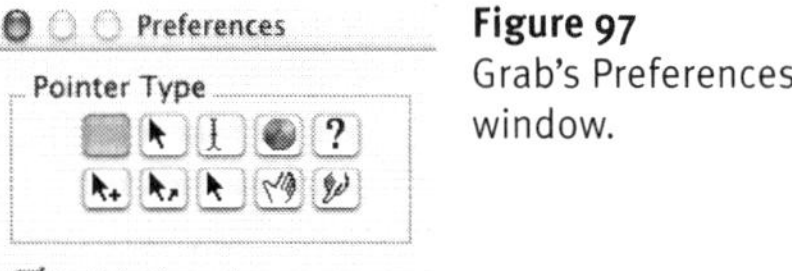

Figure 97
Grab's Preferences window.

To get information about a screen shot

1. While the screen shot's window is active within Grab (**Figure 92**), choose Edit > Inspector (**Figure 94**), or press ⌘ 1.
2. View information about the screen shot in the Image Inspector window that appears (**Figure 95**).
3. When you are finished working with the Image Inspector, click its close button to dismiss it.

To set Grab preferences

1. With Grab active, choose Grab > Preferences (**Figure 96**).
2. Set options in the Preferences window that appears (**Figure 97**):
   - ▲ **Pointer Type** is the appearance of the pointer when it is included in the screen shot. The first option hides the pointer.
   - ▲ **Enable Sound** turns on the camera shutter sound effect to confirm that a screen shot has been made.
3. When you are finished setting preferences, click the Preferences window's close button to dismiss it.

Installer

Installer enables you to install software in Apple Installer document files. In most cases, this program will launch automatically when you open an Installer document. You can, however, launch Installer and use its Open dialog to locate and open an installer document containing software you want to install.

✔ Tip

- Not all software uses Apple Installer document files. Some software has its own installer or uses the Vise installer.

Figure 98 Use this Open dialog to locate, select, and open an Installer document file.

To install software with Installer

1. Open the Installer icon in the Utilities folder (**Figure 1**).
2. Use the Open dialog that appears (**Figure 98**) to locate and select the Installer document you want to install.
3. Click Open.
4. Follow the instructions that appear onscreen to install the software.

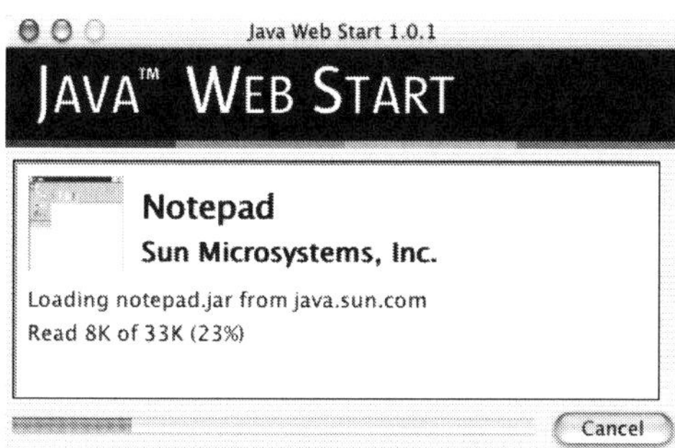

Figure 99 Java Web Start displays a status window as it prepares to launch a Java application from the Web.

Figure 100 Here's one of the demo applications available from the Java Web site: Notepad.

Java Web Start

Java Web Start is an application that enables you to run full-featured Java applications from within a Web browser window. You simply click the link for an application to put Java Web Start to work. First, it checks to see if the application exists on your computer. If not, it downloads it. Next, it checks to see if the downloaded version is the most recent. If not, it updates it. It caches the program's information so the program can be launched at any time. Finally, it loads the application and displays its windows, menus, and other interface elements.

✔ Tips

- Java Web Start was created by Sun Microsystems, developer of the Java programming language. As this book went to press, it was a brand new technology. You can learn more about it and run demos at java.sun.com/products/javawebstart/.
- Java Web Start works with files that have the .jnlp extension.
- Java Web Start is brand new in Mac OS X 10.1.

To launch a Java Web Start application

1. Visit a Web page with one or more links to Java Web Start applications.
2. Click an application link.
3. Wait while Java Web Start launches and prepares to run the software. It displays a status window as it works (**Figure 99**). When it's finished, the application appears (**Figure 100**).

To launch downloaded Java Web Start applications with the Application Manager

1. Open the Java Web Start icon in the Utilities folder (**Figure 1**) to display the Java Web Start Application Manager window.
2. If necessary, choose View > Downloaded Applications (**Figure 101**). The window displays all downloaded applications that are available to run (**Figure 102**).
3. Select an application you want to run and click the Start button. The application launches.

✔ Tip

- You must have an Internet connection for Java Web Start to check for updates to the application. If it cannot check for updates, it will not launch the application.

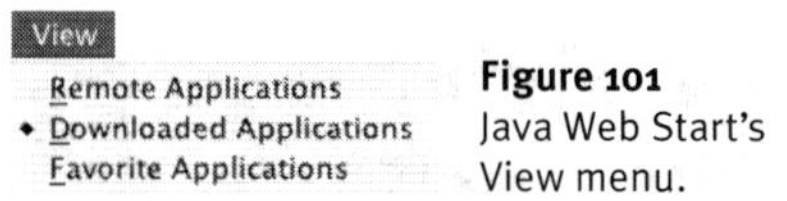

Figure 101 Java Web Start's View menu.

Figure 102 The Downloaded Application view of Java Web Start's Application Manager shows all applications that have been downloaded to cache.

Figure 103 The Printer List window with two printers.

Printers
View Printer List
Add Printer ...
Show Queue ⌘O
Make Default ⌘D
Close Stylus COLOR 740 ⌘W
Delete
Configure Printer ...

Figure 104 The Printers menu includes commands for working with the Printer List and individual printers.

Print Center

Print Center is an application that enables you to manage printers and print jobs. It has two main components:

- **Printer List** window (**Figure 103**) lists all of the printers your computer "sees." Use this window to select and configure printers.
- **Printer Queue** window lists all of the print jobs sent to a specific printer. Use this window to check the status of and cancel print jobs.

✔ Tips

- Print Center replaces the Chooser and Desktop Printer Utility software that were used for the same function in Mac OS 9.x and earlier. Desktop printers are not available in Mac OS X.
- Printing and using the Printer Queue window to work with print jobs is discussed in detail in *Mac OS X: Visual QuickStart Guide.*

To display the Printer List window

1. Open the Print Center icon in the Utilities window (**Figure 1**).
2. If the Printer List does not appear automatically, choose Printers > View Printer List (**Figure 104**).

✔ Tip

- If a question mark appears beside a printer in the Printer List window, you may need to install printer driver software for that printer. Printer drivers are covered in *Mac OS X: Visual QuickStart Guide.*

To add a Printer

1. Click the Add Printer button in the Printer List window (**Figure 103**).

   or

   Choose Printers > Add Printer (**Figure 104**).
2. A dialog sheet appears. Choose an option from the pop-up menu (**Figure 105**) to indicate the type of printer connection.
3. If you chose AppleTalk, wait while Print Center looks for printers and displays a list of what it finds (**Figure 106**). Select the printer you want to add and click Add.

   or

   If you chose LPR Printers using IP, enter an IP address or domain name and set other options in the dialog sheet (**Figure 107**). Then click Add.

   or

   If you chose USB, Print Center displays a list of USB printers connected to the computer (**Figure 108**). Select the printer you want to add, and click Add.

   The printer appears in the Printer List (**Figure 103**).

✔ Tips

- You only have to add a printer if it does not already appear in the Printer List window (**Figure 103**). This needs to be done only once; Mac OS X will remember all printers that you add.
- In step 3, if you chose AppleTalk and your network includes AppleTalk zones, you must select a zone from the pop-up menu that appears in the dialog (**Figure 106**) to see a list of printers.

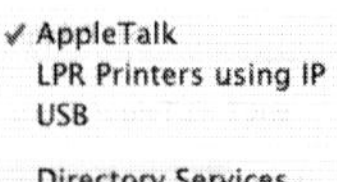

Figure 105 Use this pop-up menu to choose the type of printer connection.

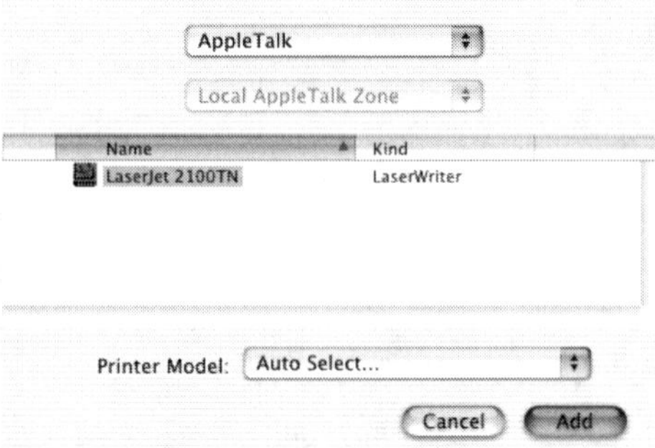

Figure 106 Options for adding an AppleTalk printer, ...

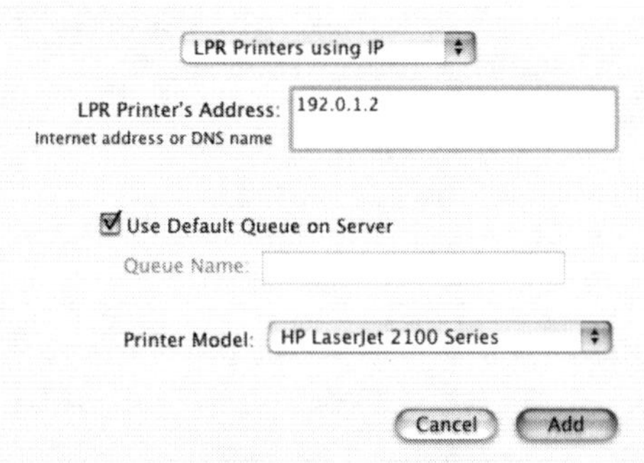

Figure 107 ...an LPR Printer using IP, ...

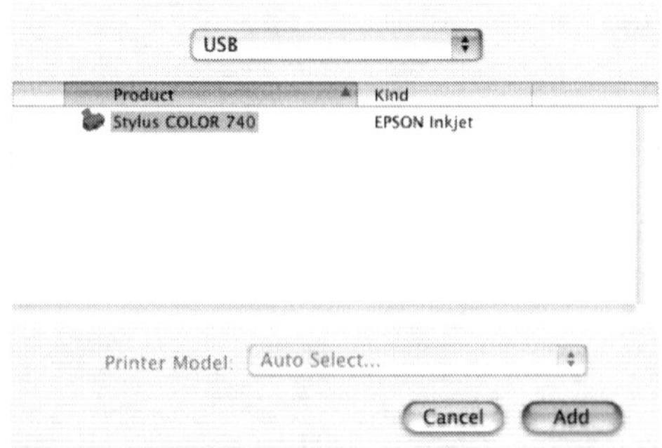

Figure 108 ...and a USB printer.

- If your AppleTalk or USB printer is properly connected but does not appear in step 3 (**Figures 106** and **108**), you may have to install printer driver software for it. Printer drivers are discussed in *Mac OS X: Visual QuickStart Guide*.
- If you're not sure how to set options for an LPR Printer using IP (**Figure 107**), ask your network administrator.
- When adding a printer, it's a good idea to choose the appropriate printer from the Printer Model pop-up menu (**Figures 106** and **107**). This assigns a specific PPD file for the printer and helps ensure that Mac OS X can take full advantage of the features the printer has to offer.

To delete a printer

1. In the Printer List window (**Figure 103**), select the printer you want to delete.
2. Click the Delete button in the Printer list window (**Figure 103**).

   or

   Choose Printers > Delete (**Figure 104**).

To set the default printer

1. In the Printer List window (**Figure 103**), select the printer you want to set as the default.
2. Choose Printers > Make Default (**Figure 104**) or press [Cmd D].

   A bullet appears beside the printer you selected, indicating that it is the default printer (**Figure 103**).

✔ Tip

- The default printer is the one that is selected by default when you open the Print dialog.

Process Viewer

Process Viewer enables you to get information about the various processes running on your computer. You may find this information helpful if you are a programmer or network administrator or you are trying to troubleshoot a computer problem.

✔ Tip

- A *process* is a set of programming code that performs a task.

To see a list of processes

Open the Process Viewer icon in the Utilities folder (**Figure 1**). The Process Listing window appears (**Figure 109**).

✔ Tips

- To sort processes in the Process Listing window (**Figure 109**), click the column you want to sort by. You can reverse the sort order by clicking the tiny button above the vertical scroll bar.
- To show only specific groups of processes, choose an option from the Show pop-up menu (**Figure 110**). The list changes accordingly.
- To see more information about a selected process, click the triangle beside More Info at the bottom of the dialog. The dialog expands to show information about the process in two tabs (**Figures 111** and **112**).

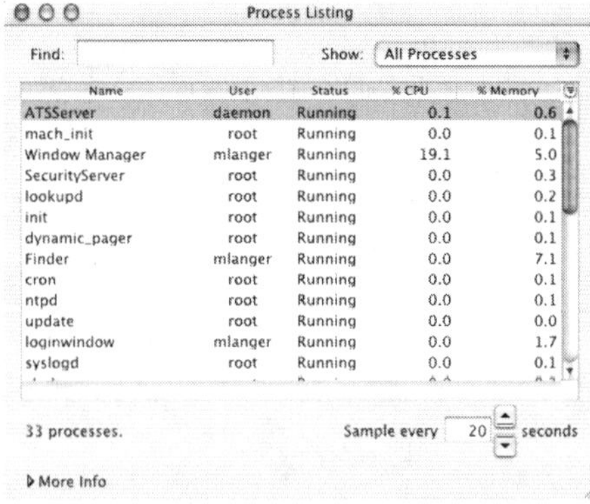

Figure 109 The Process Listing window shows a list of all processes running on your computer.

✓ All Processes
User Processes
Administrator Processes
NetBoot Processes

Figure 110
Use the Show menu to choose the type of processes to display.

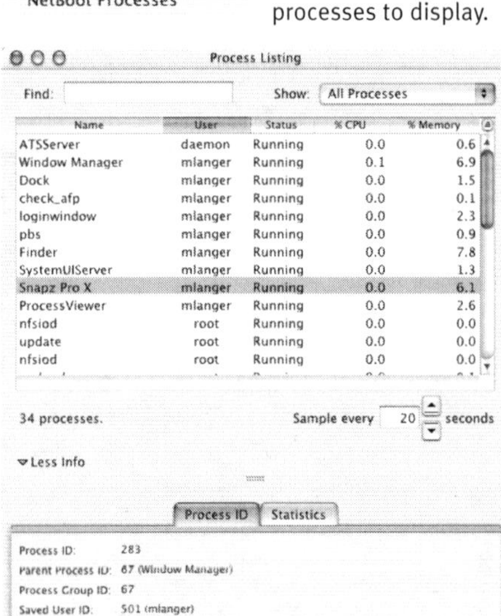

Figure 111 You can display additional information about a selected process in the Process ID tab...

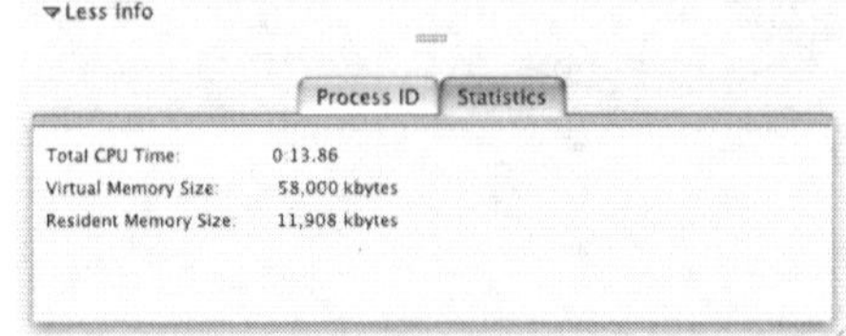

Figure 112 ...and Statistics tab at the bottom of the window.

Figure 113 Drag the icon for the compressed file onto the StuffIt Expander icon.

Figure 114 StuffIt Expander's File menu has only one command.

StuffIt Expander

StuffIt Expander is a file compression utility that expands files compressed or encoded with StuffIt (.sit), Zip (.zip), BinHex (.hqx), Tar (.tar), and other schemes. Files distributed over the Internet are commonly compressed or encoded to bundle multiple files into one file and reduce download times.

✔ Tips

- Developed by Aladdin Systems, Inc., StuffIt is a standard compression scheme for Mac OS computers.
- StuffIt Expander does not compress files; it only decompresses them. To compress files, you need a program such as StuffIt Deluxe, which is available on the Aladdin Web site, www.aladdinsys.com.

To expand a compressed file

Drag the icon for the compressed file onto the StuffIt Expander icon in the Utilities folder (**Figure 113**). When you release the mouse button, StuffIt Expander launches, expands the file, and quits. The expanded file appears in the same location as the original (or in another location specified in StuffIt Expander's preferences).

✔ Tips

- Another way to expand a file is to launch StuffIt Expander by opening its icon, choosing File > Expand (**Figure 114**), and using the dialog that appears, to locate, select, and open a compressed file.
- When properly configured to work with Internet applications, StuffIt Expander will automatically expand downloaded files as they are received.

To set StuffIt Expander preferences

1. Open the StuffIt Expander icon in the Utilities folder (**Figure 1**).
2. Choose StuffIt Expander > Preferences (**Figure 115**) to display the preferences dialog.
3. Click the Expanding icon to display its preferences (**Figure 116**). Set options as desired:
   - ▲ **Expand Archives** expands files with .sit, .pkg, .arc, .bz, .cpt, .dd, .gz, .lha, .rar, .tar, .Z, and .zip extensions. You can turn on the **Delete after expanding** check box to automatically delete the original file after it has been expanded.
   - ▲ **Expand Encoded Files** expands files with .hqx, .bin, .pf, .as, and .uu extensions, as well as those encoded with MIME/Base64 encoding. You can turn on the **Delete after expanding** check box to automatically delete the original file after it has been expanded.
   - ▲ **Expanded StuffIt SpaceSaver Files** expands files compressed with StuffIt Deluxe's SpaceSaver feature.
   - ▲ **Continue to Expand** expands compressed files within compressed files.
   - ▲ **Ignore Return Receipt requests** processes files regardless of the presence of a return receipt request.
   - ▲ **Scan for viruses using** enables virus scanning with the virus protection software you select from the pop-up menu. (The software you select must be installed to use this feature.)
4. Click the Joining icon to display its preferences (**Figure 117**). To automatically join compressed files that were segmented, turn on the **Join Segmented Files** check box.

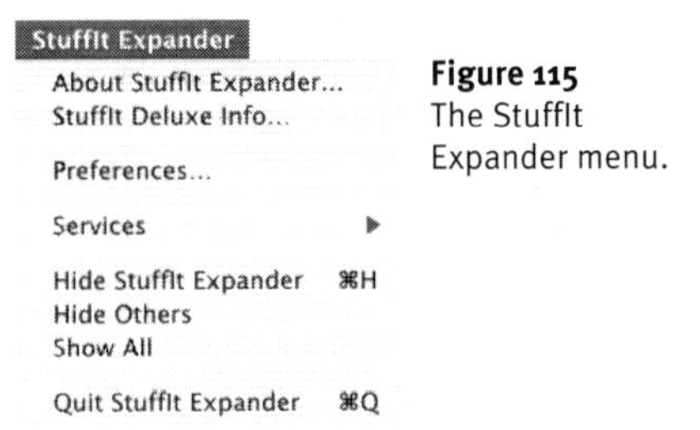

Figure 115 The StuffIt Expander menu.

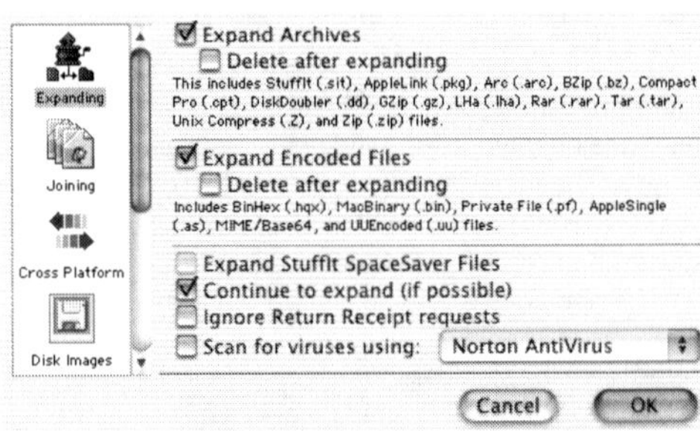

Figure 116 StuffIt Expander's Expanding preferences.

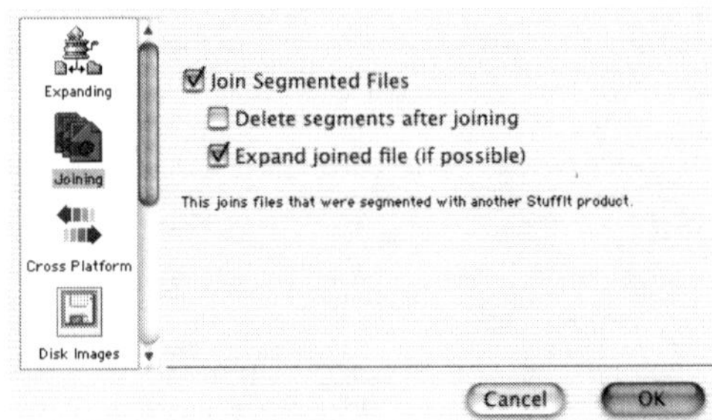

Figure 117 StuffIt Expander's Joining preferences.

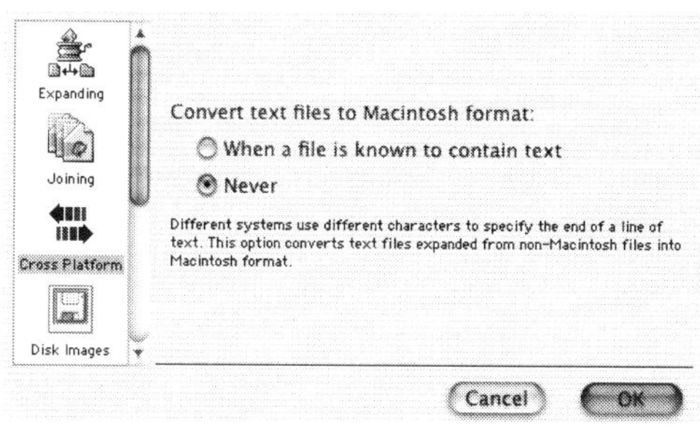

Figure 118 StuffIt Expander's Cross Platform preferences.

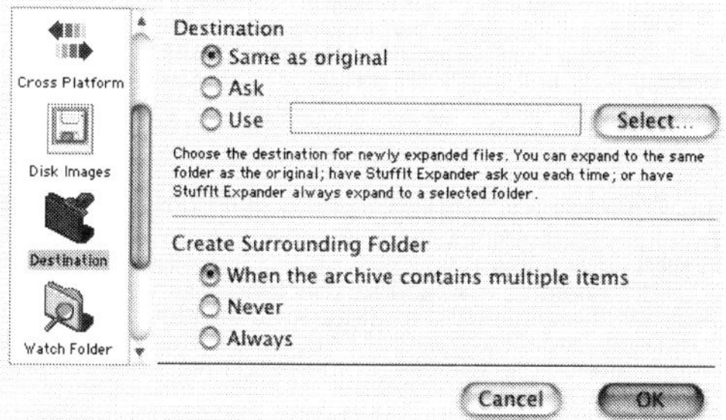

Figure 119 StuffIt Expander's Destination preferences.

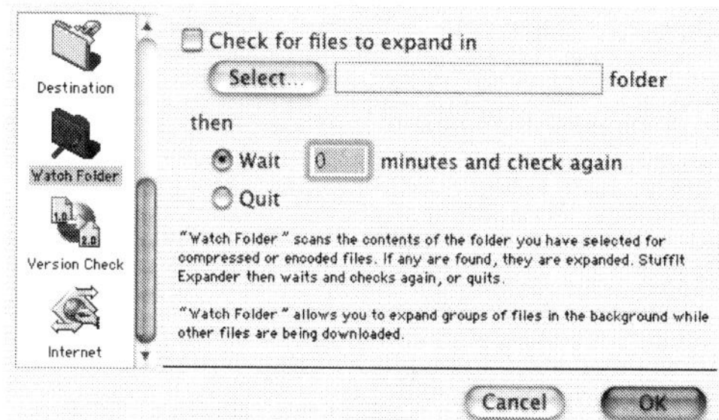

Figure 120 StuffIt Expander's Watch Folder preferences.

You can then turn on the **Delete segments after joining** check box to automatically delete the original files after they have been expanded and joined. You can also turn on the **Expand joined file** check box to expand files that, when joined, are compressed.

5. Click the Cross Platform icon to display its preferences (**Figure 118**). Select a conversion option for text files:
   - **When a file is known to contain text** automatically converts text files to Mac OS format.
   - **Never** does not convert text files.
6. Click the Destination icon to display its preferences (**Figure 119**). Set options as desired:
   - **Destination** is the location in which expanded files should be saved. If you select Ask, StuffIt Expander will display a Save As dialog each time you expand a file. If you select Use, you can click the Select button to choose a disk location.
   - **Create surrounding folder** specifies whether StuffIt Expander should save expanded files into a new folder.
7. Click the Watch Folder icon to display its preferences (**Figure 120**). To automatically expand files in a specific folder, turn on the **Check for files to expand in** check box. Then click the Select button and use the dialog that appears to select a folder in which compressed files will be stored. Select one of the radio buttons to determine what StuffIt Expander does after compressing files: **Wait** waits the number of minutes you specify before checking again; **Quit** quits.

Continued on next page...

Continued from previous page.

8. Click the Version Check icon to display its preferences (**Figure 121**). To automatically check for new versions of StuffIt Expander while you are connected to the Internet, turn on the **Allow Version Checking** check box.
9. Click the Internet icon to display its preferences (**Figure 122**). Turn on the check box beside each compression or encoding scheme you want StuffIt Expander to handle when downloaded from the Internet. To quickly turn on all check boxes, click the Use StuffIt Expander for all available types button.
10. Click OK to save your settings.

✔ Tips

- Very large files are sometimes segmented so they can be sent over the Internet as a series of smaller files.
- Text files created on non-Mac OS computers sometimes include characters that are not used in Mac OS.
- StuffIt Expander's Disk Images preferences do not apply to Mac OS X.
- The Watch Folder feature only works when StuffIt Expander is running.

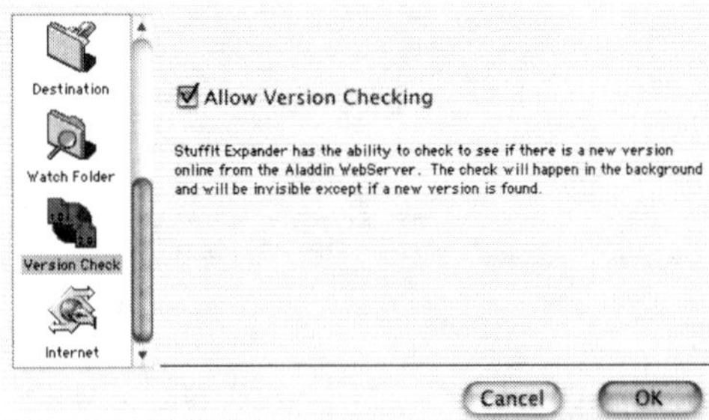

Figure 121 StuffIt Expander's Version Check preferences.

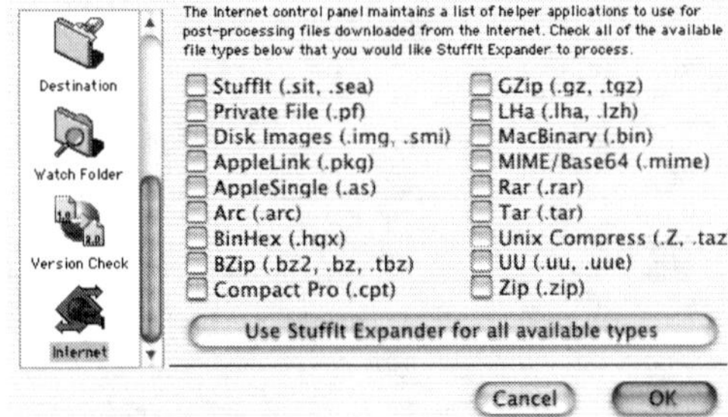

Figure 122 StuffIt Expander's Internet preferences.

Setting StuffIt Expander Preferences

SPEECH FEATURES

Speech Features

Like previous versions of Mac OS, Mac OS X has two speech-related features:

- **Speech recognition** enables your computer to "listen to" and understand spoken commands and act on them. It uses the Apple Speakable Items speech recognition system and works with AppleScripts called Speakable Items.
- **Text-to-Speech** enables your computer to read text aloud using a variety of digitized voices.

In this chapter, I tell you how to configure and use these two features.

✔ Tips

- AppleScript is discussed in **Chapter 7**.
- Macintosh computers have always have the ability to speak. The very first Macintosh introduced itself verbally when it was unveiled by Steve Jobs in 1984.

Speech Recognition

The Mac OS X speech recognition feature enables you to issue verbal commands to your computer. Although there are a number of predefined commands that you can use, you can also create your own commands.

✔ Tips

- Speech recognition requires a microphone (either built-in or plug-in) to work.
- The speech recognition feature works best in a relatively quiet work environment.

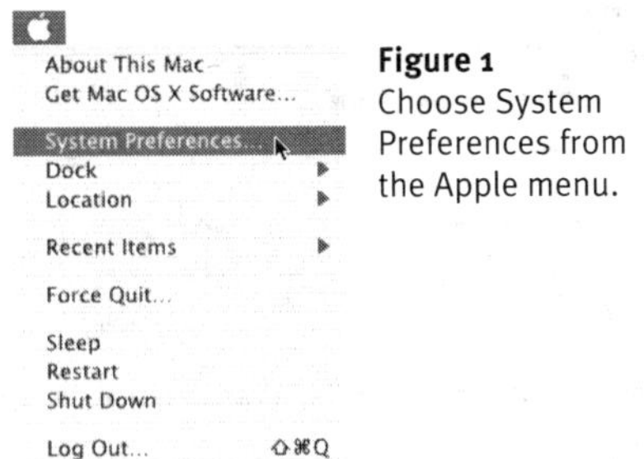

Figure 1 Choose System Preferences from the Apple menu.

Figure 2 You can open System Preferences by clicking its icon on the Dock.

To enable & configure Apple Speakable Items speech recognition

1. Choose Apple > System Preferences (**Figure 1**).

   or

   Click the System Preferences icon in the Dock (**Figure 2**).
2. In the System Preferences window that appears, click the Speech icon (in the System area) to display its options.
3. If necessary, click the Speech Recognition tab (**Figures 3** and **8**).
4. Choose Apple Speakable Items from the Recognition System pop-up menu. (It may be the only option.)
5. If necessary, click the On/Off tab to display its options (**Figure 3**).
6. Select the On radio button.
7. A dialog sheet may appear with instructions for using Apple Speakable Items (**Figure 4**). If this is your first time using this feature, read the contents of the dialog and click Continue to dismiss it.

   The round Feedback window appears (**Figure 5**).

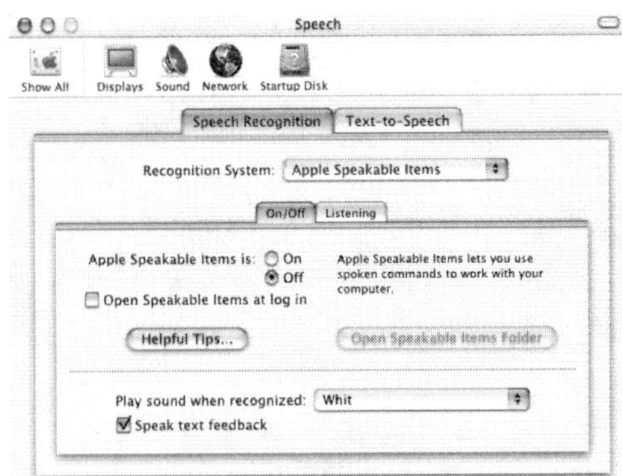

Figure 3 The On/Off tab for Speech Recognition settings in the Speech preferences pane.

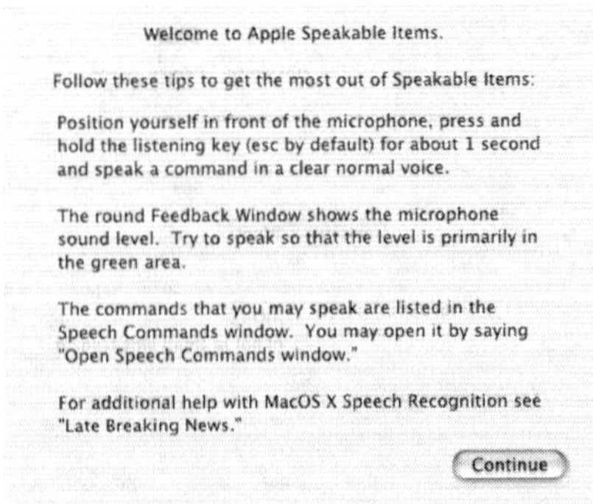

Figure 4 This dialog sheet provides brief instructions for using Apple Speakable items.

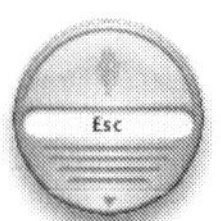

Figure 5 The Feedback window.

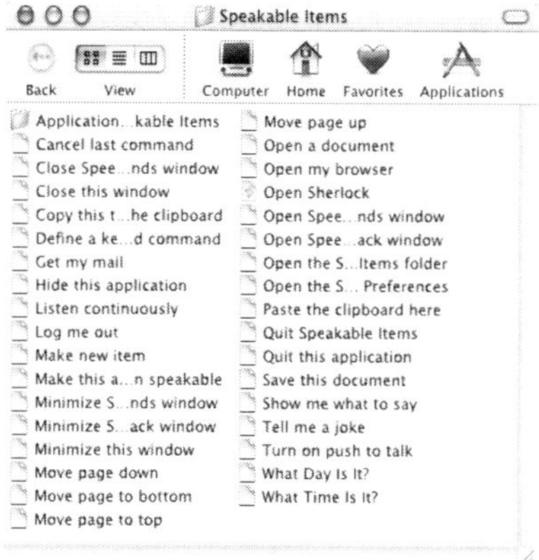

Figure 6 The contents of the Speakable Items folder.

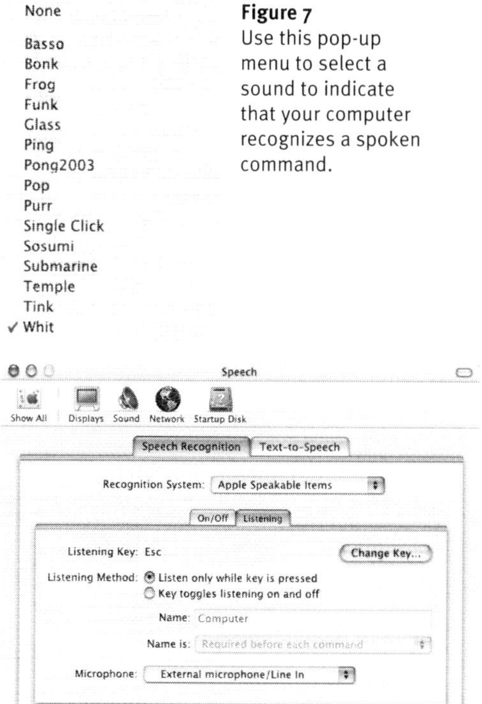

Figure 7 Use this pop-up menu to select a sound to indicate that your computer recognizes a spoken command.

Figure 8 The Listening tab of the Speech Recognition settings in the Speech preferences pane.

8. Set options and click buttons in this tab as desired:
   - ▲ **Open Speakable Items at log in** opens the Speakable Items folder when you start or log in to your computer.
   - ▲ **Helpful tips** displays the dialog sheet with information about speakable items (**Figure 4**).
   - ▲ **Open Speakable Items Folder** opens the Speakable Items folder (**Figure 6**).
   - ▲ **Play sound when recognized** enables you to select a system sound to play when your computer recognizes the spoken command. Choose a sound from the pop-up menu (**Figure 7**).
   - ▲ **Speak text feedback** instructs your Mac to speak the text of any feedback that results from your spoken command.
9. Click the Listening tab to display its options (**Figure 8**).
10. Set options as desired:
    - ▲ **Listening key** is the keyboard key you must press to either listen to spoken commands or toggle listening on or off. By default, the key is [Esc], but you can click the Change Key button and use the dialog sheet that appears (**Figure 9**) to enter a different key and click OK.
    - ▲ **Listening method** enables you to select how you want your Mac to listen for commands. **Listen only while key is pressed** requires you to press the listening key to listen. **Key toggles listening on and off** uses the listening key to turn listening on or off. If you select this second option, you can enter a name for your computer (the default name is Computer) and use the Name

Continued on next page...

Continued from previous page.

is pop-up menu (**Figure 10**) to specify whether the name must be spoken before each command.

▲ **Microphone** enables you to select which microphone you will use to issue commands. The options vary depending on your computer model and the microphones attached to it.

11. Choose System Prefs > Quit System Prefs (**Figure 11**), or press [⌘ Q].

✔ Tips

- Each user has his or her own Speakable Items folder, which can be found at /Users/*username*/Library/Speech/Speakable Items.
- For best results, either set the Listening method to Listen only while key is pressed or require the computer name before each spoken command. Otherwise, your computer could interpret background noise and conversations as commands.
- An external microphone—especially one on a headset—will work more reliably than a built-in microphone, such as the one on the front of an iMac monitor.

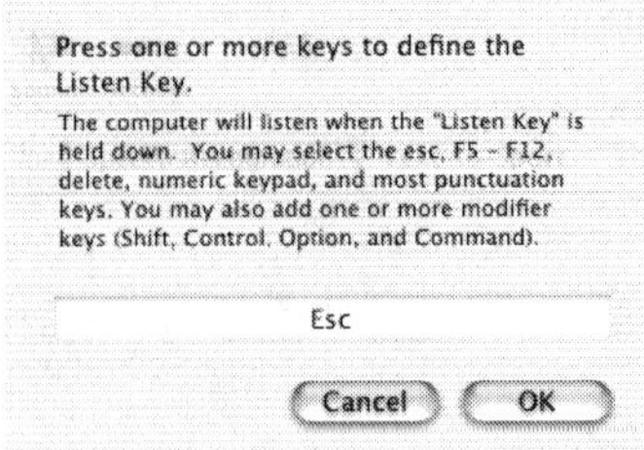

Figure 9 Use this dialog sheet to select a different listening key.

Optional before commands
✓ Required before each command
Required 15 seconds after last command
Required 30 seconds after last command

Figure 10 This pop-up menu enables you to specify how the computer name should be used for listening.

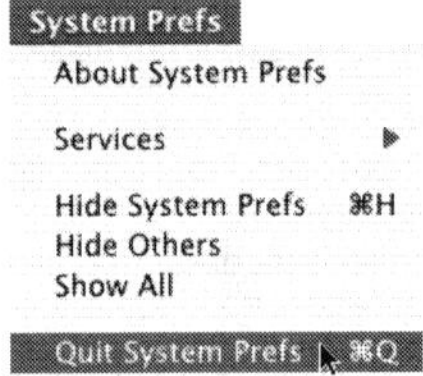

Figure 11 When you are finished setting Speech preferences, choose Quit System Prefs from the System Prefs menu.

Figure 12
When your computer recognizes a spoken command, the command appears above the Feedback window.

Figure 13
When a command has feedback, the response appears beneath the Feedback window.

To use Speakable Items

1. Hold down the listening key and speak the command you want your computer to perform.

   or

   Use the listening key to turn listening on, then speak the command you want your computer to perform. If the computer name is required before or after the command, be sure to include it.

2. If your computer understands the command, the sound you specified during setup will play and the command will appear above the Feedback window (**Figure 12**). The command is executed (if possible).

   or

   If your computer did not understand the command, nothing happens. Wait a moment and try again.

✔ Tips

- The technique you use in step 1 will vary depending on how you set up speech recognition. Consult the previous section for details.
- The Speakable Items folder (**Figure 6**) contains all preprogrammed Speakable Items. Each file corresponds to a command. Say the file name to issue the command.
- The Application Speakable Items folder inside the Speakable Items folder (**Figure 6**) contains Speakable Items commands that work in specific applications.
- Be sure to speak slowly and clearly when issuing commands.

Continued on next page...

Continued from previous page.

- If it is not possible to execute a command, nothing will happen after the command appears above the Feedback window. For example, if you use the "Close this window" command and no window is active, nothing will happen.
- If the command you issued results in feedback (for example, the "What Day Is It?" command) and you set up speech recognition to speak feedback, your computer displays (**Figure 13**) and speaks the results of the command.
- To add a Speakable Item, use AppleScript to create a script for the command. Save the script as a compiled script in the appropriate location in the Speakable Items folder. Be sure to name the script with the words you want to use to issue the command. **Figure 14** shows an example of the AppleScript used for the Open Sherlock command. AppleScript is discussed in **Chapter 7**.

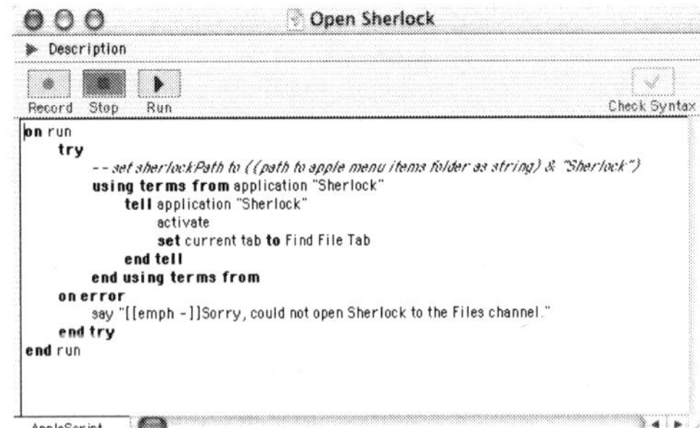

Figure 14 A Speakable Item is nothing more than a compiled AppleScript script.

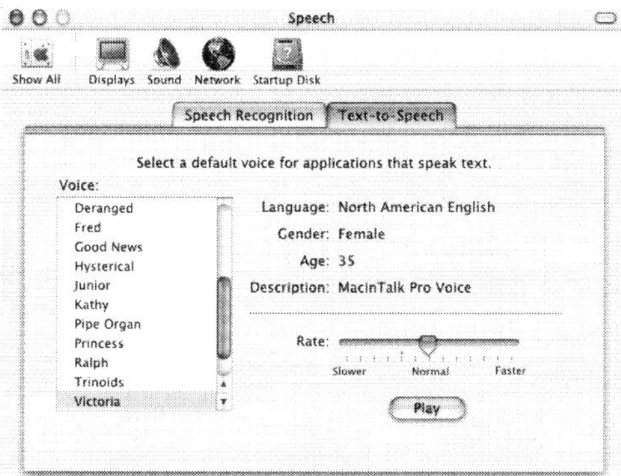

Figure 15 The Text-to-Speech tab of the Speech preferences pane.

To configure text-to-speech

1. Choose Apple > System Preferences (**Figure 1**).

   or

   Click the System Preferences icon in the Dock (**Figure 2**)
2. In the System Preferences window that appears, click the Speech icon (in the System area) to display its options.
3. If necessary, click the Text-to-Speech tab (**Figure 15**).
4. Select one of the voices in the Voice list. The description on the right side of the window changes for that voice and your computer speaks so you can hear it.
5. To change the speed at which the voice speaks, use the Rate slider. You can then click the Play button to hear the effect of your change.

✔ Tips

- As you try some of the voices, you'll see that some of them are more fun than practical.
- The settings you make in the Speech-to-Text tab affect any application that can speak text.

To hear your computer read to you

1. Open the TextEdit icon in the Applications folder (**Figure 16**).
2. In the TextEdit document window that appears, enter the text you want to hear (**Figure 17**).
3. Choose Edit > Speech > Start speaking (**Figure 18**). Your computer reads the text you typed.

✔ Tips

- Be sure to include punctuation in what you type. The text-to-speech feature will use punctuation to insert pauses as necessary.
- Sometimes you have to spell words a little differently to get correct punctuation. For example, my name is pronounced better by most voices when typed "Ma-ree-ah."

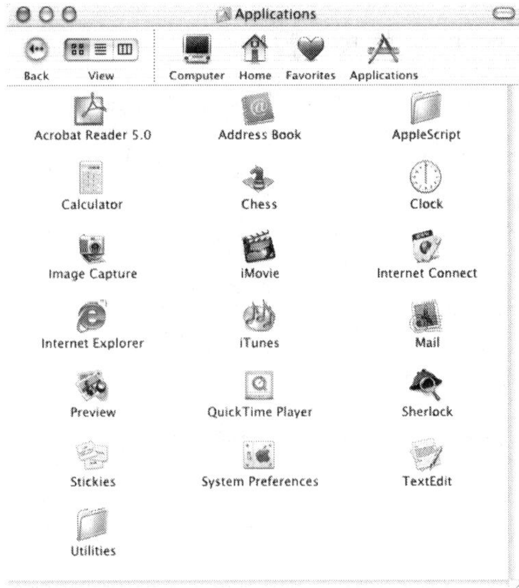

Figure 16 The Applications folder's contents.

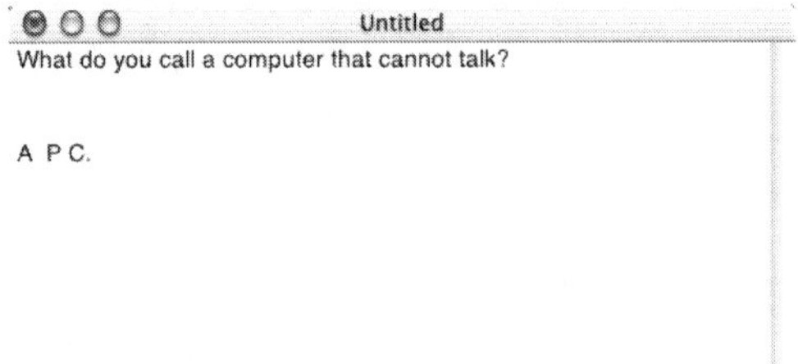

Figure 17 Type the text you want to hear into a TextEdit document window. (My Macs have always tried to be funny.)

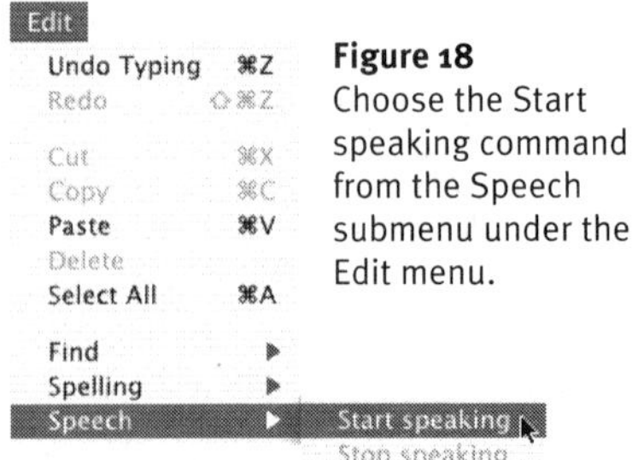

Figure 18 Choose the Start speaking command from the Speech submenu under the Edit menu.

iDisk

Go
Computer ⌥⌘C
Home ⌥⌘H
iDisk ⌥⌘I
Favorites ▶
Applications ⌥⌘A
Recent Folders ▶
Go to Folder... ⌘~
Back ⌘[
Connect to Server... ⌘K

Figure 1
One of the best things about iDisk is that you can access it with a menu command right in the Mac OS X Finder.

iDisk

Apple has embraced the Internet revolution and encourages Mac OS users to get connected to the Internet. One of the ways it does this is with iDisk.

iDisk is 20 MB of private hard disk space on an Apple Internet server that you can use to store files and publish a Web site. But rather than deal with complex FTP software to access your iDisk space, Apple gives you access right through the Finder's Go menu (**Figure 1**) and within Open and Save As dialogs.

This chapter explains how to set up, connect to, and use iDisk.

✔ Tips

- To use iDisk, you must have an Internet connection. I explain how to set up an Internet connection and connect to the Internet in *Mac OS X: Visual QuickStart Guide.*
- iDisk is a great place to store secondary backups of important files. For example, if you're a Quicken 2002 user, you probably let Quicken automatically back up your financial data at the end of each Quicken session. But also consider putting a copy of the data on your iDisk space as an off-premises backup for added protection against data loss.
- You can purchase additional iDisk space from Apple if you need it; visit the iDisk home page for details: idisk.mac.com.

Setting Up an iTools Account

To use iDisk, you must have an iTools account. *iTools* is a collection of Internet-based utilities and other features provided by Apple Computer on its mac.com Web site. iDisk is one of these features.

In this section, I explain how to set up an iTools account.

Figure 2 The iTools home page.

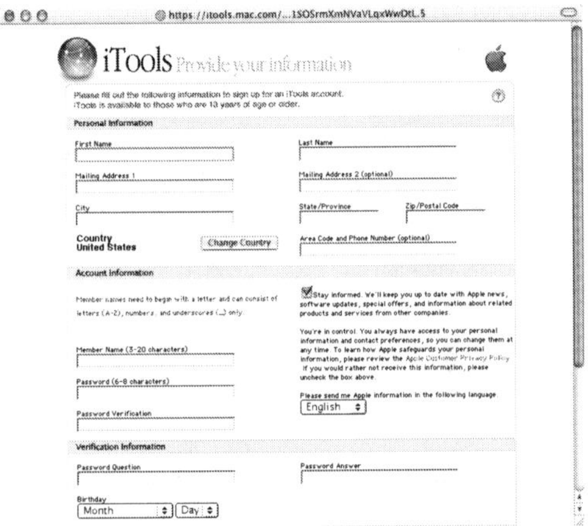

Figure 3 To register for iTools, you have to provide some information about yourself.

✔ Tips

- You may have already set up an iTools account when you registered Mac OS X. If so, you can skip the instructions here.
- iTools is free; all you need is an Internet connection and a Web browser.
- You can learn more about iTools at itools.mac.com or in *Mac OS X: Visual QuickStart Guide.*

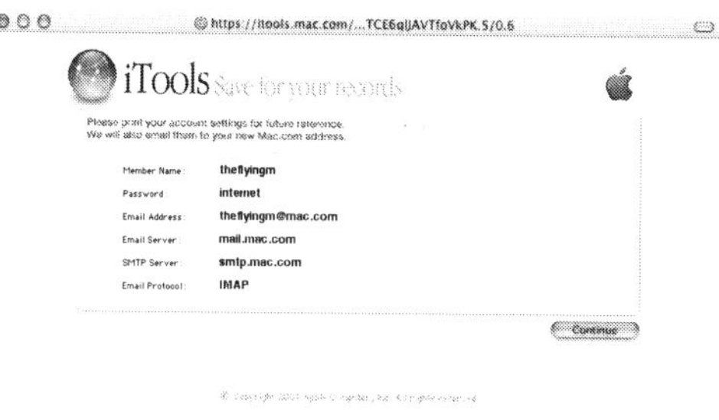

Figure 4 When your registration information has been accepted, iTools displays your login information.

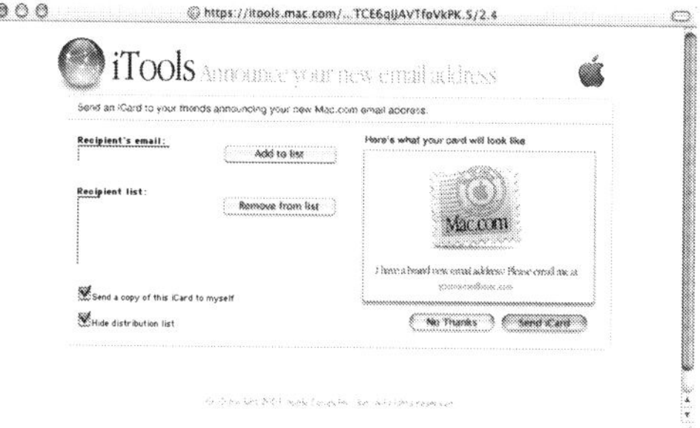

Figure 5 If you plan to use the mac.com e-mail account that's part of iTools, use this window to tell your friends about your new e-mail address.

Figure 6 At the conclusion of the sign-up process, this window appears.

To set up an iTools account

1. Launch your Web browser and use it to view http://itools.mac.com/ (**Figure 2**).
2. Click the Sign Up button.
3. Enter the requested information in the iTools Provide your information window that appears (**Figure 3**).
4. Click the Continue button at the bottom of the page.
5. Write down (or print) the information in the iTools Save for your records window that appears (**Figure 4**). It includes your member name and password.
6. Click Continue.
7. The iTools Announce your new e-mail address window appears next (**Figure 5**).
   - If you want to use the iTools mac.com e-mail account, follow the instructions in this window to send e-mail to your friends to announce your new e-mail address.
   - If you don't plan on using the iTools mac.com e-mail account, click No Thanks.
8. A Congratulations window appears next (**Figure 6**).
   - To explore iTools, click Start using iTools.
   - To start working with iDisk, quit your Web browser.

To configure Internet preferences with iTools information

1. Choose Apple > System Preferences (**Figure 7**), or click the System Preferences icon in the Dock (**Figure 8**).
2. In the System Preferences window that appears, click the Internet icon in the Internet & Network row to display the Internet preferences pane.
3. If necessary, click the iTools tab to display its options (**Figure 9**).
4. Enter your iTools member name and password in the appropriate edit boxes.
5. Choose System Prefs > Quit System Prefs (**Figure 10**) or press ⌘ Q.

✔ Tip

- If you created an iTools account when you registered Mac OS X, the iTools tab of the Internet Preferences pane (**Figure 9**) will already contain your iTools login information.

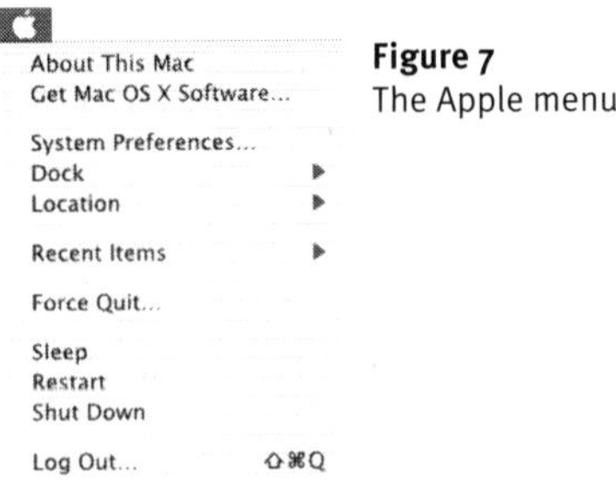

Figure 7 The Apple menu.

Figure 8 The Dock.

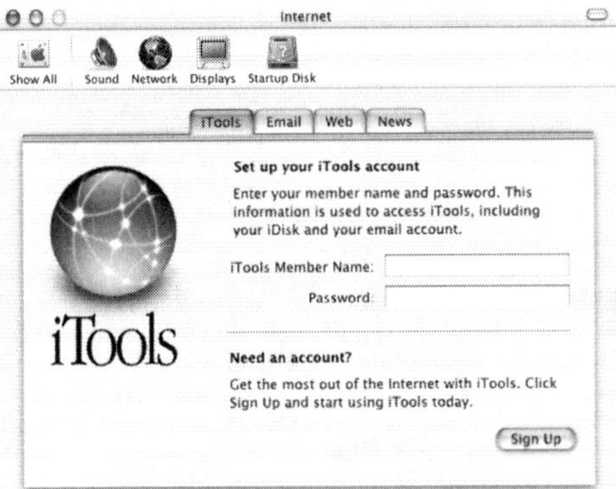

Figure 9 Use the iTools tab of the Internet preferences pane to enter iTools login information.

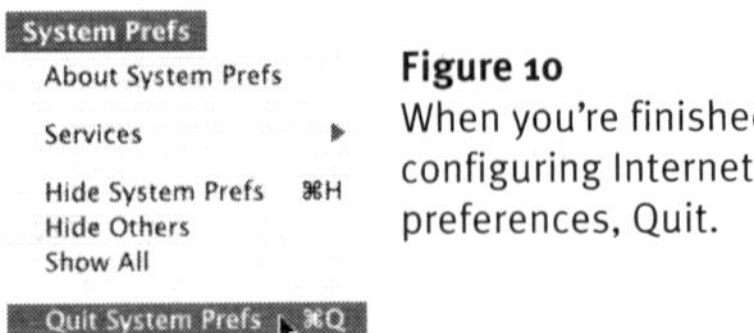

Figure 10 When you're finished configuring Internet preferences, Quit.

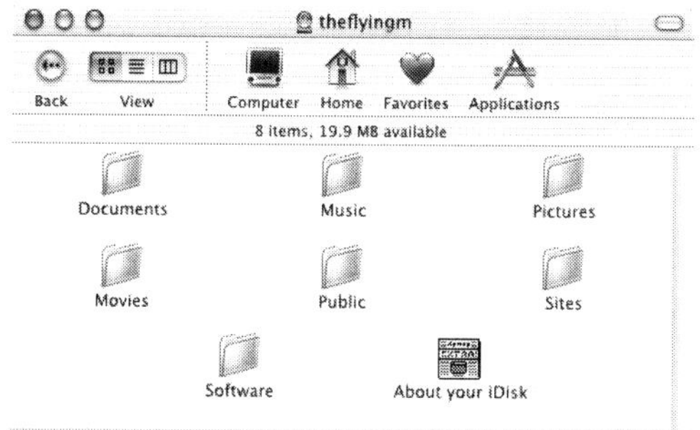

Figure 11 The contents of your iDisk home folder.

Using Your iDisk Storage Space

Your iDisk storage space (**Figure 11**) is preorganized into folders, just like your Mac OS X home folder:

- **Documents** is for storing documents. This folder is completely private; only you have access to it.
- **Music**, **Pictures**, and **Movies** are for storing various types of media. By storing multimedia files in these folder, they're available to other iTools programs, including iCard and HomePage.
- **Public** is for storing files you want to share with others. This folder can only be opened by an iTools member who knows your member name.
- **Sites** is for storing Web pages that you want to publish on the World Wide Web. HomePage, an iTools program you can explore on your own, automatically stores Web pages here. You can also create Web pages with another authoring tool and publish them by placing them in this folder.
- **Software** is a read-only folder maintained by Apple Computer. It contains Apple software updates and other downloadable files that might interest you. The contents of this folder do not count toward the 20 MB of disk space iDisk allows you—which is a good thing, because many of these files are very large!

Your iDisk home folder also includes a SimpleText file called About your iDisk, which has more information about iDisk. You can open this file with SimpleText, a Mac OS 9.x application, or with TextEdit, a Mac OS X application.

To open your iDisk storage space

1. If necessary, connect to the Internet.
2. Choose Go > iDisk (**Figure 1**), or press Option ⌘ I.
3. Wait while your computer retrieves information about your iDisk home folder contents. This can take a while, depending on the speed of your Internet connection.

   When the information has been retrieved, the contents of your iDisk home folder appear in a Finder window (**Figure 11**) and an iDisk volume icon with your account name appears on the desktop (**Figure 12**).

✔ Tips

- If a dialog like the one in **Figure 13** appears after step 2, you haven't entered your iTools member name and password in the iTools tab of the Internet preferences pane. I explain how to do that earlier in this chapter.
- The status bar of the Finder window (**Figure 11**) tells you how much space is left in your iTools storage space. To display the status bar, make sure the window is active and then choose View > Show Status Bar (**Figure 14**).

Figure 12 A volume icon representing your iDisk storage space appears on your desktop while you are connected to iDisk.

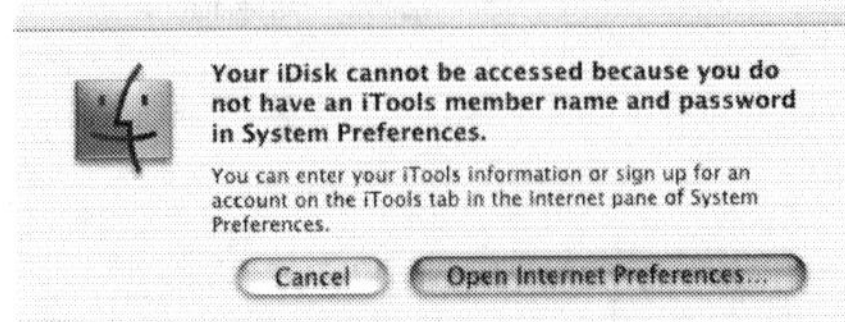

Figure 13 This dialog appears if you do not properly configure the Internet preferences pane.

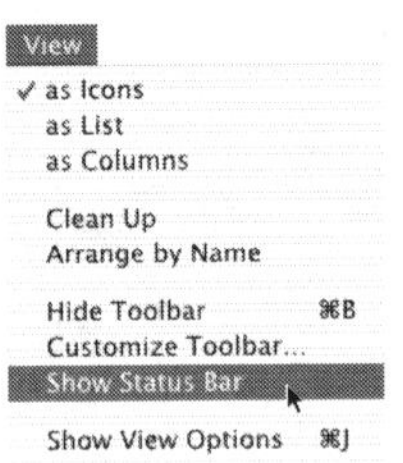

Figure 14 Displaying the Status Bar is as simple as choosing a menu command within the Finder.

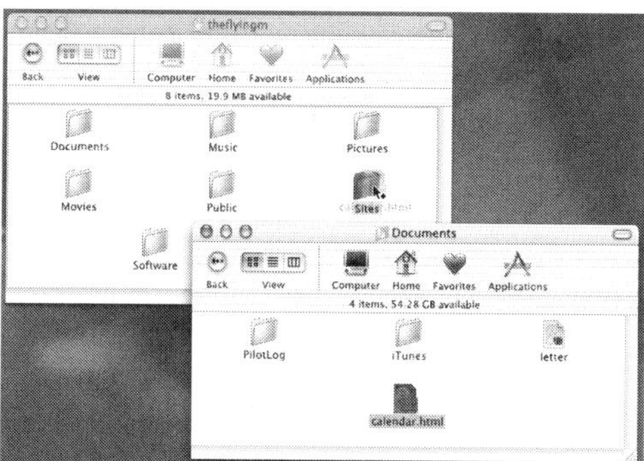

Figure 15 Copying a file to or from iDisk is as easy as dragging its icon.

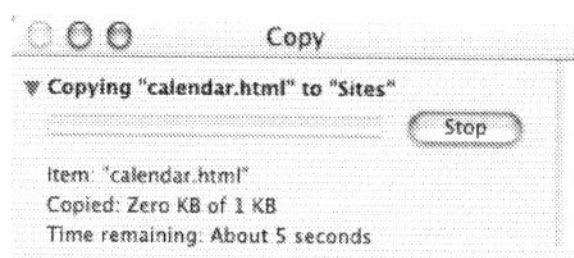

Figure 16 A Copy progress dialog appears as a file is copied.

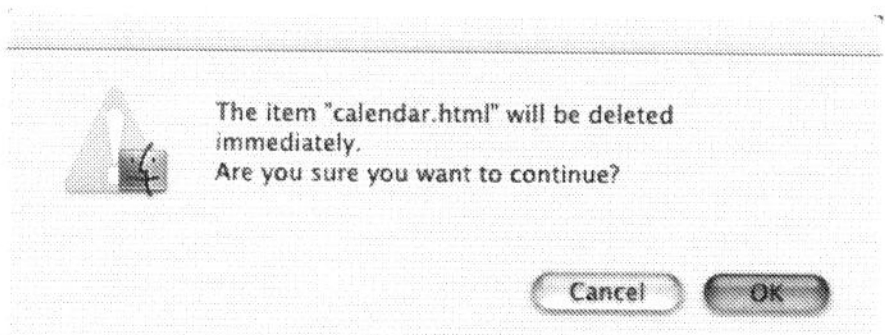

Figure 17 When you delete a file from your iDisk storage space, it is immediately removed.

To copy a file to your iDisk storage space

1. Drag the icon for the file onto the iDisk folder or into the iDisk window in which you want to copy the file (**Figure 15**).
2. A Copy progress dialog appears (**Figure 16**). When it disappears, the file has been copied.

✔ Tips

- It takes longer to copy a file to your iDisk storage space than to a hard disk or local network disk. This is because the file is uploaded to the iDisk server at the speed of your Internet connection.
- You cannot copy files into iDisk's Software folder.

To copy a file from your iDisk storage space

1. Drag the icon for the file from the iDisk window into the local or networked folder window in which you want to copy the file.
2. A Copy progress dialog appears. When it disappears, the file has been copied.

✔ Tip

- It takes longer to copy a file from your iDisk storage space than from a hard disk or local network disk. This is because the file is downloaded from the iDisk server at the speed of your Internet connection.

To remove a file from your iDisk storage space

1. Drag the icon for the file to the Trash.
2. A dialog like the one in **Figure 17** appears. Click OK. The file is deleted and its icon disappears.

To save a file to iDisk from within an application

1. Choose File > Save As (**Figure 18**).
2. In the Save dialog that appears, click the Where pop-up menu to display its options, then point to iDisk.
3. A submenu with iDisk folders appears (**Figure 19**). Choose the folder in which you want to save the file.
4. Enter a name for the file in the Save as box.
5. Click Save. The file is saved to the folder you selected in your iDisk storage space.

✔ Tip

- It takes longer to save a document to your iDisk storage space than to a hard disk or local network disk. This is because the file is uploaded to the iDisk server at the speed of your Internet connection.

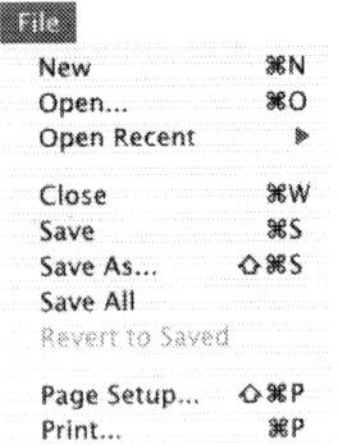

Figure 18 Like most other applications, TextEdit's File menu includes commands for saving and opening files.

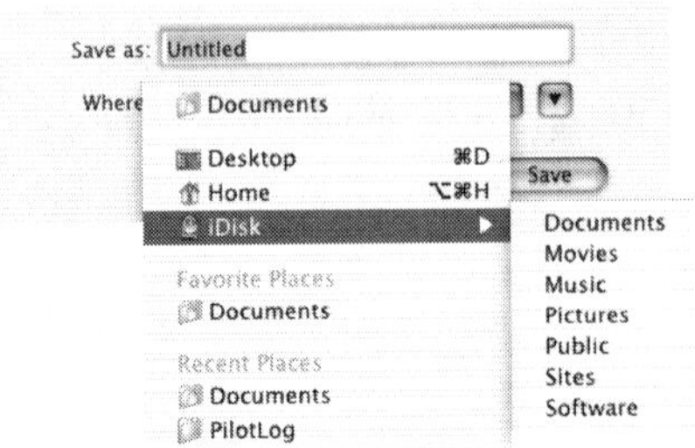

Figure 19 Use the Where pop-up menu to select the iDisk folder in which you want to save the file.

To open a file on iDisk from within an application

1. Choose File > Open (**Figure 15**).
2. In the Open dialog that appears, click the From pop-up menu to display its options, then point to iDisk.
3. A submenu with iDisk folders appears (**Figure 20**). Choose the folder in which the file you want to open resides.
4. In the list of files (**Figure 21**), select the file you want to open.
5. Click Open. The file is opened in a document window.

✔ Tip

- It takes longer to open a document on your iDisk storage space than on a hard disk or local network disk. This is because the file is downloaded from the iDisk server at the speed of your Internet connection.

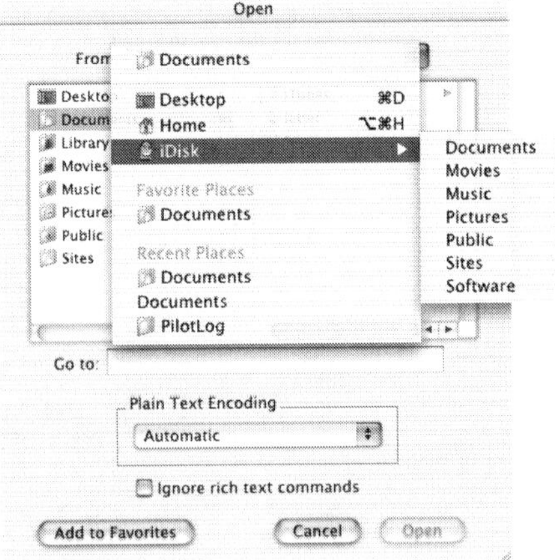

Figure 20 Use the From pop-up menu to open the iDisk folder containing the document you want to open.

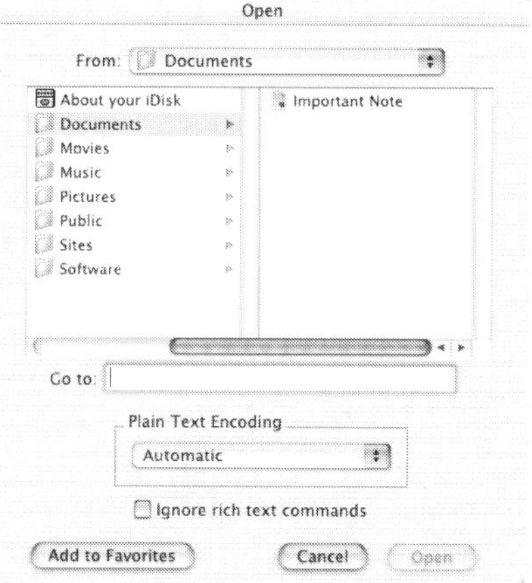

Figure 21 You can display the contents of your iDisk storage space within an Open dialog.

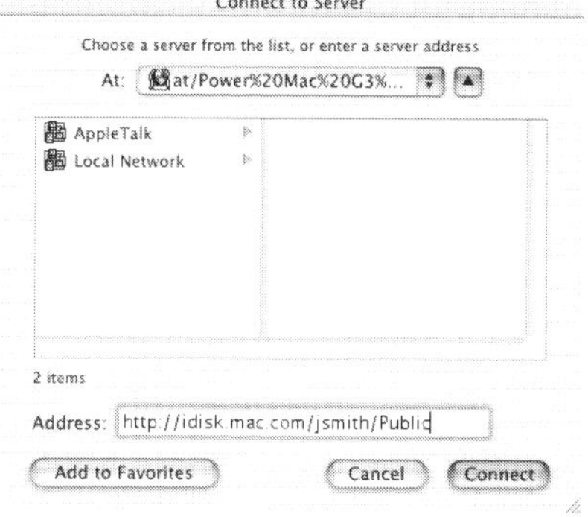

Figure 22 You can use the Connect to Server dialog to open the Public folder for another iTools member's iDisk.

Figure 23 An icon for the Public folder appears on your desktop.

To open another iTools member's Public folder

1. Choose Go > Connect to server (**Figure 1**) or press ⌘K.
2. In the Connect to Server dialog that appears, enter the following URL into the Address edit box:
   http://idisk.mac.com/*membername*/Public
   where *membername* is the iTools member name of the member whose Public folder you want to open (**Figure 22**).
3. Click Connect.
4. An iDisk volume icon for the Public folder appears on your desktop (**Figure 23**). Double-click the icon to open the folder and display its contents (**Figure 24**).

✔ Tips

- Although you can copy files from another member's Public folder to your hard disk as instructed earlier in this chapter, you cannot copy items into the other member's Public folder.
- You can give your Public folder's URL (see step 2 above) to your friends so they can access your Public folder.
- I tell you more about URLs and Internet addressing in *Mac OS X: Visual QuickStart Guide.*

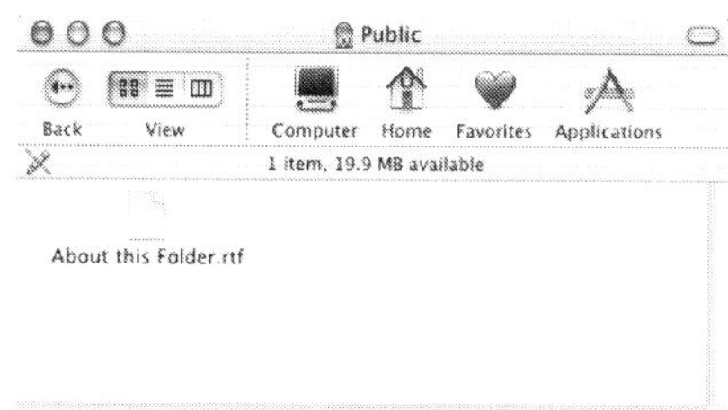

Figure 24 Double-clicking the Public folder's icon displays the contents of the folder.

To set up a Web site on iDisk

1. Use your Web browser to access the iTools home page, itools.mac.com. Then click the HomePage link and, if necessary, log in to iTools. The HomePage home page, which should look something like **Figure 25** should finally appear.
2. Follow the instructions you see online to build a Web site using HomePage. The files are automatically stored in the Sites folder within your iDisk storage space.

or

1. Use your favorite Web authoring tool to build a Web site.
2. Following the instructions earlier in this chapter, copy the Web site into the Sites folder in your iDisk storage space.

Figure 25 The home page for the iTools HomePage feature.

✔ Tips

- The URL for your Web site will be http://homepage.mac.com/*membername*/ where *membername* is your iTools member name. If you want to display a specific page within the sites folder, include it in the URL, for example, http://homepage.mac.com/*membername*/calendar.html.
- A complete discussion of HomePage and Web authoring is beyond the scope of this book. You can get online help for using HomePage as you use it. For more advanced Web authoring, I recommend that you obtain a good Web authoring software package and follow the instructions that come with it to build a Web site.

Menus & Keyboard Equivalents

Menus & Keyboard Equivalents

This appendix illustrates all of the Finder menus and provides a list of corresponding keyboard equivalents for Mac OS X 10.1.

To use a keyboard equivalent, hold down the modifier key (usually [⌘]) while pressing the keyboard key for the command.

Menus and keyboard commands are discussed in detail in *Mac OS X: Visual QuickStart Guide.*

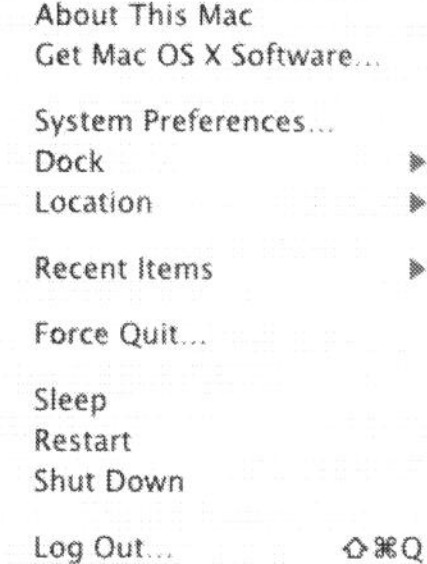

Apple Menu

[Option][⌘][D]	Dock > Turn Hiding On/Off
[Shift][⌘][Q]	Log Out

Finder
About the Finder
Preferences...
Empty Trash... ⇧⌘⌫
Services
Hide Finder ⌘H
Hide Others
Show All

Finder Menu

[Shift][⌘][Delete]	Empty Trash
[⌘][H]	Hide Finder

File Menu

⌘ N	New Finder Window
Shift ⌘ N	New Folder
⌘ O	Open
⌘ W	Close Window
Option ⌘ W	Close All
⌘ I	Show Info
⌘ D	Duplicate
⌘ L	Make Alias
⌘ R	Show Original
⌘ T	Add to Favorites
⌘ Delete	Move to Trash
⌘ E	Eject
⌘ F	Find

File

New Finder Window	⌘N
New Folder	⇧⌘N
Open	⌘O
Close Window	⌘W
Show Info	⌘I
Duplicate	⌘D
Make Alias	⌘L
Show Original	⌘R
Add to Favorites	⌘T
Move to Trash	⌘⌫
Eject	⌘E
Burn Disc...	
Find...	⌘F

Edit Menu

⌘ Z	Undo
⌘ X	Cut
⌘ C	Copy
⌘ V	Paste
⌘ A	Select All

Edit

Can't Undo	⌘Z
Cut	⌘X
Copy	⌘C
Paste	⌘V
Select All	⌘A
Show Clipboard	

View Menu

⌘ B	Show/Hide Toolbar
⌘ J	Show/Hide View Options

View

✓ as Icons	
as List	
as Columns	
Clean Up	
Arrange by Name	
Hide Toolbar	⌘B
Customize Toolbar...	
Hide Status Bar	
Show View Options	⌘J

Go

Computer	⌥⌘C
Home	⌥⌘H
iDisk	⌥⌘I
Favorites	▶
Applications	⌥⌘A
Recent Folders	▶
Go to Folder...	⌘~
Back	⌘[
Connect to Server...	⌘K

Go Menu

Option ⌘ C	Computer
Option ⌘ H	Home
Option ⌘ I	iDisk
Option ⌘ F	Favorites > Go To Favorites
Option ⌘ A	Applications
⌘ ~	Go to Folder
⌘ [	Back
⌘ K	Connect to Server

Window

Zoom Window	
Minimize Window	⌘M
Bring All to Front	
Fonts	
Documents	
✓ Macintosh HD	

Window Menu

⌘ M	Minimize Window
Option ⌘ M	Minimize All Windows

Help

Mac Help	⌘?

Help Menu

⌘ ?	Mac Help

INDEX

Symbols

A

INDEX

D

INDEX

E

F

INDEX

H

I

J

K

INDEX

INDEX

Q

R

S

T

U

V

W

X

Z

INDEX

OS

X

X
The Little Mac OS X Book
Robin Williams

MARIA LANGER
MAC OS
ADVANCED
X

M A C
9 1 1
chris breen

The Macintosh Bible

ETHAN WILDE
APPLESCRIPT
FOR APPLICATIONS

iMOVIE
FOR MACINTOSH
2